Ten pound Poms

Manchester University Press

We dedicate this book to Marisia and David Hammerton, and Lilli and Bryn Thomson, who are living the challenges and opportunities created by their fathers' migrations

Ten pound Poms

Australia's invisible migrants

A. James Hammerton
and Alistair Thomson

Manchester University Press
Manchester and New York

distributed exclusively in the USA by Palgrave

Copyright © A. James Hammerton and Alistair Thomson 2005

The right of A. James Hammerton and Alistair Thomson to be identifed as the authors of this work has been asserted by them in accordance with the Copyright, Designs and Patents Act 1988.

Published by Manchester University Press
Oxford Road, Manchester M13 9NR, UK
and Room 400, 175 Fifth Avenue, New York, NY 10010, USA
www.manchesteruniversitypress.co.uk

Distributed exclusively in the USA by
Palgrave, 175 Fifth Avenue, New York, NY 10010, USA

Distributed exclusively in Canada by
UBC Press, University of British Columbia, 2029 West Mall, Vancouver, BC, Canada
V6T 1Z2

British Library Cataloguing-in-Publication Data
A catalogue record for this book is available from the British Library

Library of Congress Cataloging-in-Publication Data applied for

ISBN 0 7190 7132 1 *hardback*
EAN 978 0 7190 7132 4
ISBN 0 7190 7133 X *paperback*
EAN 978 0 7190 7133 1

First published 2005

14 13 12 11 10 09 08 07 06 05   10 9 8 7 6 5 4 3 2 1

Designed in Ehrhardt with Gill display
by Max Nettleton FCSD

Typeset by Koinonia, Manchester

Printed in Great Britain
by CPI, Bath

Contents

List of figures

Unless otherwise indicated, permission for use has been granted by the named person or persons in the photograph

List of tables

Acknowledgements

This book results from the integration of research projects at the University of Sussex in Britain and La Trobe University in Australia, which brought together two rich archives of testimony from British migrants in Australia and return migrants in Britain. Our primary and immeasurable debt is to the hundreds of people who contributed to those archives, with written life stories, published works, photographs and, in many cases, recorded interviews. The stories told by our informants extend from the tragic to the triumphal, with a huge variety of familiar and extraordinary experiences in between. Because of the size of the archives, especially that at La Trobe with some 1,300 contributions, we are unable to acknowledge everyone by name, but in the Bibliography we list all the interviewees and a selection of written accounts. As in all books based on an extensive body of testimony, we have been unable to do justice to all the compelling stories we have gathered; this is a matter of regret to us and in no way reflects on the unique significance of the stories we have been unable to use. The pressures of space required us to make difficult selections, but all our contributors ultimately helped to shape the final product. We acknowledge the enormous generosity and enthusiasm with which they supported our attempts to tell their stories and shared our conviction that the wider history of postwar British-Australian migration had not been adequately told.

In other ways the book was a shared enterprise. It is a product of the profess-ionalism and industry of a group of dedicated research assistants and inter-viewers, with whom it was a delight to work. Michelle Arrow, Cathy Coleborne, Criena Fitzgerald, Helen Gardner, Carole Hamilton-Barwick, Susan Hutton, Mandy Rooke and Lani Russell would be any researcher's 'dream team' and we hope they will be pleased with our use of the product of their labours. Others have provided valuable help, discussion and advice, notably Graham Dawson, Siân Edwards, Megan Hutching, James Jupp, Russell King, John Lack, Michele Langfield, Jim Mitchell, Mark Peel, Eric Richards, Dorothy Sheridan, Marion White, Sara Wills and Janis Wilton. Alison Welsby was an enthusiastic supporter at Manchester University Press. For financial support the La Trobe project is indebted to the Australian Research Council, La Trobe University's large Central Grant Scheme, to Alan Frost of the then Department of History and to John Salmond. The University of Sussex project was funded by generous grants from the British Academy and the Arts and Humanities Research Board, and benefited from the support of academic and clerical staff colleagues (including Sue Brown, Sarah Davies and Sadie Graham) in the Centre for Continuing Education. We also acknowledge the generous donation of Adam Coffman's and Paul Neuburg's collection of migrant letters from the 1997 Pulse Production television programme project, *The Ten Pound Poms*.

List of abbreviations

ABC   Australian Broadcasting Corporation
BBC   British Broadcasting Corporation
BHP   Broken Hill Proprietary Limited
GP   General Practitioner
NHS   National Health Service
SBS   Special Broadcasting Service
UK   United Kingdom
UKSA   United Kingdom Settlers' Association

A note on punctuation of interviews

The transcription of oral history interviews is not an exact science; the transcript is a written translation of an oral account. In the transcribed extracts from interviews that are included in this book we have sought to represent the richness of the spoken account as effectively as possible. Words that were emphasized by the speaker are reproduced in *italics*. Only extraneous words that do not significantly affect the meaning of a passage, such as false starts or 'ums' and 'ahs', have been deleted. A pause by the narrator is denoted by a set of dashes (---). Editorial deletions from within a sentence of the transcript are denoted by the use of three ellipses (...); longer deletions are denoted by the use of four ellipses (....). Explanatory editorial insertions are included within square brackets [ ]. Pseudonyms are used in the few cases where an interviewee has requested anonymity.

Introduction

Sylvia and John Cannon: a migration life history

On 2 June 1961, Sylvia and John Cannon boarded the *Canberra* in Southampton for their ten pound passage to Melbourne.[1] Compared to their forebears on other trips undertaken over the previous fourteen years they were fortunate indeed. This was the maiden voyage of the brand new P&O liner; unlike most assisted migrants they were not put into sex-segregated quarters but, through a friend, were given a two-berth cabin with a porthole. The rare treat added to the Cannons' excitement and sense of anticipation now that their journey was at hand. The excitement continued throughout the voyage, enhanced by celebration of their first wedding anniversary at Gibraltar. Although the *Canberra* suffered mechanical troubles en route, Sylvia and John recall the three-week voyage as an uninterrupted holiday, with the exotic reception of traders in ports like Naples, Aden and Port Said magnified by the splendour of the new liner. As the pilot ships guided them into each port, Sylvia recalled, 'they would have streamers coming and they would have bands, you know, and music played.... And so everywhere we went it was like we were heralded ... and people would be there waving and it was exciting as anything ... the excitement of each port, and people being pleased to see us.'

By 1961 more than 360,000 British assisted migrants had taken the same journey as the Cannons in various standards of comfort.[2] Although their shipboard conditions were often less luxurious than those on the *Canberra*, most of them remembered the voyage as the journey of a lifetime. Indeed, since many had grown up between the wars they had bitter memories of Depression hardships, the war itself and the grimness of postwar austerity to contrast with a world cruise with unlimited supplies of food and entertainment. For that first generation of 'ten pound Poms' this was the dramatic prelude to their new life as Australian immigrants. But by the 1960s the assisted passage scheme was drawing in a generation of younger adults without memories of the Depression. Postwar shortages and the rigours of rationing were becoming a distant memory, and Britain itself was undergoing rates of growth which had begun to produce higher standards of living. In these circumstances migration was more likely to be stimulated by a sense of heightened expectations than desperation to escape austerity. The Cannons, both born in 1938, stand between these two generations and their life stories suggest elements of both patterns.

If John and Sylvia were spared memories of the Depression, their childhood recollections of the war and its aftermath still did much to shape dramatic 'before and after' scenarios as they looked back on their histories. Both came from close-knit families in the East End of London, and their earliest memories concern family relationships within sharply contrasting experiences of the war. Sylvia, for example, remembered air raid experiences in Manor Park as 'sheer terror'. One night her mother missed the warning siren. Sylvia awoke in the night as the bombing began, and she was rushed through the garden in the middle of a raid, 'the search lights and the bombs coming and I can remember everything shuddering around us and being thrown down into the shelter'. She picked up her mother's terror, and suffered panic fears into adulthood of dying and being left alone, and 'terrible nightmares all my life'. By contrast, John remembers the war mostly as a 'jolly time' in a series of air raid shelter episodes at the bottom of his East Ham garden; he would poke his head out to watch searchlights reflecting on the clouds and hear anti-aircraft guns, all with 'no sense of fear'. His equanimity was encouraged by the general sense of bonhomie in the shelter, with a population made up entirely of children and women whose husbands were away. The women's laughing, joking and singing sheltered the children from fear of the threat of imminent destruction from overhead. Indeed, John's memories of the war are dominated by the omnipresence of women. After his father left,

all the women seemed to get together in the house that I was living in, in East Ham, and so all the women were together, including Grandmother. And I was brought up by women.... And I remember other children coming on the scene, and I remember women saying certain things, and breast-feeding.... I remember the women being extraordinarily strong.... I think the women were really good for each other. In some ways it was *beneficial* to have the men gone!

At the end of the war John's father appeared to him as a stranger in uniform. And while he thought it was hard for his mother to return to a 'more subservient role' after the war, the effects were enduring and 'what she experienced in those days, stood her in great stead when my dad died'. In his own life, though, the war had left John with an enduring sense of dissatisfaction with conventional expectations, which contributed to his willingness to emigrate. 'In a sense, the deprivation that the war brought made me want more, made me want things which I knew were available before the war.' John's aspirations were also fired by a determination to break the mould, by comparison with his father, who had risen from private to captain during the war and became a manager at work but never left his 'grotty' factory or their tiny East End terrace house; 'he never moved out, and that's where one of my peculiar ideas took place'.

Sylvia's lasting wartime terrors were compounded by the death of her father in 1949 when she was 11, and of her mother when she was 18, a time when 'I was not very confident and yet I was finding myself'. After she met John at 16 she soon became attached to his close-knit family and, after the death of her mother, moved in with them while he was away on national service, well before their marriage in 1960. If this provided Sylvia with a level of comfort and security, it became constraining once they were married. 'I felt suffocated, and I really wanted to get out and become our own family.' But housing was still scarce and Sylvia and John could not achieve their goal of home ownership; the only house they could afford 'was *miles* away outside of London; it would have taken hours to travel to and from'. So when Australian friends at work, almost simultaneously, tempted them with visions of excitement and opportunity in Australia, they jumped at the chance. Since as yet they had no children, the decision was an easy one. In their case there was no hint of the disagreements which bedevilled so many couples when a reluctant partner, most often the wife, nursed resentments and homesickness for years after their arrival. Sylvia had no close family to bid farewell, so the moment of leaving, beckoning 'happy adventure', was easy. John too was caught up with the excitement of anticipation, though he did have an emotional parting with his parents, compounded in his later memory by his father's death before he could return: 'I remember hugging my father when we said goodbye. It was the only time I ever did hug him as an adult! And, I didn't see him alive again. I went home to his funeral and I saw him lying in his coffin in the front room of this East Ham house that I'd lived all my early days.' But any lingering doubts at the time were soothed by Sylvia and John's agreement, characteristic of the more youthful generation of the 1960s, that they would stay in Australia only for the required two years, move on to Canada and eventually return to England.

The Cannons' idyllic dreams, which were sustained by the delights of the ritual visit to King's Park in Perth during a Fremantle stopover, were brought down to earth abruptly upon their arrival in Melbourne. Transported in a 'prison-type bus' to their first housing in the Melbourne Exhibition Building compound, a short-term holding station, they experienced the shock of hostel austerity and the stock provision of knife, fork, spoon, mug and toilet roll: 'we used to call it "the concentration camp"'. The urgent priority of the search for work loomed large. Both were white-collar workers, and because John had worked for Ford in London he promptly arranged an interview for a sales position in their Geelong office. He was faced with a pre-dawn departure to allow for travel, which rigid hostel lock-up rules did nothing to accommodate.

1 Sylvia and John Cannon on their honeymoon in 1960 shortly before leaving for Australia

2 John Cannon in 1962 with his first car 'outside our "Home" – half a Nissen hut!' at Geelong Hostel

3 Sylvia and John Cannon in 1963 soon after arriving in Fremantle. The Falcon was
a company car

4 Sylvia and John Cannon in 2002 on the Swan River foreshore with Perth city in the
background

I had no idea about Australia and transport and where Geelong was, and the morning of the interview, I had to get dressed up in my pin-stripe suit, which I brought from London with me, and I couldn't get out of the bloody place, because everything was locked. This was very early in the morning, the sun hadn't come up, and I had to climb over a huge great gate, with barbed wire along the top.

While the Cannons' first job searches, both with Ford, were successful, tight finances and a job transfer back to Melbourne dictated living in a series of hostels before they were able to move to a flat in East Hawthorn, where 'life really took off'. Until then the hostel experience stood in stark contrast to the more congenial atmosphere at work (though, ironically, Sylvia confronted some anti-British hostility in her first job at Ford). They made friends rapidly among John's Australian workmates rather than their British hostel neighbours, most of whom, they decided, were 'whingeing Poms' waiting to return to Britain. Sylvia recalls that 'we made this decision that we wouldn't get friendly with any British people, and we'd get out and we'd try to make friends with Australians'. The Cannons' experience is a reminder that hostel discomforts were not simply a matter of bureaucratic regimentation and isolation. Lack of sympathy even with British neighbours could be one of the strongest motives for escaping hostel conditions when working life was pointing in more inspiring directions.

Once settled in their Hawthorn apartment, the Cannons supplemented their incomes by 'moonlighting' on weekends for a real estate agent, selling blocks of land in Doncaster. This inspired them to buy one of the blocks and build for themselves. No sooner had they realized their dream of home ownership than John, barely three years after arrival, was offered a lucrative promotion and transfer to Perth. Sunny Perth, the envy of most of John's workmates, was even more enticing, and boosted their increasing resolve to stay permanently. Sylvia recalls her satisfaction with making new friends and a realization that the two year compulsory period was a clever Australian strategy, 'because within the two years, people were just acquaintances, after that they became friends, and for me that was a difference … to help me to settle'.

Life in the West, however, was far from stable. Before long John tired of working for others – he had always wanted to 'better himself' – and entered a succession of car dealing partnerships, one of which took them for eighteen months to remote Cunderdin, some 150 kilometres east of Perth, where they learnt the trials of bush-living. For Sylvia especially this required a new level of adaptation: 'I had to learn to wear a hat and gloves to belong to the Country Women's Association. I was supposed to bake cakes and make jams, and you had to get used to snakes coming up between floor-boards and huge spiders.' Here, in searing summer heat, the first of three children was born. After several years of trying to conceive, 'the actual birth of this child was like a miracle to us'. Sylvia promptly and deliberately withdrew from the workforce and devoted herself to her children. But like so many women migrants, who seemingly pioneered a more 'modern' approach to blending work and mother-hood, when her youngest son was only 4, she began – tentatively – her 'journey' back into the workforce. At the same time John's job changes were mirrored by frequent residential moves, as they boosted their income by buying and renovating houses and trading up, so that they experienced a succession of Perth suburbs.

If return to England remained a possibility, it was put to the test when they decided in 1966 to visit John's family 'to show our newborn son off'. But even though the visit lasted for a year, and John worked selling photocopiers, their commitment to life in Australia never wavered. They had kept their house in Perth and Sylvia found that her newly developed independence was challenged by again living with John's mother, so that for her Australia repre-sented personal autonomy and development. Far from contemplating resettle-ment in England, within the year they had decided to go back to Perth, and John's sister and husband had decided to join them. The family networks of the extended Cannon family were now transnational. John's mother was not pleased – 'she says, "If I can find the guy who discovered Australia I'm going to kill him!"' – and in the years to come Sylvia and John and the children would make frequent family visits to England.

For many migrants who stayed in Australia the founding story of their migration could end here, with modest prosperity ahead and proud recollection of adaptation, struggle to succeed and the making of a new Australian family embodied in successful children and promising grandchildren. But for the Cannons there was a further chapter ahead. By the late 1970s Sylvia had begun her own dream of re-education and became a psychotherapist with a large counselling agency. In the mid-1980s John became dissatisfied with running car dealerships, embarked on a university degree course and then began a private counselling practice as a psychologist. At the time of the interview each had a separate counselling practice. Unusually for British migrants, the Cannons, at considerable temporary sacrifice, thus lifted their social status as well as their material well being. It was rare for adult British migrants to under-go such a radical change in occupation and status, and not surprisingly this has enhanced their sense of appreciation for their opportunities in Australia.

For Sylvia this is a story about disentanglement from the conventional gender roles of the 1960s:

I think Australia has given me the opportunity to make changes away from family. It is a place where there's been for me extreme change, extreme turmoil, extreme pleasure, and it's about *wonderful* people – mixtures of different people. I have arrived as a woman at a different place because of living in Australia than I really believe that I could ever have done in England.

John agrees that their evolving relationship was central to adaptation to the new country. 'There's a new whole series of stories about how our married life changed, and how I changed; and how Sylvia wasn't prepared to put up with what she'd always had, and how traumatic all those changes were, and the threat of the marriage ending, and then it coming good again and it becoming better than it's ever been.' But for John, the greatest achievement of his emigration to Australia is 'my work…. Because Australia allowed me to become who I really wanted to be. I fit here really well, especially in so far as being my own boss.'

I can see us as being extraordinarily lucky in what we have experienced and what we have. We have been born in the time of development which has been so fantastic. I've seen war and I've seen deprivation and ration books and I've seen plenty and I've seen advances and I've watched these kids of ours grow up and so I feel particularly very, very lucky, privileged, in fact. And yet, I still have this strange feeling about wanting to be back there.

The Cannons' rapid social mobility, their move from the lower middle class to the professions and their frankness about their relationship perhaps differentiates them from the bulk of adult British migrants, mostly from skilled working-class backgrounds. In some respects their history is closer to that of the children of migrants. But their account echoes abiding themes in the experiences of two generations of assisted British migrants in its attachment to that earlier life in Britain, their sense of migration as a life-changing event and the story of transforming changes in the new land.

The Cannons, like many migrants, are still pulled between the land of their birth and their adopted home, and their life stories express this tension in different ways. Sylvia doubts that she could ever live with the 'grey skies' and 'claustrophobic' attitudes and way of life in England. For Sylvia, children have been the 'stabilizing part for me in Australia, because they're Australians and that makes me feel as though this is where my home is'. But John still expresses ambivalence about his Australian identity. He hates the heat of the Australian summer 'with a passion', and is deeply attached to England as the land of his heritage: 'I go back quite regularly and when I do … it gets into your soul. And the more I think about this, the more I realize what the Aborigines are talking about when they have a connection with the land, because … the countryside, and London itself, fills me with joy and pleasure.' Family, on the other hand, ties the Cannons to Australia, and in its emphasis on the complicated bonds of family we will find that their story echoes a central theme in the memories of postwar British migrants. John knows that he cannot now return, that the Australian family is too important for himself and Sylvia, but 'if it were not for my children being here, I think I would move back to England'. Though John Cannon has settled in Australia, his life story, and the personal identity which it defines, is less comfortably assimilated.

'Ten pound Poms': the invisible migrants

This book draws heavily upon the life histories of migrants like Sylvia and John Cannon, and uses the rich detail of personal and family stories to enrich our understanding of postwar British emigration to Australia. The Cannons were among more than one and a half million Britons who left for Australia in the quarter century following the Second World War. Most of the migrants came under an assisted passage scheme through which adults travelled to Australia for just £10 whilst children travelled free. These British immigrants comprised one of the largest planned migrations of the twentieth century, and they became known to most Australians as the 'ten pound Poms' (the term was misleading since, as Scottish and Welsh migrants are quick to insist, the word 'Pom', whether used in a derogatory or affectionate sense, refers to English migrants exclusively). Throughout the postwar period more Australian immigrants came from Britain than from any other country (it was not until 1996 that Britain was pushed into second place by settlers from New Zealand), and though Australia's massive postwar immigration scheme included large numbers of migrants from other, non-English-speaking countries, throughout the 1950s and 1960s the British comprised never less than a third and at times more than half of all settler arrivals.

And yet the British were to become 'invisible migrants', in a number of ways.[3] The British had controlled and dominated the European settlement of Australia in the eighteenth and nineteenth centuries, and thus ensured the predominance of the English language and the adaptation of Australian cultural and political life to British ways. It was assumed that twentieth-century British immigrants would assimilate easily and thus 'disappear' into such a familiar society. And it was certainly true that with a few significant exceptions (such as the new suburb of Elizabeth in Adelaide), the postwar British immigrants did not form geographical and cultural enclaves, and were barely noticeable as a distinct group in the Australian population. Conversely, most mid-century Australians still regarded themselves as members of the British race and Empire (in law, all Australians were British subjects until 1984) and Australian governments of all political complexions preferred British immigrants precisely because, as Immigration Minister Harold Holt claimed in 1950, 'this is a British community, and we want to keep it a British community'. It was assumed that the British migrants would fit easily into Australia's 'British way of life'.[4]

There were times, however, when the postwar British were a highly visible migrant group. At the outset of the assisted passage scheme in 1947 much was made – in both Britain and Australia – of the importance of migrants from Britain; over the next two and a half decades the Australian government sought to sustain the proportion of British migrants by extensive advertising in Australia as well as Britain, for example through the 'Bring Out a Briton' campaign of the late 1950s. When British migrants protested about conditions in the migrant hostels of the 1950s and 1960s, they created a furore in the Australian press and parliaments and acquired the nickname of 'whingeing Poms'. When it became clear that a large number of the British assisted passage migrants were returning home, Australian commentators and politicians lamented the failure of these migrants and were appalled at the wasted investment in their migration (by contrast, British commentators blamed Australia's 'false' advertising). The federal government commissioned a report into 'The Departure of Settlers from Australia', and funded several major research projects about the British migrants, most notably Reg Appleyard's long-term study of one cohort of migrants who left Britain in 1959.[5] For a time, researchers and politicians recognized that the British faced similar challenges to other immigrants, and tried to understand how they responded to these challenges.

Yet the prominence of the postwar British immigrants in Australian politics and research was short-lived. Australia could never obtain British migrants in the desired quantities, and was forced to look elsewhere for the immigrants who were essential for postwar reconstruction. European war refugees arrived in the late 1940s, and were followed by waves of migrants from non-English-speaking countries, at first from central and western Europe, then from southern Europe and the Mediterranean rim. These non-English-speaking refugees and migrants precipitated the most dramatic transformation in twentieth-century Australian history, as a predominantly monocultural society was transformed – slowly and painfully – into a multiracial and multicultural nation.

The problems faced by non-English-speaking settlers – and their social and political impact upon Australia – far outweighed concerns about British immigrants. These 'New Australians' – as the non-English-speaking settlers were labelled – necessarily became the primary focus of political debate, media attention and social research. In Australian popular imagination and policy formulation, the term 'immigrant' was increasingly equated with the New Australians who came from non-English-speaking countries, and very often the British were not regarded as 'real immigrants'. One telling sign of this almost unconscious attitude is suggested by the catalogues of many Australian libraries, which use the index headings 'migrant' or 'migration' for memoirs by postwar migrants from non-English speaking countries, but not for memoirs by postwar British migrants. When Australians talk and think about migrants, for the most part they mean migrants from non-English-speaking countries. A parallel argument can be made for Britain, where the focus of interest in the last forty years has been upon black immigrants rather than white emigrants or immigrants.[6]

Historians have also neglected postwar British migrants. In 1988 Reg Appleyard updated his earlier study of the postwar British migrants, but his co-authored book *The Ten Pound Immigrants* is the only significant published history of these migrants.[7] General histories of Australian postwar immigration tend to move quickly past the British in order to focus on the more dramatic and challenging story of the New Australians and the journey to a multicultural Australia.[8] Even more striking is the comparative neglect of British migrants in local studies and community histories. In the 1970s and 1980s a large number of projects were initiated around Australia – by migrant and ethnic community associations, literacy projects and government agencies – to record and publish the oral histories and written testimony of non-English-speaking migrants. These projects were part of the agenda of multicultural politics, and aimed to present hidden histories that would illustrate the particular difficulties, needs and struggles of migrants from non-English-speaking backgrounds. With one or two notable exceptions the ensuing publications have ignored the British migrant.[9] As a group, British migrants were not perceived to have stories of political significance or commercial value.

British migrants often internalized this sense of political and historical insignificance so that few wrote or told the stories of their migration. Those who have produced memoirs – mostly in the last decade or so – have usually self-published with small local presses or have simply made photocopies for family and friends. Apart from a handful of accounts by British migrants who have achieved public significance in their time in Australia,[10] these are usually books written by 'ordinary' people who are reviewing their lives in old age and whose main purpose is to make a record for members of their families.[11] Though migration provides one significant storyline for these memoirs – a point of rupture, opportunity and even transformation – in comparison with many narratives by migrants from non-English-speaking countries, these accounts are not, on the whole, written in order to assert the distinctive experience of this particular migrant nationality, and they have not had a wide readership or influence.

One aim of this book is to recover the history of these 'invisible migrants' through the memories of British postwar migrants like Sylvia and John Cannon. When we began to collect British migrant life stories in the mid-1990s we soon discovered that many of our narrators also felt that theirs was an 'untold story'. They were enormously enthusiastic about recording their personal or family account for the historical record and about putting British migrants back into the history of Australian postwar immigration. Sarah Ricketts, for example, wrote that 'I have often felt that much has been made of the migrant experiences of non-English speakers to this country without including those who could speak the language, as though we assimilated automatically and felt no grief at losing our homeland and so on.' Joan Watson explained that she was 'delighted to get your letter and to hear that your department at La Trobe University will record that part of Australia's history, of which us Ten Pound Poms took part'.[12]

Since we began working on this book, other researchers have also begun to challenge the invisibility of the postwar British migrants. Several historians who came to Australia as children with their British migrant parents have initiated oral history projects intended to make sense of their own background and of the historical experience of their parents' migrant generation.[13] Other researchers have begun to consider the contemporary cultural significance of postwar British migrants as represented in, for example, support for Perth Glory soccer team, the annual 'BritFests' on Melbourne's Mornington Peninsula, or voting patterns in the republic referendum.[14]

This book is thus part of a growing interest in the historical experience and contemporary significance of postwar British migrants. We aim to explore the distinctive experience of the British as *migrants*, and to complicate a story which has been assumed to be comparatively straightforward and unproblematic. We are *not* arguing that non-British immigrants have received undue attention or unfairly favourable treatment. Australian attitudes and policies did discriminate against immigrants from non-English-speaking backgrounds, and the struggle for a more just and multicultural society is one of the most important chapters of contemporary Australian history. But the history of postwar immigration makes better sense if the British are included in a story which records the common and distinctive features of their migration.

For example, the British migrant experience was shaped by a number of critical developments in postwar Australian and British history. British migrants were caught up in the interdependent but changing relationship between the two countries in the second half of the twentieth century, as political and economic forces pulled them inexorably apart. The ten pound migration scheme was intended to ensure a British peopling of Australia and to enable migration to a country that was like Britain in the sun, but the migration experience became complicated in unexpected ways. British migrants confronted a country and culture that was both curiously familiar and disconcertingly strange; they wondered why 'whingeing Poms' were not automatically welcomed and respected by their Australian hosts; they were perplexed by the transformation of British Australia to multicultural Australia; and they were troubled by the fact that from the 1980s British origins and citizenship no longer conferred automatic rights in Australia.

Actual changes in each country and in the relationship between the two countries were mirrored by shifts in how each place was imagined and perceived by the other, and these perceptual changes also affected the migrants. Australians imagined Britain as a war-torn land of grim austerity; as a Coronation Street slum; or as London in the 'swinging sixties' – and responded to newcomers from Britain accordingly. Australia's image in Britain remained comparatively positive, as a place where you could raise a family in relative comfort and enjoy a sunny outdoor life, though even this image altered in subtle ways over the decades and affected migrant decisions and expectations.

The British migrant experience was also influenced by social and economic change. Working-class British migrants went to Australia hoping for a better standard of living, but they did so at a time when economic and social conditions in both countries were changing at great pace. British migrant life stories are entangled in the postwar social histories of home ownership and consumerism – the 'home of your own' with modern appliances and a new family car looms large in our oral histories – and evoke the significance of these material changes for family life and personal aspirations. The transformation of transport and communication technologies – from ocean liners and aerogrammes to jumbo jets and email – changed the ways in which migrants moved from one country to the other, and altered relationships within extended families that straddled the globe. We interviewed migrants who were unable to phone home in the 1950s because their parents lived in a British street which had no telephones, but who now correspond by email every day with their own international backpacker children.

Family life in Britain and Australia was itself transformed during these postwar decades. The assisted passage scheme assumed that skilled British male workers would staff Australia's postwar industrial reconstruction and that their wives would bear children to boost Australia's population. Yet migrant women often wanted or needed to work, and migrant marriages were challenged by the strains of migration; Sylvia and John Cannon's story points to the likelihood of change in relationships between migrant husbands and wives. A recurring theme in this book concerns the way that families responded to, and were affected by, migration. A related theme is the way in which migration could be different for men and women and was shaped by gender roles and expectations whilst at the same time challenging stereotypical roles. Of course, many aspects of family and social life that we consider here were not unique to migrants. Immigrants are not the only people with complicated histories of housing, work and family. But migration cuts across these and other aspects of personal experience, and when migrants recall these features of their life history they frequently do so through the lens of migration.

While we emphasize patterns and themes in the history of postwar British migrants, we also argue against a homogeneous history of British migration. There was a range of factors which made for startling differences in the lived experience of postwar British migration. We have already noted the contrast between the emigrants of the immediate postwar period of austerity and those who went to Australia in the more affluent 1960s and 1970s. Whatever the year, migrants who brought substantial capital resources to Australia had a much easier start in the new country than those who came with nothing; migrants who were nominated and housed by relatives or employers often fared better than the 'Commonwealth nominees' who were destined for the notorious migrant hostels. Many British migrants travelled in family groups but there was also a significant minority of young single men and women who took up the ten pound passage, often as a way of funding a working holiday. The Australian experience of these single 'sojourners' was very different from that of immigrant families. Even within families there were significant variations in the migration experience, not only between men and women, but also between migrant parents and children, or between young children and teenagers.

Another important distinction concerns settlers and returnees. Almost a quarter of the postwar British migrants returned to Britain, though some of these – like Sylvia and John Cannon – re-emigrated to Australia. Return migration adds another element to the migration story – and the rather different British vantage point for the storyteller – yet return migrants are often neglected in migration histories, which tend to focus on settlers' stories of struggle or success in the new land. Here we draw upon migrants' accounts recorded in both Britain and Australia and explore the contrasting experience of settlers and returnees.

The term 'British migrants' also conceals regional and national diversity. The great majority were English, with migrants from the suburban south east and the north western industrial conurbations predominant but bringing subtly different characteristics and attitudes to Australia. Scotland was also well represented – Wales less so – and there were notable differences between the Scottish and English migrant experience. For one, the Scots resisted the 'Pommy' label and were keen to ensure that their Australian hosts did not confuse them with English 'whingers'. The Irish – who had been numerically and culturally significant amongst Australia's nineteenth-century immigrants – were much less important in terms of numbers or influence in the second half of the twentieth century. Theirs is a rather different history, in terms of

Irish origin and of cultural and political influence in Australia, and it is not a subject of this book.

In short, British migrants cannot be presented in simple or stereotypical terms, and their differences may well be as revealing as their similarities. And of course each individual migrant life history, with its unique mix of background, aspiration and opportunity, points to common patterns whilst at the same time emphasizing an extraordinary idiosyncrasy. In the final section of this introduction we explain what we mean by 'a life history of British emigration to Australia', we note the particular contribution which migrants' own stories make to that history and we consider some of the challenges that life stories present for the historian.[15]

Life stories and migration

The migrant life stories we use in this book come from three main sources. In 1996 a BBC film crew making a documentary in Australia titled *Ten Pound Poms* put out an appeal for potential interviewees. They were flooded with over 1,200 responses from British migrants eager to tell their story. Some were long letters which amounted to condensed life histories, ranging from accounts of joy and self-congratulation to haunting tragedies; some sent in published and unpublished autobiographies or promises of them, often with sad tales of failed attempts to publish with unsympathetic publishers. Many included memorabilia, such as photographs or copies of ship papers. The film-makers used interviews with eight of these respondents and then donated the letters to La Trobe University in Melbourne. Jim Hammerton and a team of La Trobe researchers contacted all the letter writers for permission to store and use their writing, and then began to add to this rich archive by recording and then transcribing oral history interviews with over 141 of the respondents. On tape the migrants reiterated and then expanded the stories they wrote for the BBC. Many of the interviews added quite surprising dimensions – for example about personal aspirations or family relationships – that were not hinted at in the written narratives.[16]

At about the same time on the other side of the world, Al Thomson and his University of Sussex research associate, Lani Russell, were collecting accounts by migrants who had returned to Britain. More than 500 returnees responded to an appeal in the local press and regional radio and were invited to write an account of their migration experience, 'in as much detail and depth as possible'. There were guidelines for writing which suggested possible topics but emphasized that 'It is your story and we would like to hear what *you* recall as most significant'. The Sussex project collected 252 autobiographical accounts, ranging from a few handwritten pages to book-length typescripts.

Many of the accounts were accompanied by family photographs and migration ephemera, some included migration diaries and letters, and a few people even sent home movies. Oral history interviews with thirty of these returnees enabled us to explore aspects of the migration experience which had not been covered in the written accounts.[17]

The British and Australian ends of the project started separately but soon joined forces when we realized that a joint project could make best use of these complementary collections and, crucially, could include the experiences of both settlers and returnees. We added a third set of life stories after a trawl of Australian archives and libraries uncovered additional diaries, interviews and both published and unpublished memoirs by postwar British migrants.[18] In total, and not including the letters sent to the BBC film crew in 1996, just under 500 autobiographical accounts contribute to our 'life history' of postwar British emigration to Australia.

Migrant life stories illuminate migration history in a number of ways.[19] Most obviously, personal testimony enlivens the presentation of history. The stories of so-called 'ordinary people' make history more engaging and accessible for the general reader, and migrant stories like that of Sylvia and John Cannon are resonant for other migrants who make comparisons with their own experiences. The focus on individual experience also shifts the focus of history, as Joan Watson, one of the British migrants who was delighted to record her story for the La Trobe project, explains: 'So often it seems to me, the history books tell of the deeds of the higher echelons of society, the rulers, the politicians, the military top brass, the explorers, whereas the stories of ordinary people are never told.'[20]

French historian Philippe Joutard writes that 'modern migrations ... could scarcely be studied nowadays without first hand accounts from the emigrants'.[21] A central and abiding claim of oral historians of migration has been that the migrant's own story is likely to be unrecorded or ill-documented, and that personal testimony provides an essential record of the hidden history of migration. Official sources reveal the creation, implementation and contestation of migration and 'ethnic affairs' policy, and statistics enumerate patterns of movement, settlement, employment and welfare. Oral history and written life stories demonstrate the human processes of migration and show how those policies and patterns are played out through the lives and relationships of individual migrants, families and communities. Personal testimony 'allows understanding of how moving matrices of social forces impact and shape individuals, and how individuals in turn respond, act and produce change in the larger social arena'. By illuminating aspects of the migrant experience which might otherwise be disregarded, life history enables us to 'carve theory out of ... complex personal histories', to challenge simplistic theories – such as the economic 'push and pull' explanation of migration – and to reshape the ways in which migration is understood.[22]

For example, personal accounts which span the lifecourse long before migration show how prior experience – such as John Cannon's feelings about his father's fixed social position, or the distress and insecurity suffered by Sylvia Cannon after her parents' untimely deaths – might subsequently influence migrant aspirations. The intimate detail of an extended life history reveals important aspects of migration history, like the interplay between family members as they consider emigration and then confront the challenges of the new world. Within each migrant life story we can see how different socio-economic factors influence migration and can better understand, for example, connections between employment, housing and family status.

Personal testimony is also an essential source for exploring how the knowledge, feelings, fantasies, hopes and dreams of individuals, families and communities (for which scholars use the term 'subjectivities') inform and shape the migration experience at every stage and are in turn transformed by that experience. From our accounts we can begin to understand why Britons wanted to go to Australia and what they imagined they might find; we learn of the mixed feelings of exhilaration and homesickness that accompanied arrival. We can explore why some migrants begin to think of themselves as 'Australian' while others resolutely sustain a British identity or hover between the two; and we can understand the predicament of migrants who decide, in retirement, that that they want to go 'home'.

Personal feelings are often affected by public attitudes, and migrant testimony illustrates the interconnections between the two. For example, how did prospective migrants respond to the ways in which Australia was promoted in Britain? When they came together on the ship to Australia or in a migrant hostel, in what ways did they develop a collective identity as British migrants? After they settled in Australia how did they feel about the label 'whingeing Pom'? What do migrants who have retained British citizenship think about Australian debates on a republican future?

Most of the life stories we use in this book are memory stories, either written or told, and they are told from the *present* life circumstances and identity of the narrator. Thus one of the unique features of a life history of migration is that while the stories are about past experience and the history of migration, they are also about what that migration experience means in the present life of the narrator. They illuminate the contemporary significance of migration for the individual, for a family and in the wider society. Our narrators often reflect on the meanings of their migration story and its importance for their own sense of identity. For example, in their oral history interview, Sylvia and John Cannon describe their migration history, but they also contemplate how migration has shaped their lives and identities and continues to pose issues about their place in the world. Indeed, our understanding of the British migration experience has been informed by the men and women who shared their life stories and their thoughts about migration with us.

Migrant memories make for a particular type of migration history but they also pose a series of challenges for the historian. For a start, life stories are not in themselves a sufficient source for migration history. We need statistical evidence which relates the individual story to wider patterns. If, for example, several migrants report that the terrible English winter of 1947 or the Suez crisis of 1956 was a spur for their migration, was that individual response reflected in migration applications? Reference to migration policy, regulations and publicity also helps to contextualize personal experience. When an interviewee recalls the migration 'propaganda' of Australia House in London we can contrast this memory with the actual publicity material which was produced and disseminated by the Australian immigration authorities. Though migrant life stories are the primary source and analytical focus of this book, we draw upon other sources and studies which enable us to make best use of life histories, and where necessary we suggest the need for further archival or statistical research.

A second concern about life history research is that memory is an unreliable historical source because narrators remember selectively and self-censor the stories they tell, and because these stories about the past are inevitably influenced by the present circumstances and attitudes of the narrator. Every life story is a selective rendition of past events – we can never tell the whole story. Members of the same family will choose to remember different aspects of the same event and will tell rather different stories. And the migrant who returned to Britain may reflect differently upon the rights and wrongs of the original migration decision, by comparison with another immigrant who stayed and succeeded in Australia and looks back favourably on the decision. There are at least two responses to this concern about reliability. On the one hand, we can subject migrant memories to the same critical scrutiny we would apply to any other historical source. By asking gently probing questions during an interview, by listening carefully to the interview or reading between the lines of a written account, and by contrasting what we are told with what we know from other sources, we often see the ways in which the story is selective or has been revised with hindsight. With care we can distinguish evidence about past events and attitudes from their retrospective reinterpretation.

And yet we can also approach the apparent 'flaws' in memory from another direction, and ask how they might actually provide a rather different type of evidence. What a narrator chooses to recall and relate about his or her life, and the way in which the story is told, can be very revealing. The jagged

edges and contradictions of memory tell their █████████████████████
which starts with a recollection about suppor████████████████████
moments of parental anger or opposition, conv████████████████████
feelings of family members who stayed behind, bu███████████████
and guilt experienced by those who went away. T██████████████
anecdote might also be revealing. The migrant an██████████████
often tells of the moment, after two years in Austra████████████
the native flowers in her Perth garden and placed██████████
kitchen. This anecdote, and its repetition, highligh██████████
painful confrontation with an alien landscape and a se███████ ___uccess-
ful acclimatization.[23] Conversely, silence can speak lo___ __ than words. The
teenage son or daughter who had no say and little enthusiasm for emigration
is sometimes missing in the parents' account, and that absence points to a
troubling story of teenage angst and intergenerational tension which only
occasionally emerges in the comparatively safe space of the extended life history
interview – and in the teenager's own story. When we listen carefully to the
ways in which migrants tell the story of their life, the so-called unreliability of
memory becomes a resource rather than a problem for the historian.[24]

A rather different concern about life history research is that the stories we
use are unrepresentative, that our sample will be biased in some way and our
findings irrevocably flawed. Historical sources are never comprehensive and
no sample is ever fully representative. The key is to know who and what is
represented in your selection and how any significant exclusions might affect
your conclusions. The British migrants who recorded their life stories for us
were, like most respondents to oral history projects, 'willing' subjects, perhaps
more likely to be satisfied than disaffected with their migration experience or
to have a strong desire to tell their story because migration had a major impact
upon their lives, for better or worse. But with this caveat, on the whole the
richness and diversity of experience evident in the accounts we collected
outweighs the risk of sample bias. Furthermore, the different origins and forms
of the life stories in our archive – from settlers in Australia and returnees in
Britain, oral histories and written autobiographies, contemporary diaries,
letters and photographs as well as retrospective accounts – offset concerns we
might have about a sample based upon a single approach. Finally, and as a
double-check, a simple quantitative review of the interviews we recorded
confirms that, for the most part, they match the characteristics of the postwar
British migrants in terms of regional origin, social class and family status.[25]
The most notable absences are accounts from people who migrated later in
life and who are no longer alive to tell the tale – though we know that because
of the rules of the assisted passage scheme there were only a relatively small
proportion of emigrants aged over 45, most of whom were parents and

extended families. At points throughout this book we draw
...es from within our archive of migrant narratives, for example as
...y of illuminating the reasons for migration and return. These are not,
...ctly speaking, 'representative samples' and they are not intended to
provide numerical 'proof' for our arguments, but they do indicate patterns
and themes that we explore in more depth and detail through the life histories.

Life stories also offer an alternative to the study of a representative
sample. While it is important to know if there are significant gaps within the
archive, and to discover patterns of common behaviour and attitude across the
sample, the single life story can, by itself, illuminate the migration experience.
Anthropologists often refer to the 'telling case', a single case study which
might not be typical or representative but which offers deep and intimate
insights and which suggests new questions which might be taken to other
sources. The migration life history of Sylvia and John Cannon is the first of
several detailed case studies of a single migrant or a migrant family which we
use throughout the book to illustrate particular aspects of migration in
greater depth and to highlight the dynamic relationship between individual
experience and social forces.

One final possible criticism about the use of personal testimony as a
historical source is that the story is often told to the researcher and might be
unduly influenced by that relationship. When we collected written accounts
and recorded life history interviews we tried to offset this influence by
encouraging migrants to write or tell their stories in their own terms and in
response to open-ended questions. But of course every storyteller is affected
by an audience and the key is to be alert to the relationship and its influence.
For example, when Lani and Al began to collect accounts by return migrants
in Britain they worried that their Australian origins – apparent as soon as they
spoke on the phone – might be off-putting for people who had negative
memories of their time in Australia or might persuade them to tone down
their criticisms so as not to offend. This concern proved unfounded: people
were delighted in the interest in their migrant past and happy to speak about
good and bad times. Indeed, Lani and Al found that their own knowledge of
places in Australia often sparked off detailed and enthusiastic recollection. In
most of the interviews conducted for this project – in both countries – we
were impressed by the extraordinary frankness and generosity of men and
women who were willing to relate even the more troubling aspects of their
migration histories, and to go beyond their initial written correspondence and
offer deeply reflective life histories.

The other side of this coin is that our own life histories as migrants
brought each of us to this project and have affected the relationships we have
formed with our respondents and the themes of our research and writing.

Jim as an 11-year-old child followed a familiar path of many postwar British migrants, not to Australia but to Canada. In 1949 his family boarded the venerable *Aquitania* and emigrated from Sheffield to Montreal. The seven-day winter sea journey, which terminated in Halifax, was a brief and chilly interlude compared to the Australian voyage, but it was enough to instil in him a sense of the vast distance and the huge undertaking his parents had initiated. In the new country he rapidly adopted Canadian ways. But observation of his parents gave some inkling of the stresses of the migrant's condition. Although the family was cushioned from initial hardships by accommodation with his mother's relatives, tensions were rife and money scarce, and the family briefly celebrated 'freedom' when, after six months, they moved out of shared housing into a rented duplex. Still, Jim's mother suffered bouts of homesickness for her brothers and sisters which clouded the family's outlook. Recovery from this was slow and painful, and the fact that father adapted more readily to an enthusiastic Canadian identity while mother remained steadfastly attached to all things English (even the tomatoes never tasted the same!) was never far from the surface of family life.

Jim and his sister were told regularly that it was for them to make the best of the opportunities of the new country, and ironically it was Jim's educational path which took him to an academic job in Australia, twenty years to the day after arriving in Canada. Only some years later when he married and had his own children did he begin to experience personally some of the anguish of the migrant condition, as his children, their grandparents and wider extended family only saw each other a few times in a decade. The dilemma of being attached to three countries yet belonging fully to none became more acute with each overseas visit, and played some part in his long-term academic interest in migration history. In this project the long exposure to the stories of other British migrants has been a further exercise in self-discovery. While Jim is cautious about identifying too easily with surface similarities in quite different contexts, sharing a migrant identity with informants has often been an immeasurable asset in interviews, and a further spur to reflection about the dilemmas of his own transnational family.

Al's migration has taken him in the opposite direction. Born in Victoria in 1960, within a few months he was travelling by sea with his parents and older brothers to England, where his Australian army officer father served as a staff instructor at Camberley. Returning to Australia in 1963 they were evacuated from the *Canberra* when it caught fire in the Mediterranean. Among the many assisted passage migrants on that same dramatic voyage was Mrs Mullard, a young Surrey woman who helped out with the Thomson sons and whom, in turn, the Thomsons sponsored to Australia. 'Mrs M' became part of the family. Her Australian Englishness, and her regular trips between

Canberra and Camberley – where her English family wanted her to care for ageing relatives – became part of Thomson family folklore.

In 1983 Al left Melbourne for a year of postgraduate study in England. Like the postwar generation of young and single British sojourners in Australia, he was excited by the prospect of a year abroad but fully intended to return when the year was up. But whilst living in Brighton he fell in love and, after months of indecision, decided to live in England. In the classic migrant pattern, once he had his own children these family ties and then schooling made return to Australia much more difficult – though it remains a tantalizing prospect.

In Brighton on the south coast, Al's Australian background and accent have often prompted strangers in shops or on public transport to tell their own story of migration to Australia and return to Britain, or to recall relatives and friends who took up the ten pound passage ('You might know my uncle Ted?'). These casual conversations sparked off research to record such stories in more depth. In the course of the research Al was often reminded of aspects of his own, unintended migration: for example, the acute homesickness of the first years in England; an undiminished longing for the landscape and seascape of eastern Australia; and the practical and emotional difficulties of living in a transnational extended family. At times such experiences helped him to empathize with the stories he was told and offered personal ways of understanding. In turn, researching and writing this book has enriched Al's understanding of his own migration – not least in thinking anew about the desire for and difficulty of return.

A guide for readers

The chapters of this book are arranged in three parts, which follow the rough chronology of the migrant life history. Part I focuses on the period leading up to arrival in Australia. In Chapter 1, 'Imagining Australia', we explain the origin and nature of the assisted passage scheme and explore the ways in which prospective migrants imagined their destination and a different future for themselves. Chapter 2, 'Leaving Britain', considers the ways in which life in Britain before and during the Second World War affected subsequent migration decisions, and then examines aspects of postwar life that induced Britons to take up the assisted passage and discusses the practical and emotional challenges of leaving. Chapter 3, 'Between two worlds', evokes the extraordinary setting of the migrant ship (and later aeroplane) and how migrants' relationships with other passengers, and with exotic places and people in the ports of empire, affected their ideas about migration and about themselves.

As its title indicates, Part II considers the immigrant life of 'Britons in postwar Australia'. In Chapter 4, 'Strangers on the shore', we describe arrival in Australia and ask how the British responded to a country that seemed both 'very familiar and awfully strange'.[26] The Commonwealth migrant hostels offered an especially stark place of arrival, and Chapter 5, '"Butlins without the laughs": life on the hostel', explores hostel lives and grievances. Working life looms large in the ways in which British migrants recount their Australian stories – whether in terms of adapting to Australia, dazzling success, battling and survival or a sense of wounded failure – and is the focus of Chapter 6. The prospect of better family fortunes and a home of one's own impelled many Britons to Australia, and Chapter 7 explores the 'Suburban dreams and family realities' of the immigrants' everyday life. Younger, single migrants did not always intend to make their future in Australia, and Chapter 8 considers the less settled stories of these sojourners and the relationship between mobility, affluence and the aspirations of postwar youth. A significant number of 'boomerang migrants' returned to Britain and the final chapter of Part II assesses the causes of return and, in particular, the significance of homesickness and family ties.

Part III focuses on the contemporary significance of postwar British migration to Australia, for individual migrants and in the two societies, and explores the relationship between 'Migration, memory and identity'. In Chapter 10, 'Coming "home"', we examine the consequences of return and the ways in which the years in Australia are remembered by, and significant for, migrants living back in Britain. The concluding chapter focuses on postwar British migrants in Australia today and considers how they now reflect on their migration and identify themselves in relation to both Britain and Australia at the start of a new century.

Notes

1 Unless otherwise noted, information relating to Sylvia and John Cannon derives from an interview conducted in Perth for the La Trobe University project in 2000 (see Bibliography for full details).

2 Appleyard, *The Ten Pound Immigrants*, p. 160.

3 Charlotte Erickson coined the term 'invisible immigrants' to describe Britons who emigrated to the United States in the nineteenth century, in her 1972 book *Invisible Immigrants*. Our use of the term 'migrant' encompasses the 'emigrant' and 'immigrant' experience as well as the return process.

4 Quoted in Appleyard, *The Ten Pound Immigrants*, p. 28.

5 Committee on Social Patterns, Commonwealth Immigration Advisory Council, *The Departure of Settlers from Australia, Final Report*. This report considered all migrant returnees but much of the research focused on the British. For the research projects, see Appleyard, *British Emigration to Australia*; Richardson, *British Immigrants and Australia*.

6 A rare exception is Paul, *Whitewashing Britain*.

7 Appleyard, *Ten Pound Immigrants*. Mark Peel's *Good Times, Hard Times: The Past and the Future in Elizabeth* is an exemplary local study of the predominantly British postwar Adelaide suburb of Elizabeth. Betka Zamoyska's *The Ten Pound Fare* does not tackle the historical issues in any depth. Nor does Alan Whicker in *Whicker's World Down Under*.

8 For example, Wilton and Bosworth, *Old Worlds and New Australia*; Lack and Templeton, *Bold Experiment*; Peters, *Milk and Honey*. An important exception to neglect of the British in early general studies of immigration was James Jupp's 1966 study, *Arrivals and Departures*.

9 Exceptions include Allery, *Elizabeth*; Gray and Young, *The Ten Quid Tourists*. Several migration anthologies include a single British story: Lowenstein and Loh, *The Immigrants*; Henderson, *From All Corners*; Hawthorne, *Making It in Australia*.

10 See, for example, Scott, *Changing Countries*. Mary Rose Liverani's autobiography *The Winter Sparrows* is an exception, an extraordinary account by an 'ordinary' migrant which was critically and commercially successful.

11 See, for example, Snuggs, *I Came a Migrant*; Preston, *Blowing My Own Trumpet*; Sharp, *The Beginning to the End 1920–1993*; Skowronski, *I Can't Think of a Title*; Towler, *Look Mum, I Can Speak Australian!* Others have been published in Britain, including: Frost, *It Wasn't So Bad After All*; Upton, *To the Undiscovered Ends*; Hill, *Corrugated Castles*.

12 Sarah Ricketts to BBC, 26 November 1996; Joan Watson to A. James Hammerton, 4 January 1998. These letters are held in the La Trobe University Archive (see note 17).

13 Carole Hamilton-Barwick, 'In search of a voice that is silent: narratives of postwar British women immigrants' (PhD in progress, La Trobe University); Annie Rule, 'Keeping the money under the soap' (PhD in progress, University of Western Australia); Sara Wills, 'Knowing their place? A social and cultural history of British migration in late twentieth century Australia' (ARC Fellowship project in progress, University of Melbourne); Emma Greenwood, 'The importance of British stock: apartheid South Africa and (White) Australia, c. 1945–1960' (PhD in progress, Australian National University); Peel, 'Dislocated Men: Imagining "Britain" and "Australia"'.

14 See, for example, Stratton, 'Not Just Another Multicultural Story'; Brabazon, *Tracking the Jack*, especially ch. 6; Jupp, 'Post-war English Settlers in Adelaide and Perth'; Jupp, 'From New Britannia to Foreign Power'.

15 By 'life story' we mean any account of personal experience, whether recorded in a diary, a letter, a memoir or an oral history interview. By 'life history' we mean, firstly, a person's attempt to tell the 'whole' story of their life and, secondly, a particular type of history, exemplified by this book, which draws primarily upon life story sources.

16 Paul Neuberg (producer), *Ten Pound Poms*, Pulse and Touch productions, BBC 1, 14 April 1997. See also Hussey, 'Making Television Oral History'; Thomson, 'Ten Pound Poms and Television Oral History'. Further details about the La Trobe University archive and project are in Hammerton and Coleborne, 'Ten-Pound Poms Revisited: Battlers' Tales and British Migration to Australia, 1947–1971'. The La Trobe project was led by Jim Hammerton, and research assistants over the years include: Catherine Coleborne, Helen Gardner, Carole Hamilton-Barwick and Amanda Rooke.

17 The University of Sussex return migration collection will be archived in the Mass-Observation Archive at the University of Sussex. Citations of accounts collected by these two projects use the abbreviations 'US' and 'LU' to distinguish those held in the University of Sussex and La Trobe University archives. A full listing with archival references is in the Bibliography.

18 In 1998 Al researched migrant narratives located in Australian collections. For a survey of these accounts see Thomson, 'Recording British Migration'.
19 On the use of oral history and life writings in migration research see Thomson, 'Moving Stories'.
20 Joan Watson to A. James Hammerton, 4 January 1998, LU.
21 Joutard, *Ces voix qui nous viennent du passé*.
22 Benmayor and Skotnes, 'Some Reflections on Migration and Identity', pp. 13–14.
23 Jolley interview, Battye Library, OH2268; Jolley, 'Interview with Candida Baker', Mitchell Library ML MSS 4880/27 item 5, p. 3.
24 On the interpretation of oral history interviews see Perks and Thomson, *The Oral History Reader*.
25 See Appendix for further details.
26 Susan Jack written account US.

Part I
Emigration

Imagining Australia

In the late 1940s, Fred Ford, a young father who worked as a fitter and turner in Salford, began to imagine a different life in Australia:

After six years of war, there was still rationing. It was impossible to buy a house even if you had the money for one. I had no home of my own. I had a wife and two small babies and I had to live with my mother. The circumstances were difficult. An advertisement in the *Manchester Evening News* prompted me to apply for a £10 assisted passage to Australia. The publicity was impressive. I had a dream of a different country and a different life, one which would be better for my children.... I imagined I would be going somewhere that was sunny and clean, that there would be plenty of leisure time. It would be ideal for a young family and there would be no problem getting a job or a house.[1]

Fred Ford's memory encapsulates two interconnected forces which impelled Britons to emigrate to Australia in the quarter century after the Second World War: difficult circumstances in Britain and the tantalizing promise of Australia. Every emigrant makes an extraordinary decision. Uprooting yourself and perhaps your family and travelling half way around the world to settle in another country is never easy, and the decision is driven by significant motivating factors. Disentangling those motivations and explaining that decision is a serious challenge for the historian of migration. There is rarely one single and simple explanation. More often there are several different and interconnected reasons of greater or lesser significance, some with a long and complex personal history, others a response to a more immediate concern. The prospective migrant may be pulled in different directions; within a migrant family the various factors will have different significance and there may well be conflict over the final decision.

This opening chapter explores the attraction of Australia for prospective migrants. We explain how the ten pound scheme enabled working-class Britons to realize an Australian dream, and consider the ways in which Australian immigration authorities sold emigrants an image of Australia that resonated with pre-existing British ideals and aspirations.

'Emigrate to Australia for £10'

Assisted passage migration from Britain to Australia predated the ten pound scheme but was transformed by the urgent demographic needs of postwar Australia.[2] Throughout the nineteenth century Australian colonial governments were forced to provide financial assistance for many British immigrants in order to offset the disadvantages of the long sea voyage and to compete with other migrant destinations such as North America. Between 1860 and 1919, 45 per cent of all British immigrants were assisted by Australian governments. In the interwar years the British government and the white Dominions of Australia, New Zealand, Canada and southern Africa developed an Empire self-sufficiency scheme which linked migration, investment and tariffs to counter economic competition from other countries. The Dominions would export primary produce to Britain on preferential terms in return for capital, manufactured goods and migrants to farm the uncultivated hinterlands of Empire. Under the Empire Settlement Act the British and Australian governments subsidized the costs of selected migrants – the first time that the British government had contributed to the fares of emigrants to Australia. Between 1921 and 1933 over 200,000 Britons arrived in Australia under this scheme, but it was undermined by the Depression of the 1930s and by a declining demand for agricultural labour as Australia became a more industrial nation.[3]

Amongst British policy makers the idea that British interests were served by a strong and interdependent Empire and Commonwealth, and that emigrants from the 'mother country' could reinforce the British character and loyalty of the imperial outposts, continued into the immediate postwar years and underpinned British support for a new assisted passage scheme.[4] But the greatest enthusiasm came from Australia. While postwar housing shortages and the pressing demands of ex-servicemen at first tempered support for immigration within the other Dominions, in Australia the war had forced a dramatic reassessment of national priorities. The Australian nightmare of invasion from the near north had almost come true and, with Britain unable to help, Australia's wartime Labor government had been forced to look to the United States for protection from Japan. In the past, Australian Labor had been wary of immigration, but 'populate or perish' was the new national mantra, as the government determined to develop a strong industrial base and fill the vulnerable empty spaces of a vast continent. In 1945 Arthur Calwell, the first minister at the new Ministry of Immigration, declared that the Australian economy could sustain 2 percent population growth every year, but that only half of that amount would be met by a declining birth rate. Immigration would make up the balance, with an annual intake of 70,000 immigrants that would increase as the total population increased.[5]

From the outset, it was intended that the bulk of these immigrants would be British, and that the postwar immigration scheme would sustain the British character of Australian society. In 1946 Calwell argued that 'for every foreign migrant there will be ten people from the United Kingdom', and in that year the two countries forged the United Kingdom–Australia Free and Assisted Passage Agreements, which became operative on 31 March 1947.[6] Under the schemes ex-servicemen were granted free passages paid by the British government, and the British and Australian governments would each make an equal contribution towards subsidizing the fares of selected citizens who would only pay £10 per adult and £5 for each child aged between 14 and 18, whilst younger children went for free (by the 1960s all children up to the age of 18 went for free). Australian migration officials would select migrants and be responsible for their placement and support in Australia. Assisted passage migrants were expected to remain in Australia for at least two years, and if they returned within a two-year period they would be required to reimburse the balance owed on the outward fare.

The assisted passage scheme generated a euphoric response in Britain. At one point in 1947 over 400,000 Britons were registered at Australia House in London for assisted passages. The greatest obstacle to meeting this extra-ordinary demand was the severe postwar shipping shortage. Calwell and his staff embarked on determined and successful negotiations with British officials to obtain converted troopships for the migrant trade, in order that 'no berth for a British migrant would be lost', and by 1949 ship-owners had guaranteed berths for up to 400,000 British migrants over the next five years.[7]

Although the basic format of the British–Australian assisted passage migration scheme barely changed over the next quarter century, there were significant changes in the funding and circumstances of Australian postwar immigration. Within British politics the desire to 'people the Common-wealth' with British stock was offset by increasing concern that emigration was draining Britain of the skilled workers and young families which it needed for its own postwar reconstruction. Worst of all, Britain was paying for these people to leave! In 1950 Britain reduced its contribution to the assisted passage scheme from an equal share to a maximum of £25 per adult emigrant. The following year the British government decided to limit its total annual contribution to the scheme to £500,000, and in 1954 this was reduced to £150,000 per year (enough to subsidize the fares of about 1,000 migrants), a figure that was maintained until 1972.[8]

Of far greater significance for Australian postwar history was the fact that Britain simply could not supply sufficient migrants to meet Australia's economic needs. Thus humanitarian feelings were only part of the reason why Australia accepted 170,000 European displaced persons between 1947 and

1953; the International Refugee Organisation provided shipping for these refugees and agreed that Australia could place them for up to two years in jobs that were essential to postwar reconstruction. By the early 1950s the initial rush of British assisted passage migrants had subsided and Australian immigration authorities looked to other sources in order to reach immigration targets and sustain economic growth. They turned to the Baltic states and northern Europe in the early 1950s and then to Italy, Greece, Yugoslavia and other southern European and Mediterranean countries throughout the 1950s and 1960s. By 1948 Calwell accepted that Australia would never achieve the ten to one ratio between British and foreign migrants and instead settled on the ratio of two to one. By 1951 the government settled for a British proportion of 50 per cent, though this would only be achieved in the peak years of the 1960s.

When the number or proportion of British migrants dropped, the Australian government extended and varied the scheme to sustain the British contribution. In the 1940s Australia had prioritized single skilled migrants nominated by Australians who could provide them with accommodation. By 1952 a Commonwealth Nomination Scheme opened up migration to Britons who could not find a personal sponsor and offered accommodation in migrant hostels. Single migrants and couples without children were preferred, but when their numbers diminished the scheme was extended to encourage British migrant families. In the late 1950s British enthusiasm for emigration to Australia waned as economic conditions improved in Britain and when Australia's reputation as an immigrant country was tarnished by controversy over conditions in the migrant hostels. To counter this trend Australia opened additional migration offices in British provincial cities and abolished the £5 fare for teenagers. In 1957 the government announced a 'Bring out a Briton' scheme which was intended to inspire Australian families to sponsor British migrants, and in 1959 the 'Nest Egg' scheme offered further incentives for Britons who could bring a minimum of £500 with them to Australia and pay for their own housing when they arrived.

Whilst in the immediate postwar years Australian immigration authorities had sought migrants with the particular skills required by the national economy, by the late 1950s there were almost no skill restrictions. British immigrants needed to be in sound health and, ordinarily, under the age of 45. They were also expected to be white. Britons of mixed race had very great difficulty in being accepted as immigrants for 'White Australia'.[9] But apart from these limitations almost any single adult or family wishing to emigrate from Britain was welcome in Australia. With so few restrictions the 1960s has been described as 'a halcyon period' for British emigration to Australia, with British migrants comprising just under 47 per cent of Australia's immigration intake for the decade.[10] In the peak year of 1969 almost 80,000 Britons came to Australia.

Table 1 Percentage of UK migrants in Australia's migrant intake

	Total settlers	Total UK settlers	Unassisted UK settlers	Assisted UK settlers
1945–49/50	379,560	175,138	92,287	82,851
1950/51 –1959/60	1,174,081	405,946	118,146	287,800
1960/61–1969/70	1,339,469	623,344	44,252	579,092
1970/71–1979/80	956,765	341,565	119,379	222,186
1980/81–1981/82	228,720	70,271	58,792	11,479
Total	4,078,595	1,616,264	432,856	1,183,408

Note: for much of the period the small and declining number of Irish immigrants are included within the UK figures, and before 1959 the statistics do not distinguish permanent and long term movement from settler movement.
Sources: Appleyard, *The Ten Pound Immigrants*, p. 160; Department of Immigration, *Consolidated Statistics, vol. 1*, 1966, pp. 32–3.

In the quarter century after the Second World War Britain remained the single most important source for Australian immigrants, and yet in these same decades Australian society was transformed by the dramatic and unprecedented influx of migrants from non-English-speaking countries. In 1947 only 1.9 per cent of the Australian population had been born in a non-English-speaking country; by 1991 this figure had ballooned to 15.2 per cent.[11] The creation of a multicultural Australia was a begrudging transformation, required by economic and demographic needs and cutting across Australian racial sympathies. From the 1940s through to the early 1970s there was sustained and bipartisan Australian support for the pre-eminence of British immigrants. At the first national Citizenship Convention in 1950 Harold Holt, Calwell's successor as Minister of Immigration in the new Liberal government, announced plans for 200,000 immigrants in the coming year; half of these would come from Britain, 'in order to retain, as much as possible, the fundamental composition of the population'.[12]

Australia preferred British migrants and offered them a privileged status by contrast with migrants from non-English-speaking countries. Though other countries secured different types of assisted passage schemes, conditions on British migrant ships were much more comfortable than those deemed suitable for refugees and assisted migrants from other countries. Australia's Nationality and Citizenship Act of 1948 created the category of Australian citizenship but it also made a clear distinction between 'aliens' and British subjects. The British could apply for Australian citizenship after one year of residence whereas 'aliens' had to wait five years. Even if they did not take out Australian citizenship, British migrants, unlike 'alien' migrants, enjoyed most of the benefits of citizenship. They could vote in Australian elections and move in and out of the country without restriction. They were entitled to all the social security benefits available to Australians except the age pensions (after 1953 a reciprocal agreement required the Australian government to top up a British pension to the Australian level). When the Commonwealth began to provide hostel accommodation for British migrants in the early 1950s it was usually better than the accommodation intended for other migrants.[13]

Throughout the 1960s Australian–British relations changed as Britain's economic and political ties shifted towards Europe and away from the Commonwealth, and as Australia forged closer trading links with its Asian neighbours. After Britain joined the European Community in 1972 both countries removed the right of almost unimpeded entry from one country to the other. At the same time Australians were increasingly questioning the White Australia policy and the preference for, and favoured treatment of, British migrants. With the election of Gough Whitlam's Labor government in 1972 the special privileges accorded to British migrants came to an end, and over the next decade Australian governments progressively dismantled the assisted passage scheme until its demise in 1982. At the same time, the economic crisis of the mid-1970s caused a dramatic cut in Australia's immigrant intake, and the proportion of British migrants declined. More significantly, the percentage of British assisted migrants within the total of assisted migrants plummeted, from 52 per cent in 1977 to just 12 per cent in 1980. After 1979 prospective Australian immigrants – including the British – were judged according to how many points they scored in terms of age, education, occupation, English language capacity and connections with Australia, and after 1982 all immigrants had to pay their own way. The British dream of assisted passage to a new life in Australia was over.

There is no doubt that the ten pound scheme was a significant factor in the postwar emigration decisions of many Britons. For most migrants, and especially large working-class families for whom the standard fares to Australia were prohibitive, the scheme made emigration possible. In 1952, for example, the real cost of shipping a British migrant to Australia was about £120, and in 1965 the full fare for a family of two adults and three young children was about £600. In the 1940s, when the average male manual worker's weekly wage was about £7, it might have taken some time for a working-class family to raise its own subsidized contribution to the fares, but by 1960 the average male manual worker's weekly wage had doubled to well above the cost of an assisted passage. The £10 contribution was never a significant obstacle to emigration and, more importantly, the subsidy made emigration affordable.[14]

The assisted passage scheme also gave Australia a competitive edge over the other destinations for British postwar emigrants. Without the ten pound scheme Australia would have struggled to compete with Canada – which was much closer to home – or indeed with the 'New Towns' that were being built around the edges of British metropolitan centres and which also offered a better life for workers and their families. New Zealand – another competitor in the emigration market – had its own assisted passage scheme, though many migrants recall that New Zealand was more selective than Australia or that the terms were less attractive.[15]

Emigration-minded Britons sometimes surveyed the different migration options in the white Dominions, and apart from the cost of passage, several viewpoints recur in the decision-making of migrants who chose Australia: Canada was too cold; New Zealand was too choosy; and southern Africa had racial problems.[16] In 1964, for example, Scottish electrician John Hardie was unhappy in a temporary job after redundancy and began to think of emigration for himself and his family. John had relatives in New Zealand but was told that it would take at least two years to be accepted by New Zealand:

I thought well I'm not working at this job for two years and sat down and wrote the letters, Canada House, Australia House, South Africa House, and give them their due Canada came back and says, it was the winter, and their idea was that a lot of the people come in from the forests and work in the towns in the winter and then go back out in the spring time, so he says you'll be really struggling to get work. Fine, the guy was honest. At that time South Africa was just started apartheid-type situation, well there's no way I'm running about with a screwdriver in one hand, a gun in the other, and Australia *was* exactly six months to the day I wrote the letter that we flew from Scotland, exactly six months.[17]

Who were the 'ten pound Poms'?

About one and a half million people emigrated to Australia from the United Kingdom and Ireland between 1945 and 1982 (for much of this period statistics did not include a separate figure for the Irish, who were a small and decreasing percentage of the total). In the immediate postwar years between 1945 and 1958 there were about 300,000 UK emigrants to Australia, and in the peak years of a sustained high intake – from 1959 to 1975 – 925,675 people came to Australia from the UK and Ireland. The vast majority of the British postwar emigrants to Australia – about 90 per cent in the 1960s – travelled under the assisted passage scheme. The number of personal and Commonwealth nominees varied each year, but in 1959, for example, the proportion of Commonwealth nominees was just slightly higher than that of personal nominees.[18]

So who were the men, women and children who took up the assisted passage to their imagined Australia? For a start, we know that these migrants were mostly young people. The grandparents of migrating families and older people with exceptional skills were amongst the few exceptions to the age restriction of 45. Only 7.6 per cent of Appleyard's sample of 1959 emigrants was aged over 45 compared with the 36.8 per cent of the UK population at the time, and 38.5 per cent were under 15 years of age by comparison with 23.3 per cent of the UK population. The great majority of the assisted passage migrants – about 84 per cent – were members of family units, whilst about 16 per cent were single persons, fairly evenly divided between single men and women.[19]

The regional origin of the British assisted passage migrants mostly matched the population distribution of the country, but with some significant exceptions. Rural areas were substantially under-represented amongst the migrants, who were much more likely to come from cities and towns. The Welsh were also under-represented (3.2 per cent of the migrants as against 5.8 per cent of the population) by comparison with the Scots, who were more likely to emigrate (13.7 per cent of the migrants as against 10.3 per cent of the population). Of the British migrants about 84 per cent were English, with the largest number coming from the London and the south east (25.4 per cent against 24.5 per cent of the population) and the north west (15.1 per cent against 14.4 per cent of the population).[20]

These migrants were, according to Appleyard, 'by no means the ne'er-do-well of British society'.[21] Almost none of them came from unemployment and few were impoverished. They were not unduly drawn from the poorer inner city areas, and in fact were more likely to come from the suburban fringes of British cities and provincial towns. About a third of migrant families already owned or were buying a house in Britain (this matched home ownership levels for the general population in the late 1950s), and of those in rented accommodation about half lived in council houses. Overall the skill and income levels of the adult migrants were above the British average, though very few had tertiary education and members of professions requiring higher education were under-represented. Most migrants had left school with only the basic qualifications, though many of the men had acquired further training through apprenticeship in a trade. For example, between 1963 and 1973, 46 per cent of the men were 'craftsmen and production process workers', and 41 per cent of British migrant women workers had clerical skills. In short, the migrants came from Britain's aspiring working and lower middle classes, and British immigration did indeed provide the skilled and semi-skilled workforce that Australia needed for postwar reconstruction.[22]

It is much harder and perhaps more risky to generalize about the character or personality of the postwar British migrants. Research by Alan Richardson in the 1950s, which contrasted a sample of eighty British married men who were about to emigrate to Australia under the assisted passage scheme with a matched sample of eighty non-emigrants, suggested that the emigrants were distinctive in several ways. They were less likely to have close ties with their extended family or to a particular locality. They were more likely to have 'energetic, out-going personalities', and they gave the impression that 'they felt themselves to be more in charge of their destinies and less the pawns of fate than did the non-emigrants'.[23] None of these trends is particularly surprising; it was harder for people with close family ties and strong local roots to leave the country, and the decision to emigrate half way around the world required a bold intent. But the migrant life histories we examine through-out this book enable us to go further, and to see the workings of individual character and family dynamics within a context of social, economic and other factors which influenced the migration decision. They help us to understand the lure of Australia and the desire for a better life which made the ten pound passage such an attractive offer.

Selling Australia

By 1966, a social survey in Britain confirmed that Australia was the favoured destination for British families with serious thoughts of emigration.[24] The ten pound scheme had given Australia a competitive edge, but Australian immigration authorities had also worked hard for twenty years to persuade Britons to travel to the other side of the world. Most ten pound Poms recall the alluring publicity for the assisted passage scheme, ranging from billboards and newspaper advertisements urging Britons to 'Walk Tall in Australia', through to glossy information leaflets and film nights which portrayed sunny Australia in glorious technicolour. Australia House in London sold a potent image of Australia.

Australia and the Migrant, for example, was a newsletter for prospective migrants issued by the Australian News and Information Bureau at Australia House. Number 22, of March 1948, led with extracts from an article from the *Brisbane Telegraph* in which new British immigrants gave their impressions of settlement in Queensland. These migrants most liked 'your sunshine, your open spaces and your candour'. A young man from Tottenham who was now working on a pineapple plantation and hoped to buy his own farm enjoyed 'the complete absence of class distinction and red tape. Australians are blunt, they call a spade a spade.' A carpenter from Lancaster who was building his own home in Queensland advised that 'this country offers plenty of oppor-tunity to those who are willing to work'. The British migrants were 'bewildered … by the meat and fruit-filled windows of our shops', and Mrs Jefferis, a mother of four from Cardiff, explained that it was 'heart-breaking to see so much food here when you know what your people have to suffer at home'. Mrs Jefferis also noted that the Australian housing shortage was one of the few 'dislikes' of the British migrants, and could 'not understand why there should be a serious housing shortage in a country growing so much timber'. As if to offset this hint of a problem, another item in the newsletter asserted that 'Australia is building thousands of new homes to meet the housing shortage'. Other articles featured the expansion of factories and job opportunities, and the ways in which British immigrants were welcomed to Australia and helped to settle. In short, 'Our new settlers seem satisfied with Queensland. And if they don't know it already, Queensland is satisfied with its new settlers.'

This type of publicity worked. Ron Warden, an Australian journalist based in London between 1949 and 1953, recalled that in these years of post-war austerity Australia was 'almost synonymous with migration': 'Australia's publicity, we found, had caught the imagination of a great part of the country. It added up to two things – sun and meat.'[25]

Australia Invites You, published by the Chief Migration Officer at Australia House on behalf of the Department of Immigration, offered 'a summary of what Australia offers emigrants from the United Kingdom', and the tenth edition of 1959 was an attractive fold-out leaflet studded with photographs of Australian life (see Figure 5). On one side a bold heading emphasized 'Australia for Your Children's Future', whilst smaller print explained the assisted passage schemes available for different categories of British migrants and the application and interview procedures. The reverse side highlighted eight reasons why Britons should 'Emigrate to Australia for £10'. Australia was a vast country with 'Room for Millions More', at least half of whom would be British. The half a million Britons who had come to Australia since the war had found a 'British Way of Life' amongst people 'who are predominantly of British Isles stock'. Australia had a 'High Standard of Living' and a 'very high proportion of families have motor-cars' while 'most families own their own homes or are buying them'. Industrial 'Expansion in all Directions' ensured 'good employment prospects for immigrants', and 'Farming in Australia' offered 'plenty of scope for British migrants "on the land"'. British migrants were covered under special conditions for 'Social Security and Health' with a 'well-subsidised health service, modern hospitals and a generous system of social security', and the high standard of 'Education in Australia' was guaranteed by free primary, secondary and technical schools and bursaries for higher education. Finally, 'Australia's Famous Climate' enabled 'people of all ages' to 'enjoy the long outdoor season' and 'some of the finest surf and bathing beaches in the world'.

Whilst this written text offered an enticing inducement to emigration, the subliminal message of the twenty accompanying photographs suggested three main reasons for emigration to Australia: a sunny outdoor lifestyle

Room for Millions More

Australia is 32 times the size of Great Britain, but has only 10 million people. Planning to take millions more, she wants at least half to be British. As well as open spaces with fine sheep, cattle and dairy country, the immigrant sees vast natural resources and industrial expansion in all directions—expansion that spells opportunity and a future.

Expansion in all Directions

There are good employment prospects for immigrants. As well as long-established fields of employment, hundreds of millions are being spent on new oil refineries, motor car plants, blast furnaces, steel mills, chemical and textile industries. A tremendous hydro-electricity and irrigation scheme is being carried out. Immigrant workers are welcome.

A British Way of Life

More than half a million British people have gone to Australia since the war. They found a British way of life and a welcome from a people who are predominantly of British Isles stock. Below is a young British migrant family out for Saturday morning shopping in one of the older suburbs on a typical sunny day.

Social Security : Health

A well-subsidised health service, modern hospitals and a generous system of social security all contribute to good national health standards for young and old. British migrants are covered under special conditions for the social service benefits (maternity child endowment, unemployment and sickness benefits, pensions, etc.) and for the health scheme.

Australia's Famous Climate

Famous for its sunshine, Australia also has some of the finest surf and bathing beaches in the world. For a big proportion of the population, they are close at hand for weekend and holiday recreation. There is a wide range of climate over the various parts of the continent, but the average is temperate. People of all ages enjoy the long outdoor season.

Education in Australia

Education of high standard is provided in free primary, secondary and technical schools run by the State Governments. For those who prefer private schooling, denominational or otherwise, there are many excellent establishments. Bursaries and subsidies enable children of suitable ability to go on to Universities and to other advanced levels.

High Standard of Living

The standard of living is amongst the world's highest. The Federal basic wage for adult males in Sydney at March 1959 was £13.8s., and slightly lower in other States. However, the average weekly earnings of all male adults was £18.15s.0d. a week last year. A very high proportion of families have motor-cars; most families own their own homes or are buying them.

Farming in Australia

Many thousands have emigrated to Australia in rural occupations and have done well there. There is still plenty of scope for British migrants "on the land". You can apply for an assisted passage on a personal nomination, or, if you are an experienced farm worker, Australia House may be able to consider you (with family) on an employer's nomination.

Emigrate TO AUSTRALIA FOR £10

(seven photographs); modern cities, services and industries (eight photographs); and the benefits to families with young children (five photographs). By the late 1950s, with increasing economic prosperity and the end of rationing in Britain, the comparison of austerity Britain and abundant Australia was no longer appropriate. Australia was now sold as a country where young families would prosper in a modern society with familiar British characteristics but a superior climate and lifestyle.

'I had a dream of a different country'

British migrants have vivid recollections of this rosy portrayal of Australia, and many of them recall that the publicity had a significant influence upon their decision to emigrate. Kathleen Upton remembers the 'bleak, wet and utterly miserable' Coronation Week on the Sussex coast in June 1953 when her husband Ron suggested 'What about Australia?' Ron was commuting to shiftwork for the Railways and he and Kathleen had little time together. Their daughter Vivienne suffered from asthma and a doctor's suggestion of a warmer climate had prompted Ron's first thoughts about emigration. He returned from Australia House laden with brochures: 'All the pictures depicted endless sunshine, blue skies, white sandy beaches, surf riders and bikini-clad girls. Paradise!' For Kathleen, living in a tiny flat with 'wet bed linen draped across the kitchen' and struggling to make do with low wages and rationing, 'the prospect of unlimited food was a dream, and the thought of warm weather for most of the year, where fuel would be a minor problem, enticing'.[26]

Different types of emigrants responded to the Australian publicity in different ways. For example, our interviews and other research confirm that young single migrants – who often anticipated a working holiday in Australia and did not have to worry about children or the long-term future – absorbed little about Australia apart from the usual stereotypes of sun, surf and wide open spaces and, at best, a slightly more calculated knowledge about Australian wage rates.[27] Grace Turnbull, a young nurse who went to Australia in 1948 fired by a desire for freedom and adventure, imagined 'beaches and the sunshine!' and was persuaded by 'the girls at the hospital' not to pack her umbrella with its 'beautiful owl handle': '"You won't need that! You're going to Australia! It never rains over there!" [laughter] We've been to Sydney twice recently and we've had to buy umbrellas.' Ten years later another nurse, Avis Williamson from Nottingham, used the ten pound scheme to travel the world on a working holiday. An uncle in Adelaide had told her that there were jobs for trained people and that pay was better than in England, and from the publicity she knew that 'they had kangaroos, sunshine, plenty of fruit, and that was about all'.[28]

By contrast, prospective migrants with children were likely to investigate their Australian future with more care, and Commonwealth nominees, who did not have a personal sponsor in Australia, were especially dependent upon the information provided by Australia House. Appleyard's research in 1959 suggested that migrant families were reasonably well-informed about wages and house prices in Australia but often 'seriously over-estimated' their ability to save sufficient money to buy an Australian house within a planned time period. Prospective migrants often knew most about directly relevant economic factors, though it was very difficult to make comparative judgements about wages and purchasing power (which were on the whole better in Australia) or about taxation, health, welfare and housing (which probably favoured working-class families in Britain), and easier to accept the common belief that ordinary families were better off in Australia.[29]

British migrants often knew even less about Australian politics and geography. They confused the states and capital cities (when John Clark and his family were directed to Adelaide in 1951 they had no idea where it was; in 1968 David Bailey assumed that Queensland was a town), and though they knew Australia was a big country they had little idea of actual distances (John and Eileen Fairbairn imagined that they would be able to get a taxi from Melbourne to visit friends in Sydney). A high percentage of emigrants knew that Robert Menzies was the Australian prime minister, but more than half presumed that he led a Labor government, perhaps influenced by the stereotype of Australia as a classless society.[30]

Some migrants who were distrustful of the Australian publicity (or of the naive enthusiasm of an emigration-minded spouse) conducted rather more rigorous research before making such an important decision. When Margaret Hill's husband came back to Liverpool from overseas military service 'he'd got this idea of sunshine and warmth and being able to swim in blue waters and he wasn't at all happy about coming back to dull old Merseyside'. He sent for brochures from Australia House and tried to persuade Margaret to emigrate. At first she resisted his persuasion but after several bad winters with sick children in an unheated house her doctor suggested they would be better off in a warm climate and she agreed to go. But first she determined to find out more about Australia:

I mean I knew Australia was big but I had no idea it was so big. And I'd been listening to all these rumours and all these stories that he was telling me and I thought no, no, no, no, so I wanted to find out, and because — we had a questionnaire from the immigration people to say where would we like to go, and I thought, I'm not just going to say anywhere, I need to know, 'cause with him being a painter and decorator, we need to be somewhere where there's going to be a likelihood of him getting a job. So I went to the local library, I left the kids with a friend and trotted off to the library and got all these books out about Australian cities and just read. I mean I was only there for a day but I just had a look at the cities. And I decided that we needed to be nearer to Sydney or Canberra or Melbourne. So that's what we made our preferences, Sydney, Canberra or Melbourne, but of course they sent us to Adelaide, didn't they.[31]

Prospective migrants who tried to find out more about Australia through independent reading were often frustrated by the paucity of appropriate books. Even librarian migrants struggled to find useful and informative literature. In 1959 Elizabeth Jolley came to Perth with her children and husband Leonard, who was taking up the post of librarian at the University of Western Australia. They knew 'very little' of Australia before they left Glasgow: 'Books were confusing and contradictory. Pringle's *Australian Accent*, then not long published, nearly caused us to cancel our passage. Perhaps we misread it. It presented to us a picture of a rigidly conformist country with not much religion but almost obligatory church going. Almost all we were told about Australia – even the impossibility of purchasing cotton underwear – proved false.'[32]

Actual contact with Australia and Australians was much more important than books as a source of emigration information and influence. Servicemen who had been stationed in Australia during the war were able to make their own comparisons. Alf Floyd had docked in Sydney with the British navy at the end of the war and stayed with a family on a farm in New South Wales: 'I loved the country; I loved the country.' Back in England he 'wasn't settling down too well at all' and made plans to emigrate with his wife Dorothy and their young son. The terrible winter of 1947 confirmed his decision: 'Snow was up there, cistern in the toilet froze solid, couldn't open the door for the snow, and I thought, oh, that sunshine, I kept remembering it, yes.'[33]

More often, Britons learnt about Australia from others who knew the country. Bernard and Vera Makewell, for example, were frustrated by poor prospects of promotion at work, but the catalyst for their emigration in 1954 was Bernard's sister, who was nursing in Australia:

And of course all the Australians were coming to England for the Coronation, and she'd say: 'You go and stay with my brother', and on the Coronation eve we had a houseful of Australians sleeping everywhere, and that, they were so persuasive, about coming out here, what a great place it was, I think that sort of successfully talked us into it. And there was one lady, who: 'I'll sponsor you! You can come and live with me for a while', and this, that and the other, and I think that really started it.[34]

Emigrants who were sponsored by relatives or friends in Australia were greatly influenced by the sponsor's portrayal of the country. When Ron and Kathleen Upton decided to emigrate they wrote to several friends of friends looking for a sponsor and were delighted to receive an offer from Jean, an

English migrant who had settled in southern Queensland and who extolled the beauties of the tropical seaside: 'Utopia had nothing on that particular patch of Queensland!' (utopia turned out to be a 'squalid room' in a decrepit, insect-infested house in the middle of nowhere).[35]

Of course personal connections provided more than just information, and most sponsors were more helpful than Jean. For a significant proportion of British emigrants, strong encouragement from relatives, the likelihood of practical and personal support and a desire for family reunion on the other side of the world were major factors in the migration decision. As more and more British migrants settled in Australia the importance of family reunion increased. For example, chain migration to Australia was part of the family history of Margaret Parkinson, a trainee teacher on the Merseyside in the late 1950s:

When we were growing up there had always been talk of emigrating to Australia. Two of my father's sisters and one of his brothers had gone to Australia when he was only 3 years old and their children were nearer in age to him than they were to me. My mother also had two sisters living there and these two and their families had visited England a few times so we had heard many tales of the great weather and the good life that was to be had there. One of my sisters, a nurse, emigrated with another of my father's sisters in 1953 and then my older brother, an electrician, went in 1955. In 1957, just before I was due to complete my college course and my younger brother was about to leave school, our parents asked if we would accompany them to Australia. We both said yes and so the application was made.

Upon their arrival in Sydney in February 1958, 'there was a welcome party for us with over fifty relatives there, most of whom we had never met before'.[36]

Apart from personal stories and published information from Australia House and other sources, the expectations of prospective migrants were shaped by the range of ways in which, over many years, the idea of 'Australia' had seeped into British culture and consciousness. Children were taught that Australia was an imperial outpost of 'convicts, sheep, rabbits and kangaroos' (as James Saxton recalls from his schooling in Essex in the early 1950s). Australia was memorable because it was so different. In Michael Peters's schooling 'Australia remained a land … mentioned only for its unusualness…. The boomerang, the primitiveness of its natives, the extraordinary percentage of Catholics, its export of brains, talent and wool and the seemingly inexhaustible supply of little men who could hit balls with triangular bits of wood for days at a time.'[37] Romantic notions about a pioneering rural life in the Australian outback seem to have been particularly resonant for mid-century British school children. In 1939–40 Dorothy Wright 'did' Australia in school geography:

I was entranced. All that sunshine, those enormous areas of waving corn, sheep by the million, open spaces, horse riding and so on and so on. I think as an 11-year-old I was in a very romantic phase and saw myself as a 'tough guy' living the great free outdoor life. Then in the summer of 1940 came a cable from relatives out there: 'Send the children to us.'

Although this overseas evacuation never eventuated, Dorothy's yearning for that other world increased when she read the letters of an ancestor who had gone to Australia in 1850. In the late 1950s she and her husband Mike began to get 'itchy feet' after the birth of their first child, and Mike wanted to further his engineering career by getting experience away from England and 'head office'. 'Glowing reports' from a friend who had emigrated to Sydney and who agreed to act as a sponsor made up their minds. Dorothy Wright's story is like that of many migrants for whom the ten pound scheme rekindled childhood dreams of adventure in other worlds, whilst at the same time offering an answer to adult desires or frustrations. 'We only wanted to see the world, we were not disillusioned with England, we did not see emigration as a way out of housing or other problems. *We just had itchy feet!* And so we went.'[38]

Pathe newsreels about royal tours and late night radio broadcasts of Test cricket matches in Australia sustained the image of a country which was almost British. Yet the return visits of Australian cricketers, tennis players and other sporting legends suggested that the abundance, warmth and open space of Australia was building a rather different breed of Britons. In 1948 Brian Ward's London classmates congregated in the school hall to hear radio reports of the cricket matches between England and Bradman's Australian 'Invincibles', and in the same year 'impressionable teenager' Valerie Proverbs's interest in Australia was ignited by the batting exploits of the dashing 19-year-old Neil Harvey, and she concluded that all Australians 'played cricket and rode horses'.[39] Young emigrants anticipated that they, too, would be transformed by the adventure and opportunity of a young, outdoor country.

In wartime Britain and during a decade of postwar austerity Australia figured prominently in childhood dreams of exotic abundance. When the parents of six-year-old Bruce Bates announced in 1951 that the family was leaving Wolverhampton for Australia he was 'very excited at the prospect of this great adventure':

What I do recall very clearly, however, is being shown a photograph in a very old fashioned geography textbook, showing pineapples growing in a field and absolutely relishing the thought of going outside and cutting one whenever I wanted. I now realize that we were then experiencing the period of postwar austerity in England and I can still remember taking ration books to the local shop to get sweets and that the only tropical fruit I can remember eating at that time was black, dried banana. It is little wonder, therefore, I suppose, that I so relished the prospect of 'free' fresh pineapples! To me, going to Australia was every bit as exotic and exciting as the tales from the Arabian Nights.[40]

There were at least three overlapping ways in which British postwar emigrants imagined Australia. Firstly, immigration officials presented a British way of life for young families in a modern industrial nation. In the immediate postwar years this publicity emphasized the comparative abundance of Australia and a safe distance from the troubles of Europe. By the 1960s Britons were beginning to enjoy economic prosperity and immigration publicity now focused on the good life in Australia's sunny outdoors climate.

Secondly, popular culture and schooling offered a more romantic and usually rural image of Australia, as a place for outdoor adventure and personal transformation. But lurking on the other side of this pioneering 'bush legend' was a third, darker image of a more primitive and even threatening country. In the 1950s, Londoner Betty Preston read a book about Australia that 'gave a hair-raising description of black men with bones through their ears and very scantily dressed' and concluded there would be no electricity in Australia: 'We sold our Hoover and my electric sewing machine and things like that, and came here expecting to see something like the edge of beyond.'[41] Elizabeth Jolley wondered if the house that awaited them on the campus of the University of Western Australia might 'be on some rugged field miles from anywhere and I might have to walk and carry water'. In postwar Glasgow, teenager Mary Rose Lavery had heard that Australia was full of 'blackfellows and bananas', and 'snakes and spiders and savage heat.... So I never mentioned to my friends that my mother was wanting to go to Australia. I didn't want their sympathy.'[42]

Prospective ten pound migrants invariably drew upon these resonant if somewhat contradictory British preconceptions about Australia. The idea of 'Australia' ignited their interest in emigration and informed their decision. This imagined Australia would be part of the cultural baggage of hopes and expectations that British migrants transported to their new home – where it would be confronted by the more complex realities of Australian society.

In this chapter about the ways in which Australia was sold to and imagined by prospective migrants we have also glimpsed hints of emigrant disaffection with Britain: the damp and squalid living conditions of Margaret Hill's 'dull old Merseyside' or Kathleen and Ron Upton's home on the south coast; Alf Floyd's misery during the frozen winter of 1947; Fred Ford's belief that he would never afford a home for his family in Salford; and John Hardie's dissatisfaction at work. In the next chapter we draw upon personal accounts by British migrants to illuminate the world they left behind and to explain why they wanted to leave.

46   Emigration

Notes

1 Ford written account US.
2 This summary of the origins and development of the postwar assisted passage migration scheme draws substantially upon the detailed history in Appleyard, *The Ten Pound Immigrants*, pp. 1–44. See also Appleyard, *British Emigration to Australia*; Bosworth, 'Australia and Assisted Immigration from Britain'. For statistical details about migrant intakes see Hugo, 'Migration Between Australia and Britain'.
3 Roe, *Australia, Britain and Migration*.
4 See, for example, Barker, *People for the Commonwealth*.
5 Appleyard, *The Ten Pound Immigrants*, p. 9.
6 *Ibid.*, p. 10.
7 *Ibid.*, p. 24.
8 See Bosworth, 'Australia and Assisted Immigration from Britain'; and Paul, *Whitewashing Britain*, pp. 25–63.
9 See Maggie and Robert Smith interview US; Attwood written account US.
10 Appleyard, *The Ten Pound Immigrants*, p. 39.
11 Hugo, 'Migration Between Australia and Britain', pp. 24–5.
12 Quoted in Appleyard, *The Ten Pound Immigrants*, pp. 28 and 33. See also Lack and Templeton, *Bold Experiment*, pp. 2–72.
13 Appleyard, *The Ten Pound Immigrants*, p. 39; Jordens, *Redefining Australians*. Note that Irish citizens were also excluded from the 'alien' category.
14 Jenkins, *We Came to Australia*, p. 69; Appleyard, *British Emigration to Australia*, p. 57.
15 Appleyard, *British Emigration to Australia*, pp. 159–60. See also Hutching, *Long Journey for Sevenpence*, p. 10.
16 Comparative figures for United Kingdom emigrants (from Paul, *Whitewashing Britain*, p. 31) include: Southern Rhodesia, 1946–60, 82,178; South Africa, 1946–57, 125,676; Australia, 1946–60, 566,429; New Zealand, 1946–60, 151,730; Canada, 1946–1960, 582,787.
17 Hardie interview US.
18 Appleyard, 'Post-War English Immigrants', pp. 314–16.
19 Appleyard, *British Emigration to Australia*, pp. 118–22. Appleyard's figures for 'unaccompanied migrants' were based upon the years 1955 to the mid-1960s.
20 Appleyard, *British Emigration to Australia*, pp. 109–45; Appleyard, *The Ten Pound Immigrants*, pp. 51–3. See also Hugo, 'Migration Between Australia and Britain', pp. 9–23.
21 Appleyard, *The Ten Pound Immigrants*, p. 51.
22 Appleyard, 'Post-war English Immigrants', p. 316.
23 Richardson, *British Immigrants and Australia*, pp. 16–23.
24 *Ibid.*, pp. 14–15; Appleyard, *The Ten Pound Immigrants*, p. 54.
25 Warden, *Vale Enchanting*, p. 127.
26 Upton, *To the Undiscovered Ends*, p. 2.
27 See Appleyard, *The Ten Pound Immigrants*, pp. 60–1.
28 Grace Turnbull interview LU; McDermott interview US.
29 Appleyard, *British Emigration to Australia*, pp. 155 and 192–201.
30 Clark interview LU; Bailey interview LU; Fairbairn interview LU. Richardson, *British Immigrants and Australia*, p. 15.
31 Hill interview LU. According to Appleyard's research (*British Emigration to Australia*, p. 155), books, magazines and newspapers were the main source of information on Australia for about 13 per cent of Commonwealth nominees like Margaret Hill.

32 Jolley, 'Tricked or Treated?', in *Central Mischief*, pp. 66–8. Very few British migrants recall using any of the commercially published emigrant guidebooks, which are often more revealing about their author's prejudices than about life in Australia. See, for example, Lewis, *Shall I Emigrate?*; Jenkins, *We Came to Australia*; Tribe, *Postmark Australia*.
33 Floyd interview LU.
34 Makewell interview LU.
35 Upton, *To the Undiscovered Ends*, p. 3. See Appleyard, *British Emigration to Australia*, p. 155; Richardson, *British Immigrants and Australia*, p. 15.
36 Parkinson written account US.
37 Saxton, *Something Will Come to Me*, p. 124; Peters, *Pommie Bastards*, p. 130.
38 Wright written account US.
39 Ward interview LU; Proverbs interview LU.
40 Bruce Bates written account US.
41 Preston, *Blowing My Own Trumpet*, p. 20.
42 Jolley interview, Battye Library, OH 2268; Liverani, *The Winter Sparrows*, p. 3.

2

Leaving Britain

And after the war, of course, '45 onwards, people were quite, everybody had jobs in those days, and people were quite well off. There was a definite increase in standard of living and everything. And of course they were my sort of growing-up years, so I looked at them as being wonderful! I just loved being in the West End and mixing with that type of person. It just sort of seemed to be the right life for me! (Jeanne Paul)[1]

It wasn't the nicest place to be in the East End of London then. It was very dingy and lots of smog, very unhealthy, lots of poverty.... I commuted, that was another thing, that was three hours on the train every day. That was depressing too I can tell you. Off the train at Waterloo and down into the drain and off to the Bank and then from the Bank you walked to Liverpool Street or carried on, but if you wanted to save a couple of bob you walked the rest you know. There was no money, it was such a dismal place, it really was. There was absolutely no money, you were scraping all the time in the fifties. So dismal. (Nigel Heath)[2]

For the million and more people who left Britain for Australia between 1947 and the early 1970s their postwar homeland was a world of enormous upheaval and rapid change. But the change was infinitely variable in its effects on different people, and this is reflected now in migrants' diverse and seemingly contradictory memories of the years before they left. The above passages illustrate how the same period – in this case the 1950s – could be recalled as the best of times and the worst of times according to circumstances. Of course, memory of life in Britain before emigration is coloured by the nature of subsequent experiences in Australia, and, for some, by the subsequent return to Britain. Memories do help us to understand the lived experience of a changing social world, and to unpick the factors which led to emigration. But memory stories also tell us about the identity of the narrator at the time of telling, and about the meaning and significance of migration in his or her life story. Nigel Heath's account of commuting to a clerical job on the London docks evokes a dismal, claustrophobic world which contrasts in his memory with the adventures and opportunities he enjoyed in Australia as a young single man. This memory is also refracted through the disappointments of return and a feeling that perhaps he missed a chance of a better life in the new world. In Jeanne Paul's memory the bustle and hope of postwar London is fused with the excitement of adolescence, and the nostalgia of her reminiscence is deepened by her own teenage anger at being taken away from this 'wonderful' life when her family emigrated to Australia.

Most movements of mass migration are shaped by difficult conditions propelling people to leave their homes, combined with some attraction in the country of destination. These are the classic 'push and pull' factors of migration theory. In the postwar period both of these factors operated in varying degrees. Postwar dislocation, austerity and reconstruction provided millions with the impulsion to escape from a seemingly bleak future, whilst Australian publicity held out promises of opportunity and sunshine. In these respects postwar migration was similar to previous movements, like those in the nineteenth century, which saw millions leave Britain. But the Australian government's offer of free passage to ex-servicemen, and subsidized fares to other adults and children, made for a unique pattern of movement at a time when mobility in Britain was already intense, with postwar 'slum' clearances and the creation of 'New Towns' beyond the cramped metropolitan centres. It meant that offers of a new life in Australia could be taken up not simply by those desperate for a new start, but by others who might otherwise never give emigration a second thought. It could attract the young of both sexes keen to enjoy a working holiday, those chafing at undue parental control, those desperate for a chance to give unstable marriages a new start, or even those who, on a whim, seized the opportunity for a change.

For the ten pound emigrants a number of motivating factors were significant throughout the life of the assisted passage scheme: family reunion and families in crisis; personal frustrations around work and housing; the weather in Britain compared with Australia; a desire for independence, adventure or escape; the opportunity of a better life for oneself or the family and a strong sense that the better life could be realized in Australia. Cutting across these factors are at least two important distinctions about the migrants and about the postwar Britain they left behind which recur throughout this chapter. First, single migrants (and some migrant couples without children) often emigrated for reasons that were very different to those of migrant families. Secondly, the context and causes of British emigration in the decade or so after the war were very different from those operative from the later 1950s onwards.[3]

Historical understanding of the reasons for emigration is not an exact or predictive science. From our archive of migrant life stories we can distinguish significant patterns and themes. Most importantly, these life stories highlight the complexity of the migration decision and the interplay between diverse factors within different contexts. The migration stories also remind us that very often the roots of emigration – particularly for that first generation of emigrants in the 1940s and 1950s – lie deep within the family and social histories of prewar and wartime lives. The first sections of this chapter explore how these 'pre-histories' – of interwar poverty and then the dramatic impact of war – influenced postwar emigration.

The long shadow of Depression and poverty

Memories of the postwar generation of British migrants reach back as far as three generations, in some cases to a world before the First World War, a premodern society closer to conditions of the Britain of the nineteenth than of the twentieth century. Stories told by those who left Britain in the decade after the Second World War range from those with backgrounds of poverty to relative affluence, but many routinely describe conditions of a lost world utterly alien from the modern comforts of Australia and Britain at the end of the twentieth century.

Grace Turnbull, for example, remembers her childhood of the 1920s and 1930s in a series of villages in Wiltshire, Buckinghamshire and, mostly, Northamptonshire. Her stories could almost have been taken from a Thomas Hardy novel. Grace's early life followed a deeply traditional pattern. Like most of her generation she left school at 14, and for several years worked as a domestic servant until war broke out, when, against the wishes of her parents, she trained as a nurse. Her early memories were idyllic ones in which a close-knit family and community, home grown rural produce and the childhood freedoms of village life outweighed the primitive living conditions of a thatched cottage household without running water, with dry non-flush outdoor toilets and the ever-prying eyes of neighbours.[4]

Traditional rural life, and its imminent demise, is epitomized in her recollection of the communal killing of the village pig. Grace had not actually seen this practice, but it was ingrained into her memory of village conversation because of its recent abolition when her family moved to East Haddon, Northamptonshire:

And just before we went there, everybody kept a pig, in the backyard. So, every time, everybody worked it so everybody killed their pig at a different time, and they'd share around! Process. But then the government, just before the War, brought out this thing that you weren't allowed to keep a pig in the backyard; it was unhygienic! Oh, and there was a lot of work; that hurt more than anything else, you know, because they'd been used to their pigs and the proceeds from it, and everybody had the bacon hanging in the kitchen, so you see, yes. I mean it was unhygienic, but they existed.

If the prewar abolition of backyard pig-keeping heralded the coming of modern life to Grace's village, the war was the catalyst for her own leap from rural traditions, against the scepticism of her family, and for a transformation in aspirations and opportunities that would lead her to Australia. The war, she said, 'changed it, completely, you see. Because I had to do something, so I decided well I'm, I'm not going down, I'm going up! ... So I just applied [to train as a nurse] and had to sit the exam and, so it made a lot of difference; it changed my life. Or else I would have probably wandered on, and wandered on, and met a boy and – if I'd met a boy, I don't know.'

By 1948 Grace had had enough of being a ward nurse at Kingston Hospital, though she declined an opportunity to retrain as a district nurse: 'We looked at them, my friends and I, and thought we're going to turn into those dowdy creatures! [laughter] Actually they were very nice, but I mean we were young, and ...! And I thought oh well, I'd like to travel.' Grace applied for a nursing job with P&O but discovered that they had a waiting list 'of about a thousand', and then she heard about the ten pound scheme:

So I went up to Australia House and put my name down, and I got accepted practically straight away! So! So I thought well, ten pounds, I'll come out there and stay two years, and I can go on to America or somewhere like that, and go round the world! Because they said you only had to stay two years, you see. I didn't come out to stay in Australia! [laugh] I was cheating, I suppose! And that's why I migrated.

How these early experiences are remembered plays a large part in the building of people's own personal histories of migration. For John Clark, born in 1919 in the Scottish village of Pownall in Kinrosshire, rural life as a child was remembered as sheer hard work, carrying water for the washing and wood for the fire, and cutting kindling, all before breakfast. His childhood milk-and paper-run, the long walk to school and later work on a farm at 14 – 'a boy doing a man's job' – served in his memory as a training ground for the hard work which enabled him to make a success of his life in Australia. Whether remembered with nostalgia or revulsion these stories of a distant rural past help to define the world of difference in lives changed dramatically by the momentous experience of migration. They provide the sharpest contrasts we encounter in the stories migrants tell about their lives in two countries.[5]

At the same time we need to remember that rural life was a minority experience for postwar emigrants. From 1947 the Australian government stressed that it was seeking, above all, skilled workers to build up its urban industrial base. Publicity was therefore routinely targeted at urban workers, married or single, but especially couples with young families. Overwhelmingly these were the people who seized the opportunity of the ten pound passage from urban centres across the country. Their memories naturally differ markedly from those of people brought up in the country, but for urbanites who lived through the Depression of the 1930s and earlier there are equivalent tales of a world long forgotten. Poverty, and its effect on family life and personal opportunity, is a recurring theme in prewar working–class life histories. The impact and memory of poverty profoundly influenced the migration decisions of the first generation of postwar British emigrants.

Both enduring poverty and the progressive loss of her small family dominate Ethel Ledgett's memories of growing up between the wars, and these now reinforce her sense of the change resulting from her move to Australia. Born in Portsmouth in 1921, she remembers no time before the Second World War when her father, an unskilled labourer, was in regular work or her mother in good health. Her mother 'couldn't even buy me a Christmas present, I was an only child, you know, so poor, and then being near the navy dockyard, and my father couldn't get work in those days after the First World War'. The relentless stresses of poverty and making do provoked the one incident of violence between her parents that Ethel remembers:

I never saw them fight much, but I did see her go for him with a knife once, because he'd lost the only half a crown she had, because she sent him out for something, shopping, and that's all she had. And that sticks in my mind now, I've forgotten how lucky we are, you know, there I am with a bag of fruit there, I'm only on a pension, but I can still live well.

The meagre family income came mainly from her mother's part-time cleaning, supplemented by occasional means-tested welfare provisions of flour and sugar. But when Ethel was 11 all that ended abruptly with the death of her mother from tuberculosis. This catastrophe prompted her father to send Ethel to live with his sister in the Kentish Town suburb of London. Here Ethel continued to live on the edge of subsistence, in a six-room house with four families, through the peak years of the Depression:

My auntie only had one room, with a gas stove on the landing, shared with people in the next room, three in the other room and a tap of water running on the next floor down, and the toilet on the ground, bottom floor. And people won't believe it, will they? ... And then wonder why you don't have baths! I mean, you had to have a top and tail, you know! That's what I remember.[6]

Like the great bulk of her contemporaries, Ethel left school, unwillingly, at the age of 14, and like her mother and generations of women before her she became a live-in domestic servant, working fifteen hours a day. After three years she was able to join her father, who had moved to London in a relationship with a man. Here she could revive her tenuous family connection and take much preferred work at Selfridges. She could also, for the first time, experience something of the freedom of youth, enjoying the work and finding 'mates' of her own age, one of whom, Bruce, she eventually married in 1942. By that time the war had revolutionized her life. After her home was bombed she moved into war work, training at Leicester and then becoming an aircraft inspector at the Hucknall Rolls Royce factory in Nottinghamshire. Like so many of her age group she experienced the war as liberating:

Well, I got a bit of a better job. I was in regular money and had more freedom, we worked long hours but we used to go to dancing two or three nights a week, all for a shilling, you know, and to the cinema, and I met a more, big circle of friends. So, I know it sounds awful to say, there was advantages … especially for women, there was a lot more freedom, you see.

Marriage, though, brought another major turn, and further instability, in Ethel's life. Her husband was on active service throughout the war, by 1944 she was pregnant, and she experienced a succession of moves, living with her in-laws, where her son was born in 1945 ('a D-Day baby as his father came up from Southampton on twenty-four hours leave prior to D-Day'!) and then with her own father. After her husband was finally demobilized they returned to London, where they suffered the chronic shortage of housing, again having to live with others. Bruce returned to retail work and Ethel, caring for her baby and working as live-in housekeeper for a retired parson, began to feel hemmed in by the full-time demands of her family and the parson; meantime, her carefree husband, whom she nicknamed 'Sir Andy Capp', enjoyed his recreations. These constraints meant that the prospect of a new life in Australia came as a welcome relief.

Well, I was, I was quite pleased because, in a way, it was exciting to me, and I've always been interested in other countries. And I was working, see, in a house then, and for six years I looked after this parson, retired parson, and he wanted four meals a day. I mean I was tied down, my husband was still free to go to his regimental things, right, and at Easter he would go down to what he called 'Bisley', the shooting, oh, and I got stuck home you see with Keith, my son and the parson, and I hated those times, you know. Because, well I didn't have any local friends, and so to me it was excitement, coming out here. I always remember sitting in bed, reading all the brochures when we applied to emigrate here.

Australia for Ethel came to represent adventure, by contrast with the circumscribed life she knew in England, limited by housing scarcity and the demands of others. When the Ledgett family finally, by mutual consent, emigrated to Sydney in 1956 and settled in the suburb of Chatswood, Ethel quickly returned to her retailing career, working for Grace Brothers department store and cultivating a network of supportive friends and neighbours. Looking back she was convinced that she 'had a more adventurous sort of life here' while at the same time describing herself as 'a bit of a suburbanite really'. Her life in Australia, as a mother, a worker and 'mixing with people', recalled the relative freedom she had enjoyed as a single woman during the immediate prewar and early war years, contrasting starkly with those constricted years in England after the war. Interestingly, Ethel, now an active and independent widow, speaks with greatest pride of her virtually uninterrupted working life, and points to her two granddaughters who have combined their careers with family responsibilities. This coexists with wistful regret over the fact that the main correspondence with her father consisted of him asking her for money. Looking back, though, she is in no doubt that the escape from postwar Britain opened the way to success and fulfilment in Australia she could not have dreamed of in England.

Ethel's story is neither typical nor commonplace; by definition individual life stories blend the uniquely personal with the more common patterns which define their times. Her lifelong working career, for example, sets her apart from many women who gave up work to care for their children in these years, although even here the patterns are not so clear as we might expect.[7] We will encounter many cases of women, before and after migration, who continued to work through marriage against their preference to stay at home. But if we step away from the individual detail of Ethel's story we can see echoes of events, issues and processes which governed the early lives of so many of her contemporaries: the impact of poverty and war; young teenagers forced to leave education prematurely; discontent with postwar austerity; stressful family dynamics and the idea of Australia as an escape route, whether from austerity or controlling families.

Depression experiences shaped the memories and outlook of working-class migrants who had lived through the 1930s. We need to remember that at the time these conditions would have seemed perfectly normal to young people who had no prior memory of relative prosperity (and that they were not so very different to conditions experienced by working-class Australians who lived through the Depression). 'We didn't know it as hard up at all' is a routine comment on recollections from between the wars, and, except for cases of serious family dysfunction, most people recall happy childhoods from this difficult period. But their experiences could motivate young people obsessively to seek avenues of self-improvement, and the resulting ambitious drive might easily translate later into a willingness to emigrate. This could mean a long struggle at a time when the school-leaving age for most was 14. John Fairbairn, for example, came from a family of ten children in Kelso, Scotland. His father's steady work as a master baker kept the family fed throughout the 1920s and 1930s, but their large numbers made for scarcity and overcrowding in a small four-room flat. Each child was expected to take part-time work while still at school to supplement the family income, and as they grew older the pressure to leave home early was overwhelming. John's chances of breaking this mould were heightened when, at 14, he 'won the Dux medal, presented by the Duke of Roxburgh', which came with a scholarship for the local high school. The opportunity, though, was not enough to guarantee John an education 'because of the conditions at home and the need for everybody to work, as soon as they could.... It was more important that I get a job.' In retrospect John came to think that this was no bad thing, since the editor of the *Kelso Chronicle*, noting his 'penmanship' skills, promptly engaged him as a cub reporter. This opened up a successful career in journalism, interrupted by more than five years in the army just after his marriage. The same drive prompted him to apply for a job with the *Launceston Examiner* in 1950, the beginning of his family's life in Australia.[8]

War stories and disrupted family lives

Family themes loom large in migrant memories, but are bound up closely with conditions of the time. It would be surprising if the enormous disruption in daily life caused by the Second World War did not have lasting effects on family and marital relationships, which, in turn, would influence life trajectories and the possibility of emigration. The routine appearance in a minority of our files of illegitimacy, loss of parents, adoption and desertion before the sharp rise in divorce from the 1960s challenges any cosy assumptions about a postwar 'golden age' of family life.[9] Wartime ordeals like child-evacuation, bombing destruction, husbands' absences and lone parenting for women in times of scarcity left few people without scars, although the effects could vary between those whose marriages were virtually destroyed and those who were brought closer together. For couples married on the eve of the war the return to 'normality' could be a welcome prospect. After working in her husband's newspaper job throughout the war, Eileen Fairbairn was 'quite pleased to be out of it ... I got back to ordinary things after that'. Peacetime brought with it the prospects of new social life and adventure, and the resulting 'itchy feet' for a better life together could lead logically to thoughts of emigration.[10]

But the corrosive effects of the war could produce quite different results. In some cases the long habits of women managing a household alone could later translate into a permanent shift in the family balance of power, with women continuing to make the important decisions, unchallenged by compliant husbands happy to return to a quiet life at home. Margaret Reardon recalls her own enhanced duties during the war as the eldest sister, 'the overpowering sense of responsibility to my sisters. Looking after them'. But the greatest postwar change was between her parents, with her mother carrying on her custom of command and management without any hint of resistance or dispute from her father. At the time her father explained his deliberate refusal to interfere with his wife's child rearing, for example, by reference to her wartime practice. 'She's done such a fantastic job by herself with these children,

who am I to say anything.' His wife's role as the family decision-maker
extended well beyond child discipline. In 1951 it was she who made the
decision to emigrate to Australia, against the wishes of her husband, who left
Edinburgh in the role of the 'reluctant migrant', a reversal of the
conventional stereotype of migration decision-making.[11]

At another extreme the disruption of war years could set marriages on a
course of alienation and conflict. The well-worn images of a postwar return
to close-knit family harmony and a low divorce rate in the 1940s and 1950s
often belied the fact of some marriages and family relationships which were
deeply unhappy, with couples struggling for years against persisting wartime
resentments. Bunty Davis tells the story of a young London Jewish family on
the eve of the war that was affected deeply in this way. Her own memories of
the war are of a childhood seared by cruel evacuation experiences on a farm,
where she and her elder brother were 'treated like slaves'. Her experience
contrasts with that of her younger brother, who went to a much kinder family
and became so well-integrated that return home after the war caused conflict
between the two families. But Bunty's main family story is about her parents.
From the start her mother resented the fact that her father, always eager to
travel, had enlisted immediately on the outbreak of war, which made for a
five-year separation. With father away at the war and mother working as a
full-time waitress, the evacuated children rarely saw their parents, and her
mother lived effectively as a single woman. It was common knowledge that her
mother conducted a series of affairs, some with American servicemen, and
this led to lasting tensions in her marriage after the war. The subsequent family
life seemed to be dominated by the resulting resentments.

And we went back before my father got home from the War, and my mother had
lots of men friends during the War. I — she had many affairs, and even when we
got home there was a man locally that she was having an affair with, and I think
my father found out, and I think that caused a lot of friction, forever, right
through the years. And I think, even till he died, I think that was always a thing in
the family. And I remember them arguing, well, he had a girlfriend when he was
away, too, so that five years' separation was a very big thing for my family, it made
a big hole.[12]

These wartime effects on the family were bound up with their emigration
to Melbourne in 1949. The material consequences of the war were hard
enough. Bunty's father had been a self-employed barber, but returned to find
his shop destroyed by bombing and faced lasting difficulties trying to start
again. There was a drawn-out struggle to regain custody of their youngest
son, and his parents were now hostile to his wife. 'My father's parents always
were very angry with my mother for what happened during the war, because
they lived close by. And the Americans used to come up and visit my Mum.'

In their district of Hackney the possibility of emigration – to Canada, South Africa, New Zealand and America as well as Australia – was a common subject of discussion, and so it emerged gradually as an opportunity to escape from all these difficulties.

Fundamental problems faced by families such as Bunty's are rarely resolved by emigration. Life in Australia, far from improving discordant marriages, sometimes drove them to divorce, and we will see later that 'problem families' could be particularly susceptible to return migration. Bunty's parents seemed to be headed in that direction. The five-year separation 'didn't draw them closer, it pushed them apart', and that was as true of their lives in Australia as in England in the 1940s. Bunty, too, found the tensions of family life so difficult that she married early to escape, and only after leaving home did her relationship with her father, also damaged by his long absence, improve. But her parents, deeply committed to family life, stayed together permanently, and, in spite of the ongoing arguments, thrived within a close English-Jewish community in the Melbourne suburb of Elwood. Their experience is a reminder that the outcome of migration is rarely complete, with possibilities of family break-up, return or simply a delicate ongoing coexistence always in prospect.

We would expect that the war itself might form one of the most crucial influences on the lives of young adults who decided later to emigrate. Obviously the war impacted upon the whole population to some degree, whether as child evacuees, women who turned to war work, victims of bombing or those who lost family members. But for those who served in the armed forces, especially in direct combat, the after-effects could be traumatic and enduring. This theme is a compelling one, and its implications for marriage and family life after the war have engaged novelists and historians alike. Melvyn Bragg's recent semi-autobiographical novels, *The Soldier's Return* and *A Child of War*, play on the inability of a traumatized soldier to adapt to his family and civilian life after his chilling experiences in the Burma campaign.[13] In Bragg's story, Sam, the returned husband and father, is alienated from his narrow Cumbrian community and family, oppressed by his unrewarding work and outlook, and seeks wider horizons by planning to emigrate to Australia. His wife, transformed in subtle ways by the greater independence she experienced in wartime work and lone motherhood, enjoys a much deeper attachment to her home, community and women friends, and the prospect of leaving them for Australia prompts a 'terror ... over which she had no control'.[14] The theme is a familiar and persuasive one, although we will find infinite variation in the ways in which both men and women responded to the after-effects of war trauma.

The story of Albert and Anne Lougher provides a fascinating variation on this theme, and illustrates how the effects of war experience could merge seamlessly with the desire to emigrate. Albert was born in London in 1920, and described himself as a 'real cockney', brought up in the harsh conditions of poverty we have already seen. In fact, despite his large family of nine siblings, his father's frequent unemployment as a painter and 'long periods of pawn shops', there were some mitigating factors in those early years of struggle. While Albert was at school two older sisters were already employed at a plastic factory and the 15s. a week they each brought in were crucial to their mother's capacity to manage. 'There were times when I'd see mum with a cap, she always wore a cap, she'd put the money in the cap and look at us with kindly eyes for the first time. Terrible wasn't it?'[15]

A more crucial factor was that in 1928 Albert's family moved from the slums of Paddington to a council house in Willesden, then still on the edge of a rural belt. For the overcrowded Loughers this move to a house 'with three big bedrooms and a great big garden' brought a vital change in their fortunes, though for young Albert and his close siblings – 'all ragamuffin merchants, kids from the slums' – the move was not entirely welcome. 'Suddenly we got this lovely bathroom with a heater, and the council done it, I mean I must be fair, and Dad got chickens and we, blimey it was beautiful, you know, but then we would have gone back to the slums without any — .'

Albert's school experience recalls John Fairbairn's story of missed opportunity, and echoes that of countless children of his generation. For a brief moment it seemed that he might break out from the cycle of poverty when he passed his exams for the local grammar school. But when he visited the school and found that uniforms were mandatory, 'my Dad said you'll have to bloody pack that in, he said, I can't even buy you a cap'. Leaving school at 14, Albert's prospects again brightened when a 'Lady Visitor', friendly with his mother, found him a job as an office boy on Fleet Street with *Boys' Own Paper*. There the editor and staff cultivated him to the point where he was able to contribute a regular 'office boy's column'. Eventually they sponsored him to apply to become a cub reporter on the *Daily Express*, but, once again, the requirement of a training fee of 10s. a week brought him up against the stark realities at home. 'I went home, I could hardly wait, and I got home and Dad said, "No mate, I can't give you ten bob".'

After a few years working for an automotive firm in a variety of white-collar and manual jobs, Albert was in line for a reserved occupation when the war broke out and the company, a feeder for Rolls Royce, converted to aircraft manufacture. But in 1940, much to his employer's annoyance, Albert, envious of two older enlisted brothers 'seeing a bit of the world', promptly left and joined the army. While 'seeing the world' he was captured at Tobruk in 1942 and transported to Macerata, Italy. On a sudden, lone and hazardous impulse, he escaped and eventually joined the Italian resistance, where he became known as 'Nostra Pepe', renowned locally for his part in raids on German supply camps. He was recaptured by the Germans, sent to a labour camp outside Dachau and put to work in slave labour conditions building Farben's poison-gas factory. Finally, after brutal concentration camp treatment and high-risk attempts to sabotage the project, Albert was liberated and demobilized in 1945 and returned to a war-weary England which he felt had little to offer him. The experience left enduring physical and psychological scars and a profound alienation from postwar British society:

I was absolutely lost, absolutely lost. The friends that I'd known, a lot of them hadn't gone in the army, and when I came out, I mean even when I met Anne, I wasn't right and they'd whack me on the back, 'Hello Albert' and 'Glad to see you're back and have a beer'. And I was very bitter and lost because … after all that hardship, all that fighting I came out with ninety quid. Five years, I came out with ninety quid. They were earning nineteen pound a week…. I used to walk round and it's funny you know I wished I was back … oh I was absolutely lost, buggered! I really wanted to end it a couple of times. Well I wanted to get out of it. The people that I respected were dead. My brother had died and he was two years older than me, and the people that went away with me were all dead. I mean, what the hell was I doing back there? It wasn't my world; I should have died when they died.

Albert had to contend with this alienation of the battle-scarred war veteran along with ill-health and the social and physical dislocation of London, which seemed to limit the opportunities he had sought so energetically before the war. Fortunately the army offered him a year's training course as a watchmaker, followed by employment in the army ordinance depot, and it was as a watchmaker that he emigrated to Australia in 1954.

Albert attributed his recovery after the war to his partnership with Anne – his 'saviour'. They had met at a dance at the Cricklewood Palais late in 1945 and married in 1947. Anne's father was a regularly employed tailor, the family owned their own home in Colindale, north London, and drove a car. They were part of that large segment of the moderately prosperous suburban lower middle class whose fortunes remained relatively stable throughout the 1930s and 1940s, so it is hardly surprising that Anne's childhood was a more sheltered one. But her more comfortable background created tensions, during and after their courtship, when her parents insisted that she could do better than Albert. His account recalls the class and family stresses he lived through – part of the routine tensions of class mobility and mixing after the war – as well as the tight financial position facing the new couple.

Her mother never really liked me, bless her. She … thought Anne could have done better. And not only that you see, I wasn't earning much, the army, I came out very, very badly bashed about … and I wasn't earning much. It was only a couple of quid, while you learn. Then her mum and dad, I mean let's face it, they, to me they were real poo poos, you know, I mean, her mother thought here's a right merchant.

Even with Anne working, the housing shortage after the war forced them to live with her parents, adding in-law tensions to the familiar postwar trials of low incomes, rationing, shortages and cold winters. Capping all this for Albert was a sense, bound up with bitterness about his war fortunes, that the class system was again rearing its head: 'I could feel it coming back and I didn't want any more of it; I thought I'd done my whack and yet I had to cap in hand. And I mean who the hell were they you know, and they'd got away with making lots and lots of money and I'd come out with nothing, yes I resented it, very much.' The prospects were not bright, particularly in the light of the Loughers' undaunted ambition to get ahead. Albert admitted that his marriage to Anne had given him a leg up in the world, and if anything this boosted his aspirations. 'We realized ... we were on the lower end of the middle class ... but we were ambitious, we wanted our own home, we wanted not to live in London, we wanted to live out of London, past Hampstead.' Recalling

6 Anne and Albert Lougher on board the *New Australia* in 1954: 'you were all on the migrant boat and you were all going to make a fortune mate... It was so much optimism and it was wonderful'

this time, Albert returns again and again to that sense of optimism against the odds, a feeling that they were embarking not just on a quest for prosperity, but on a mode of life quite different from that of their parents. Noting his attitude to sharing domestic tasks with Anne, he insisted that he came 'from a new generation, not like my dad'.

In retrospect Albert's outlook seems to have been tailor-made for seizing the opportunity of emigration, and when his army friend sent letters to him from Melbourne he began to urge a sceptical Anne to make the move. Like so many other hesitant wives, Anne was reluctant to leave her family, but finally consented on condition that they go for no more than the minimum two years required to qualify for the ten pound assisted fare. In the event, her parents ultimately joined Albert and Anne in Sydney. This was a subject of lasting guilt for Albert, so that years later he still regretted the way he had persuaded Anne to desert her family.

And let's face it … I was a very, very selfish man, and when they came I realized the love that they had for Anne, and for me. And it made me realize what I'd done, you know. What I'd done is turfed them out of their life and Anne's life, we should have stayed with them you know.

These wistful regrets came much later; at the time both Albert and Anne were more preoccupied with escaping from the bleak outlook which faced them at home. The powerful message conveyed during their visit to Australia House, that Australia could transform their lives, shaped their attitude to the new country, although forty-four years later it was recollected with tongue in cheek: 'Everything was marvellous you know, I mean, they wanted migrants. You know it really looked like the land of plenty, and the weather was nicer, they showed you the beaches and the countryside.' During the four-week voyage (see Figure 6), expectations were heightened further by the general sense of the land of opportunity awaiting them:

You were all on the migrant boat and you were all going to make a fortune mate. It's going to be a bit hard, but we'll keep together, this is our address and phone number, when you make your money let us know. It was so much optimism, and it was wonderful.… Because they were like us, see, a lot of them had children. But they were optimistic in every sense, 'We're going to a new country.'

It is difficult to disentangle Albert's unbounded sense of optimism about his Australian expectations from the palpable feeling of frustration and defeat which he conveys in his story of the postwar years. By the time the Loughers left England in 1954 their fortunes were beginning to improve; they were both working, as yet childless, Albert was a qualified watchmaker and they even owned a car, 'an old bomb I bought for ten quid'. The cold and damp climate was still an irritant, as was the continuation of rationing and housing scarcity, but Albert and Anne were beginning to benefit from the mid-1950s expansion of the British economy.

If we are to understand the outlook that drove emigrants like the Loughers to leave we need to look beyond the well-known material hardships to the pervasive psychology of gloom which gripped so much of postwar Britain, which for many people persisted well past the worst years of austerity. In Albert's case his bitterness can be related directly not only to a deep sense of injustice arising from his war experience and subsequent disillusionment, but also from his memory of prewar setbacks in employment. In so many migrant stories this sense of postwar despair is contrasted with later good fortune in Australia in a vindication of the decision to emigrate.

Indeed, we should note that memories of deprivation and difficulty in Britain achieve a particular significance in the life stories of the first generation of postwar immigrants who settled in Australia, like the Loughers, precisely because the transformation of their lives and fortunes is typically explained in terms of migration. (This compares with non-migrants or returnees who point to improving living standards in either country as an explanation for the change in their own fortunes.) These men and women often divide their lives between a British, pre-emigration time of hardship and gloom, and an Australian, post-emigration period of achievement and prosperity. Their story fits well with the tale of the classic battler conquering misfortune, and Albert and Anne's account of their life in Australia continues in that vein, recounting their ultimate fulfilment against the obstacles of anti-British taunting and business failures. Common to most of these stories until at least the late 1950s, even when they are unrelated to war service, is a sense of hopelessness and lack of opportunity in Britain.

'England was an *awful* place': postwar austerity and gloom

Britain in the decade after the end of the Second World War is a grim memory for most migrants. James Saxton was 15 when he emigrated from Essex with his family in 1951:

The post-war world, as I recall, was a pretty dismal place to grow up in. A colourless, featureless world of 'make do and mend'. A world of 'Utility' this and 'Utility' that. A world of shabbily dressed, pinched faced mums, perpetually forced to queue for an illusive [sic] 'something'. A world of self-righteous politicians who kept making biting forceful speeches which all boiled down to we, the public at large, working harder and being fed less…. A sense of futility permeated our lives. We, as a nation, had given our all and then some – so where was our reward?[16]

Of all the well-remembered hardships persisting well into the 1950s the housing shortage was one of the most pervasive, and it often provoked thoughts of emigration. The bombed out craters in city streets were vivid reminders of lost housing, and stir collective memories of a bleak existence which the much heralded 'postwar reconstruction' never seemed to remedy. Kathleen Barrand, who left Rainham, Essex, with her family in 1949 at 16, still associates those scenes with more general deprivations.

As everybody will tell you, England was an *awful* place, even in 1949. Now I can remember … the bombed-out houses, still all there, and the grass all growing in them, and the food was awful, and … when I say rations … Australians went: 'Oh yes! We were, had rations too!' But they have really no *idea*…. I mean I'd never tasted ice cream or lemonade until I came, you know.[17]

The search for independent housing was most acute for young couples, often requiring, as we have seen, cohabitation with parents for years, creating tensions which could put the marriage at risk or prompt otherwise improbable thoughts of escape. In 1952 Tom and Beryl Walker, only recently married, had high hopes of saving to buy their own house. To avoid the hazards of cramped living space and lack of privacy at Beryl's parents' house in Weymouth, they lived in a caravan in rented ground on a nearby farm – with 'no facilities, ablutions'. The caravan was a common strategy at the time, preferable for many in small towns to living with parents or in the semi-public space of boarding houses.[18] But close-knit families living nearby could still control young couples facing an uncertain future, as Beryl's story illustrates:

We were living in a caravan, hoping one day to own a house, but once the baby was born I had to live with my mother…. It was snowing, and my younger sister came down and said, 'Mummy says you've got to come home, she won't have you living in this caravan in this cold weather'…. It was really quite cosy but my mother said, 'No you've got to come home'…. The day he was born Tom came into the hospital with the papers for us to sign for us to come to Australia, and as I say, within six months we came. Because for a simple reason we knew we would never get a house, we had nowhere to live, and I'd always lived with my mother. So we thought wonderful opportunity, so over we came.[19]

For Tom and Beryl the chronic housing shortage was inseparable from family constraints on their hopes for an independent marriage, and Australia represented a bright prospect of resolution, in which their dream of home ownership was connected to freedom from parental interference. For those in large cities, the problem may have been less dramatic but no less pressing. The hopes of a way out for most were set on reaching the top of the long waiting list for a council house. At a time when the idea of home ownership was alien to most working-class people the lure of the council house was taken for granted.

'This is what you did in those days,' Elizabeth Gray commented, 'people didn't buy houses.' Elizabeth was among the fortunate few (like Albert Lougher) whose family had made the move to a council house before the war, when they left an old house in Bethnal Green for a new one in Chingford, with all the luxuries of indoor bathroom, toilet and hot water. So she was doubly fortunate when, soon after her own marriage in 1948, she was able to move from two small rooms to a Chingford council flat.[20]

These housing moves, whether dating from the 1930s, 1940s or 1950s, are invariably recalled with pleasure, the first hints of a higher standard of material comfort. One can detect here occasional glimpses of the rising expectations which led so many to aspire to more decent housing and to higher standards of living more generally. From the 1950s and 1960s they came to be represented more dramatically by New Towns like Stevenage and Milton Keynes.[21] Even the often rigid distinction between those yearning to own their own home and those aspiring to no more than a comfortable council house became blurred as conditions gradually improved.

Housing was not the most significant motivation for emigration to Australia, and it represented different needs and aspirations at different times: from the desperate responses to acute shortages in the decade after the war through to the ideal of home ownership which began to take root in the late 1950s. Yet housing stories recur throughout British migrant narratives, and Australian publicity – which promised a home of your own – struck a resonant chord of British hopes and dreams.

If housing was a central and enduring concern after 1945, it was easily magnified by other events, which could combine to reinforce the sense of malaise and lack of faith in the future. At a time of high demand for skilled employment during postwar reconstruction this dissatisfaction was rarely driven by unemployment. Much more significant was a contrast between employment aspirations – which were heightened by the end of the war and the expectation that work opportunities and living standards would improve – and the disappointment and frustration which seemed to characterize many working lives in this period. Difficulties and dissatisfaction at work (mostly though not exclusively experienced by male workers) – such as being passed over for promotion, the possibility of retrenchment or a sense of boredom or limited prospects which is often characterized as a being in a 'rut' – figure in our accounts as the single most important triggers for emigration, as indicated in Table 2.

Fred Marchinton's pre-migration history illustrates some of the ways in which postwar optimism and hope could turn to restless dissatisfaction. Fred had grown up in a struggling single-parent family in interwar Leeds, after his mother died of tuberculosis when he was 6. He completed an apprenticeship

Table 2 Factors cited as influencing the emigration decision

	Family 1945–58	Single/ couples no children 1945–58	Family 1959–	Single/ couples no children 1959–	Total
Prior experience of Australia	2	1		1	4
Disillusioned with postwar Britain	6	3		1	10
Unsettled ex-service(man)	5	2	2		9
Particular political crisis	1		1		2
Problems at work	7	7	8	7	29
Australian career prospects / job offer	5				5
A personal rut or crisis	2	2	2	4	10
Housing difficulties	2	2	3	1	8
The weather	9	4	8	1	22
Health issues (especially children)	6				6
Marital problems	1		2	1	4
Seeking independence from family	1	1	4	2	8
Already distant from family		2	3	2	7
Reunion with family in Australia	9	4	4	3	20
Strong encouragement from Australia	7	2	9	2	20
Australian immigration publicity		1			1
Long-term attraction of Australia	3	5			8
Previous travel experience	1	3	5	1	10
Opportunities for oneself		7		1	8
Opportunities for family and children	5		14		19
Concerns about children's education	2		2		4
Travel – adventure – working holiday	1	6	3	9	19
Total	75	52	70	36	233

Note: in this table we use a sample of 89 migrants or migrant families as an aid to explore factors which influenced emigration. This sample was based upon accounts for which we had detailed versions in electronic format, and comprised the first 29 La Trobe University interviews that were transcribed; all 30 University of Sussex interviews and 13 received written accounts; and 17 other published and unpublished written accounts. Though not pretending to be a scientific sample, we have no reason to suppose that it is significantly skewed, and it does suggest patterns that we could explore through the life histories. The sample comprised 28 families and 16 single migrants or childless couples that left Britain in the immediate postwar years 1945–58, and 28 families and 17 single migrants or childless couples that left Britain between 1959 and the mid-1970s. In total there are 56 migrant families, 14 couples without children and 19 single migrants (we group together single migrants and couples without children as in many cases their behaviour was similar). Of these, about a third (29) were Commonwealth nominee families who spent time in a migrant hostel; 13 were young single migrants or childless couples who did not have a personal nominator and who found their own accommodation in Australia; another third (29) were nominated by friends or family members; and 14 were nominated by employers or others organizations. Two were not on the assisted passage scheme, and the mode of assistance of the remaining two is unclear.

in sheet metal work and was in and out of employment during the 1930s, when he became an active trade unionist and, for a time, a member of the Communist Party. He married Mary in 1936 and they managed to save to buy their own flat, then a semi-detached house where one daughter was born at the beginning of the war and another at its end. War service as a Royal Marine Engineer Commando included mine-clearing at D-Day and an NCO promotion to train other soldiers, and Fred recalls his wartime contribution with great pride. Upon demobilization in 1946 he started a small business partnership making metal implements, but as the business prospered and grew it became increasingly stressful and Fred became 'irritable and impossible'. In 1950 he asked his partner to buy him out and returned to factory work, but 'I was restless and couldn't settle down, the job was just a job and I wasn't content.... Arriving home [after a short holiday] and being confronted with the gloomy prospect of years of drudgery of working in similar factories to the one I was currently employed, Mary and I talked things over and decided to take the plunge and emigrate to Australia', following Fred's older brother Roy who had emigrated with his family in 1948.[22]

The emigration of single men and women might also be triggered by frustration at work. Jessie Frost had taken up a nursing career after her father was bankrupted during the Depression. During the war she worked as a mid-wife in the Midlands, and when the war finished a nursing mentor in London invited her to train as a nurse tutor. Jessie was delighted by this encouragement and then terribly disappointed when she was forced to decline the offer because she could not afford the £150 college fees: 'And she said, "In that case, I have to put you in the General Ward. You can't stay in the midwifery department." And that's when I started planning to come to Australia. I had been in contact with my uncle and aunty and they kept saying, "Are you coming?" '[23]

Frustrations at work and the perception of limited prospects in Britain were important motivating factors for single men and women, yet there were significant differences between the ways in which young men and women perceived their Australian future in the decade or so after the war. Jessie Frost was going to join her relatives in Australia 'just for a holiday' – 'I just came because I had the attraction to come here, to visit' – and was 'over the moon' when she realized that it would only cost £10. She told her disapproving mother, 'I'm only going for two years, I'll be back.' Almost invariably, young single women who took up the ten pound scheme in these immediate postwar years saw Australia as an opportunity for travel and adventure. Often these were women who had gained a degree of independence from their families through wartime mobility and work. With nursing qualifications or secretarial skills single women knew they would find work in Australia, but career development was rarely a primary motivation.

By comparison, young single men who used the ten pound offer in the immediate postwar years were much more likely to consider Australia as an opportunity to improve their prospects and as a place of settlement. In this regard their migration motivations parallel those of many married men, though the latter usually associated their own prospects with opportunities for the family and children. In 1949, 21-year-old Archie Shaw couldn't see 'any prospects' in his shift work as a messenger boy for Manchester's *Daily Mail*. When he read about the assisted passage scheme Archie decided that Australia was 'an opportunity, I'll go and see what I can do somewhere else'.[24]

As we shall see, by the 1960s young single men also began to imagine the Australian sojourn as an opportunity for travel and adventure, but in the first decade or so after the war a male work ethic, reinforced by a potent collective memory of poverty and insecurity during the 1930s, prescribed emigration as an opportunity to 'better oneself'. By comparison, work and career did not have such a central place in the identities and aspirations of many young women, who were able to imagine their Australian opportunity in very different terms. Indeed, in the immediate postwar years young single women pioneered the 'working holiday', as we shall see in the discussion of these 'sojourners' in Chapter 5. Table 2 confirms the different motivations of single men and women who went to Australia before 1959: all seven who cited 'opportunities for oneself' were men; all six who cited 'travel, adventure or a working holiday' were women.

In the decade or so after the war, widespread political disenchantment with the state of postwar Britain exacerbated personal frustrations about housing and employment and bolstered the drive for a new start. George Adam, who was a policeman in Edinburgh by the early 1950s, still blames Attlee's Labour government for the postwar stagnation which drove him to leave in 1956, insisting that 'it was politics that made us come here'. By 1955 he and Connie had two children 'and things were getting worse, and worse, and worse in Britain, mainly because of the nationalization that had taken place. Unemployment was rife and of course, as unemployment is rife so crime increases'. George separates his own career prospects from the more general outlook: 'The occupation future was no problem at all; it was just the — I couldn't stand what they had done to Britain, and I couldn't see Britain being able to pull itself up, not even by its bootlaces; it still hasn't.' The Attlee government also had to bear the brunt of resentments over rationing, and often still does, despite its loss of power in 1951. In George's story this is allied with a more general political grievance, and his bitter memory of the rationing regime in Edinburgh extends it to 1956, two years after its official cessation in 1954. 'I mean — so one of the, one of the things that got right up our nose, Connie was wild about it as well, we still had the ration books, in 1956!

And stuff was rationed that had never been rationed during the war. I mean Churchill never had potatoes or bread rationed.'[25]

While George Adam and others criticized postwar rationing and nationalization, another perspective is provided by Albert Lougher, who pointed the finger at the resurgence of the British class system and all its inequities. Though these contrasting explanations for British postwar stagnation derived from very different political attitudes, in each case the perceived opportunities of Australia – a new start in a new country – were an enticing alternative to the old world.[26]

Besides British domestic politics, the postwar insecurities of Europe and the Cold War – from the Berlin Airlift in 1948 through to Suez in 1956 – contributed to a general pessimism about the future of Britain and to a widespread spirit of emigration mindedness. In Margaret McHugh's mind there was no doubt that 'the reason that we came to Australia in the first instance was because of the Suez crisis'. Her husband 'Mac' had been in the airforce, 'and we thought things were boiling up for some sort of action and we'd just finished with the ... war so we didn't fancy another experience like that, so we, we toyed with it really for quite a long time'. The McHughs were not alone in their worries about Cold War threats in the northern hemisphere, heightened by the Suez crisis and compounded by further irritants like the reintroduction of petrol rationing.[27] The surge in migration to Australia in the years following 1956 testifies to a sense of alarm and a feeling, however illusory, that Australia – with Melbourne as the host of the 'friendly' Olympic Games in 1956 – might offer an escape from the nuclear threat.[28]

Family complications delayed the McHughs' emigration decision until 1961, but these were soon swept aside by more prosaic matters:

It was the weather which did it in the end, because we had this little house in Somerset and the rain used to run down the windows, and it used to look like an aquarium, you know, and the rain running down all the time and, so we just decided we'd had enough what with wars and rumours of wars and the weather.

In migrant memories miserable British weather is a thread that circles around other personal and political factors for emigration. Sometimes the weather sparked first thoughts of change; sometimes it was the last straw. In a few cases – almost invariably involving sickly children within the first decade after the war – the British climate was a primary motivation for emigration. For example, Betty Preston, who had refused to join her serviceman husband when he was demobbed in Australia immediately after the war, relented in 1952 when a doctor advised her that her asthmatic daughter would be better off in a different climate. More often, the weather became important in migrant decision-making when combined with other grievances. The terrible winter of 1947 stands out in these stories, particularly because it was associated with food rationing and fuel shortages which led to drastic cuts in heating at a time of greatest need. This was also a political turning point, prompting some former Labour supporters to question nationalization policies. Dorothy Rooms's recollection captures the mood of the time and how it could easily stimulate thoughts of escape:

Oh, in the end we saw this thing about emigration. And 1947 was a shocking winter, the sea froze at the edges down south. Snow was…. Oh, it was terrible. What with the shortage of food, and the terrible winter, everybody was fed up. And my husband said, he said, 'We're going to have to get out of this.'[29]

The winter of 1947 is justifiably remembered for its extreme severity and its social and political impact throughout North and South. But it has no monopoly on the place of the weather in migrants' feelings about the Britain they left behind. The role of the weather as the 'last straw' on top of a range of grievances continues throughout stories of the 1950s and 1960s. Most often bad weather figures prominently in a vividly recalled moment of dissatisfaction, in which a decision based on other complaints was crystallized. Irene Spencer from the South Wales village of St Athan recalls that in 1965, 'Ah the weather was the main thing, and it was just a day to day existence'. As a young woman during the war Irene had enjoyed an exciting life as a trainee nurse, but she had never completed her training and was now working part time at a café in the school attended by her young son Alan, whilst husband Ray worked as an auxiliary plant operator at a local power station. For Irene the dismal weather captured the mood of her own dissatisfying life.

Anyway [laughs] we were living in, we had this council house in St Athan and it's been *pouring* for a solid week…. And I was sitting there looking out of the window and I thought, I can't stand this any longer. I thought I'm not going to end my days in a small village like this with the terrible weather we're having here and I think there's got to be more to life than this…. To tell you the truth Ray's mother used to call in once a week at least, on this particular day, every Thursday, she used to call in before she went down to the village to get her pension, and I know at this one day it was *pouring* with rain and I just watched her walking her way down the village and I thought to myself, that's how I'm going to end up. Going down the village once a week like that for my pension. And I thought, no way, there's a life out there and I'm taking it. And that's what, how it happened actually…. So I went down to go get a daily paper and lo and behold there was my answer. Ten pound Poms wanted, emigration, there was my answer. Ray came home from work and I said, 'We're going to Australia.' … Off we went to Australia, and *never* ever regretted it.

Irene's story points to the personal and metaphorical significance of the weather. At the time the unceasing rain contributed to Irene's sense of imprisonment in her 'dreary existence'. Through the rain she could see her future self following in the footsteps of Ray's mother, forever doomed to a claustrophobic village life. Not surprisingly the weather, that proverbial British cliché of complaint, remains as an iconic memory when seen against Irene's very positive experiences of sunny Perth. Perhaps most significantly, this story is framed by Irene's return to South Wales with Ray and Alan after only four years in Perth. Thirty years later this return is still Irene's deepest life regret. Her emigration story resonates with frustrated hopes and the unspoken fear that perhaps she did not escape the 'dreary existence' after all.[30]

Affluent fifties and swinging sixties: a new generation of emigrants

By the mid- to late 1950s Britain was emerging from a decade of postwar austerity and gloom. Harold Macmillan's legendary phrase of 1957, 'Most of our people have never had it so good', which circulated widely during the 1959 election, acknowledged the growth of affluence which was nurturing social mobility, a thriving popular culture and the youthful search for new experiences and adventure.[31] These trends form the background for memories of a quite different kind of Britain, one focused on economic prosperity and material comforts, leisure and excitement and a more pronounced generation gap, all of which could stimulate emigration. The emigration motivations of this second generation of ten pound Poms were often very different from the motivations of emigrants in that first decade or so after the war.

For most working-class families the 1950s and 1960s were years of increased economic security, and this slow but significant transformation resonates throughout the accounts of migrants who emigrated in this period. There were significant regional and even seasonal variations. For example, by the 1960s unemployment was twice as high in Scotland as it was in England and Wales, and the decline of Scottish heavy industry contributed to the disproportionately high rate of Scottish emigration.[32] But in much of the country there was still plenty of decently paid work for skilled tradesmen, and mothers with young children had less need to take on paid work outside the home (and experienced considerable social pressure to confine themselves to home and family). Many working-class families had now moved on to new council estates or were even beginning to buy their own homes in the suburbs and New Towns.

These were also years of massive expansion in the production and consumption of new consumer goods, especially home appliances, and these, too, are significant markers of relative affluence in memories of the Britain left behind.[33] Of the 1940s and early 1950s there is a wide consensus that 'in those days' people lacked the new goods like telephones, television, refrigerators and cars, and this denoted a different mode of premodern social life. The new television, for example, could be a proud indicator of change and success, as it was for Marion Kells's family in Wolverhampton when her father bought one just in time for the 1953 Coronation, 'and half the street coming in, and my mother feeding half the street, you know. Because that's the way things were in those days .... And because the television was such a novelty, and everybody thought my father was rich because he could have bought this television.'[34] Stories of domestic acquisition in the 1950s and 1960s point to the dawning of an age of comparative material well-being amongst working-class Britons, but these stories also serve other, metaphorical, purposes. They mark the end of the premodern world of Depression, war and austerity. In some cases the stories highlight the success through hard work of one's own family and imply that this drive and ambition fuelled their emigration. And for migrants who settled in Australia the rather extraordinary memory of a street with a single telephone or television evokes the contrast between the premodern Britain they left behind and the modern, affluent Australia they made their home – while overlooking the fact that such changes were part of the social history of both countries in the postwar years.

By the 1960s the onset of cheap package holidays in the Mediterranean was also beginning to transform working-class leisure and contributed to a widening interest in different countries and a sense of alternative futures. For example, in the late 1960s young Brighton couple Keith Whittle – a power station worker – and his wife Gill, who worked for a wholesale chemist, enjoyed several holidays in Spain 'when package holidays were starting up':

And it was exciting, wasn't it? I mean, even going to Spain for a couple of weeks was a, because before then people didn't really fly a lot, did they? .... that most probably put the bug in, you know, in your mind. You thought oh, I quite enjoyed that, so – And then to go to Australia just for ten pound, that was an even bigger adventure! [laughs][35]

How then, in this period of comparative and growing prosperity for working-class families, to explain emigration, and indeed the fact that the 1960s was the peak decade of postwar emigration to Australia? In part, the explanation lies with a variety of factors which frustrated rising expectations and sustained a continuing pessimism about the future in Britain.

For example, the series of financial crises from the middle of the 1960s, commonly labelled 'the squeeze and the freeze', imposed financial austerity even in times of relative affluence. In 1966 the *Daily Sketch* ran a series, 'The Search for a Better Life', highlighting the motives which were driving record numbers of Britons to leave for Australia, Canada and South Africa. Each country had its distinctive attractions, but regardless of destination all the interviewed emigrants agreed that economic pressures in Britain, notably high taxes, high prices and an inability to save for the future, had spurred them to leave. The personal accounts cited by the *Sketch* played on that common media image of Britain as a highly taxed land of stifled initiative. Ian Pullen's story chimed with the stereotype perfectly. An aircraft mechanic who had gone to Australia, he admitted that

I can earn a decent salary in Britain, say £28 a week. But I can't save. I can't own my own home – not till I'm middle-aged, anyway. I'd just get a mortgage and spend the rest of my life paying it off…. I want a business of my own, but what chance is there in Britain? You can work as hard as you like but you can never save enough, because the more you earn the more taxes you pay.[36]

If this focus on high taxes and lack of opportunity played to a prominent political agenda of the time against the Wilson Labour government, it also played a part in the thinking of many potential migrants. As we have seen, the foundations for this attitude were laid during the 1940s, but it continued to influence the ways in which many people thought about their society in the 1950s and 1960s.

The onset of black immigration in the 1950s marked one of the most far-reaching changes in postwar Britain and contributed to white pessimism about the future of the country. Not infrequently, stories about the early incursions of West Indians and Pakistanis into urban areas revive negative memories about black ghettos and 'taking over' that are similar to the racial discourse of the time.[37] Few people now attribute their actual emigration to these changes, although race might be cited as a contributing factor. Londoner Connie Ward admitted that 'that was one reason I *was* glad to leave England, because whenever you went on a plane, a train, you were the only white person. It used to aggravate me. I think a lot of people were aggravated by it.'[38]

But if the wider contexts of social and political change were influencing the emigration decisions of working-class families, most often it was a particular difficulty or frustration – against the backdrop of raised expectation – which triggered thoughts of emigration. In the 1960s there was no longer a stark contrast between austere postwar Britain and the imagined abundance of Australia, but there was a subtle and yet potent sense of a better life elsewhere which could be readily achieved through the ten pound scheme.

We can see this pattern if we return to the story of Ray and Irene Spencer. For Irene, emigration was precipitated by the weather but grew out of dissatisfaction with her 'dreary existence' and dead-end future in South Wales. Ray recalls that before they made the decision he took the information about Australian migration to work and in his spare time read about the sunny climate and the fantastic wages offered in the mining industries of north-western Australia. At the power station he was earning average wages but 'was still having to find money at the end of the week':

We were paid on a weekly basis and there was ... too much week left at the end of your money, as they say. Mind you we were trying to run a car at the same time, I suppose, but we managed but we were always pushing for the Christmas time and things like that, really couldn't afford to go on a holiday or whatnot, so we were living from week to week all the time.... I heard all this good money was being earned in Australia, and I thought well here's a chance, put ourselves out of the rut and get some, get onto our feet you see, cash wise. So that's what really pushed me, was the thought that I could earn better money in Australia in a better climate.

Underpinning Ray's decision was a dream of owning his own home – a dream that had been forged in a poverty-stricken childhood in a coal-mining village during the Depression and that he now believed could be realized in Australia.[39]

For families like the Spencers, economic and employment frustrations triggered thoughts of emigration, but the decision was often influenced by a deeper, personal sense of malaise – life in Britain was a 'narrow' or 'dreary' existence – and the belief that Australia offered change and excitement as well as better opportunities. In short, the magic of the ten pound scheme was that it offered – at least in prospect – an easy answer to existential concerns and enabled working-class families to try out Australia as an alternative future. In this regard these migrants of the 1960s are little different to their precursors in the immediate postwar years.

There was, however, one significant difference in the emigration decision-making of families in the latter period, when the improved economic circumstances of Britain required more careful calculation about family prospects in the two countries. The *Daily Mail* journalist Peter Black met up with a group of British migrant families in Adelaide in the mid-1960s and believed he had 'caught the essential character of this postwar migration from Britain of which the impelling force is a sober appraisal of personal conditions in Britain, tinctured by the pressure of Australia House's artful propaganda'. In fact, by this time large, average-income families were probably no worse off – in financial terms – in Britain.[40] But it was enormously difficult for prospective emigrants to make an effective comparison when there were so many variables and when they faced such complicated and even contradictory information. Often a perception that the family would be 'better off' in Australia – or at the very least could make a new and promising start in life – was the key.

The Farnfield family exemplifies this type of behaviour. In the 1950s, Don and Dorothy Farnfield raised three sons in the south coast town of Bexhill where Don worked as a painter and decorator. In 1959 they moved to Ilford in Essex where there was excellent schooling for the boys and plentiful work for Don – and for Dorothy who returned to work part time as a cleaner after her sons were all at school. In 1964 one of the boys was doing a school project about Australia and Don suggested that they all go up to London to collect some information and illustrations for the project. At Western Australia House 'we started to read about the jobs and the housing and the climate' in the newspapers laid out on a bench. One of the boys said 'couldn't we go to Australia?', 'And of course we said no [laughs], and then when we came back and we were talking about it on the train coming back.... the boys persuaded us *a lot* to think seriously about it.... and we kept going back, about once a month we would take a trip up there and have another look'. In the course of these trips the Farnfields researched their prospects in Australia, including details about employment, housing, education and healthcare. 'We knew that it wouldn't be like some of the papers printed it. It wasn't a land of milk and honey', but 'we both thought that, for the three boys it would be a better opportunity perhaps there than here'.[41]

Sponsorship by the Western Australian Employers' Federation guaranteed a job for Don and a house for their first four months, and they joined the Blue Cross Society to ensure health cover in Australia. Both sets of grandparents thought emigration was a mistake and were very upset about the loss of their grandchildren, but Don and Dorothy had already established their own strong and independent bond – 'we together are quite strong' – and decided that they should grasp this opportunity for themselves and above all for their children: 'our parents had never really *been* anywhere, they'd remained in England. They hadn't ventured.... but the opportunity was there for us to take so had it not worked right, well so be it.'

The Farnfield family story evokes many of the key themes of family emigration in the 1960s. The Farnfields had already established their independence as a family unit during their prior move to Essex, and geographical mobility was linked to social and economic improvement and a willingness to seek adventure and grasp change. Dorothy recalls with laughter that 'it was just the gypsy in both of us that kept us travelling around'. The ten pound scheme made emigration affordable for a family of five, yet Don and Dorothy carefully weighed up their prospects in each country and concluded that Australia offered their three sons the best prospects. For the Farnfields – and many other migrant families – emigration to Australia was, above all, an investment in the younger generation.[42]

Youth culture and the search for adventure

Young single men and women, and adventurous couples without children, had a very different attitude to their use of the ten pound passage to Australia in the 1960s. If they imagined a better life in Australia it was not necessarily a life of economic security for themselves and their children. The search for adventure was part of the transformation of youth culture and aspirations which sprang from increasingly widespread affluence (see Figure 7). We have seen how, in the 1940s and 1950s, young single women on the assisted passage pioneered the working holiday. By the 1960s young men had begun to shed conventional expectations of work and career and were also beginning to use the scheme for travel, adventure and personal change. The roots of this

7 'Penny and I in Trafalgar Square after our interview at Australia House for the Assisted Passage Scheme', February 1970. Penny was rejected on health grounds but Marion Rajan (on the left) spent five years in the 1970s working and travelling around Australia before returning to England in 1976. Like many young men and women of her generation, Marion used the assisted passage scheme for travel, adventure and personal change

change can be found in the transformation of youth culture from the 1950s, as ballroom dancing was displaced by rock and roll and the young were attracted to the excitement and fashions stimulated by an assertive youth movement and made possible by an increase in disposable income.[43] David Bailey, a London teenager and 'Teddy boy' in the 1950s, typically recollects the era of the Beatles and the 'swinging sixties' with great enthusiasm. 'I reckon it was a really good time in the '60s. I loved the '60s you know, everything about it. The Beatles and this, that and the other.... I wouldn't have missed that for anything in the world, it was a great time.'[44]

David Bailey's generation routinely refer to the Beatles as the iconic memory which marked Britain in the 1960s, and this is now underlined by their feeling that they participated in a time of deep social change. As Christina Daly, a Londoner born in 1951, put it, in the 1960s 'everything was happening wasn't it? ... The clothes, the music, you know it was, and it was such an optimistic time then ... that was really, well, when youth took off. And it was a very, very optimistic very nice time.'[45]

And yet although 'everything was happening' for young people in Britain in the 1960s, this same sense of excitement and adventure rubbed off into aspirations for travel and personal development which were, in turn, made possible by the ten pound passage scheme. Asked about the main reasons for going to Australia in 1973, Christina Daly recalls that 'it was just a sense of adventure really':

And just wanting to ... well we wanted to travel, both of us did, and we didn't have any money and we thought, well maybe we could go out there, okay, [whispers] bit of a long way away ... and earn some money so that we could finish travelling around. Because my husband wasn't a particularly career-orientated at the time either. He didn't have this big, you know, forty-year plan of where he was going and what he was doing or anything like that. So I think it was wanting to do something different.

John Daly is representative of many young men in the 1960s and 1970s who took the assisted passage as a passport to travel and adventure rather than as a career opportunity. This new generation of young men were less tied to expectations of career and family – or rather, they wanted to enjoy themselves before they settled into a more traditional role, and could afford to do so because of the comparative prosperity of the period and because of the assisted passage.

Other factors influenced this young couple. John Daly worked for IBM in the city of London but was relocated to Portsmouth, which he and Christina both found rather dull after the excitement of London in the 1960s.

Well *because* we didn't have any money, this is going to sound awful now, and we *were* down in Portsmouth at the time and it was *really* – and we didn't have much money and this place was freezing – it was so cold this flat we had and I remember because it was pouring down with rain and we were sitting there in our coats thinking this is a *joke*, you know, we thought we're going to have to go travelling, we're going to have to do something, and so I had a relative in Canada and I said, 'Oh you know, we could go to Canada'. And John's going, 'Oh it's freezing there, it'll be worse than here', you know. 'Oh all right.' So he said, 'Oh we'll go to South Africa', and I said, 'Absolutely no way, I'm not setting foot in South Africa, you know it's apartheid system over there, *no* way'. So, 'All right then'. So we said 'We'll try Australia'. I mean the thought processes of youth [laughing], 'Yes write off to Australia House, see if they'll have us.'

Upon being told that Australia wasn't taking single migrants at the time, John and Christina married in 1972, then passed their migration interviews and medical examinations without caring too much about the fine details: 'we're gaily going round telling people we're going to Australia they're saying to us, "Do they have a good pension fund over there?" And "What's the health service like?", and we're like, "Don't know, haven't got a clue, only going for two years" [laughs].'

Family relationships exerted a more subtle influence on John and Christina's plans. John, a 'whiz kid at IBM', had never been very close to his family and they 'didn't even *enter* into his decision-making processes'. Christina's mother was 'beside herself, but then she never, she'd never ever looked at me as a person'. As a child in working-class south-east London in the 1950s, within a close network of extended family, Christina had 'always felt claustrophobic there and stifled and, this sounds awful, misunderstood. I didn't feel that I fitted in there.… And from an early age I can remember thinking I'm getting out of here, this is *not* where I intend to be spending the rest of *my* life.' As a child she avoided the rough and tumble of the streets and escaped into books – which her parents thought very odd – and dreamed of travel and far off places. When she left school at 17 her father found her a clerical job with a London city branch of the insurance company he worked for. She met John and left home at 19, and arrived in Sydney at the age of 22. The ten pound scheme enabled Christina to live out her childhood fantasies and to escape the world of her family and upbringing. The proposal of a time-limited, two-year working holiday pacified parental resistance.

The desire for adventure and change, and for a life different to that of working-class parents who seemed to be trapped in the grind of work, home and family, inspired many young people – including couples without children like the Dalys – to take up the ten pound fare. Permanent settlement might be an outcome of the move but it was much less likely to be a definite intention than it was for families with children. Some of these 'sojourners' settled in Australia, some returned to Britain; all were transformed by their experience.

The family dynamics of emigration

We have already seen – in the case of Albert and Anne Lougher or Christina Daly – that emigration could be a painful and even contested issue with families. How the actual decision to leave was made in the family context tells us much about the intimate dynamics of marriage and family life. While there are many overlaps, three patterns can be discerned in the relationship between husbands and wives as they made their decisions about migration. The first is the 'reluctant wife' in the mould of Melvyn Bragg's novel *The Soldier's Return*, in which the husband is driven to leave but the wife is terrified of leaving her friends, wider family and community; the second pattern is close consensual agreement; and the third is a reversal of Bragg's story, with the entire process in Britain and Australia being driven by the wife's initiative. In the latter two patterns informants most often narrate their story – or sometimes their parents' story – as one in which each was committed to a close-knit companionate model of marriage. But few, if any, of these stories adhere to a consistent and predictable line of marital dominance and subordination, nor do they reveal conformity to postwar governments' promotion of traditional ideals of domestic life based upon a conventional male breadwinner and home-based wife and mother. In 1964 economic historian Reg Appleyard discerned one 'common pattern': returned soldiers who had met Australians during the war were often 'at the threshold' of migration in 1945, but their wives remained resistant until their children reached secondary school or leaving age in the 1950s, when anxieties about their children's future tilted the balance in favour of emigration.[46] Appleyard's version is certainly consistent with common post-war gender stereotypes, but it hardly does justice to the enormous diversity of stories told by the migrants themselves, or to the complex and shifting dynamics of family relations.[47]

The persistence of the image of the wife as the 'reluctant migrant' has not gone unchallenged in histories of migration, even in accounts of the nineteenth century.[48] Still, it is a common theme in many accounts by women and children, and is central to some poignant stories of women's fears of leaving the security and support of family and neighbourhood in Britain, and of homesickness and painful adaptation in the new country. A telling example is that of Margaret Hill, who left her Liverpool home for Australia in 1956, under great protest, and pregnant, and after many fights with her controlling husband. This is how she described the decision:

And I said to Jim, 'We'll wait until I have the baby', and he said, 'No we'll go while we can, I've heard rumours this immigration scheme's going to stop, we'll go now while we can.' And I said, 'No, no', I didn't want to go. And, and most of my memories of that are just of controversy, of not wanting to be involved in any of it, between he and I. In the end it was just me being so tired of everything, arguments and packing and having to give away things that I couldn't pack, and him saying, 'Oh don't take that, don't take that.' I'm just getting rid of stuff and getting rid of stuff and getting rid of stuff, you know stuff that you'd worked for and you'd got together in your glory box when you're saving to get married and all this and just having to get rid of stuff, and family heirlooms just having to go. And, then all of a sudden, just being on a train and unload, and just being tired, I was bone tired. To do all that and be pregnant was really exhausting, really wears you right down, it wore me right down and I was just tired to the middle of my bones and it took me a long time to recover. But having said that, once I'd got here and I settled, in the long run, I settled and made myself a life here and he is still bitter and unsettled and discontented.[49]

While stories like this conform to the stereotypes of the dominant husband with his submissive and reluctant wife, the larger narratives are rarely so straightforward. Margaret Hill eventually agreed to emigrate when a doctor convinced her that their sickly children would be healthier in Australia. In her account of their life in Australia she emerges as a powerful advocate for the welfare of her children and, ultimately, is transformed from put-upon wife to independent working woman and single mother. Her conclusion that it was she who made a life for herself while her husband remained 'bitter and unsettled and discontented' should warn us that power dynamics in marriage are rarely encapsulated by a single moment like that of the emigration initiative.

This subtle mixture of agency and subordination is more pronounced in accounts from both individuals and couples who present their decision as a consensual one, which could conceal a good deal of persuasion on either side. The postwar climate of chronic housing shortage, rationing and uncertain employment, not to mention periodic power and fuel shortages, added a quite unique urgency to mutual decisions about a couple's future. A similar urgency surrounded the surge in 'emigration mindedness' at the times of the 1956 Suez crisis and the financial crises of 1966–68. In this context lingering doubts about a partner's decision might easily be overcome. Beryl Walker, we recall, overcame a reluctance to leave her mother, in 1953 and with a new baby, because she saw no way out of the grim prospects of living in a caravan in Weymouth or sharing a house with her parents, and accepted her husband Tom's view that the children's future would be brighter in Perth. But the mechanics of this agreement hardly reflected the balance of decision-making in the marriage. Beryl described forthrightly how she had insisted that Tom leave his dead-end work in his mother's grocery shop in Bristol (for which he only received 'spending money') in order to escape from his family to Australia. And when his mother followed them to Perth and once more took him on in a new grocery shop she established there, it was again Beryl who prised Tom away from the dreaded family connection and sought other employment for him. 'We had a bit of an upset in England because I made Tom leave the family business.... The same old problem seemed to surface' in Perth, she remarked. And Beryl sustained their early years in Australia by running a boarding house as well as managing Tom's career.[50] This postwar generation is frequently forthright about an identification with the trend towards greater domestic sharing and intimacy, often defined as 'companionate marriage', as distinct from the more traditionally separate roles of their parents' generation. Like all deep social changes this was slow and subtle, but provides an early marker of ways in which marital relations were changing in the second half of the twentieth century.

The conventional male-dominated stereotype of emigration decision-making within a marriage is utterly confounded by those cases in which the wife took the initiative, occasionally against the opposition of her husband, and often defiant adolescent children. Joanna White was quite forthright about the reasons for persuading her husband to move in 1961:

For myself, I loved adventure and travelling. I'd already done a lot of travelling in Europe and – couldn't get enough of it and whilst my marriage, at that stage, was very happy, he was very entrenched as a Londoner, Cockney, absolutely Cockney Londoner, and I could see that our future was pretty ordinary and so my hidden agenda I suppose was to drag him out to Australia and hope that both our lifestyles would improve and there would be new opportunities.[51]

One of the most colourful accounts is that of Margaret Reardon, who emigrated with her family from Edinburgh in 1951, at the age of 16. Margaret's mother is the hero of a story of her family's struggle against the odds to do well in Australia and rise above what she feared would be a dismal future in Edinburgh, where her father was stuck in unskilled work in a grocery shop. The resistant husband had tired of overseas postings during the war and wanted simply to return to a quiet life in Edinburgh (in stark contrast to Melvyn Bragg's model of postwar soldiers' alienation). Margaret's mother eventually persuaded him, under quiet protest, to go along with her emigration plan. She was, Margaret felt, 'very brave ... to embark on this voyage because she was going on, I'd say, a dream ... she made all the arrangements for getting a sponsor, accommodation and a job for father'. All this had to be accomplished despite what Margaret called 'that friction' whenever the brown envelopes arrived from Australia House. When, within twenty-four hours of their arrival in Australia, the family suffered the disaster of father's prearranged farm job collapsing, miles into the country from Sydney, she again described her mother as the consummate manager who tried to negotiate with the reneging employer, left the farm and sought new work for father and accommodation for the family. And so it continued throughout the story of their lives in Australia, with father the permanent reluctant migrant and mother fighting fiercely for her family's welfare. Recalling this contrast, Margaret attributed it to the impact of wartime on her parents' attitudes: 'Mum was more the decision maker in big issues like coming to Australia, because, I think, Dad left that to her because of the five year gap, because she made all the decisions.'[52]

Figures like Margaret's mother appear routinely in our stories; they are often linked in the narrators' minds to specific regions, like London and the urban north west, in which adult children describe their cockney or northern mothers, for example, as the 'matriarch' of the family, or the 'top sister' from a large family, with habits of command, managing the family's enterprise in both Britain and Australia.[53]

These brief examples are just that – anecdotal illustrations of a diversity of decision-making processes in family relations generally, and migration in particular, which invariably had profound effects on later family fortunes. But they represent something more significant for our understanding of the shifting dynamics of marital relations in the postwar years. At the very least these stories provide evidence for alternative models of masculinity and femininity in the family context which were being talked about, however tentatively, during the late 1940s and early 1950s. How far those habits of sole authority, employment and management which women acquired during the war years persisted into the postwar decades and were passed on to their children is much discussed but still not resolved. But the kind of evidence presented in these migrants' stories does at least suggest that all the pressures after 1945 for men and women to return to a traditional division of labour had little relevance to couples' actual practices. Accounts by both men and women unsettle the notion of a postwar British population resistant to social change or simply conforming to the stereotype of dominant breadwinner father and passive wife and mother.

Entangled with the emigration decisions and disputes of husbands and wives were serious intergenerational tensions. The grief and pain of elderly parents who were losing children and grandchildren to the other side of the world is a searing, guilty memory for many migrants. Some parents of emigrants responded to the loss of their children and grandchildren with selfless acceptance and silent grief; others were sullenly resentful or even bitterly resistant. They grieved for the loss of loved ones, they hoped but also feared for their family's uncertain future in Australia, and they worried about their own fate without sons and daughters to care for them in their old age. In turn, emigrant sons and, especially, daughters were torn between the needs and demands of ageing parents (and, in some cases, their own need for parental support) and the chance of a better life for themselves and their children.

In 1966, according to Maureen Hands, 'while you were watching the World Cup, the Hands family were sailing to a new life in Australia'. A Stockport mother of two young children and pregnant with a third, Maureen vividly recalls 'the last time I went to see my Mum and Dad'.

We took the girls and we had something to eat with them. I don't know how I got through it. My poor Mum was crying all the time but she tried not to let me see her. When it was time to leave we all kissed each other and my Dad said, 'You're doing something that none of the family have ever done, but you'll be alright. It will give your children a better chance in life.' Julie and Lesley just didn't understand that they wouldn't see their Granddad and Grandma for a long time. My Dad was quite pleased that I would have a baby born in Australia, saying it would be a 'little Aussie'. They walked to the gate with us. Some of the old neighbours were outside their doors, all shouting their best wishes. I couldn't look back. I knew if I did I wouldn't go. My Mum told me afterwards that my Dad watched till we were right out of sight. I felt as if I was deserting them; however would they manage without me being there? The fact that they had nine other children didn't matter. I felt they needed me. Twelve months later in Australia I realised it was me who needed them, all of them. I'd never been so lonely in all my life.[54]

Sandra O'Neill's story highlights the competing loyalties within a family as it was tested by emigration. An only daughter growing up in Birmingham in the 1950s, she became a rebellious teenager and 'horrified' her parents when at 16 she became engaged to builder Brian who was six years older. Sandra's parents reluctantly agreed to the marriage on the condition that Brian and Sandra first saved up to buy their own house, which they did. By the time Sandra had two small children and had moved into a larger house in Sutton Coldfield, the conflict with her parents had been resolved and they were 'wonderful' grandparents. But Brian started to have affairs and Sandra was desperately unhappy. When she became pregnant for the third time, 'all I could think of, that I was absolutely trapped.... And then that was when he kind of said, "We need to get away from everything, and start again, it's not going to work." So it was at that time then that the Australia thing came about, yes.'

Sandra had no desire to go to Australia, but Brian was determined: 'I still did want the marriage to work, and he sort of said to me, "If we kind of go, it will be a completely new start. There'll be no outside interference, you won't be able to run back to your mother, you won't be able to have anyone influencing you, telling you what you should do and what you shouldn't do. There will be just us. And you know, it's a great opportunity."' Not surprisingly,

Sandra's parents were 'distraught'. They knew the marriage was in trouble and worried about what would happen if it broke up in Australia, and they were desperately unhappy to be losing their only child and grandchildren: 'as far as they were concerned, they perhaps would never see any of us again. That was the situation at the time.' But for Sandra, 'as much as I loved my parents, the overriding emotion was that I'd got to try and make this marriage work, and if it meant moving to a new country, to a new life, well so be it, that's what I'd got to do'. In 1972 the O'Neills flew to Perth, and Sandra's mother, 'she just took to her bed for a whole week and she couldn't speak to anybody, talk to anybody, she was just beside herself'.[55]

Other parents resented and opposed their children's decision to emigrate, and even campaigned for their return from Australia. Sickly 7-year-old David Casson, for example, emigrated with his parents from Northampton to Adelaide in 1950 after a doctor advised that 'I had to be relocated to a warmer climate with better food if I was to survive'. But 'both sides of the family … thought that travelling 12,000 miles was a stupid idea when I just needed "fattening up" and my mother's family were plotting to get us back home, even before we left, on the grounds that her mother would be ill one day!'[56]

Of course some families took grandparents with them or brought them out once they were themselves settled in Australia. In 1968 the Watkins family of Sussex was disillusioned with Harold Wilson's Labour government and decided that the three sons 'would benefit from a freer and more egalitarian society', though Christine Watkins was 'not happy leaving my mother who was so sad and looking after a very sick husband'. Six years later Christine's widowed mother joined them in Sydney and lived in the 'granny flat' which they built as an extension to their three bedroom fibro house. But more often parents stayed behind and the transnational dislocation of families was a continuing source of grief, guilt or regret and, as we shall see, a powerful pressure for return.[57]

Family ties, however, were not always so strong, and not all emigrants were tested by these competing loyalties. We have already seen how wartime disruption might weaken family links, and thus make emigration easier and less painful. Jessie Frost had grown apart from her parents during and after the war when she worked as a nurse, and especially after her father had died and her mother remarried. When she decided to take the ten pound passage to Australia in 1948,

Mother said, [laughs] 'I don't know why you're going there.' No she wasn't, she didn't approve. But I said, 'I'm only going for two years, I'll be back.' In any case, I had very little to do with my home because I didn't like my stepfather. I didn't disapprove of him, it was her choice, but he seemed to upset my home, you know. And they were happy together so it was nothing to do with me.[58]

Young single women often used the 'two-year rule' to convince parents that they were not leaving forever. But for some, the ten pound scheme simply reaffirmed a wartime separation from parents, whilst for others it provided an alternative to marriage as a way of escaping from parental constraints.

The postwar mobility of young working-class families who were moving to the suburbs and New Towns and seeking economic and social improvement within Britain – exemplified by the Farnfield family – also contributed to an independence from the extended family which, in turn, eased the more dramatic move to Australia. In more extreme cases emigration was an asser-tion of independence from the tiresome constraints of a domineering family relationship. We have seen how the postwar housing shortage made young couples like Tom and Beryl Walker or John and Sylvia Cannon desperate for independence in a home of their own, away from the interfering presence of in-laws. Similarly, Eileen and Fred Hay decided to leave Aberdeen shortly after they were married in 1960, 'partly as we thought we would be better off financially and partly we could be totally independent – mainly from my mother'. As a child Eileen had 'found living at home very restrictive as my mother was a very dominant person who liked everything done her way'. Now that she was married Eileen wanted to make her own life, and the ten pound passage to Australia was the answer.[59]

British migrant stories highlight the transformations in family lives and relationships during and after the Second World War. The unique relation-ships within each family shaped emigration decisions and disputes but were, in turn, influenced by the changing patterns of family life. Whilst close and supportive relationships within extended family networks were a significant and continuing pressure against emigration, other young couples had already weakened these family ties or used emigration to confirm their independence. By wrenching many families out of the wider networks of kin and community, the assisted passage scheme contributed to the emerging pre-eminence of the nuclear family.

Excitement and trepidation: the mixed emotions of migrant children

Migrant accounts resonate with the distant voices of parents and grand-parents who grieved over the emigration of their children and grandchildren. In our archives we can also hear at first hand from children and teenagers who followed their parents to the other side of the world, and begin to comprehend the distinctive feelings and attitudes of these young migrants. In official discourse – and in the guilt-tinged memories of some migrant parents – migration was for the good of the children, who would 'adapt very quickly to an Australian life style with its emphasis on outdoor living and a freer way of life'.[60] Our migrant children travelled with the security of parents and siblings, unlike those other, very different 'child migrants' who were sent from British children's homes and orphanages to uncertain futures in Australia.[61] But they rarely participated in the emigration decision and they now recall a confusion of feelings.

The youngest children swung between excitement and bewilderment. In 1951, 11-year-old Pauline Rooms was 'thrilled to bits' when her mother took her into Manchester to buy her first new coat, for the trip to Australia. She was 'very excited and not concerned about leaving any friends or family behind', but her eagerness was tinged with a fear of the unknown:

I really had no concept of the distance we were about to travel. I imagined Australia to be a little bit like the Tarzan films, with jungle, animals, natives etc., I could not imagine going to school or my parents working. It frightened me when my aunt said things like, 'What happens if one of you becomes ill. You will have no medical care, no doctors or hospitals to care for you.'[62]

For 8-year-old Judith Addison, emigration was a terrible shock which wrenched her out of a safe and secure life in the Lancashire town of St Helens:

My family lived in a very small semi-detached, in an estate built mid-1930s. Dad worked for Pilkington Brothers, the glass people. My mother did not work. My brother and I attended school. My brother was in the Scouts and I was in the Brownies. Life seemed very straightforward, school, Sunday school, Sunday lunch (which we called dinner) listening to the radio (*Ray's a Laugh*, *Life with the Lyons*, *Take if from Here*). Mum was a good cook. After Sunday school we usually all met up at Auntie May's house for Sunday tea, and possibly a game of cards afterwards (Rummy, Newmarket, stuff like that).

When Judith's parents decided to emigrate in 1951 she had 'had very little idea what was going on or why. I was only told we were going a few weeks before the event. There were never any family discussions about whether we should go, or if there were I was not aware of them. It came as a great shock to me to learn that I would be leaving my home, family, friends, school etc. for the other side of the world. I remember going to Liverpool to have the injections for travel and not really knowing what was happening.' Judith's only memory of the train trip from St Helens to Manchester and then down to Southampton evokes her feelings of loss, fear and confusion: 'Some friends came as far as Manchester to see us off. I remember sitting in the compartment by myself as the others stood by the doors and windows of the train, feeling absolutely devastated (although then I did not know the word). I do not remember the rest of the train journey.' In Judith's memory the feeling that emigration to Australia was a dreadful interruption to the safe world of her Lancashire childhood was heightened by a second disruption when the family left Australia after only two years and returned to St Helens.[63]

For many young children the fear and confusion of emigration was eased by the comforting presence of parents and older siblings – though the degree of comfort depended upon the extent to which parents recognized their concerns and offered solace and support. Older children and teenagers experienced a rather different confusion of feelings, influenced by their own enthusiasm for a life in Australia but also by impending loss of the networks and relationships of an emergent and independent adolescent identity.

We have seen how Don and Dorothy Farnfield's three sons, aged 13, 11 and 7, actively encouraged their parents to emigrate. In 1950, 14-year-old John Jordan, whose father was thinking of going alone to Australia to set up a base for the family, was just as keen:

I was pushing my dad towards going all the time … I wanted to go desperately, I was saying, 'When are you going to go dad, when can you go dad, are you going to do this dad, are you dad, oh when? Let's get you on a slow boat', because there was an old song at the time, 'I want to put you on a slow boat to China', and I just changed the words and said, 'I'd like to get you on a fast boat to Australia' [laughs].[64]

Other teenagers had more mixed feelings. When the Lavery family in Glasgow received confirmation of their passage to Australia, 13-year-old Mary Rose and her younger siblings 'somersaulted all over the beds and threw the pillows up in the air. "We're off to see the beaches, the wonderful beaches of Aus." Then we ran out of the house half dressed and knocked on all the doors and windows like Wee Willie Winkie.' Mary Rose's mother had been dreaming and scheming for years to get her family to Australia and away from the grey poverty of the Glasgow docklands, but Mary Rose was ambivalent about the decision. She had passed a qualification exam for a 'posh' secondary school, and feared for the loss of her new found friends and self-worth:

'What do you need tae go there for, anyway?' I asked, catching the crumbs from the edge of the table. 'Mah Da's getting good work noo, and ah like Bellahouston. The teacher wants me to finish my story.' Increasingly, every day, despite my attempts at self-flagellation, I was rediscovering my own worth.[65]

Sometimes teenage reluctance developed into outright resistance. In 1951, 16-year-old Scot Margaret Reardon had just won a scholarship to continue at high school when her mother finally persuaded a sceptical Mr Reardon to take the family to Australia. Margaret 'used to go to school and think about it and start crying. I'd have the Nuns coming up and saying,

"There, there, you know, it might never happen", and all this sort of thing, you know. Because I used to think, gosh, I'm going to leave this, I can't believe it you know.' During the emigration interview at Australia House in Edinburgh Margaret, asked for her opinion of Australia, almost ruined the family's chances:

I said, 'I don't want to go'. And Mum looked at me, and he said, 'Well you're honest', and he said, 'What do you expect to find over there?' and I said, 'I don't really care'. That was the two answers. And, I just saw this look, my sister's there, my Mum, this is it, that's the finish, we've had it, we're not going, you know, they're not going to ... and she said, 'When they're this age they're — ', just tried to smooth it over, you know. But I could just see this big man just grinning at me [laughs]. [66]

A few older teenagers successfully asserted their independence. John Jordan's elder brother had just started university and refused to go to Australia with the rest of the family, but was allowed to stay only when his grandmother agreed that he could live in England with her. But young men and women who had left school (though not home) and had started work were still legal dependants of their parents until they were 21 and were, for the most part, expected to emigrate with their families. In 1965, 19-year-old Maureen Carter was 'grossly unhappy' about leaving a good job in Neath to go to 'a blackfella place':

But being the eldest of ten children, and being very young for my age, being emotionally bound to my family, a strict Catholic family where you, in those days 'honour thy father and mother' was almost the most important commandment, so there was no way I could have, at 19, stayed in Wales. [67]

Some reluctant teenage migrants made the most of their Australian experience. Others continued to resent the loss of their British adolescence and identity, or felt an absence in their Australian lives which might ultimately propel them back to Britain. In later chapters we shall see how intergenerational tensions – between emigrant families and their parents, and within emigrant families – complicated settlement and sometimes sowed the seeds for future discontent

'We came to Australia': the Jenkins family and the logistics of leaving

The practicalities of emigration were comparatively straightforward for young single migrants or couples without family responsibilities or worldly goods. But for families, leaving Britain was almost never easy. Once a decision had been made, the migrant family faced a series of bureaucratic obligations and the bewildering challenge of selling up, settling affairs, packing and preparing to sail. The emigration of the Jenkins family in 1965 illustrates the complex logistics of leaving.

Thomas Jenkins started work in 1947 as a journalist in Dundee, where he met his wife Barbara ('Babs'), a senior nursing sister. In 1956 he joined the *Sunday Express* in London, rising to foreign editor in 1961. By 1965 Thomas and Babs, both aged 35, had a mortgage on an 'above average semi-detached house' in Walton-on-Thames and three children under the age of 7. With an income close to £3,000 per year, family holidays in the Mediterranean and West Wittering, and a love of London restaurants and the Surrey countryside, the Jenkinses were comparatively well-to-do; in certain respects their financial and cultural resources and middle-class attitudes made for a migration experience which was significantly different from that of working-class families.

Yet Thomas Jenkins was a thoughtful and perceptive journalist, and when he realized how little practical and emotional guidance there was for prospective migrants he determined to write an account of his own family's migration as a guide to others. The Jenkinses kept 'notes and letters and diaries and documents and photographs; everything that might add up to a true record of our experiences. We heard other's experiences, and recorded them.' In 1968 the *Sunday Express* featured extracts of Jenkins's migration story and in 1969 *We Came to Australia* was published in London. By comparison with autobiographies and interviews recorded many years later, which recall moments of striking significance but are often vague about the practical details of emigration, Jenkins's more contemporary account – based upon detailed records and intended as a guide for others – conveys the practicalities of emigration in precise detail.[68]

His own family's experience confirmed for Thomas Jenkins that emigrants 'rarely have ONE good reason for migrating. They have several.' The move from Scotland nine years previously had been 'a valid rehearsal for our big jump' and had weakened family and cultural roots. In Fleet Street Thomas was unhappy with the intense competitiveness at the top of the profession and becoming bored with an office job; a rare foreign assignment to Saudi Arabia confirmed 'with certainty how distasteful was the prospect of going back to my desk, to the 6.27, to the rut'. At home the idyllic village feeling of Walton was being ruined by developers and their bulldozers. And 'Britain itself had so many troubles, so many crises. Whichever government was in power, it warned of hard times, tightened belts, higher taxes.' A cold, wet summer holiday at West Wittering in 1964 exacerbated this disenchantment. By contrast, a meeting with the press officer for the visiting premier of Western Australia in 1963 had introduced Thomas to Australia as a country that 'was beautiful, potentially rich and blessed with a superb climate'. In 1965, two days after his return from Saudi Arabia, a meeting with another Australian journalist who extolled the potential of Perth made up his mind: 'As he talked, I suddenly felt sure that this was the place for us.' That night Thomas talked it over with Babs – who 'made it clear to me where she saw her first loyalty – with me. I could remember her grinning and saying "Whither thou goest, old fruit .... "' – and then wrote to a contact asking for a job on the *Western Australian* newspaper.[69]

Australia's migration programme was, according to Thomas Jenkins, 'one of the wonders of the modern world', and the title for his chapter about emigration procedures – 'Through the Machinery' – indicates the efficiency and, for some, the challenge of this bureaucracy. On 23 July 1965 the *Western Australian* offered Thomas a job. Two days later he applied for assisted passages and on 16 August the family was called to Australia House for an immigration interview. Their preparations for the interview highlight both the importance of the occasion and the Jenkinses' preconceptions about Australian attitudes to the British: 'Babs, choosing a dress, muttered, "Not too short, showy or sexy". I shaved as if for my wedding and dithered pitifully over a tie (not old school or regiment, not a bow or too tweedy, in case it suggested snobbery or arty-craftiness, or something).' In the event the children ran riot, the interviewer criticized Thomas for putting the house up for sale and giving notice at work before they had been accepted for emigration, and they began to worry that acceptance was not automatic.

The Jenkinses need not have worried. Australia House was unlikely to reject a young family with plentiful savings and Australian employment secured for the breadwinner, and after a successful medical (including mandatory X-rays in case of tuberculosis) the letter of acceptance arrived on 8 September. Thomas and Babs were asked to surrender their passports for two years in return for 'documents of identity' (thus ensuring they could not return within two years without paying the balance on the outward fare) and to submit vaccination certificates and their £20 contribution to the fare; had they paid the full amount the boat trip would have cost the family £595 8s. Within a few weeks the Jenkinses were notified that they would be sailing on the P&O vessel *Oriana* from Southampton on 5 December 1965.[70]

By comparison with the Jenkins family, other British migrants have mixed memories of their dealings with the emigration 'machinery', depending upon their own status or delays that were caused as officials sought to match applicants with available shipping and employment needs in Australia. The young and healthy (and impatient) often recall the official interview and medical examinations as 'superficial' or 'perfunctory'.[71] However, in one regard at least the Australian authorities were particularly careful. Dorothy Wright recalls that in 1959 she and her husband Mike went for a migration interview in Guildford and left their baby son asleep at his grandparents' house. The interviewer demanded to see the baby: 'We had not realized that the White Australia policy in operation at the time, meant us and our baby, too! So we had to drive the man to Mike's home so he could just check that we weren't trying to smuggle a black baby into Australia. Amazing!' A similar anecdote is repeated in numerous accounts and has no doubt become something of an urban legend, highlighted in memory because of the surprise at the time and because the story recalls a notorious aspect of Australian migration policy.[72]

Australia also filtered out applicants with health problems that might be a burden on the state, and if there was any doubt the medical examination was rigorous. For example, Albert Lougher underwent three medical inspections because of the disabilities he had incurred as a prisoner of war, was also quizzed about why he and his wife had no children, and was relieved to be accepted after two years of uncertainty. In 1971, 19-year-old Kate Rowe, a recovering anorexic and drug user, was referred by the Australian authorities for psychiatric testing but managed to lie her way through to acceptance. Northumberland mother of three Mary Dickinson was recalled for a second medical examination because the results of her chest X-rays had been inconclusive. Her husband Matt's journal for 1955 records 'Another ordeal for Mary, but they get over, once more we were waiting, waiting, WAITING'.[73]

The Dickinsons waited almost a year between application and sailing date, and Matt later recalled that 'When trying to emigrate, the period of waiting can be very trying on the nerves. Every post might be the one which carries the news, good or bad.' After confirmation of acceptance, Australia House tried to provide at least a month's notice of the shipping date (sometimes it was less) and emigrants were urged not to make plans about their house or work until the date was confirmed. When the notification finally arrived there was often a stressful period of frenetic preparation.

Once Thomas Jenkins had a job offer in Western Australia, and whilst the Jenkinses were waiting for confirmation from Australia House, they used this head start to find information about Australia that would aid their preparations. Thomas would later write that too many emigrants tackled their venture 'with suicidal carelessness'. He was suspicious of the seductive 'soft sell' of official immigration material, and instead sought advice from contacts in Australia and by reading Australian newspapers. 'I doubt if there was any sort of organized build up of information in our minds. It came piling in – land prices, mortgage difficulties, freight charges, huge fridges, surf, sharks, and all – and then settled, like silt, in our minds. We picked out what we could act on, and let the rest lie.' Apart from a highly selective impression of Australian culture and society, the Jenkinses benefited from practical advice about what to leave behind and what to bring with them. They were advised to bring furniture, household utensils, whitegoods, toys and clothing, because it would cost less to send these items by sea than it would cost to buy them in Australia, and because Australian replacements would be of inferior quality. A woman friend in Perth wrote to Babs, 'There is nothing much wrong with Australia that Marks and Spencers and Sainsbury's could not put right. My advice is to get kitted out at Marks and Spencers and also to buy plenty of shoes.'[74]

Of course the Jenkinses' enquiries related to their own middle-class concerns (about ballet or private schools, for example) and, perhaps more importantly, presumed a level of financial resources unavailable to many migrants. They could afford the 'economics of freighting – if it will cost more to replace than it does to freight, take it' – and thus for £230 were able to pack most of their household goods into a huge 225 cubic foot wooden box and send them by sea freight to Australia where 'today they are all round us, comfortable and comforting'. Apart from this psychological comfort, the Jenkinses benefited from considerable long-term savings on replacement costs (they also saved about £200 by freighting their car to Australia, but lost out in the long run because they could not get spare parts).[75]

By contrast, the Dickinson family, like many British migrants who had little in the way of savings, had to make do with their hand luggage and a free allowance of baggage which would be stored in the ship's hold (20 cubic feet per adult and 10 cubic feet per child, with an additional 6.5 cubic feet for the family – for which they had to pay £10 22s. for rail freight to the docks). In these circumstances, decisions about what to take could be heartbreaking. In 1950, Betty Preston's husband was 'officer in charge of packing' and they were limited to bare essentials. Having to leave behind her books was Betty's 'first heartache', and each child was rationed to a small parcel of personal items.[76]

Items that could not be taken to Australia were given away or sold, though as Matt Dickinson noted, 'Selling up for migration is a real game of chance'. By making careful deals with neighbours and sales rooms the Dickinsons lost very little against original purchase prices and even made a little profit on some items (in 1952 Dorothy Rooms and her husband made a healthy profit on their carpets and furniture because of postwar shortages). In 1958 Margaret Parkinson's father sold their worldly possessions and for the first time in his life had £100 in the bank; Eileen Hay and her husband managed to save £100 after 'selling up' in 1961 and they thought they were rich. Based upon his survey of migrants in 1959 (when the average weekly wage of the British male manual worker was just over £13), Reg Appleyard calculated that each family expected to transfer a median of £289 to Australia. At the time this might have seemed a small fortune for a working-class family, though most later realized that it covered only the bare essentials of setting up a home in Australia. Families who had their own home to sell took a larger capital sum to Australia – a median of £829 in 1959 (in 1965 the Jenkinses sold their house for £6,250 and made a tidy profit). Selling a house in limited time was extraordinarily stressful, but provided the deposit for a mortgage on their home in Australia. As we shall see, this would prove to be a hugely significant head start for an immigrant family.[77]

The Jenkinses' last feverish weeks in England are recalled in a chapter in *We Came to Australia* titled 'On the brink'. Apart from selling their house and arranging temporary accommodation with friends, packing their belongings, and buying essential items for Australia, Thomas and Babs needed to sort out personal insurance, tax and health benefits, and to arrange money transfers into an Australian bank and purchase travellers cheques:

As the pace quickened and we struggled with the multiplying aspects of our migration, a thought struck me. I was living on the telephone, typing endless letters, making outrageous use of the free time my employers gave me, I wondered how the hell the average migrant contrives at all to get to the ship on time. I had the benefit of a fair education and administrative experience. What of the barely-literate labourer, with no telephone, typewriter, and precious little time? People like this either have more organizing skill than I give them credit for, or they leave a good deal of mess behind.

And, in this hectic round of practical details and lists, there was the 'sweet sorrow of parting'. Thomas's parents were dead but Babs's siblings and widowed mother lived nearby. When they told Babs's mother of their decision she wished them well, whilst holding back her tears, and they in turn promised to build a room for her in their house in Perth (she took up their offer for a four-month holiday but decided to return to be with her other children in England).

The last night in England, and a meal with close friends and family, became a poignant memory:

Granny and Alice and Babs and Shirley all cried, Bill and Robin and I felt like it, but did what men always do when the women cry on occasions like this, and made gruff jokes. Babs' mother said 'I'll never see you again', then regretted it and said: 'Don't pay any attention. Have a lovely time ... ' as if we were going to Wittering for the week. Hugs, hard handshakes. 'Take care of them', they told me.... We peeked in on the children, sleeping defencelessly. Did they understand, in any way, what day of their lives tomorrow would be? Then we went to bed, not thinking. For, as T. S. Eliot says, 'Human kind cannot bear very much reality.'[78]

Notes

1 Paul interview LU.
2 Heath interview US.
3 There is one further distinction, noted by Appleyard, *The Ten Pound Immigrants*, p. 57, but less obvious within our material, that by comparison with personal nominees, Commonwealth nominees had higher levels of dissatisfaction with their British lives (they were less likely to be drawn to Australia by personal connections).
4 Grace Turnbull interview LU.
5 Clark interview LU.
6 Ledgett interview LU.
7 See Summerfield, *Reconstructing Women's Wartime Lives*.
8 Fairbairn interview LU.
9 For example O'Neill interview US; Elizabeth Gray interview US; Gray interview LU; Adams interview US; Kells interview US; Shaw interview US; Pickett interview US.
10 Fairbairn interview LU.
11 Reardon interview LU.
12 Davis interview LU.
13 Bragg, *The Soldier's Return*; Bragg, *A Son of War*.
14 Bragg, *Soldier's Return*, p. 316.
15 Lougher interview LU.
16 Saxton, *Something Will Come to Me*, p. 108.
17 Barrand interview LU.
18 See also Williams written account US.
19 Walker interview LU.
20 Gray interview US; see also Jordan interview US.
21 Marwick, *British Society Since 1945*, pp. 30, 88, 194; Clapson, *Invincible Green Suburbs*; Finnegan, *Tales of the City*.
22 Marchinton, 'Three Score Years and Ten', MS 11700, p. 108, Box 1872/7, State Library of Victoria, La Trobe Australian Manuscripts Collection.
23 Frost interview LU.
24 Shaw interview US.
25 Adam interview LU. See also Clark interview LU.
26 Lougher interview LU.
27 Appleyard, *The Ten Pound Immigrants*, pp. 47–8.
28 McHugh interview LU.
29 Rooms interview US. Preston, *Blowing My Own Trumpet*, p. 20. On the winter of 1947 see especially Robertson, *The Bleak Midwinter*, pp. 157–62, and Floyd interview LU; Clark interview LU.
30 Spencer interview US.
31 Marwick, *British Society Since 1945*, pp. 110–11.
32 Bain, 'Post-war Scottish Immigration', p. 669.
33 Benson, *The Rise of Consumer Society in Britain*.
34 Kells interview US.
35 Keith and Gill Whittle interview US.
36 *Daily Sketch*, London, 25 October 1966, p. 8.
37 For example Paul interview LU; Bailey interview LU; Britton interview LU; Lougher interview LU; Ward interview LU.
38 Ward interview LU.

39 Spencer interview US.

40 Black, *The Poms in the Sun*, p. 209; Appleyard, *The Ten Pound Immigrants*, pp. 46–61.

41 Farnfield interview US.

42 Appleyard, *The Ten Pound Immigrants*, pp. 46–61, also notes a demographic bulge of British postwar babies coming to maturity in late 1950s which increased parents' concerns about employment prospects for their teenage children.

43 Sinfield, *Literature, Politics and Culture in Postwar Britain*, pp. 152–8; Marwick, *British Society Since 1945*, pp. 131–5, 142–4.

44 Bailey interview LU.

45 Daly interview US.

46 Appleyard, *British Emigration to Australia*, pp. 168–9.

47 Based on a survey of 82 transcribed interviews from the La Trobe University Archive, an analysis of testimony about family decision-making reveals that the most common practice was consensual agreement, reported in 69 (83.7 per cent) cases. Among these 29 (35.4 per cent) were initiated by husbands with their wives' willing agreement, 10.9 per cent by wives with husbands' agreement, and among 31 (37.8 per cent) neither could recall who first expressed the idea, with both equally enthusiastic. Only in 11 (13.4 per cent) cases was the decision attributed to the husband against a wife's reluctance and 2 (2.4 per cent) to the wife against a husband's reluctance. In a further 3 cases divorced or widowed women initiated the decision with children (there were no cases of widowed fathers emigrating with their children).

48 For example Haines, *Emigration and the Labouring Poor*, p. 257.

49 Hill interview LU (Margaret Hill has made minor amendments to the transcript of this extract to clarify the meaning of her account); also Hill, *Corrugated Castles*.

50 Walker interview LU.

51 White interview LU.

52 Reardon interview and correspondence, LU. For other examples of wives who took the lead in emigration, see: Elizabeth Gray interview US; Hurst interview LU; Liverani, *The Winter Sparrows*.

53 See also Howell interview LU.

54 Hands written account US.

55 O'Neill interview US.

56 Casson written account US. Reg Appleyard (in *The Ten Pound Immigrants*, p. 86) explains that of his 1959 sample of 452 migrants, in at least 66 cases a parent was strongly opposed to the emigration; he argues that the language of survey responses suggests that the extent of opposition was even greater.

57 Watkins written account US.

58 Frost interview LU.

59 McGarrity written account US.

60 Norman Hoffman, Regional Director (Migration), Australian High Commission, London, quoted in introduction to Zamoyska, *The Ten Pound Fare*, p. xxii.

61 On child migrants see Humphreys, *Empty Cradles*; Paul, *Whitewashing Britain*, pp. 35–7; Sherington and Jeffery, *Fairbridge*; Gill, *Orphans of the Empire*.

62 Stanyer written account US.

63 Qureshi written account US.

64 Jordan interview US.

65 Liverani, *The Winter Sparrows*, pp. 188–9 and 163–4.

66 Reardon interview and correspondence LU.

67 Carter interview LU.

68 Jenkins, *We Came to Australia*, p. xvi.

69 *Ibid.*, pp. 22–53.
70 *Ibid.*, pp. 66–9.
71 See Proverbs interview LU; Tomlin interview LU; and Pickett interview US.
72 Wright written account US. See also Upton, *To the Undiscovered Ends*, p. 4; O'Neill interview US; Elizabeth Gray interview US.
73 Rowe interview LU; Lougher interview LU; Dickinson, 'Our diary of our migration', State Library of Victoria.
74 Jenkins, *We Came to Australia*, pp. 47, 74 and 41.
75 *Ibid.*, pp. 58–61.
76 Preston, *Destination Australia*, p. 3; see Hill interview LU.
77 Dickinson, 'Our Diary of Our Migration', State Library of Victoria; Rooms interview US; Parkinson written account US; Appleyard, *British Emigration to Australia*, pp. 57 and 211.
78 Jenkins, *We Came to Australia*, pp. 62–82.

3

Between two worlds

Leaving home

Leaving Britain was a potent emotional experience. The migrant's farewell event at the railway station or on the docks is detailed in vivid journal entries and is etched in memory, where it is shaped into a story which evokes the meanings and significance of emigration. In November 1954, 15-year-old Graham Little left London for Melbourne with his parents and younger sisters. He bought a new journal to record his 'Memoirs of a Trip to Australia on *S.S. Strathnaver*', and started to write down his feelings, 'even before we left England':

Amidst all the regrets and fears I was immensely excited to be going to Australia, in fact impatient to be off. On November 2nd, 'How I wish that we were on our way now!' and on the 4th, 'I could hardly eat my lunch for excitement'. I enjoyed trying to picture Melbourne, 'Maybe there are still trams there – I hope so, because I love them!' This is the diary that discovered the exclamation mark!

As the *Strathnaver* left Tilbury docks it was lit up by bonfire night celebrations on shore at Greenwich, and Graham began to feel the loss of his youthful life and of the security of childhood and England:

I stood watching it all for over an hour. I felt like I was leaving a party, my own party, just when all my friends were there and starting to enjoy themselves. I hoped they knew I wanted to be with them, that I didn't want to go, that I wanted to stay and do all the things we used to do. I wrote my first shipboard entry in the diary at ten, not sure if we'd quite cleared the Thames, feeling sorry for myself. I was too sad to write more than a note, and a short prayer, and anyway they served breakfast at 8.15 in the morning.[1]

Graham Little's journal captures the turbulent teenage emotions of departure, as he swings between excitement and trepidation and senses the end of childhood security, the frustration of his burgeoning English life, and the dreams of an Australian future. This mix of confused and even contradictory emotions is common in stories of leaving, though several types of emotion predominate. For some the tangle of feelings had a numbing effect. Maggie Smith explains why she and her husband Robert felt 'empty' and 'brain dead' in the days leading up to their departure from Edinburgh in 1965:

'I suppose you were saying I don't want to go but at the same time you were saying I want to go. The excitement of going was there but the sadness of leaving was there too so they were both fighting each other, that's probably what made you brain dead.' Scottish teenager Mary Rose Lavery could barely comprehend her own feelings as the train carrying her family and other emigrants pulled out of Glasgow station while a piper played 'Will ye no' come back again?': 'I wiped my eyes with my knuckles and stared down the platform into the darkness ahead of the engine, feeling absolutely desolate. If I'd been an Arctic wolf I would have howled and howled drearily and bleakly. For what, no one knew. I, least of all. But misery pressed crushingly on my chest.'[2]

Many others were hugely excited, almost overawed, by the momentous significance of departure and by the milling crowds at the railway station or the grandeur of a great ocean liner leaving the docks. For 6-year-old Bruce Bates in 1950, travelling to Australia was 'the equivalent of what going to colonise Mars might be today':

I remember the awe that I felt at seeing the size of the ship, the P&O liner *Maloja*, and going aboard up the gangplank. The ship seemed very crowded and the thing that I noticed first was the very distinctive smell – a mixture of paint, wood (from the deck) and oil. I had a very strong sense that we were unlikely ever to return to this country, or to see relatives and friends again. The sense both of setting off into the unknown and of embarking on a voyage of no return was very strong. This was very much more the case then than it would be today, as the world has 'shrunk' so much. I do remember the amazing scene as the ship departed. There was a band playing, hundreds of people on the quayside waving frantically, shouting and weeping, and people on board throwing thousands of coloured streamers down to those ashore, as though reluctant to finally let go. As the ship pulled away from the jetty I remember the streamers breaking and watching for the last one to snap – the signal that our ties with the past had been broken and that our great adventure had finally begun.[3]

For many emigrants, excitement and anticipation were clouded by feelings of sadness or guilt about parents and other relatives who were being left behind, and whom they might never see again (see Figure 8). Joan Pickett recalls that the moment when she and her friend Jean caught the midnight train from Manchester to London and Tilbury docks in 1960 was like a scene from the film *Brief Encounter*:

My father was standing there with his raincoat and his trilby on, and he sort of kissed us and he said, 'Well, come back if you can, but if ... don't worry about us, you do what you want to do.' And my mother was crying of course. And we were crying. [laughs] And the train pulled away, and my father sort of disappeared into this cloud of smoke, and I never saw him again.[4]

8 Phyllis Cave sent us this evocative photograph from November 1969 of 'My husband's family seeing us off at Southampton. They are the group at the right with a lady in the check coat, man with child, the three to their right and one in front of his brother with the camera'

Most painful of all were the departures where family members refused to come to the station or the docks because they were still bitterly opposed to the emigration or because they simply could not bear the parting. Joan Pickett's much-loved older brother, for example, just could not face the farewell scene at Manchester railway station.

Emigrants who had mixed feelings about migration felt the pangs of leaving most sharply. Teenagers were sometimes angry that they had not been party to a decision that pulled them away from the life that they were beginning to create for themselves, and could be desperately unhappy. Other emigrants were tormented by second thoughts. In 1966, as the *Fairstar* slowly pulled out of Southampton docks and people started shouting and throwing streamers, young mother Maureen Hands grieved about leaving Manchester and deserting her parents: 'Even with so many folk around it was as if I were on my own. My throat was tight, my chest full of pain and the tears began to fall as England got smaller and smaller. If you have never left England by sea you won't realize how green and beautiful it is.'[5]

Departures are infused with feelings about the places as well as the people you are leaving, and the British landscape and weather is a significant metaphor in migrant accounts, expressing deep feelings about emigration; England was especially green and beautiful for Maureen Hands because she did not want to leave. In 1946 Albert Walker left his young bride in Chesterfield and set off by train to Plymouth and thence to Australia, where he hoped to carve out a new life for them both. Desperately sad and lonely after leaving Marjory, and anxious about his uncertain Australian future, the emotions of leaving were heightened by 'a journey made so lovely by the glorious Spring weather we were having at the time'. 'England is so lovely in Spring. Everything is happy and the country smiles at every turn. This made it much more difficult to leave, and I thought of all those lovely places I had seen ... and wondered whether I should see the like again and whether one day I should return and see them again.'[6]

By contrast, 15-year-old James Saxton's 'greatest desire had been to get out and see the world for as long as I could remember', and his enthusiasm about leaving England in 1951 rings loud in this description of Waterloo Station: 'there were over a thousand of us, all clad in our new utility clothing. It was a drab grey day in a drab grey station'. Writing in 1969, after several successful years in sunny Perth, journalist Thomas Jenkins uses the same metaphor to encapsulate his memory and feelings about emigration: 'The rain was falling on Southampton in slanting grey veils. The docks were grey. The water was grey. We were not sad, not torn, just glad the waiting was over and we were on our way. We took a last look at the land of our fathers. It looked wet.'[7] Green and grey are resonant colours in British emigrant narratives. At one level they simply describe the country and its weather on the day of departure, but at another level they symbolize contrasting feelings, of regret at leaving Britain or anticipation of a fresh start in a sunny new land.

Ship stories

Graham Little and Albert Walker were among many British migrants who recorded the sea voyage in a diary or journal. The voyage was a special time and a significant rite of passage with a definite beginning and end. Many passengers wanted to create a record, either for themselves or for friends and relatives, of a momentous event which was often their first overseas trip. On board ship the migrants had the time for reflection and writing which was not so readily available in everyday working and domestic lives in Britain or Australia. Many were writing a journal for the first time and few ship journals continued into the busy months after arrival.[8]

The journal provided an intimate reflective space, and through writing the diarist could begin to make sense of the tangled feelings and extraordinary experiences of migration. Thus for Graham Little, 'on the day before leaving, it's all up and down, waking in excitement then having qualms, then again thinking but I wouldn't miss it for the world', and in his diary he writes, 'That is how it has gone on all day. Just at this minute I am wishing we were embarking today – I think!' Yet even the intimate diary often has a real or imagined audience in mind. Graham Little hoped that 'the imaginary reader will enjoy the humour' of his diary. Ulster nurse Margery Black, travelling to Australia in 1949, recorded her thoughts and impressions in a duplicate book and at each port of call she posted copies back home. Matt Dickinson, the Co-op grocer from Northumberland travelling to Melbourne with his wife and three children in 1955, produced his journal as a guide for his brothers, who were also considering emigration, and thus his account includes careful descriptive passages about what they should expect – and what they should bring – as they travel to Australia.[9] A diary was not necessarily a private account, and the prospective audience influenced the story that was told.

Emigrants also wrote about their voyage in letters and postcards, though in these very public missives they often took great care not to worry their readers. Dorothy Wright sailed to Australia on the *Fairsea* in 1959 with her husband Mike and 18-month-old son, but her trip was ruined by seasickness. Dorothy's letters and postcards make passing reference to being 'a bit low', but 'they certainly don't tell the full story…. I could never tell mother about staggering out to the toilet block, trying not to slip in the sick of other people who had not reached there in time.' Norma Palin, a young mother from Liverpool, 'wrote glowing letters home' from the *Oronsay* in 1956, 'about the new things and people that I was seeing. I later learned that all the neighbours would gather to hear the letters and my sister would read them all aloud. Some of these people had never been over the River Mersey, and here was one of their own thousands of miles away on an ocean liner.' In fact, with two small children to care for, Norma 'had little time to enjoy the adventure and wonder which was unfolding all around me…. The ship touched many exotic ports, I was left on board to care for my babies, whilst my husband went ashore with the throngs, he came back with stories which kept me in writing material for days after.'[10]

Written memoirs and oral history interviews offer another perspective on the sea voyage. In retrospect, migrants like Dorothy Wright and Norma Palin reflect upon what they could and couldn't write in letters home, and they sometimes offer thoughtful and even critical explanations of their past attitudes and behaviour. Writing in 2000, Dorothy Wright concludes that the 'prejudices as expressed in my letters appal me. How racially prejudiced I was. How ignorant of the conditions of really poor people in Port Said and Aden. I hope I am different now.' By contrast, sometimes memoirists self-censor attitudes about race or status which were common fifty years ago but which are no longer socially or politically acceptable.

Memories of the sea voyage are often detailed and vividly sensual – like the rich smells of paint, wood and oil recalled by young Bruce Bates. But by comparison with contemporary letters and diaries they are less able to provide the 'minute by minute' bulletins which record how thoughts and feelings changed during the course of the voyage. Memory tends to frame the story of the voyage in particular ways: for example as a luxury cruise or a nightmare at sea; as an event marred by seasickness or enlivened by romance. Some retrospective accounts focus on a single 'iconic' memory – for example, the misery of departure or the first plate-load of food piled up in front of an English child used to rationing – and use that story to convey the main theme of their emigration, as the start of a personal disaster or as an introduction to a land of plenty. These well-rehearsed memories are revealing about the enduring significance of the voyage in memory and identity. One resonant, oft-repeated memory of the migrants' sea voyage to Australia is that it was the holiday of a lifetime.

A 'floating grand hotel'

At the end of the Second World War, Australian immigration plans were hampered by a severe shipping shortage. Under the 1946 agreement the British government agreed to provide a number of old British liners for assisted emigration to Australia. Most of these were hastily refitted troopships, and conditions on board could be austere. In 1951 8-year-old Judith Addison sailed with her parents on an ex-troop carrier, the *Asturias*, and she recalls that 'facilities were basic' and it was 'hardly a luxury liner'. For 14-year-old John Jordan in 1950 the *Cheshire* 'was horrible', 'almost a tramp steamer', with eight-berth cabins full to capacity and total segregation of the sexes, without air conditioning, swimming pools, cinema or other organized entertainment. John was bored until they reached 'interesting places' like Port Said. In 1956 Anne and George McLanaghan sailed on the last voyage of the old *Moreton Bay* before it was scrapped, and 'it was a disgrace'.

The more historically aware passengers realized that even these conditions were a great improvement on those suffered by nineteenth-century emigrants; Dorothy Wright notes that her own voyage was not 'half as terrible' as the six-month voyage of her ancestor William Wilkins back in 1850; 'his pregnant wife died on the way'. Even in these early postwar years, many migrants – especially the young and single – made their own fun and enjoyed the trip despite the austerity. Twenty-year-old Ron Penn recalls that a hundred migrants signed a letter of complaint about conditions on the *Orion* in 1947, but he had no grievances and enjoyed a 'very happy' trip in the company of young, single passengers.[11]

The food on board the postwar migrant ships was almost never a cause of complaint. The contrast between food-rationed Britain and the abundance of food on the ocean voyage and then in Australia is a pervasive theme in the memories of the first wave of postwar migrants (see Figure 9). Young James Saxton recalled that his fellow passengers of 1951 were spending a fortune in the ship's shop because they assumed that supplies would run out. As for many migrants, the first meal on board became a resonant memory: 'A steward appeared at my elbow and I ordered egg on toast, and I was shocked to receive not one, but two whole eggs. This was the first time in my life I could recall seeing two eggs on one plate! I could not conceive that food rationing was no more a part of our lives.'[12]

By 1957 the last of the old British Ministry of Transport vessels had been phased out and British assisted passage emigrants travelled on newer commercial liners, including ships owned by the British P&O and Orient lines but also foreign-flag vessels such as the Italian Sitmar fleet. These new ships, and older vessels which had been substantially refitted so that they could compete in the migrant trade, were, as Graham Little recalled, like 'floating grand hotels'. Most had several decks of cabin accommodation and a separate deck for amenities, which included lounges, shops, bars, a playroom and a writing and reading room, and one or more large rooms for dances and other social events. On deck there was at least one swimming pool and space for outdoor games and deckchairs (and for 'canoodling' on the upper decks in the dark, as Matt Dickinson recalls). Dickinson's journal lists the great variety of activities which were organized – sometimes by the crew but often by passenger committees – to ward off boredom; there were cinema shows, dancing, Sunday evening entertainments, divine service with a church choir (which the Dickinsons joined to practise carols for a Christmas service), a record club and a whist drive, schooling in the morning and games in the playroom for the children, a pantomime, a ship's concert and special celebrations for Christmas, New Year and the crossing of the date line, and, finally, a Landfall Carnival Dance. For the Dickinsons, Christmas Eve 1955 was a night to remember:

The best part of the evening, for me, was after the concert, we were on the sun deck, it was a beautiful night, with the sea, a smooth swell, a nearly full moon, making a silver path across the sea, over the loud speakers came the recorded sound of Christmas Carols played by some cathedral bells. Our three bairns, safely asleep in their bunks, tired out from the excitement of the day. The Italian steward keeping an occasional check to see that they are all asleep.[13]

In the first decades after the war British working-class families almost never holidayed abroad, and they had rarely enjoyed the luxury of tea in bed and waiter service at mealtime. On the *New Australia* in 1953, 7-year-old Vanessa Seymour 'had the *best* fun on boat, and my mother also says that the

9 Rosa Rance eating her first watermelon on the *Orcades*, April 1951. As teenager James Saxton recalled, 'I could not conceive that food rationing was no more a part of our lives'

best holiday that she ever had was the boat coming out, that it was just lovely — Mind you, it was probably the only holiday she ever had, you know, in those years.' Six-year-old Bruce Bates was 'free to explore and enjoy life' on the *Maloja* in 1951.

And what a life it was! We led a most privileged existence. We were, after all, being treated to a world cruise on a well-equipped liner, complete with servants, who cleaned and tidied our rooms, cooked and served our meals and in every other way tended to our needs, and all for the princely sum of ten pounds a head! For a working class family like ours, coming from the austerity of postwar Britain, it was like a fairy tale come true.[14]

Not all the migrants were able to enjoy their luxury cruise. Dorothy Wright recalls that 'emigration leaflets had led us (well, me) to believe we would enjoy new friendships, concerts, games, film shows, dancing and other deck diversions. They were available, but I was not well enough to enjoy them.' Seasickness seemed to strike at random – older ships which had no stabilizers were the worst – and though some migrants only suffered a short burst of sickness, usually in the wild waters of the Bay of Biscay and before they found their sea legs, others endured a month of misery. Kathleen Upton's voyage on the *Orsova* in 1954 was 'a disaster: whenever the ship was actually moving, I felt ill'. For Frances Akehurst seasickness on the *Georgic* in 1955 was 'one of the worst nightmares I have ever been through'; she lost a stone and a half in weight and even now cannot sit on the top of a double decker bus because when it goes around a corner 'my mind goes back to that ship'. Catherine Barber recalls that in 1964 her ship was nicknamed *'Fairsea, fairsick'.*[15]

Despite the travails of seasickness, in their self-contained world the migrants forged new relationships with fellow passengers. Betty Preston – a woman with impressive organizational skills who became secretary to the social committee on the *Ormonde* in 1952 – recalls how a group gathered around her family to have an evening cuppa: 'it was a very gay gathering too. There is nothing like a friendly cup of tea to clear away shyness.'[16] Often sharing the same table at each meal, groups of migrants developed new friendship networks. These friendships sometimes outlasted the voyage and provided significant emotional and practical support as the migrants established new lives in Australia, though such links were often broken by the Australian government's policy of waiting until the ships arrived in Australia before deciding where Commonwealth-sponsored migrants were most needed. Margaret Hill, the young mother from Merseyside who had been such a reluctant emigrant, recalls the dilemma for new friends on the migrant ships:

But myself and everybody else, the thing that really bothered us ... We never knew which ladies we were going to be friends with because we didn't know which friends we were going to be able to take with us to where we were going.... and we spent a lot of time talking about, 'But I might not see you again', and we were telling each other's backgrounds and talking to each other where we'd come from, what we'd hoped to do, whatever, whatever, whatever. But we were always thinking, 'But I might not see you again'.

For single men and women – and for some who were married – the voyage was a romantic opportunity. Margery Black, the middle-aged nurse from Ulster travelling on the *Georgic* in 1949, noticed that the ex-navy officers at first 'kept aloof from this ignorant mass of "bods"', but were soon 'casting their roving eyes round for possible voyage acquaintances'. Within a week she was enjoying sherry in the boardroom and started walking out each evening with one of these officers, while the crew and the stewards began to fight over other migrant women. On the *Empire Brent* in 1949, 'Lancashire lad' Sydney Hart befriended a young stenographer from London. 'The close association of shipboard life had convinced me without a shadow of a doubt that life without her would be pretty nearly unbearable', and not long after their arrival in Sydney Miss Daniel became Mrs Hart.[17]

One of the more important social distinctions on the migrant ships was that between families with children and young single men and women. The

Manchester medical secretary Joan Pickett and her travelling companion Jean teamed up with other single travellers on the *Oronsay* in 1960 and found that 'the young people' had their own active social life and 'didn't have a lot to do with the families who were going out':

You see, we weren't really true migrants in that sense, we were joining in with this, but we honestly didn't feel that we were going out to settle in a new country, we were going out to *try* a new country, and if we liked it, we'd stay. But, we didn't have as much to lose as some of these other people, they'd sold their homes and everything. Some of them were quite worried. But that didn't apply to us you see.[18]

On many migrant ships men and women were segregated (ostensibly to ensure the optimum use of space and facilities), and families were often divided, with father and older sons in one cabin, and mother, daughters and young sons in another, sometimes on a separate deck. The segregation of assisted passage families was almost universally unpopular. On the *New Australia* in 1954, Albert and Anne Lougher had not expected to be separated, but 'suddenly Anne was whizzed away with five other ladies and I was whizzed away with five other blokes' who wanted 'to get into the beer'.

That wasn't for me at all, I'd been all with the army, I didn't want all that…. All I wanted was to be with Anne. I wanted to be with Anne, we wanted to talk, hold hands, cuddle if you like, and know that, how can I put it to you, that we'd done the right thing. I mean Anne had left her mum, she'd left her friends. Oh yes, she was crying.[19]

Many migrants joke about the arrangements that some couples made – with temporary room swaps and shared keys – to find opportunities for intimacy. The newly married Blackmores soon attracted the solicitous concern of other passengers: 'they used to say to us, well I think there might be a spare lifeboat there. Then you'd look in there and there'd be another couple in there and you'd go along and find another one.'[20]

For families, childcare was a more serious concern. Matt Dickinson, who was separated from his wife and three children under the age of 5, had a pragmatic response – 'What it really means is that I sleep on D deck and live on A deck' – but plenty of other men enjoyed the enforced freedom from responsibility for small children. Even on the most modern ships parents with babies and toddlers – and especially women with absent husbands – had an arduous voyage. Mothers were saved the drudgery of cooking and cleaning but clothes still had to be washed, in difficult circumstances. Gwen and Cliff Good sailed on the *Fairsky* with three young sons in 1963; Gwen recalls that she had 'four white shirts and all their underwear and all these nappies to hand-wash every day, so that kept me quiet most of the morning, hanging them out, and then you had to watch them because if you weren't careful you lost your nappies' (not lost overboard, but taken by other passengers!).[21] Parents needed to accompany children to separate meal sittings, and though older children were often free to roam, young children needed to be watched at all times. The ship was a dangerous place, and it could also be an unhealthy place as childhood infections 'spread like wildfire' and parents had to cope with children suffering from chicken pox or flu.[22] Maureen Butts was left distraught when her 20-month-old daughter contracted measles during an epidemic on the *Fairsea* in 1959; her child was placed in quarantine and all parental contact forbidden for ten days.[23] With healthy children, the playroom or an hour of schooling could offer temporary respite – though some parents recall that the playrooms were chaotic and unsatisfactory, and few children remember much in the way of schooling. A friendly steward might occasionally keep an eye out for a sleeping baby, but most parents (often mothers) were bound to their small children. For many young parents the fun wore off and the voyage became hard work. Matt Dickinson's initial diary entries are full of the excitement of the trip and the fun to be had by his three small children. Twenty-seven days out from England, it is a different story:

I should like to make one thing clear concerning a voyage of this type, that it is not the perfect holiday, beneath sunny skies, with quiet rest in comfortable deck chairs. This is an illusion and an even bigger illusion when you have children. Consider things yourself, there are 400 children under the age of twelve on the boat, there goes your peace and quiet. About 1000 odd adults, and there goes your deck chairs, unless you sit tight. A playroom for children is provided but it is 10 yd by 5 yd and has one nurse with the patience of JOB. With children you are constantly under tension, with the ships rails and innumerable stairways and heavy steel doors to guard against. Children also take badly to the cramped, unnatural style of living, after an open country life.[24]

'Our sort of people'?

The migrant ships brought together Britons from diverse social and regional backgrounds, and four weeks of enforced proximity sharpened awareness of social class and cultural difference. The majority of assisted passage migrants were skilled and semi-skilled workers and their families, and the cultural life which was provided, and which they generated for themselves, was a seagoing version of the delights of Blackpool and Brighton. Some of the more middle-class migrants who had taken the cut-price assisted passage rather regretted the cut-price fellow passengers with their working-class ways. Wendy Jay, an old girl of Cheltenham Ladies' College, emigrated with her husband and two children in 1952, and she recalls that the passengers on the *New Australia* were 'mostly from the north of England, or the London area, sort of Cockney area; we just didn't feel we had anything in common with them, there were no sort of country people round.... I *hate* to be snobby about this, but I remember turning to my husband and saying, "Oh, God help Australia!"'

On the *Georgic* in 1949, Ulster nurse Margery Black soon lost her patience with the boorish crowds and the noise of 'awful', ill-disciplined children:

Those having no intellectual resources are not enjoying this trip. I have just heard a woman saying 'Everyone is bored stiff aren't they'. A lot of people sit inside and play cards all day. Others just sit. And the children scream round & round.... This trip is wasted on about 90% of the passengers. They can't adapt themselves or relax and bring their disgusting English habits with them. The mania for queuing ... Everyone grumbles like hell and smacks their children to breaking point, are bored to death so gossip & slander one another. I am beginning to agree that people without intellect should be made to work hard as they can do nothing constructive when they are idle.[25]

In the account Thomas Jenkins wrote about his trip in 1969 he concluded that the other migrants were not 'our sort of people':

We would, it appeared in reality, have bingo every second night, a meeting for the purpose of forming a camera club, a dice-race meeting, a musical quiz and a sing song.... there were far too many people – 1,700 in tourist class – and not too many of them seemed to be our sort of people. No doubt the programme of entertainment had been designed for them.

Jenkins's high hopes for the commodore's cocktail party were shattered by the crush and 'orgy' of the event – though 'I expect quite a lot of people were delighted to be there' – and he and his wife eventually found cultural solace in the cinema programme which is 'excellent and up-to-date', by playing scrabble in the library in the evenings, and in their discovery of Australian wines – 'the mind connects wine with civilization and we were happier for our discovery'.[26]

At sea there were class distinctions by fare as well as class distinctions in the mind. Whilst some of the migrant ships were single tourist-class vessels, other commercial liners carried both assisted passage migrants and full-fare travellers in tourist class as well as first-class passengers. Thomas Jenkins was upset to discover that there was an 'apartheid at sea' which divided the cinema into first-class and tourist-class passengers, and he and his wife felt that they were in the wrong class. Patricia Drohan recalls the class differences on the *Orsova* when she emigrated as secretary to her Ballarat employer, Mr Anderson, in 1958. The Andersons were in first class, though the two daughters often visited Patricia in tourist class because 'they said they're all frumpy up there, and they could come through to our end of the ship but I couldn't go through to theirs'. Meanwhile, Patricia made friends with Valda, an Australian who had paid to return home and now enjoyed better accommodation than the ten pound migrants: 'I went to their cabin, and they got a porthole and you found the benefit of fresh air! "Oh, we don't get one where I was", about seven or eight decks below sea-level! ... Yes, there was, a definite distinction.'[27]

Most ten pound migrants had little sympathy for other assisted passengers, like Margery Black or the Jenkinses, who had first-class pretensions. On the *Otranto* in 1951 the Mancunian mother Dorothy Rooms had no time for the 'toffee-nosed' migrants who said they had sold businesses but were 'just spoofing about that'. Annie Barkas from South Shields recalls a similar type on the *Fairsea* in 1960:

There was some snobs on that ship, you know, the English. Like some of them, [in posh voice] 'Oh, I belong to the Rotary Club!' And then the Queen announced she had Andrew, and this fella stood up, he said: 'To the Queen!' And this Yorkshire fella said: 'Ah, sit down, ya silly bugger!' [laughs] ... and me husband said to me, 'I think they're just the same as us, on the ten pound passage'.[28]

Occasionally these class tensions were expressed in terms of regional or ethnic difference, such as Wendy Jay's distinction between 'country people' and cockneys and northerners, or Ulster-woman Margery Black's acrid comments about the 'disgusting English habits' of the working class. Certainly, these migrant ships carried people from throughout the British Isles. Matt Dickinson shared his cabin with 'two scotch lads, a cockney, a Yorkshireman, an Irishman, a lad from Birmingham and myself, a Geordie', and in his journal he pasted a photograph with the following caption:

A View of the table showing the table steward Simone Torlorice from Genoa. The left hand side of the table is the Hobbs family from Devon, the Dickinsons from Northumberland, Ould Bob, a Yorkshireman and the Cutts family. Young Bob, occupies the head of the table, from Kent. On the right of the table is Bert and Family from Canterbury & Chas Hetherington & Family from Birmingham.[29]

British migrants noted the distinctive characteristics of passengers from different parts of the country. Sydney Hart was a proud Englishman and Briton yet he also distinguished himself from his cabin mates as 'a Lancashire lad' who 'isn't glib-tongued in describing his inner-most feelings'. Matt Dickinson enjoyed the regional banter and humour of his cabin mates and remarked that 'Having a considerable number of Irish on board, being born comics, as well as a lot of scotch, with their own type of dry humour and dances, we are well equipped for the unexpected.' More often than not the distinctive regional and ethnic characteristics of British passengers are portrayed with humour and good feeling, and as a proud affirmation of a common British identity. Twenty-four days out from England, Dickinson described a talent and community song night on the *Fairsea*; it comprised songs from all over the British Isles, including 'a great burly, rough looking scot' who sang a heartfelt and unaccompanied 'Bonny Strathyre' which 'carried you back to those fells' so that 'more than one scotch heart would have had an ache in it'. 'One amazing thing' is that there were no Welsh volunteers for a Welsh song, but the assembled passengers made up for this by singing in unison a rousing rendition of 'Land of Our Fathers'.[30]

The migrants were meeting other Britons and recognizing what they had in common as well as their distinctive characteristics. But they were also bound together by their shared identity as migrants. Maureen Carter from Neath found that there were very few Welsh, Scots or Irish on the *Castel Felice* in 1965, and yet the sea voyage banished her Welsh stereotype of the English as an unfriendly race: 'We were all in the same boat! We were all ten pound migrants trying to get somewhere on the cheap!' West Midlander Sandra O'Neill made special friends with two couples on the *Northern Star*, one from Worthing on the south coast and the other from Scotland, and found that they all had a 'common goal …, everybody was going, everybody was talking about the future, and their hopes'.[31]

Nor were there significant tensions between the British and other nationalities on the migrant ships. Most ten pound migrants remember their stewards – of Goan, Italian or other racial origin – with great affection. Only a few recall difficulties when they shared the voyage with migrants from other countries. About 300 Greeks joined British migrants on the *Orontes* in 1956, and Maureen Carr, who was 14 at the time, recalls that 'we had to have them moved, couldn't eat with them any longer, couldn't eat with them…. They were rather peasant type ones that would come down to dinner in their dressing gowns, you know, until they were told off. And they used to put the salad and the food in the middle of the table and dig in.'[32]

By contrast in 1970 the Whittle family from Brighton enjoyed the company of a 'very nice, very friendly' group of Italians on the *Fairstar*, though they noticed that unlike most of the British migrants the Italians were emigrating in 'huge family units': 'There were brothers, sisters, aunties, uncles, grand-dads, grandmas.' Families like the Whittles and the Carrs were learning about other nationalities – and in turn about themselves and their British characteristics – through such exchanges. But more often the British did not share their ships with other migrants. The most significant cultural exchanges, and a dramatic assertion of British identity and eastern difference, occurred in the ports of call.[33]

'The Empire was a bar of soap'

A British imperial identity – though sometimes challenged within the ship along the fracture lines of class and ethnicity – was reinforced by the migrants' confrontation with 'the natives' as they traversed the harbours of empire. The emigrants' journals are remarkably frank in this regard, and offer a window on to postwar British racial and imperial attitudes. For some migrants, the sea voyage conjured up a powerful collective memory of Britain as a maritime nation. At Plymouth Hoe, Albert Walker 'did enjoy the feeling of standing there and imagining the feelings of those who first sighted the Spanish fleet'. Upon boarding the *Empire Brent* in Glasgow in 1949, ex-navy man Sydney Hart reflected that 'Maybe the ghosts of Francis Drake, Captain Cook and Anson were beckoning me on.... I could smell the assorted tangs of Singapore and the fragrant East, together with the thousand other odours that in combination spell adventure and romance.'[34] Historical and literary imagination, and generations of imperial schooling, had fostered a collective cultural memory which migrants used to make sense of their own voyage.

In part, British migrants experienced their journey and stop-overs as excited tourists, and were delighted to see places they had imagined but never dreamed of visiting. Even the train trip across Britain towards the port of embarkation offered some migrants a first view of the country beyond their own region. The Dickinsons travelled from Northumberland to London with wide-eyed enthusiasm for new places, and when they stopped off in London, 'Trafalgar Square, with the pigeons, is a sight that everyone who passes through London tries to see. Glenise and David were thrilled, but David was bent on killing one'. Throughout the voyage Matt Dickinson wrote with pleasure and interest about changing climatic conditions, sealife and birdlife, and about the places that they visited along the way.[35] For Irene Tyas, sailing on the *Canberra* with her husband Cliff and two daughters in 1966, 'It was so fascinating, it was, to me it was so unreal ... I kept thinking, no, it's not happening to me.' In Naples the Tyas family were bussed up Mount Vesuvius and visited Pompeii; in Port Said they watched Arab boys diving for silver coins thrown overboard by the passengers; in Aden they bought duty-free electrical goods they had been told they would need in the migrant hostel – a toaster, a kettle and a tape recorder – and then got off the back streets 'pretty sharpish' when an Arab girl threw a stone at 8-year-old Melody; in Ceylon they marvelled at working elephants and then took tea and cakes in the wicker chairs of an elegant hotel, 'the old colonial thing'. Even now, almost forty years later and living in a council house near Nottingham, Irene sees these places on television and exclaims with delight, 'I have actually been there, and I've seen the elephants and I knew exactly what they were talking about. And it was great, it really was.'[36]

The migrants were eager shoppers, whether trading by rope with vendors bobbing in small crafts around their ship in Port Said, or visiting the bazaars and duty free shops that proliferated around the ports. In Colombo in 1951 the extended Saxton family from Essex went ashore for the first time and their self-appointed local guide led the unwitting tourists to a jewellery shop: 'The sales staff ambushed us. And Pop cried out in exasperation, that we were emigrating to make money, not to spend it! Outside the store, Pop offered our guide ten bob to piss off.'[37]

The glimpse of 'the orient' was a potent experience for many migrants (see Figure 10; see also Figure 39 on p. 353). As the Jenkinses sailed out of Naples, with the ship playing popular British tunes, 'A cool voice beside us said, "Edge of the known world. What now, eh?".... We felt much more emotional then we had done when we left Southampton.... The words so exactly mirrored our thoughts'. The North African coastline, Port Said, the Suez Canal, Aden and Bombay or perhaps Ceylon – the route of the migrant ships evoked resonant British imperial images and understandings about the Middle and Far East. As their ship passed Mecca, Matt Dickinson noted that from here the followers of Mohammed 'swept across NORTH AFRICA, spreading Islam by fire and sword'. When the 'beautiful spectacle' of the North African coastline receded, 'As the bloke on the Pictures would say "We leave Algeria, Land of Mystery and Romance" or should it be intrigue.'[38]

One way in which migrants comprehended these lands was as an exotic and mysterious world steeped in history and redolent of ancient civilizations. As Thomas Jenkins passed through the Suez Canal in 1965 he wrote in his diary that 'Beyond the banks, I see a mysterious woman shrouded in black moving among the palm trees. None of them, so far, has a water jar on her head, but otherwise the biblical picture is perfect.' In 1949, also at Suez, Sydney Hart was greeted by 'the usual sights: the ever-lasting caravans, the clumsy-looking but highly efficient Arab dhows that had flitted to and fro the centuries when we Britons were still learning how to handle clumsy coracles!'[39]

Yet the ancient civilization and biblical history of the Middle East was almost invariably contrasted with its present-day, post-imperial squalor. Empire is a thread which runs through the migrant stories, and it was usually an empire which brought order, cleanliness and efficiency to lands which were now reverting to their previous squalid and corrupt state. Emigrant stories not only traversed the ports of empire; they charted – through British eyes – the quarter century of an empire in decline. Anchored in Malta's Valetta harbour in 1949, Sydney Hart admired the imposing sight 'of our own Mediterranean Fleet at exercise' and praised 'the island that had thrilled the civilized world by its unbelievable stand against the overwhelming, evil forces of Nazism and Fascism'. On the Suez Canal in 1955, Matt Dickinson spotted

10 Brothers Bruce and Alvyn Bates on the dock in Aden, 1950, with their ship the *Maloja* in the background. Bruce reminisces that travelling to Australia was 'the equivalent of what going to colonize Mars might be today'. Alvyn recalls that 'although the temperature must have been in the high 90s Bruce had a long sleeved shirt buttoned up with a tie, long woollen socks and black plimsolls! I cannot remember what "Mr Cool" had in his left hand'

the monument to the 1914–18 Empire War Dead in the Ismalian Campaign:

To see that Monument standing there, with a background of sand and salt marsh, brought right back that memory of school days, learning,

'THE SAND OF THE DESERT IS SODDEN RED.

RED WITH THE DEAD OF A SQUARE THAT BROKE

THE GATLING'S JAMMED AND THE COLONEL DEAD

THE REGIMENT BLIND WITH DUST AND SMOKE'

And they are still doing it. Two Grenadier Guardsmen were on the boat at Port Said, seeing someone, and today as we passed up the canal we saw two English soldiers on a jeep, patrol part of the canal embankment.[40]

Migrants often compared the ports still under British control with those which were newly independent. As the *Fairsea* passed through the Suez Canal Matt Dickinson remarked in his journal, 'When you have seen the Egyptian Army or Police you realise what a good soldier the TOMMY is. We had Egyptian Police and Army Officers on board at Port Said. The Police, wearing Luger automatics, but pathetically musical comedy in appearance.' Fourteen days out they arrived in Aden (which was still a British protectorate) and 'The first thing that impresses you on landing, is the absolute smartness of the Aden Police in their Khaki shorts and shirt and a black belt with a brass buckle and the black fez and black puttees and sandals. They look really efficient.' In Aden one year previously, teenager Graham Little had made the same comparison: 'Prompted by my father, but how he knew isn't clear, I gave the Aden police higher marks than the ones in Egypt.'[41]

The post-imperial Middle East was not only inefficient; the politics of the natives who had taken over were dismissed as rather ridiculous. British emigrants, steeped in imperial ideology, were unable to comprehend the causes and nature of Arab nationalism. Remembering his migrant voyage of 1949 from the vantage point of 1957, Sydney Hart recalled of Port Said – 'the gateway to the East' – that 'Then, as now, the times were somewhat turbulent, though no hint was apparent of the surprising moves that were to be made later, when Egyptian nationalism ran wild.' Thomas Jenkins had spent a year of national service in Egypt, where he 'had grown to dislike the Egyptian people very much. Since then there had been Suez.' As they passed the Egyptian coast in 1965 he wrote to a friend that 'if you were foolish enough to land, you'd find a bunch of Nasser's hooligans throwing lead at you out of Czech machine guns'.[42]

Arab politics and society were misunderstood and ridiculed by British migrants but the Arab world could also be deeply threatening. Ports were closed because of the 'troubles'; soldiers with machine guns patrolled the docks; Arabs threw stones and made rude gestures as the migrants visited their ports or sailed through the Suez Canal. Mostly the meetings were brief and the migrants could escape to the security of the ship, but just occasionally the threat felt very real. In 1949 14-year-old Bunty Davis was sailing with her family on the *Largs Bay* when it caught fire in the Suez Canal. The passengers were put ashore in Aden for three and a half weeks and housed in an army barracks where women and men were in separate quarters: 'it was quite dangerous because it was –– the Arabs used to try and invade the women's quarters so they eventually had to separate us into families'.[43] Only very rarely was there the opportunity or shared language to develop any real under-standing of these societies and their people. When the Rooms family from Manchester stopped off in Ceylon in 1951 they decided to visit the zoo and on the way they befriended Mr and Mrs De Silva and their little girl, who was being educated in an English-language school. The De Silvas invited the Roomses to share their picnic hamper, and over lunch confided that they also wanted to emigrate to Australia but had not been accepted because of their colour. The Roomses agreed to send some photos they took of the two families, and in return the De Silvas agreed to send them some tea, which had been rationed in England and was a precious gift. More typical was the attitude of the Roomses' eldest daughter, who had refused to leave the ship in Colombo because she was frightened 'when she saw the Indian natives on the docks'.[44]

The East: exotic, inefficient, rebellious, threatening and, perhaps most of all, dirty. When the Dickinsons went shopping in Aden (recorded and recalled as a scorching, fetid hell hole by most migrants) 'the squalor of some of the shacks is an eye opener to western eyes and so is the smell'. For many British migrants, the ship was a safe haven, a capsule which quarantined and protected them from this squalid, threatening world. The Jenkinses visited Port Said:

Immediately we were under assault from men and boys ... like vultures round a kill.... The place felt and smelled dirt-poor and diseased. The people – we never saw a woman – kept up their pleading, menacing barrage.... We beat our way back though the remaining ranks of pleading brown hands (it was rather like a nightmare flag day). When *Oriana*'s fat British walls closed around us, we felt visibly relieved.[45]

As Graham Little recalled, 'the thing that frightened us in all these places was the same thing that frightened us at home, the poverty and the dirt.... The Empire was a bar of soap, Lifebuoy or the then wonderfully carbolic Pears. Being British was being clean.'[46]

The cultural historian Simon Gikandi writes that 'the other' was 'a constitutive element in the invention of Britishness' (as it was in the invention of other western imperial identities) and that expressions of a distinctive British or English identity have often been most fervent at times of doubt or difficulty for national identity. British postwar emigrants' fleeting contacts with, and repulsion from, the oriental 'other' – at a time when migration was unsettling personal identity and national affiliation – reinforced and reshaped their sense of themselves as British, and as the representatives of a country and empire which stood for order, progress and good hygiene.[47]

No-man's-land

The 12,000 mile voyage to Australia – typically four weeks though the Mediterranean and Suez and across the Indian Ocean to Fremantle – impressed upon the migrants the great distance between Britain and Australia and the huge gap they were opening up in their lives. To keep track of their where-abouts and yet locate themselves in relation to 'home', some charted the distance they travelled each day and recorded their inexorable movement away from British time. Graham Little 'liked to keep remembering that we were in a ship and sailing across famous seas or, on another scale, only a speck in the ocean, hardly bigger than the birds who dropped down from the sky when the scraps were thrown out in the ship's wake. I liked to picture us as a pencil line stretching further and further across the charts to the underside of the world.'[48]

Despite such attempts to mark time and space, the sea voyage was also a liminal period, as the migrants moved between the two countries and their two lives. In 1959, Bournemouth woman Ivy Skrowronski left for South Australia with her Polish refugee husband and two children. In 1986 she wrote about their time at sea:

One never reads what happens to migrants during the journey to their new country. Temporarily homeless, plunged into a no-man's-land between countries, it is a very strange feeling indeed. One door has closed behind them, another remains unopened, but the prospect of three weeks on a ocean liner for £10 per head, with children travelling free, is enough to tuck their worries away for a while.[49]

The ship was 'no-man's-land' – 'our own little bubble in time and space' – an extraordinary site of constriction *and* freedom, and an opportunity to live outside the routines of everyday life. Teenagers like Graham Little and children like Bruce Bates revelled in this 'new kind of home' where they were not bound by the regulations of school and family and could roam almost at will. Adults for whom holidays had at best been an annual week at the British seaside shed the routines of work and domesticity for a whole month (though as we have noted, for mothers of young children there was no easy escape). In this strange and temporary world the migrants enacted carnival rituals which turned customary social roles and codes upside down. At the Crossing of the Line ceremony the court of King Neptune took control of the ship and

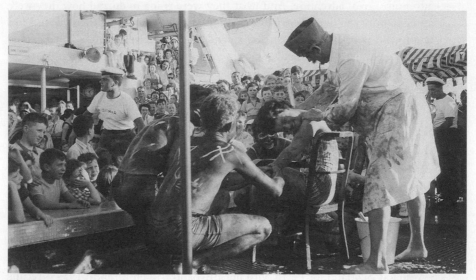

11 Cornelia Smurthwaite sent us this photograph from the *Fairsky* in 1959, when the court of King Neptune took control of the ship for the 'crossing the line' ceremony and passengers were blacked up as natives and in other exotic costumes before being dunked in the swimming pool

passengers were blacked up as natives and in other exotic costume before being dunked in the swimming pool (see Figure 11). Sydney Hart recalled the 'brutal orgy' as unwilling passengers were dragged from their hiding places and thrown in the water, though others like 10-year-old Ralph Price on the *Cheshire* in 1951 remember that it was 'all good fun'. Dressing up and cross-dressing – for the date-line rituals of King Neptune and in pantomimes and cabaret – were almost everyday events on board ship. 'Twenty-three days out' – as the relentless stretch of the Indian Ocean was taking its toll – Matt Dickinson described the 'Honeymoon Express' race: 'The sight of big built Scotchmen, trying to put Brasseirs and Rollons [sic] on, or trying to get them off. Or the sight of small built lasses getting into oversize men's pants and fastening the braces, and sock suspenders is really unbelievably funny.'[50] 'All good fun', though the sexual themes and inversions of such displays, and the recurrence in contemporary accounts of terms like 'orgy' and 'canoodling', hint at an unusual degree of sexual tension and activity which was unleashed in these strange, temporary surroundings.

If the sea voyage allowed passengers to laugh at social roles and even transgress conventional identities, it also offered a time for reflection, about emigration and about themselves. John Jordan recalls that his parents and the other migrants on the *Cheshire* in 1950

used to have informal and formal sort of meetings I think on the ship about what they were going to be faced with and they all felt like they were part of an adventure, great adventure. And what they were going to do and how they were going to work and there were people of similar types who would then say ... I'm a chippy, I'm a brickie, I'm a so and so and so and so, let's think about forming together, getting a bit of land somewhere, building, this sort of thing. All these plans were being made in the ample time you had to make them in six weeks across the world. And we all felt, I know I did, that we were part of some sort of pioneering adventure really.[51]

Some migrants wanted to learn more about their destination. Each migrant ship carried an information officer who organized talks and film shows about Australia, though few migrants recall learning much of great value. By contrast Australian passengers returning home from the 'old country' were eagerly pumped for information about their country, and they offered a taster of Australian character.

Above all, a month at sea offered a significant opportunity for reflection about migration and its dramatic reshaping of the lifecourse. Elizabeth Jolley – who left Scotland for Perth with her husband and children in 1959 – recalls the potential of the ocean voyage for memory and imagination, for desolation and for hope:

But for all, the voyage remains a physical and emotional experience which cannot be erased. At some point in the journey the migrant is hit by the irrevocable nature of his decision. Even if he starts back as soon as he reaches his destination he will never be the same again.

Suddenly there was, during my own long journey, the realisation that the world is enormous. During a day when the ship was waiting in the Great Bitter Lake, the calm expanse of colourless water, with its lack of concern for human life, caused a sense of desolation more acute and painful than anything experienced during the first term of boarding school. Memory followed memory; the stillness of willow trees along soft green river banks and deep grass in water meadows where sweet-breathed cows, straying close to the field paths, waited to be herded for milking. Then there were the field flowers, the cow parsley, purple thistles, nettles and the dock leaves so close to the nettles, a remedy for stings. And there were grass-covered graves with groundsel growing at the edges in a walled cemetery. All these images came from a time far removed from the time preceding the voyage. We had long left the Midlands and had encountered the cold hostility of Edinburgh and the apparently more affable but essentially exclusive world of Glasgow. We should have been experienced migrants. The strangest of all was the vision of my father walking alongside the ship waving farewell as he used to walk and wave alongside the train every time I left for boarding school. And ridiculous as it was, I wanted to rush back to him, to hear his voice once more. But which of us can walk on water, I mean, long distance.[52]

Though migrants might be troubled by such reflections as they took the long sea voyage to Australia, the no-man's-land of the boat was, essentially, a secure temporary home. For teenager Graham Little, the *Strathnaver* had become a safe haven, a world of its own which offered life without care. When the ship reached Fremantle and then skirted the Great Australian Bight towards Melbourne the immigrants began to worry about their arrival in Australia, and 'as they lost interest in the life of the ship, the life we'd created and enjoyed together for more than a month, it petered out and I was feeling very sad'. Young Graham 'felt a sort of chill, knowing the voyage was effectively over' and he dreaded leaving the safety of the ship. He confided in his friend, the quartermaster, Mr Kelly, 'who, like some sort of ship's psychiatrist, got me off the boat that linked me to England and planted my feet on Australian soil'.[53]

Flying to Australia

The quarter century after the Second World War was the last great age of oceangoing migration to the New World, which ended as aeroplanes became bigger and faster – and flights became less expensive – during the 1960s. Elizabeth Jolley recalls that in the late 1950s and early 1960s, 'The arrival of a great ship was an occasion', and she laments that 'Very few ships come now except the container ships and who would throw streamers and sing to a container?'[54] The introduction of the jet passenger plane in 1960 made air travel a realistic alternative; throughout the 1960s an increasing proportion of British migrants took the plane – encouraged by Australian immigration authorities who wanted as many British immigrants as possible and offered assisted passage by air at no extra charge. In the early 1970s the jumbo jet spelt the end of migration by sea and many of the ocean liners were sent to breakers yards, whilst others were converted for the luxury cruise trade. On 19 December 1977 the last shipload of British assisted passage migrants arrived in Sydney on the *Australis*.[55]

British migrants on the earliest flights to Australia remember an exciting adventure and think of themselves as aviation pioneers. The first migrant flights had some similarities with the sea voyage. In 1959 Bristol television engineer Bert Adams was offered a job in Adelaide. Bert's new employer wanted him to start work as soon as possible and agreed to fly Bert, his wife Marjorie and their four sons to Australia. The Constellation plane stopped eight times along the way and the trip took the best part of a week. At Singapore the Adamses were able to leave the airport and explore the city, and Marjorie's memory of the open sewers echoes concerns about dirt and hygiene expressed by seagoing migrants of the time. On the plane one of the stewards looked after the 15-month-old Adams baby, and his older brothers visited the cockpit and were thrilled by an extraordinary experience which 'they've never forgotten'.[56]

In 1964 John and Margaret Hardie had expected to emigrate by sea. Exactly six months after applying to Australia House Margaret phoned John at work on a Wednesday: 'She says, "I've got a flying date", a *flying* date, well most people were going by ship. "Sure it's a flying date?" "When is it?" "A week on Friday." "You're joking?"' Ten days later, after frantic packing and farewells, they were at Heathrow, which was 'a bit awe inspiring because … it's a city on its own', and boarding a British Eagle company Viscount jet propellor aeroplane with 90 other passengers. The Hardies had never seen an aircraft close up before and had little idea about what to expect or how to behave; John decided that such a special event warranted a collar and tie. Going across India the plane was rocked by a terrible storm and they were 'flung everywhere' but Margaret recalls that they didn't realize that they should be frightened. For John, it was all part of the adventure:

We were five hours with seat belts on, and I always remember that and I looked out the window – we were sitting at the window – I can still see this thing it was like a big football just hanging in the sky and it just seemed to explode and take off, and it turned out to be a ball of lightning. And, it was mad, as I say, quite an adventure.

At each of the four refuelling stops they glimpsed another world. In Istanbul their 18-month-old daughter Gillian refused to use the hole-in-the-floor toilet, and in Singapore one of the engines caught fire and they were put up in a hotel for the night and had time to look around, as John recounts:

Well what amazed, well not amazed me but surprised me, was apparently the city where the airport was, beautiful white marble buildings, but between the buildings if you looked up there was all corrugated iron where the squatters were staying between the buildings. It opened your eyes, I grew up, I really did, I began to see things in a different light and looked at things in a different way.

In Darwin the Hardies were greeted by a thunderous monsoon deluge and by the Australian authorities who sprayed the plane with a thick white mosquito repellent so that 'you was choking, the tears were running down here'. Eventually they flew into Melbourne, elated, exhausted and filthy.[57]

When migrants were offered the choice between ship or plane many opted for the four-week cruise; but some preferred to travel by air because they were eager to reach Australia as quickly as possible, because they were afraid that they would spend all their money on the four-week sea voyage, or simply because of the novelty of air travel. But as air travel became more common and more migrants flew to Australia, the novelty wore off. By the end of the 1960s the flight averaged between twenty-four and thirty-six hours and was a short but physically gruelling experience. The day after arriving in Perth by plane in 1965 Roger Kilworth explained in a tape sent back to England that 'I'm still recovering from the flight'. He described a nightmare trip – with no sleep in cramped seating, terrible noise, peculiar meals and frequent refuelling stops and delays in characterless airports – and wished that he had come by boat like other immigrant friends.[58] Air passengers arrived in Australia dazed and jetlagged, often slept through their first day in the new country and took a week to recover.

Compared to the sea voyage, flying to Australia was a rather unsatisfactory rite of passage. There was little opportunity to see the world and glimpse strange cultures. There was barely time or space to mingle with other passengers, discuss future plans or make lasting friendships. The cramped and exhausting plane trip was not conducive to extended personal reflection about the life you were leaving and the life you might make in Australia; there are very few aeroplane journals. Perhaps most importantly, migrants who arrived by plane had not benefited from a gradual period of adjustment to their future life as immigrants, and often felt bewildered and disoriented when they arrived. The sea voyage is often remembered by British migrants in vivid and extensive detail and as one of their most memorable experiences of a lifetime. For those who emigrated by aeroplane – with the exception of the earliest 'pioneer' flyers – the flight was little more than a way of getting from A to B. It is not remembered as the event of a lifetime, and it is not retold like the rich and extraordinary stories that recount the 'sailing across famous seas'.

Notes

1   Little, *Letter to My Daughter*, pp. 206–10.
2   Maggie and Robert Smith interview US; Liverani, *The Winter Sparrows*, pp. 191–2. See also Jenkins, *We Came to Australia*, p. 85.
3   Bruce Bates written account US.
4   Pickett interview US.
5   Hands written account US.
6   Walker, 'Diary', 1 April 1946, State Library of Victoria.
7   Saxton, *Something Will Come to Me*, p. 146; Jenkins, *We Came to Australia*, p. 89.
8   See Hassam, *Sailing to Australia*.
9   Little, *Letter to My Daughter*, pp. 206–7; Dickinson, 'Our Diary of Our Migration', State Library of Victoria; Black, 'Diary', 11 January 1949–14 February 1949, Mitchell Library.
10 Wright written account and undated postcards to 'Phyl and Mummy', from the *Fairsea*, and letter to 'Mummy' dated 9.12.1959, US; Palin written account US.
11 Qureshi written account US; Wright written account US; Jordan interview US; McLanaghan interview US; Penn interview LU.
12 Saxton, *Something Will Come to Me*, p. 147.
13 Dickinson, 'Our Diary of Our Migration', State Library of Victoria, p. 29.
14 Seymour interview LU; Bruce Bates written account US.
15 Wright written account US; Upton, *To the Undiscovered Ends*, p. 6; Akehurst taped account US; Barber interview US.
16 Preston, *Blowing My Own Trumpet*, p. 11.
17 Black, 'Diary', 19 January 1949, Mitchell Library; Hill interview LU; Hart, *Pommie Migrant*, p. 47.
18 Pickett interview US.
19 Lougher interview LU.
20 Blackmore interview LU.
21 Dickinson, 'Our Diary of Our Migration', State Library of Victoria, p. 20; Gwen and Cliff Good interview US.
22 See Roscoe interview US; and Lane written account LU, which describes the tragic loss of her young stepbrother overboard.
23 Butts interview LU.
24 Dickinson, 'Our Diary of Our Migration', State Library of Victoria, p. 41. See also Jenkins, *We Came to Australia*, p. 105.
25 Jay interview LU; Black 'Diary', 12, 17 and 29 January 1949, Mitchell Library.
26 Jenkins, *We Came to Australia*, pp. 105 and 89–94.
27 Drohan interview LU.
28 Rooms interview US; Barkas interview LU.
29 Dickinson, 'Our Diary of Our Migration', State Library of Victoria, p. 34.
30 Hart, *Pommie Migrant*, p. 65; Dickinson, 'Our Diary of Our Migration', State Library of Victoria, p. 35. Englishmen like Hart and Dickinson included the Irish amongst the shipboard community of 'Britons'. Ulsterwoman Margery Black had less sympathy with her English fellow passengers. Future research might unpick the

distinctive relationship between Irish and British passengers on migrant ships after the war.

31 O'Neill interview US; Carter interview LU.

32 Carr interview LU.

33 Whittle interview US.

34 Walker, 'Diary', 1 April 1946, State Library of Victoria; Hart, *Pommie Migrant*, pp. 12–13.

35 Dickinson, 'Our Diary of Our Migration', State Library of Victoria, p. 19.

36 Tyas interview US.

37 Saxton, *Something Will Come to Me*, p. 150.

38 Jenkins, *We Came to Australia*, pp. 95–6; Dickinson, '*Our Diary of Our Migration*', State Library of Victoria, pp. 21 and 8.

39 Jenkins, *We Came to Australia*, diary entry, 12 December 1965, p. 99; Hart, *Pommie Migrant*, p. 22.

40 Hart, *Pommie Migrant*, pp. 19–20; Dickinson, '*Our Diary of Our Migration*', State Library of Victoria, p. 15.

41 Dickinson, 'Our Diary of Our Migration', State Library of Victoria, pp. 15 and 23; Little, *Letter to My Daughter*, p. 219.

42 Hart, *Pommie Migrant*, p. 20; Jenkins, *We Came to Australia*, pp. 96 and 100.

43 Davis interview LU.

44 Rooms interview US. It is worth noting the contrasting experience of those migrants who sailed via South Africa, especially in the years after the closure of the Suez Canal in 1967. Their brief experiences of Durban or Cape Town were not framed by the imperial cultural memory that shaped migrant responses to the Middle East, and the strongest memories are about being disturbed by the overt racism of apartheid: see interviews with O'Neill US; Brooks US; Whittle US.

45 Dickinson, 'Our Diary of Our Migration', State Library of Victoria, pp. 23–5; Jenkins, *We Came to Australia*, pp. 96–8.

46 Little, *Letter to My Daughter*, pp. 219–21. Anne McLintock (*Imperial Leather*, p. 209) explains how the development of soap as an imperial commodity in the nineteenth century linked the Victorians' obsessions with racial hygiene and imperial progress.

47 Gikandi, *Maps of Englishness*, p. xviii.

48 Little, *Letter to My Daughter*, p. 211.

49 Skowronski, *I Can't Think of a Title*, p. 2.

50 Hart, *Pommie Migrant*, p. 25; Ralph Price written account US; Dickinson, 'Our Diary of Our Migration', State Library of Victoria, p. 36.

51 Jordan interview US.

52 Jolley, 'Who Would Throw Streamers and Sing to a Container?', in *Central Mischief*, p. 61.

53 Little, *Letter to My Daughter*, p. 225.

54 Jolley, 'Who Would Throw Streamers and Sing to a Container?', in *Central Mischief*, p. 61.

55 Plowman, *Passenger Ships to Australia and New Zealand*, pp. 7–8; Paul, *Whitewashing Britain*, p. 33.

56 Adams interview US.

57 Hardie interview US.

58 Good family audio letter to the Edwards family in Leicester, 6.8.1965, Battye Library.

Part II

Britons in postwar Australia

4

Strangers on the shore

'Very familiar and awfully strange'

Susan Jack emigrated in 1965 from a small village in West Sussex and has vivid memories of her arrival in Australia: 'We docked at Fremantle. The sky was so blue and endless. Men in long socks and shorts. The board walks and the white wooden thorough-fares. A Woolworths called Coles. Milk shakes and cool shop interiors. Women in summer dresses, yes, with white gloves. All very familiar and awfully strange.'[1] This tension between familiarity and strangeness is a central theme in the British migrant experience of Australia. Because the 'invisible migrants' spoke English and came from a country with elements of a common culture it was all too easily assumed that they would have few problems learning to live in Australia. Yet even the most subtle changes contributed to a disquieting sense of disorientation while some differences required significant adjustment. And, like all migrants, the British had to cope with the challenge of being uprooted from their own home and country and starting life in a new land.

This chapter explores the initial Australian experiences of the postwar British immigrants: how did they begin to remake their lives in the new land; what were their first impressions of the natural and human landscape; and what can their experience of disorientation and adjustment tell us about postwar Australia and about the migrants themselves? In short, how did the British respond to and deal with a country that was both 'very familiar and awfully strange'?

Immigrant arrival was a frenetic process and generated mixed feelings of anxiety and excitement. Graham Little recalls sitting on the wharf at Melbourne's Station Pier as the Little family waited with their luggage to go through customs: 'This part was exhilarating. There was a terrific bustle. Everywhere we looked there were people meeting friends, collecting their bags, pointing which way to go, this way, that way, and back on the ship others still scanning the rail for a first sight.' Some immigrants recall an orderly disembarkation facilitated by helpful migration officials; others like Matt Dickinson enjoyed the buoyant presence of welcoming crowds but complained that the official procedures were 'absolutely hopeless' and 'could have been handled much better'. In Fremantle the Jenkins family waited to be vetted by health and migration officials in 'the biggest queue I have stood in since I went to see *Mrs Miniver* during the war', and then sweated in the baking heat as they dragged their baggage through customs. Elizabeth Jolley was shocked by the intrusive rigour with which Australian officials protected their shores in 1959: the medical officers examined finger nails for the ridging which might be a side-effect of TB; required 'sleeves to be modestly rolled up a few inches for possible signs of a tell-tale rash' that might indicate an infectious disease; and asked parents if their children had hives and 'whether they have had, in the previous country, adequate food and fresh air'. A customs official 'tore his hands on the metal strips binding our crates of books in his eagerness to pursue the immorality which must be contained within the covers of *What Katy Did* and, even worse, *What Katy Did Next*'. For the Jolleys, as for so many migrants, arrival was 'accompanied by anxiety'.

An anxiety revealed by the six-year-old boy who was certain that his grandmother, left behind in Britain, was already in Australia (by broomstick, perhaps?) and waiting, he could *see* her, down there on the wharf. The hope for some familiar comfort and assurance? And the question asked by his four-year-old sister, 'Are there any lavatories in Australia?' was perhaps voicing in plain language the intangible anxiety.[2]

Australian ports provided migrants with their first sight of Australia and often made an indelible impression, offering a portent of the new land. Many would have agreed that Sydney, with its magnificent harbour, was the 'best arriving place' (see Figure 13). In 1950, 10-year-old John Jordan captured a first thrilling glimpse of the Harbour Bridge from outside Sydney Heads: 'there it is, this was Australia wasn't it? Sydney Harbour Bridge above all things, never mind, there wasn't any Opera House, Sydney Harbour Bridge typified what Australia was. It was the signature of Australia and there this place was through the hills.'[3]

But Fremantle is the port that resonates in the memories of British migrants who came by sea. Whether or not migrants planned to settle in Western Australia, Fremantle was the first port of call after the long haul across the Indian Ocean and it was, as Thomas Jenkins explains, a site of significant first impressions: 'Thousands of people through the years have gazed at its mundane sheds and cranes, examined its laconic dockers, peered at the very concrete, timber and tarmac of the wharves, for some clue to the strange unknown land to which they have committed themselves.'[4] For British immigrants the two predominant first impressions of Fremantle and the adjacent city of Perth – once they had adjusted to the dazzling light and heat – were cleanliness and abundance. When asked in 2000 about her first impression of Australia as the *Canberra* docked in Fremantle in 1966, Irene

Tyas responded, 'You could eat your dinner off the pavement. It was *so* clean, it was so spotless.' Archie Shaw has a graphic memory of his arrival in Western Australia as a 21-year-old in 1949:

as we were getting up to the docks to dock, and it was like a, a huge mural, you know. *Beautiful* it was. I thought, what a gorgeous place, you know, it is, it struck me. Really clean, and fresh, and — oh, whether it was me or not, I don't know, but … Remember back in the forties and fifties, Manchester was a right dirty hole, because it was all these fogs and smogs you know. I mean I can remember pedalling home from the *Daily Mail* on my bike with a big stream of traffic behind me, you know, all following me up the main road because they couldn't see where they was going…. There's nothing like that in Aussie is there? All this smog and fog, nothing like that, no. And so that's why it looked to me, it looked — a new world in a way, yes, suppose it did really.

In these and many similar accounts the word 'clean' has several overlapping meanings. At the most literal level Fremantle and Perth were clean towns without the mess and grime that clogged memories of British slums and cities. The air seemed to be cleaner and in the fierce sunlight under a bright blue sky the streetscapes were silhouettes of light and dark. Thomas Jenkins had a sharp sensual memory of driving out of the docks of Fremantle 'past the big sign that says "Welcome to Western Australia"':

I was taken out, blinking and stunned, into our new land. The sun was too high in the sky to see from the car. But it struck blinding flames from car windscreens and bumpers. The buildings were clean, as if bleached by the sun. The dust in the streets was pale…. Everything seemed to be very clear-cut – white light, black shadows, glint and flare of sun on chrome, traffic lights glowing dimly amid the abundant light.

'Clean' is also a cultural metaphor. If the empire was a bar of soap, as Graham Little concluded, then at first sight Australia was clean and safe by comparison with the squalor of Port Said and Aden, and British migrants were greatly relieved to discover that Australia might be just like home but with sunshine. And yet for immigrants the impression of cleanliness also represented a fresh start in a new country. At the end of his first day in Australia in 1949, after docking in Fremantle and visiting Perth, the York-shireman Sydney Hart concluded that, 'Yes, indeed, the promise of Australia seemed good. It made us feel gay and ebullient, chockful of ambitious hope. Everything that Nature possessed appeared to welcome us with the vivid freshness of youth.'[5] This promise was powerful enough to draw some migrants, like John and Sylvia Cannon and Maureen and John Butts, back to the West after initial settlement in the eastern states.[6]

For British immigrants arriving in the decade after the war the other striking first impression was the abundance of produce, and especially meat, in Fremantle and Perth shops. In 1952, Londoner Betty Preston stood 'in silent awe' looking at a Fremantle butcher shop where women were buying meat in abundance – including 'sheep cut right through the centre weighing goodness only knows how much' – and remembered how she had juggled her 10d. British meat ration. By contrast with 'the coupon enforced austerity of England' the Prestons then relished a café meal which was heaped on the plate, and the children bought as many sweets as they could afford:

We returned to the *Ormonde* feeling at peace with the world. Come what may, our first sight of Australia had been even better than anticipated and we spent the next (and last) four days at sea discussing what we had seen and planning our future for we knew now that we could, with confidence, make our home in Australia.[7]

At first sight Australia seemed to be living up to its reputation as the land of opportunity and plenty. Some first impressions made a lasting imprint and were sustained by life in the new country; others unravelled as the migrants struggled with the perplexing experience of settlement and developed a more complex and even contradictory sense of Australia.

'Would we ever have one like those?'

The temporary accommodation for newly arrived British migrants forged a second set of significant impressions of Australia. Indeed, the shock of houses and hostels which were dramatically different to anything the migrants had been expecting sometimes shattered their confidence and undermined future plans. The drive to this first 'home' from the docks or airport is etched in migrant memories: through the town and dusty outer suburbs to reach the stark gates of the old army camp turned migrant hostel; along miles of empty bush roads to a primitive hut in the country; past suburban gardens and bungalows of hopeful promise:

We drove in gathering darkness over the Bridge, up the Pacific Highway to June's house, towards what was then the outskirts of Sydney. The suburb names were strange, but musical, Turramurra, Wahroonga, Warrawee. The houses, low-built bungalows, on spacious plots, with gardens full of strange trees, bushes and flowers, looked lovely to us – would we ever have one like those?[8]

These stories resonate with the hopes and worries of arrival and are often framed by a knowledge of the consequences of a difficult – or wonderful – beginning.

Different types of British migrants had very different housing experiences in their first weeks in Australia. Young single migrants, and young couples without children, usually had the least stressful time. In the immediate postwar years single workers, mainly men, were enlisted in public works and housed in hostel dormitories where they often enjoyed the transient camaraderie of itinerant workers. By the 1960s most young single immigrants or childless couples started off in a cheap city hotel or boarding house provided by the government or private sponsor, or just as easily found their own lodgings. The experience of newly-wed Mavis and Eddie Roberts, who arrived in Perth in 1968, was typical: 'It didn't seem difficult getting started. We were young and healthy and in the sixties jobs and accommodation did not seem to be in short supply.' Twenty-year-old Mancunian Peter Barnes – who had been 'restless and impatient to see the world' – flew into Sydney with a party of young single men in 1964:

The first few days in Sydney have always been a bit of a blur – abroad for the first time, alone, jet-lagged and bloated with fizzy Australian beer. Our group was met at the airport by some matey people from the Apex organization, who bought us a few beers, delivered us to various private lodging houses and left us to get on with it. 9 Churchill Avenue, Strathfield was in the heart of the sprawling, slightly seedy western suburbs, about 7 miles from the city centre (20 minutes train ride, 4s.4d. return). It was owned by a Maltese and run by Mrs O'Reilly and a cook. There were about a dozen lodgers, up to three in a room. The majority were recently arrived young Englishmen. There was one mature Aussie, a house painter who managed to make his own space amongst this alien invasion. Mrs O'Reilly's son and daughter also lived there. We were a little like the cast of *Auf Weidersehen Pet*, with a rich variety of accents and temperaments but drawn together by the common experience of finding our feet in a strange land.

As we shall see in a later chapter, the mobility and freedom of migrants without children enabled an Australian adventure which was very different from that of migrant families.[9]

Many migrant families were sponsored by relatives, friends or employers, who were required to provide accommodation when they arrived in Australia. Not surprisingly, there was a great diversity of housing on offer. The most fortunate families were placed in their own home. When Leonard Jolley was offered the post of librarian at the University of Western Australia in 1959, the family was allocated a house on campus. Elizabeth Jolley was 'afraid that it might be on some rugged field miles from anywhere and I might have to walk and carry water.... But in fact when we got there it was in a normal suburban street and had instant gas for the hot water, something I'd never had in my life before, I'd always had to make a fire to heat water.'[10]

Other migrants found themselves in sponsored accommodation which was worse than they could have imagined. Believing that 'England was washed up and we'd be best off in Australia', Ann Hawkins had left Exeter with her panel-beater husband and four children in 1964, sponsored by the Apex club who told them that a house and job would be awaiting them in the north

Queensland town of Innisfail. Before they caught the northern train the Hawkinses had a few days in a Brisbane hostel, where the host of a welcome event put on by a local ladies' club remarked,

how pleased I must be to be in Australia 'away from tiny houses with no bathrooms and all the muck'…. Thinking about my former modern home on a pleasantly green new housing estate, I looked around at the very basic none too clean amenities at the hostel. In my eyes the accommodation was no more than a collection of wooden huts around a scrubby little lawn. The lady obviously thought we should be grateful for the communal shower rooms with rusty pipes and cracked tiles in the shared lavatories.

After a train journey through 'endless miles of nothingness', an Apex representative took them to their new home in Innisfail:

I had to fight back tears as he proudly showed us what looked like a wooden shack on stilts. Apparently it had been put together especially for us, but there hasn't been time to finish it off I thought. The walls were plain wood with no lining, the toilet and bathroom very basic, with an uncovered septic tank in the garden. It wasn't until I saw its ears move, that I realized there was a horse standing in the extremely overgrown grass in the back garden. There was not a stick of furniture to be seen, and all four children would have to share the second bedroom. As the man talked, it soon became apparent that what I saw as an unfurnished building, was in fact the way our new home was going to be, our host was actually proud of it! I squared my shoulders, mentally chiding myself for being weak. We'd just have to get on with it.

The Hawkinses soon returned to the comparative civilization of Brisbane and the Apex representative was furious: ' "What's wrong with you f*******g Poms?" he screamed. "This is the fourth family to walk out on us." '[11] Part of the problem was that some Australian sponsors assumed that British working-class families all lived in urban slums or rural poverty and thought that they were doing the migrants a great favour. British immigrants, especially those who left in the 1960s, had often been comfortably housed in Britain. They had high expectations of Australia and were appalled by the prospect of a wooden shack out in the bush.

Migrants who shared a house with their sponsor could also have an unhappy initiation. Some recall the very great effort and generosity of distant relatives or second-hand friends who gave up half their house or converted a garage out the back for the migrant family. Others describe the friction created by two families crowded into one small house. For example, Sheila Vidler and her parents, brother and grandmother all moved into an uncle and aunt's house when they arrived in Sydney in 1962, but it was 'too cramped', and after the uncle posted a list of jobs for Sheila's unemployed mother to do while she was at home during the day there was a family 'bust up' and the Vidlers moved out.[12]

Migrant families without a private sponsor were 'nominated' by the Commonwealth government and housed in a migrant hostel until they could find their own accommodation. The almost universal response of British migrants as they arrived at a hostel was one of shock. In 1963 the Crooks family from Surrey were 'profoundly shocked' at Yungabba Hostel in Brisbane by the spartan accommodation and insects 'the like of which they had never seen.... Coming from a comfortable home to this was a great, great shock. This, I think, was where the rot set in and the seeds of discontent were sown.'

Maureen Hands had two small children and was five months pregnant in 1966 when she arrived at Pennington Hostel in Adelaide:

It had been an army camp and was enormous. We couldn't see much because it was dark and raining. The first people to talk to us were two women who said that they had been there for two years and had never tried to leave the camp and get a place of their own, because they were saving to go back home. They told us that the camp was awful, the children had been ill, and there was no chance of work for anyone. They told us that hepatitis was rife because of the big, open drains that ran right through the camp. All I could think about was whatever had we done, bringing our children into this.

We were taken to our little bungalows where we had just two rooms, one for the girls to sleep in, and a sitting-cum-bedroom for Gerry and I. The bungalows were like prefabs. We were given bedding, pots, pans, cutlery, crockery and an electric kettle. We had no bathroom or toilet and we had to use the communal ones. The chap who showed us to our bungalow told us that our cases would be with us soon, but we waited and waited and they didn't appear that night. We had to put the girls to bed in their vests and knickers. Poor little things! They were so tired, they fell asleep right away!

All this time I could hardly speak to Gerry. We pulled the bed–settee out and made up the bed, and I took off my dress and shoes and climbed into bed. I turned onto my side, away from Gerry, and felt that my heart was breaking in two. I cried all night. Gerry was nearly crying with me. He had his arms around me, but we felt so lost and bewildered by everything. After a few hours, Gerry got out of bed and wrote a letter home to ask if they could get the money together, between them all, to bring us back home to Stockport.[13]

The migrant hostels offered a vision of one possible future in Australia. Most worrying were the meetings with hostel dwellers who were already determined to return to Britain, or who just could not save enough money to get off the hostel and buy or rent their own accommodation. More than any other aspect of the immigration experience, the hostels shattered British illusions that Australia would be a land of easy opportunity. The hostels were fundamental to the migration – and mythology – of British migrants, and we explore the hostel experience in more depth in Chapter 5.

Dry toilets and tin roofs

This first experience of Australian housing – in hostels or sponsored accommodation – also challenged that initial impression of a 'clean' and modern country. To British eyes timber houses with tin roofs seemed very primitive and suggested poverty rather than a practical adjustment to Australian conditions and building materials. The Whittle family arrived in Perth in 1970 and were sponsored by relatives: 'when we saw Harry and Ivy's house we got a shock! [laughs] Because they had weatherboard houses and we'd come from all brick, didn't we, and we said, "Oh, my *goodness me*, this is like a *shack*".' The wood-burning stoves and wood-chip water heaters that some migrants found in their first Australian houses of the 1950s and 1960s seemed rather 'spartan' and 'old-fashioned', as Glaswegian Catherine Barber recalls of Perth in 1964: 'before we left Britain there was this great drift away from this sort of stuff, you know, into central heating and electric fires and things like that'. Yet the opposite experience of Elizabeth Jolley just five years earlier – going from a wood-burning stove in Glasgow to a gas oven in Perth – reminds us that domestic life in each country was changing at a rapid rate, and that the pace and sequence of change varied within and between the two countries. Comparisons thus depended on the period of migration and the particular British origins and Australian circumstances of each migrant family.

Perhaps the greatest domestic shock for postwar British migrants was the Australian dry toilet – with the smelly curiosity of a septic tank sewerage system not far behind. By the mid-twentieth century most urban Britons were used to flush toilets, and when working-class families moved into new council estates they expected the toilet to be indoors. To the British working class Australia's outdoor 'dunnies' and nightcart collections – out in the bush but even in some new outer suburbs – seemed to be a step back into a squalid slum-dwelling past from which they had hoped to escape. Migrant memories abound with toilet stories. Eleven-year-old Catherine Barber 'couldn't just *believe* it at all, if you went to somebody's house and there was this dunny at the bottom of the garden, I mean … that's not anything within our ken, you know?' Another Scot, Bobby Stirling, recalls a conversation with a Melbourne workmate in the late 1960s which highlights mutual misapprehension about living conditions in each country:

'I was watching *Dr Finlay's Casebook*. Is that what the way youse live over there like, you know?' I says, 'No, that was away ––– ' 'Oh,' he says, 'that's why youse all come out here', you know, just joking. And I says, 'Well one thing we have nae got, certainly, is dry toilets.' Because I always remember going to this guy's house, and he had a dry toilet, and I remember Margaret saying to me, 'Phoo, I'm not going ––– ' I says, 'Look Margaret, just go down.' She says, 'I'm nae going down to a dry toilet.' [laughing] And, I mean it was a smashing house, but the sewerage hadn't been put on like, you know.[14]

This bewilderment in British responses to Australian housing and domestic conditions was partly due to their contradictory preconceptions of Australia, as a modern young country and yet also a primitive frontier land. Outside the front door, Australian streetscapes and neighbourhoods were just as confusing. Urban Australia certainly didn't look British and the migrants drew upon two idealized images of North America – the Hollywood idylls of the wild west and of the American suburban dream – to help make sense of what they were seeing. Walking through Fremantle in 1952 Betty Preston 'felt for all the world as if we had stepped into a wild west film, for there were the same low roof "Hotels" one sees used by the "bad men" and we expected the "Posse" to ride into view any moment'. Catherine Barber felt that Perth in 1964 was rather 'backward' but also modern in the 'Americanised' way, with shopping malls and supermarkets. On the other side of the country but in the same year, 20-year-old Peter Barnes thought that Sydney lifestyle was 'close to American movie lifestyle. I was perturbed to see policemen with guns. Road traffic seemed very fast and aggressive. The surf at the beach was thrilling but overpowering.' When Mavis Roberts took a taxi into Perth for the first time in 1967 she turned to her husband and noted, ' "this is how I imagine America to be" and he said, "It is." I thought it was a bit shabby and old fashioned but trying to be modern through big advertisement hoardings and miles of bunting and signs.'

The timing of migration, and the unsynchronized pace of change in the two countries, made for very different comparisons over the years: in the late 1940s and early 1950s many migrants emphasized the modernity of Australia by comparison with war-weary Britain; from a Londoner's vantage point in the 'swinging sixties' urban Australia seemed rather old-fashioned; by the 1970s the pendulum of comparison had swung again for migrants like Mavis Roberts, who thought that Australia 'overtook Britain' in this period:

Curiously, when we went to Australia in '67 we seemed in a way to be going back into the past a decade or two, now, back in Britain [in 1979] we seemed to be doing it again! *Britain* seemed old and shabby, Australia had not only caught up but had overtaken Britain and was a more up to date and vibrant country with innovative and imaginative developments in every field.[15]

'I couldn't open the landscape'

The natural landscape of Australia was even stranger than the human landscape of housing and streetscapes. The sky didn't seem right. Hove woman Maggie Robinson 'missed the old northern hemisphere stars' in Tasmania and could not 'obtain a reliable sense of direction' when she was driving because the sun was on the wrong side of the sky. As the *Georgic* sailed around the coast of southern Australia in 1949, the Ulster nurse Margery Black noted in her diary, 'Saw the Southern Cross. Not very impressive constellation. Don't know that I could find it again.' A few days later she drove out of Melbourne and into the Australian countryside for the first time, and concluded that the general effect of large paddocks, unregulated building and gum trees 'growing everywhere and anyhow, both separately and in clumps with undergrowth or "bush" as it is called here' was 'untidy and ramshackle' by comparison with the neat fields of home.[16]

The trees were all wrong and even the flowers didn't make sense. Elizabeth Jolley recalls that it was two years before she felt able to cut the native Western Australian flowers in her garden and arrange them in a vase in the kitchen, and that 'it took me longer to sort out the seasons. The whole year became a blur of weather that seemed the same. But after a bit I began to sense the change in the air and the change in the smells. Then I managed to separate the seasons.' The very distance and space of Australia could be disconcerting, and Jolley recalls that 'the empty remote countryside here quite terrified me and at the same time enchanted me' and that 'I was frightened when I first started driving. I was afraid I was going to get lost.'[17]

The postwar migrants, like generations of British settlers before them, strained to comprehend the alien Australian landscape through a British and northern hemisphere sensibility; thus the sky, the trees and the flowers were all 'wrong', just as corrugated iron was not a 'proper' roof and barefoot Australian children looked like neglected urchins. The landscape was profoundly foreign, and at first the migrants did not know how to make sense of it. Personal identity is anchored in the familiar, sensual signposts of the natural world – colours, smells and sounds; the brightness of the sun and the position of the stars; the taste of fruit and the feel of rain – and migrants are often profoundly disoriented in their new surroundings.

This sensual dissonance was exacerbated by the anxieties each migrant brought to their confrontation with the new world. As the writer Margaret Scott explains, 'the way you feel in yourself colours what you see around you'. Twenty-five-year old Margaret emigrated to Tasmania with her then husband in 1959. She was miserable for the first half dozen years, as the 'hair cracks' in her marriage 'burst open into black fissures' under the strain of being 'wholly dependent on one another for comfort, companionship and practical aid'. Her misery was compounded by the alien landscape of Hobart:

I didn't find it beautiful. I found it threatening. The mountain rose menacingly above the Hill's hoist. The land had no history that I could read from it. Everything looked untended, shabby, peeling, dry and horribly powerful as though the bush or the sea might suddenly rise up and casually flatten all the little wooden houses. And here too was the misery of the loss of the known, not of network and ritual but of familiar places and the sense of possession that familiarity bestows. Later I felt unhappy that I couldn't, without resorting to books, open the landscape for my children as my mother had opened Gloucestershire for me.

Eventually, Margaret explains, 'everything changed because my personal life changed', and she was converted to an intense love for Tasmania and its landscape.[18]

Depressing personal circumstances and desperate homesickness could make the strangeness of Australia's landscape seem especially hostile. Twenty-two-year-old Ann Cox emigrated from Worthing to Perth in 1971 with her husband and two young children. They had wanted to escape the British recession and make a 'fresh start', but the economy of Western Australia was 'worse than at home' and Ann's husband could not find a job in his trade and was forced to work in a hospital kitchen. Ann was 'totally isolated' at home with her children until the 'nightmare' ended after a year and they returned to England. A graphic list of Australian memories evokes Ann's unhappiness and her intense alienation from the natural environment.

1   The baby was very ill with the heat and a milk allergy. I used to lay him naked in his pram covered in wet towels to cool him down. One day I put him on the car port to sleep and came back to find him covered in cockroaches. I just screamed and screamed and neighbours had to deal with it. I lost control.
2   The first day we arrived we put my daughter on a slide not realizing how hot it would be and blistered the backs of her legs.
3   At weekends my husband used to go round the outside of the house looking for red back spiders.
4   One day when walking to the shops with the children I met a large iguana going the other way. There were kangaroos and emus at the back of the garden. The children couldn't play in the garden because of the stick insects.
5   I used to go to the shops each day by 9 o'clock and then shut myself in doors until about 4 when a wind came off the desert and cooled things down. I spent more time indoors than I ever did in England. I became an expert on Australian TV.
6   I went in the sea once – it was too dangerous with the rip, wasps, jellyfish etc. Not suitable for children at all.
7   Every day I used to stand at the window and watch for the postman – my daughter's first words were 'no post today Mummy' – and just cried. The loneliness and the homesickness were unbearable.[19]

For Ann Cox and many other British migrants insects were emblematic of the bewildering and even hostile physical environment of Australia. Snakes and sharks usually lurked out of sight, and though insect life varied from state to state and between the city and the bush, insects were everywhere and they defiled the body and invaded the sanctity of the home.

Yet other migrants relished the strangeness of outdoor Australia and were excited by the thrill of discovery. Liverpudlian Ralph Price was 10 in 1951 when his family settled on the outskirts of Perth – in a caravan in the back yard of a friend from church – and this account evokes his enthusiastic engagement with the Australian environment:

Everything was different. The very ground under your feet was different. All around our area was literally sand – just like a powder-dry beach. Your shoes sank into it and filled up, so us kids just didn't wear any, though it was really painful before your feet toughened up to the baking heat of the ground and the thorny plants. Somehow things grew quite well in it wherever it was watered. Even the sky was different – blindingly bright and completely cloudless most of the time. The night sky was totally different – with the Milky Way and Southern Cross, and all the stars stunningly clear. The Ocean was only a cycle ride away, with empty beaches, and thundering surf, and gorgeous sunsets with a path to the sun stretched out across the sea and golden, pink waves backlit as they crashed into the shore. All the plants and trees, and all the birds were different.... I was fascinated by the wildlife, and devoured every book I could get my hands on. My mates called me Dr Bug![20]

Some migrants savoured their new Australian garden, with its exotic fruit and abundant, year-round growth; many relished the Australian playground of bush and beach. Another Merseyside lad, 14-year-old John Jordan, would never forget his first visit to the beach near Wollongong just before Christmas 1950:

I can close my eyes now and I can see it all. I can see that, walking along the pathway and then the sand rose up like that and then it went down to the beach and all the people on the top of this sort of raised part of sand with their picnics and everything like that.... I'd never experienced anything like that before, people having so much fun, so relaxed and friendly and then possibly a new sort of adventure round every corner really. This is what Australia is, I'm in for some sort of change of life here because the first thing that I met was so different from anything I'd encountered in England that it was quite dramatic really.[21]

Thus outdoor Australia – alien and hostile to some migrants – might also be a place of adventure and personal transformation. Dorothy Wright was pregnant when she emigrated from Surrey to Sydney with her husband and young son in 1959, and after the birth of her daughter she suffered a misery of loneliness, homesickness and postnatal depression. She 'began to find myself again' through the slow process of making friends and as she started to appreciate the sensual pleasures of outdoor Australia (see Figures 14 and 15). On the beaches around Sydney Dorothy 'began to enjoy the lovely warm water, and the hot sun when we left the sea – no huddling shivering under bath towels, warm drinks and a good run round to warm us up as in England'. She took swimming lessons and

> visits to the beach became much, much more enjoyable, and I learnt the exhilarating joy of catching a wave, albeit just a small one, not the great surf breakers, and speeding on to the beach.... I can't begin to say how this changed my life. I never would have had such opportunities in England, nothing would have induced me into our cool (or cold) waters. But there in the warmth I blossomed.[22]

12 The Wright family embarking on the *Fairsea* in 1959. Baby Nicholas is in the arms of a Red Cross helper; Mike is wearing the long overcoat and carrying a folder; Dorothy is on his right peering anxiously up at the ship

13 Dorothy Wright arriving in Sydney, 1959. Many migrants agreed that Sydney, with its magnificent harbour, was the 'best arriving place'

14 Dorothy Wright with her baby daughter Bridget 'under our gum tree', Sydney, 1960. Following the birth of her daughter Dorothy suffered from loneliness, homesickness and post-natal depression

15 After her initial unhappiness, Dorothy Wright 'began to find myself again'. She took swimming lessons and on the beaches around Sydney started to enjoy 'the lovely warm water and the hot sun when we left the sea . . . I can't begin to say how this changed my life. I never would have had such opportunities in England. Nothing would have induced me into our cool (or cold) waters. But there in the warmth I blossomed'

Migrant and poet Andrew Caesar evokes a similar blossoming in his poem 'Landscapes'. In England 'my sensibility / was honed on pavements / rags of wind-blown / chip-papers tumbled through rows / of terraced houses and landscape was / factory chimney and winding gear'. The English countryside was a 'foreign language', 'it was the property still of / aristocrats, not for the likes / of a suburban townie / from St Helens':

> Then to Australia and the great spaces
> of bush and sea and sky; the mind
> at first, stretching, then relaxed
> each new and massive landscape
> a figure of escape, a place at last
> I told myself that I could call familiar,
> a boundless wilderness in which
> to set imagination free.[23]

As this poem suggests, it was not only the natural landscape of Australia which might set imaginations free. Australian society also offered the promise of a different way of life, and British migrants were keen to discover whether or not such promises rang true.

'We're not in bloody England now'

Of the myriad subtle differences between British and Australian ways of life, two features of Australian social relations sparked the greatest interest amongst newly arrived postwar British migrants: the apparent absence of class distinctions and the superior status of men.[24] Many working-class Britons were attracted to Australia by the image of a society in which they might not be constrained by boundaries of class and status, and they often arrived with expectations of a more egalitarian society. Essex mother Elizabeth Gray recalls that when her family disembarked in Sydney in 1959 the migrant welfare officer – a rather snobbish English woman who had preferred the company of first-class passengers – shouted at her husband, 'Gray, come and help Mr (whatever his name was) with his luggage'. Harry Gray rushed off to help but was stopped by his wife:

I said, '*Mr Gray to you and he's busy helping his wife and children with their luggage*'. And he went white, she *furiously* went off. And he said, 'You'll get us into trouble', you see he was nervous. I said, 'Don't be ridiculous, we are in *Australia now*, we're not in bloody England now, we're in Australia'. So he calmed down a bit and that passed off. But I was *absolutely* livid, they still thought they could carry on as if you're nothing. You see, this terrible – and it still exists – this class structure which *does not* exist in Australia.[25]

For many British migrants Australia did seem to live up to this reputation as a less class-ridden society. In 1955 the Northumbrian grocer Matt Dickinson formed his first impressions of Australians while working on a road gang and from the warm welcome in the country town outside Melbourne which was the Dickinsons' first home:

One thing that strikes you straight away about the Australians is the complete lack of snobbery and any form of class distinction. The average Australian treats every one as equal and darned well sees that everyone treats him as such. Even to employers or foremen, they seem to be able to have a grievance and get it thrashed out and get on with the job again, with no sign of ill feeling creeping in.

Yet Australian social relations were not always so straightforward and they sometimes confused expectations. Ivy Skowronski and her Bournemouth family settled in the Adelaide satellite town of Salisbury in 1959 and she enjoyed the 'glorious blue skies and easygoing philosophy of Australians, who are very down to earth and unimpressed by class. If someone introduced a titled personage to an Aussie, the reaction would probably be: "Gidday mate – how ya goin?" without any embarrassment.' Yet when the family moved to Woomera, Ivy was disturbed to find that social activities for workers and their families were arranged by rank and status, and that senior staff could mix in the workers' mess but that workers could not 'mix up': 'It seemed very un-Australian to me – I thought class distinction had been left behind in England.'[26]

Part of the confusion was that some migrants assumed that Australian egalitarianism – the assertion that Jack was as good as his master – meant that social class was not an issue in Australia. The more astute migrants realized that although class and other social distinctions worked differently – some compared Australia's 'moneyed class' with British social distinctions of property and birth – Australia was not a 'classless society'. Scottish school teacher Alice Galletly noted finely graded social distinctions during her years in South Australia between 1965 and 1977. On the Yorke Peninsula, in particular, she was 'made to feel very class conscious in circles of country people'. A teacher was not the social equal of other professionals such as lawyers and doctors; wealthy families sent their children to private schools so that they would 'form good social contacts which would be useful in later life'; and few Catholics attended town events because 'they were either too rich or too poor to move in these circles'.[27]

Some migrants had a related concern that in this pioneering and egalitarian society cultural life would be less well developed than in metropolitan Britain. Alice Galletly concluded that although the big cities like Adelaide had plenty of cultural activities such as theatre and music, culture was not woven into everyday life or conversation, and that many Australians, especially those who had not travelled, were rather 'shallow'. Middle-class migrants were more likely to criticize the superficiality of postwar Australian cultural life, but this concern was not restricted by class. Mary Rose Lavery, the teenage daughter of a Clydeside rigger and communist, despaired of her generous but unimaginative Australian suburban neighbours in the early 1950s; they had few books in their houses, made inane conversation and preferred to listen to the football on the radio anyway.[28] These comments are not far removed from those of contemporary Australian intellectuals who attacked the banality of postwar suburban life. The acutely observant 'outsider' can tell us something about Australian life, but the commentary tells us just as much about the narrator and his or her difficulties with Australia. The more middle-class migrants who had enjoyed the cultural life of London or British regional centres (and Australian intellectuals who aspired to that world) lamented its absence in Australia. Autodidacts like Mary Rose Lavery longed for the life of books and political conversation that were part of a radical upbringing. Other working-class migrants were delighted to escape what they perceived to be the snobbishness of British 'high' culture.

Though many migrants were impressed by the egalitarian nature of Australian society in the 1950s and 1960s, they were often critical of relationships between men and women and characterized Australia as 'a man's country'. In migrant memories this criticism is sometimes sharpened by the influence of late twentieth-century feminism. As a young woman in Sydney and Melbourne in the early 1970s, Pat Brown relished the 'new experiences' of Australia – 'BYO. BBQs. Lay-by arrangements for purchases. Counter lunches in pubs', and so on – and 'it did not occur to me then how unjust it was that women could not take out a loan to purchase property, that it was not acceptable for women to go in pubs, that men earned more than women for the same work'.[29] Yet even at the time, migrant women in particular were often shocked by their first experience of Australia's 'men only' public bars, and concluded that the 'six o'clock swill' induced by early closing was the epitome of a beer-drinking macho culture. They were also bemused by the segregation of Australian parties. In 1952, Manchester couple Dorothy and Albert Rooms were invited by a workmate to their first Australian house party:

And I got the shock of my life. We walked in, there was a piano like along there, and there must have been about six women and six men, without us. And the women were sat round a horseshoe shape round the fire, Australian women, no Brits, Australian women, were sat round the fire like that, right. The men were stood with pints there.... My husband had gone to join the men at the piano. The piano wasn't being played, just had their beers on top. So, I thought, well to hell with you, and I walked across and stood with the men, which was an undone thing in those days. The men were the men, and the women talked about their babies and their families.[30]

Some migrant women thought that male dominance in Australian society, and the stark distinctions between domestic womanhood and male public culture, had created a different type of man in Australia, and they were unimpressed. In 1965 Londoner Patricia Barnes's first impression of Australian men was that they 'seemed very selfish and had very spoilt lives. The Aussie women I knew were quite hard, and I understood why.' In 1964 west country mother Ann Hawkins was appalled by Australian men's domineering attitudes to women, and worried about the future of her daughters in Australia. When her teenage son started to mimic the behaviour of Australian men the Hawkins family made plans to return to England.[31]

Migrants' impressions of Australian gender relations – like responses to class and cultural life – were influenced by their British origins and attitudes. For women like Dorothy Rooms from the industrial north west of England the local pub had been the hub of a rich working-class social life that included men and women, and in Australia, without family or other neighbourhood networks, this was a real loss. Of course we need to be wary of crude comparative generalizations about class or gender relations in postwar Britain and Australia. In both countries social life and relationships were changing dramatically, and the nature and pace of change varied in different parts of each country. As Alice Galletly noted when she moved from Adelaide to the South Australian country town of Minlaton in the 1960s, 'The change from Adelaide to Minlaton was far more striking to me than that from Glasgow to Adelaide.'[32]

The loss of the known

The human and natural landscapes of postwar Australia were, quite clearly, not like 'home', and in their first months or even years in Australia most British migrants suffered from disorientation. Graham Little recalls that, as a teenager in 1954, starting in a new place was 'like learning to live again after someone's died'. At first 'you're up' as you enjoy the novelties of a different country. Then 'the whole forward movement palls, as if an engine has cut out. You are exhausted by the novelty, you hate everything about the place.... There's an inscription in my blue diary, right at the end, addressed maybe to the Queen herself. It says "Land of Hope and Glory shall never be Waltzing Matilda, 13.12.'54".' As a young woman in Tasmania in the early 1960s Margaret Scott was also bewildered by the 'loss of the known', of her family, of 'familiar places and the sense of possession that familiarity bestows', and of the 'network of ritual' that had guided and sustained her everyday life:

All at once I had no idea where to buy cheese or where to get shoes mended. I had no system, no tools to cope with anything, no path mapped out, no set of familiar reliable procedures. This loss made me quite manic. I was used to buying coffee already ground in sealed tins. When, in January 1960, I got back to our New Town flat and found that a tin I'd bought in a strange supermarket held unground beans, I tried to grind them in the washing machine.

Women at home often suffered the worst of this disorientation, by contrast with men and women at work, or children at school, who found new patterns and support networks in an institutional context. The experience of Thomas Jenkins's wife Babs was not unusual. While he was at work in the newspaper office she had 'to grapple with strange shops, funny money and people who speak English but in many other ways are strange'. In rented accommodation for almost six months while their own house was being built, Babs had no enthusiasm for cooking – 'a disastrous change from her normal self'.

She did not like the strange kitchen of the rented house. She could not find the energy to mount an offensive against the many strange new things in her life. Cuts of meat had the wrong names. Sugar was not so sweet – we took three spoons in a mug of coffee, compared with two in Britain. Fish was called jewfish, schnapper and cobbler. So, until the stimulus of a diamond-bright new kitchen combined with the re-emergence of her own dishes and tools from our packing cases, she withdrew into a sort of culinary shell. The renaissance was greeted by her family with acclamation.[33]

Babs Jenkins overcame her discomfort and lethargy, and began to face her Australian life with confidence, when she attained control of her own domestic space and filled it with her own familiar utensils (many migrants recall the practical *and* psychological importance of the arrival of their packing crates from home). Looking back, Graham Little is surprised at how 'easy it was to settle in', after his initial disorientation, and recalls that for a teenager 'settling in' was part of growing up with a new set of friends and becoming independent from his family.

The process of 'settling in' was different for each migrant, and varied according to their background in Britain and their deepest feelings about leaving home; the quality of their intimate relationships and of new networks of friendship and support; and the material circumstances of their life in Australia. Most important of all was a positive sense of identity and purpose and a feeling that you had some control over your life and that your aspirations were being achieved in the new country. Some migrants adapted to a new life and new ways with enthusiasm and ease. Others struggled and suffered for months and even years. 'Settling in' was never a straightforward linear process of 'assimilation'. British migrants brought familiar objects and ways into their Australian lives, and they resisted aspects of Australian life and landscape. Some started to 'fit in' and then stopped and drew back. Even now, after fifty years, migrants are returning to live in Britain because they have never felt 'at home' in Australia. In a later chapter we consider the stories of migrants who could not settle in Australia, we explore the experience of 'homesickness' and we explain why more than a quarter of British migrants returned to Britain.

'The most genuine, generous, caring bunch of people'

Networks of support and friendship made a vital contribution to the settling in process. Some British migrants had joined relatives in Australia who helped them to find their bearings, but many others were dependent on a range of official and informal support. Personal sponsors – who were responsible for providing accommodation – were profoundly significant, though as we have seen their influence could be very positive or very negative. Commonwealth nominees who were temporarily housed in migrant hostels had – as we shall see – a continuing and often troubled relationship with Australian immigration authorities and their partner agencies. But for other migrants, immigration officials usually had only a transient significance in the first few days, perhaps arranging transport to initial accommodation or setting up an interview with the Commonwealth Employment Service. Some migrants speak favourably about the initial advice and support they received from immigration officials, though others recall bad experiences of officialdom. The Upton family was almost destitute in its first weeks in southern Queensland because Lloyds Bank had forgotten to forward their £250 'nest egg' and Ron Upton could not find work near their sponsored accommodation in a remote seaside community. The Brisbane Immigration Office had offered Ron a job as a fettler out in the bush but he would not leave his family in their precarious situation. The Uptons visited the Immigration Office a second time, and though they were given an address for accommodation in the city, 'our two o'clock appointment was harrowing. The official was not in the least interested in our problems. He told us curtly that they were not a "Landing Department" and that as Ron had turned down the one job they were obliged to offer, we were "on our own".'[34] For the most part – and with the significant exception of hostel residents – the British migrants *were* on their own once they arrived in Australia, and had little to do with immigration officials.

Some migrants found their way to one of the societies which assisted new arrivals from Britain. After her arrival in Melbourne from Nottingham in 1959, the young nurse Avis McDermott saw an advertisement for the Union Jack Club in the city centre: 'It said, "Are you lonely, do you want to see someone? Go." So I went. It was for English migrants.... And they sat there, the bar was there and they sat there singing songs the same as they do in the pubs here. I thought, this is not my scene, so, I didn't go again.' In Adelaide in

1960, Manchester secretary Joan Pickett and her friend Jean were no better off with the local branch of the Victoria League for Commonwealth Friendship.

But the first evening we went, we were so disappointed. It was — I don't know how to explain it, it was literally the Victorian Society, very very old-fashioned, just a little clique of English, British people, you know, all stick together and, you know, it's us against the Australians sort of thing. [laughs] And we didn't like the atmosphere at all.[35]

Later chapters explore these British clubs and societies (including the rather different and more popular Caledonian Societies), and the associations British migrants formed and joined in hostels and suburbs that had a significant British presence. New arrivals did look to other British migrants for reassurance and support in their first months. Family members who were already in Australia were especially useful, and friendships which had been forged with other British migrants on the boat or in the hostels could become mutual support networks which shared advice about jobs, housing and schools, and provided company and reassurance. Both formal and informal British networks did sometimes become inward-looking, nostalgic for the British past and critical of the Australian present. Chris Gray recalls this effect when his family moved to Brisbane in 1956 and 'all the people we knew, my mum and dad knew … And they used to have plenty of parties between all the English people, and they was always saying, "Oh, wait till we get back to, oh we can't wait to get back to England", you know.'[36]

Some migrants avoided groups of disaffected compatriots, sensing that the mood would undermine their own attempts to settle in Australia, and instead actively sought to mix with Australians. In 1973 Christina and John Daly were relieved to escape the British 'ghetto' around their hostel in south Sydney and to make Australian friends through work and their new home on the north shore. When Ray and Irene Spencer left Perth's Point Walter Hostel in 1966 they rejected the offer of housing in Medina because they didn't want to live in 'a very British area…. It didn't appeal to me at all, 'cause there was a lot of whingers amongst them, yes, some mind, not all whingers no, but you had the odd one, they gave us migrants a very bad name as whingeing Poms.' Instead they rented a house with Australian neighbours who 'knew we were Poms and yet they go out their way to help us'.[37]

Australian neighbours, workmates and school friends provided essential advice and support for many new British migrants. They showed the newcomers around and explained strange Australian ways, and they often provided temporary furniture and other domestic items whilst migrants were awaiting their own crates of belongings from home. When John Hardie's workmates at Yallourn power station heard that the Hardies' shipment from Scotland was delayed, 'they were all round that night, cups, saucers, knives, forks, blankets'.[38] Australian friends also introduced migrants to local organizations that offered new friendships and social activities. In 1951 a Methodist minister on board the *Cheshire* persuaded the Price family that 'the West's the best', and they were soon settled in a caravan in the back yard of two of his Perth parishioners who were 'truly Aunt and Uncle' to 10-year-old Ralph Price. A contact made at church led to a job for Ralph's father, and the family's Australian life centred round the church:

It was a purely social arrangement that had very little to do with faith or a relationship with God as I recall it. But what they did profess, they did. They were the most genuine, generous, caring bunch of people I have ever come across. There was real friendship, and if anyone had a need, they were there. There were lots of social gatherings, and outings, and it must have made a huge difference to my parents getting established.[39]

'Another load of Pommie bastards'

Despite such support, some Australians made life difficult for British migrants. New arrivals often expected abuse of one form or another, especially in the latter years of the assisted passage scheme when Australian criticisms of 'whingeing Poms' were well known; after Christine Daly decided to emigrate in 1973 a Melbourne woman who worked in their London office toughened her up by calling her a 'Pommy bitch' in jest every day. Others were astonished by the contrast between migration brochures that said Australia wanted British migrants and the more negative attitudes they suffered in Australia. In 1954 Kathleen Upton and her family stopped off in Sydney for a day before catching the train to Brisbane, and were met at a reception centre by a British friend, Daisy, who accompanied them on the bus to her hostel to get a meal:

We began to leave the centre behind and as we stopped at some traffic lights I noticed a group of people making signs at us, clenched fists and facial grimaces. A little further on it happened again and this time I heard what they said. 'Another load of Pommie bastards!' I turned to Daisy. 'What do they mean? Don't they like us?' She shook her head, 'Take no notice. It is always like that. They know this is the hostel bus. You soon get used to it.' I was shocked. All the leaflets and information we had read before we left home had painted such a rosy picture. Nothing had prepared me for this. If the people of Australia didn't want us, why were we so encouraged to come?[40]

Every British postwar migrant has stories about Pommy bashing. Some remember it as just a 'wind up' or 'friendly ribbing', and recall that it was usually defused by a humorous response (Scotsman John Hardie would joke about the chains around the ankles of the Australian's convict ancestors) or by a genuine effort to mix in and accept Australian ways. Others like Kathleen Upton recall a deep-seated antagonism, and were cruelly hurt by Australian derision. Margaret Hill lived in Finsbury Hostel in Adelaide in 1956 and recalls common Australian sayings such as 'The only good Pom is a dead Pom', and 'You came out for ten pounds but you're not worth ten pounds, I'll give you ten pounds if you take ten of your mates home with you'. Local shopkeepers 'used to pretend they couldn't understand what you were talking about', as when she asked for ice cream: 'we used to call them tubs and they call them dixies here – and I'd say, "I'll have a tub" and they'd say, "If you don't know what you're talking about, well take yourself off somewhere else, you Poms should learn to speak English" '.[41]

We will see more examples of Pommy bashing when we follow British migrants into schools and workplaces and consider the tensions which erupted around the migrant hostels, but for the moment we can sketch some of the main features of this particular prejudice. In one sense it has a long history in the assertion of Australian independence from the 'mother country' and the sensitivity of native-born Australians to the comments and criticisms of British authorities, visitors and settlers. By the mid-twentieth century these attitudes had become deeply ingrained, especially within Australian working-class culture. They were reinforced in the 1930s by the Bodyline cricket series, the intervention of the Bank of England in the Australian economy, and, during the Second World War, by the widespread belief that Australia was betrayed by the British after the fall of Singapore. During the 1970s Christine Daly worked in an office in Sydney where some of the older Australian women kept 'going on about how terrible Britain had been to Australia or something and we even had a Japanese submarine in Sydney Harbour, and towards the end I just got really cross with it because my dad's best friend was killed in the war'.[42]

Postwar British immigration exacerbated these tensions. Many Australians believed that these migrants had a lucky escape from British poverty and should be grateful for their assisted passage to a land of opportunity. Australians sometimes contrasted the comparatively good deal for the British with the greater difficulties faced by other European migrants, and could not understand why it was that the British seemed to complain the most.[43] The British, in turn, were disappointed with conditions in the hostels or other accommodation, which were nothing like those promised in Australian immigration publicity. Australians were hypersensitive to British migrant complaints and to the slightest hint that British standards and ways might be superior. Mavis Roberts recalls of the late 1960s that 'Most people accepted us and wished us well but it's true to say those who had settled happily plus those Australian born didn't want to hear of unhappiness or homesickness, to them it was "whingeing". So you kept quiet if you had feelings that were negative.'

Others did complain, sometimes with good reason, sometimes because they were miserable and homesick, and they set off a vicious circle of contempt which escalated into the stereotype of the 'whingeing Poms'. The term 'whingeing Pom' was probably coined in the 1950s, and by the 1960s it had set fast as a personification for British migrants that was the antithesis of the iconic figure of the Aussie battler.[44]

Not all Britons were treated the same. Scottish and Welsh migrants vigorously asserted that they were not Poms, and almost invariably recall that the English moaned the most and suffered the worst abuse. Bobby Stirling from Kilmarnock remembers that at parties in Melbourne in the 1960s 'as sure as fate, the first person you got complaining or whingeing happened to come from England'. Edinburgh couple Robert and Maggie Smith were also in Melbourne at this time and recall that 'the Scots were lucky, we didn't get the hard time the English got. I think English people got it much harder than we did.' They explain that one reason for this difference was that English migrants were more likely to be clustered together in the hostels and certain suburbs, whereas Scots like themselves 'were more fragmented' and thus mixed with Australians more easily (their own social life centred around a Melbourne soccer club where they befriended Australians, Italians, other Scots and even one or two English). The Smiths also remember that English migrants tended to be better off than the Scots and 'maybe the reason the Scots just went out there and got on with it was because they didn't have a lot to give up so they weren't feeling sorry for theirselves, they were just getting out there and getting on with it'. There is some evidence to support each of these practical explanations of the abuse directed specifically at the English migrants, but underpinning such prejudice was a long history of Australian – and of course Scottish – disdain for English superiority and complaint, real or imagined, to which the whingeing ten pound Pom added another painful chapter.[45]

'What's a Pommie bastard mum?'

Schoolchildren probably suffered the worst of this pain. School is fundamental to childhood and growing up, and migrant children have to deal with a particularly acute educational and personal disruption when they move to a new school in a new country and confront new teachers, new friends and enemies and new ways of living and learning. British migrant children usually lost several months of schooling in the move from one country to another; they were sometimes put up or down a year because of the mismatch between the British school year starting in September and the Australian start in February; they frequently started school in Australia midway through a year when friendships were already formed and lessons well under way; and they had to cope with different styles of teaching and discipline and unfamiliar subjects and curriculum. They spoke English – which gave them a huge advantage over other migrants – but were mercilessly ribbed for their alien words and accents. Teenagers faced the greatest challenges but child migrants of all ages record the difficulty of starting school in Australia. Cliff Pester left Ashburton Secondary Boys School in Croydon in 1963 at the age of 14 when his family emigrated to Brisbane: 'Tuesday 22nd Oct. I start at my new school, Corinda High School. Do I get a culture shock or what! School here is totally different to school in England; it's so regimented. The lessons in the class I've joined are far behind those I attended in my old School. Basically I'm not very impressed.'[46]

The nature of this 'culture shock' varied according to the type of schooling experienced in England and the diversity of state-based education systems in Australia. The brightest and most fortunate British working- and middle-class children who had passed the eleven-plus exam and gained a place in the more academic, usually single-sex local grammar school some-times struggled in the less intellectual, mixed-sex rough and tumble of the Australian high school. When the Crooks family from Purley in Surrey arrived at Brisbane's Yungabba Hostel, 13-year-old Barbara Crooks was sent to the nearest high school:

I didn't think much of the school, as it was more like a secondary modern school than the grammar school I was used to. The curriculum was completely different. To my horror I discovered I would have to learn shorthand and typing! And no lan-guages on the timetable – I was learning French and German back in England. The atmosphere in the school was completely alien to me and I didn't like it at all![47]

Adjustment to a new school system was hampered by racist taunts and bullying; indeed the ferocity of the Pommy bashing suffered by many British children in postwar Australian schools is shocking. In 1964 Ann Hawkins's children started primary school in Redcliffe on the coast near Brisbane: 'The first day at school resulted in a cut lip and black eye for our eldest, which I have to say didn't appear to bother him much, and a plaintive enquiry from the youngest: "what's a Pommie bastard mum?"' Six-year-old Ray Benson from Southend wasn't too unhappy at his first Australian school in a migrant suburb on the outskirts of Adelaide, but after a year his family moved to Glenelg where there were very few migrants in his new primary school:

It was probably almost immediately that my accent was picked up on (though I must have almost lost it by then) and I was jibed as a Pommie. I can't remember what particular terms of abuse were used but there were one or two characters in the early days who regularly taunted me. I was never physically threatened, rather

16 The Williams family arrived in Australia in 1965 and Patricia sent us this photograph of her son Gary's first day at a Brisbane school – 'a barefooted "Aussie"' – in January 1966. Some British children tried to look as 'Australian' as possible to avoid 'Pommie' taunts

there was a sort of stand off where I'd be 'dared' to fight..:.. As a child I was excitable, emotional, playful, but also quiet and thoughtful. I must have been deeply hurt and confused by the blind rejection some of the kids gave me.

Ray's teachers contributed to his sense of rejection:

Remember at school once, an old woman we had as a teacher, openly made fun of me in the classroom, laughing because I said pants instead of underpants. Even the least sensitive 7-year-old would feel deeply humiliated at such treatment. These occurrences only entrenched my attitudes. I developed an Australian accent unconsciously but I always pronounced my vowels in an open southern English way and I kept hold of my English terms. And since I was a member of an English family I never thought of myself as anything but English throughout the ten years as a child immigrant. And when the school assembled to sing 'Advance Australia Fair' (I think it was that song), I wouldn't sing it.[48]

Fourteen-year-old John Jordan was a successful student at Rockferry High, a grammar school in Birkenhead, when he left for Australia in 1950.

Before he left home the excitement of emigration had reduced his interest in schoolwork and after several months off school he found it difficult to start again at Wollongong High, where there 'was a completely different schooling system'. Instead of Latin and Spanish he had to take technical drawing, the teaching of algebra was totally foreign and 'history wasn't English history'. Wollongong High was less formal than Rockferry High and there were boys *and* girls – 'never used to that'. Worst of all, 'there were certain lads, in the class that I was in, they were extremely hostile to British people', and they 'tried to pick a fight with me as often as they possibly could'. John was 'very unhappy, hated going to school, would try and find every opportunity not to go to school, whenever it was possible'. He left high school at the first opportunity and has always regretted the way in which migration destroyed his education.[49]

While children like Ray Benson and teenagers like John Jordan were casualties of the playground battlefield, many other British children tried hard to 'fit in' and 'become Australian' as quickly as possible (see Figure 16). Accent was both a mark of difference and a sign of success. When 8-year-old Lancashire girl Eileen Perfect started state school in the Melbourne suburb of Auburn in 1949 she had no worries with the lessons. 'However, I soon learned that if I was to be fully accepted I needed to speak like the other children and so unconsciously, I found that I was speaking "Australian" when at school and "English" when at home.' Five-year-old Phillip Maile from Kent started school in Melbourne in 1963 and was picked on because 'I was a Pom, and of course that's fair game … I remember the hurt and wishing it would stop'. Sport came to Phillip's rescue when he 'took to Australian Rules football with a relish and thank God a natural skill' and was gradually accepted by the other children. As time went on and he moved to high school 'my Englishness disappeared altogether, and I was now fitting in and belonging a lot easier. I was speaking with a "strine", doing very well in Australian sport, and more importantly I was supporting the Australian national sports teams, particularly against England.' Jackie Smith, aged 13, attended Salisbury High School in Adelaide in 1959, but despite its high British migrant concentration she rapidly absorbed 'this overwhelming feeling that it was not good to be English', and has never lost the habit of suppressing her Englishness.[50]

Fitting in was rarely a straightforward process, and some young migrants – like young Ray Benson who refused to sing 'Advance Australia Fair' in school assembly – resisted the powerful pull to become Australian and gain acceptance. Mary Rose Liverani's autobiography *The Winter Sparrows* offers an evocative portrait of the struggles of a young Glaswegian teenager in a high school on the south coast of New South Wales in the early 1950s. As a young child Mary Rose was a voracious reader and, despite her poor working-class background, she had won a scholarship to a 'posh' secondary school in Glasgow. At her new Australian high school Mary Rose was told by the deputy head that she'd 'be an Aussie before you can say Robert Burns' and both teachers and pupils mocked her 'appalling accent': 'I shivered in my seat. I had been speaking my very best English, the one I kept for school, and here it wasn't acceptable. "Ah'm Scottish, sir."' Fellow students complained they could not understand a word she said and cut her out completely when they discovered she was brainy as well as Scottish. She felt suffocated by the intellectual shallowness and superficial concern of the Australian students, whose eyes 'contradicted the smiles and bland tones, being narrowed with suspicion, defensiveness, a waiting for possible unpleasantness'. Her Dutch and Scottish friends from the migrant hostel had been sent to the lesser 'Home Science' school or had gone out to work, and Mary Rose was desperately unhappy and 'sick to belong to any group, no matter what, to be included in the laughter'. Gradually she made friends with other outcasts, including a bold Latvian girl who scorned the Australian pupils for their 'shoddy little minds ... unvaried in their prejudices and pretensions'. Together they decided to fight back and 'tell the truth and strike them dumb, the creeps': 'So that when the maths master roared at me: "Why don't you learn to speak the King's English!" I fixed him with a baleful eye and answered: "From whom should I learn – here — sir?" And, verily, he was struck dumb.'[51]

Even without migration, the autobiographies of teenagers like Mary Rose Liverani and John Jordan would probably still recount the jagged pain and confused exhilaration of adolescence and schooling. But migration added another layer of difficulty – and of excitement – as teenagers battled with parents who had wrested them from secure roots and imagined futures; as they lost soulmates and had to make friends all over again; and as they strained to fashion an adult identity in an unfamiliar world.

Ray Benson and Mary Rose Liverani both befriended young European migrants who shared their outcast status amongst Australian pupils. It is difficult to judge the relationship between British and European migrant children, or to compare the racism they suffered from native-born Australian children. At least the British could shed their accent and become less obvious targets, and their problems with Australian English were the butt of occasional humour rather than a painful struggle to learn and study in a new language. On the other hand, British schoolkids were rarely accepted as 'just like us' and were often isolated amongst their Australian-born tormentors, by comparison with inner-city European migrant schoolchildren – such as the Italians and Greeks – who could at least draw upon the support of other 'wogs'.

Just occasionally the British children had strength in numbers and could assert their own ways. On new estates like Salisbury and Elizabeth on the outskirts of Adelaide, postwar schools had a strong British migrant presence, as one schoolboy from Coventry recalls: 'By high school, the migrant percentage of the students was still very high, more than half, and consequently we had a very English-style school. The games played at lunchtime, the music discussed and the style of humour was, not exactly anti-Australian, but more British than anything.'[52] Though Corinda High was a 'culture shock' for Cliff Pester, there were other English pupils from a nearby migrant hostel and he spent much of his spare time at the hostel with teenagers 'from all parts of the UK'. Over the next few years Cliff got involved in the Brisbane pop music scene and joined several bands (see Figure 17). For a time in the 1960s Australian popular music was profoundly influenced by the 'Mersey Beat' and several important groups – such as the Easybeats – were formed at migrant hostels. In the mid-1960s it was good to be young and British, as Cliff recalls:

17 Some of Australia's most notable bands of the 1960s were formed by teenagers in the migrant hostels. Newly arrived from south London in 1963, at Corinda High School Cliff Pester befriended English pupils from a nearby migrant hostel and got involved in 'the Brisbane Pop Music scene'. Between 1966 and 1968 Cliff played keyboards with The Angels of St Michael Pink Doggie Do-Da Blues Band. This publicity photo is of an earlier group - 'I can't remember the name, I'm at the bottom on the left' – and evokes a fusion of the Mersey Beat and Australian outback 'every thing in a teenager's life at this time revolved around the British Pop Scene. Being English at this time in Australia held certain advantages especially within one's peer group.'[53]

'Wish you were here': the Good family discovers Australia

In April 1964, six months after arriving in Western Australia, and a couple of months before the Beatles toured Australia, Londoners Robert, Andrew and Malcolm Good (aged 13, 7 and 1 respectively) were invited to their Perth nextdoor neighbours to watch the Beatles on a new television. The correspondence and memories of the three Good sons and their parents Gwen and Cliff Good offer rich evidence about one family's discovery of Australian places, people and ways, and about the challenge of 'settling in'.[54]

The Goods had owned their own bungalow in the north-west London suburb of Northolt, where Gwen worked at home as a full-time mother and Cliff commuted to a job in central London as a carpenter and joiner at the Wellcome History of Medicine Museum. Their thoughts of emigration were spurred by television images of the Commonwealth Games in sunny Perth during the terrible British winter of 1962–63, as Gwen recalls: 'Yes, in about the November I think it was and they were all sitting in shirt sleeves with sun hats on, we were sitting freezing because the power was cut because of the shortages…. and we thought, you know, we're mad to be here.' They attended a Baptist Commonwealth Night event in Ealing (the Goods were active members of their local Baptist church), 'wrapped in our winter coats, scarves, gloves and snow boots', where a speaker showed slides of Perth: 'It looked like heaven to us! Blue skies, sunshine and green lawns – such a contrast to the cold snow and grey skies outside the hall.' At the same event the Goods befriended two young women from Perth who were staying in an 'awful' cold London lodging house and who subsequently came to live with them in Northolt. Elsie Newcombe was a keen photographer and showed them her own slides of home in Western Australia, and she and her friend Christine talked about different places so that 'in our minds, we'd been through Perth'. Elsie wrote to her mother and she, in turn, offered the Goods a room in Perth at the end of her garden so that they would not have to start off in a migrant hostel. The Goods sold their home and packed their furniture and other belongings in sixteen crates constructed by Cliff with discarded shelving from work, and sailed from England on the *Fairsky* in September 1963.

On 22 October 1963, Mrs Newcombe and her son Roy, together with the minister and other members of the Victoria Park Baptist Church, greeted the Good family at Fremantle with a huge 'Welcome Chris and Gwen' banner (they had misread Cliff's signature on letters from England). Back at her home in Victoria Park Mrs Newcombe prepared 'this big tea for us all and it was the first time Malcolm had had fresh milk since he'd left England and he just couldn't stop drinking it!' Andrew recalls feeling overwhelmed by the crowds of people at the docks and all the new people they were meeting. Gwen has a vivid memory of this first evening in Australia: 'Oh, it was very nice because there was a lemon tree in the garden and the moon was shining on it and it was a clear sky.'

The Goods' first temporary home in Australia was a large brick room the size of a double garage at the end of the Newcombes' garden. But within a couple of weeks they had made an offer of £3,100 for a house just across the back lane from Mrs Newcombe's, and at the end of November the Goods moved into 65 Swansea Street. To Gwen the house seemed 'slightly old-fashioned' with its tin roof and a toilet in the laundry area under a veranda at the back, but it was brick and solid and it was home. At first they furnished the house with 'borrowed and odds and ends' until on Christmas Eve – 'with wonderful timing' – 'our crate arrived! It contained most of our furniture, including the boys' bikes and toys, and even our wheelbarrow and lawnmower. We had it all over the garden! Because it was all straw and packing…. So we got everything organized then and set the place up a bit more comfortably.'

Over the next two years the Good family described their migration experiences in thirteen reel-to-reel audio tapes which they sent, together with

18 The Good family in their back garden in Northolt before leaving for Australia in 1963. From left to right: Robert, Andrew, Gwen holding Malcolm, Cliff, and Gwen's parents Nellie and Walter Edwards

slides and occasional letters, to Gwen's parents in Leicester. In migrant family letters one person, usually a parent, will often describe the collective experience and ascribe motivation and feelings to each family member. As a more collaborative affair, this audio correspondence enabled each member of the Good family to tell their own story, in their own terms, albeit with the parental promptings and self-censorship of the family recording context. Thus when Andrew, aged 6, takes the microphone and begins the first tape recorded for Christmas 1963 – 'Hello Nanny and Grandad' – we get a sense of what is significant for a 6-year-old who has just crossed the world and landed in a new home and school. Though father Cliff can be heard prompting in the background, Andrew speaks clearly and confidently in a piping English accent. He likes school where he is in grade 2 and his reading is getting better, and he is looking forward to the long summer school holidays, which in Australia begin with Christmas. He wishes his grandparents Happy Christmas and then notes that 'on Christmas Day I think it's going to be *very* hot'. He describes the new house and the sprinkler system in the garden, a particular source of wonder. He knows that his grandparents have just bought a car, and tells them that Dad is thinking about buying a car too. Finally, he says that it was a 'very rocky ride' to Australia, but that he played with swings and toys during the voyage and got a certificate for going to school on the ship. For young Andrew, the story of migration is about novelty and excitement, and Australia is an exotic and wonderful place.

Now in his forties, Andrew doesn't recall 'ever being unsettled'. He felt secure with his parents and brothers, and there was no great disruption to his education, which was only just beginning. With hindsight he realizes that when he started school he tried hard to 'be Australian'; singing 'Click Go the Shears' on the tape to his grandparents in Leicester is one small sign of that aspiration. On the other hand, British ways were still part of Andrew's everyday experience, in family life and in popular culture. At the start of the fourth audio letter in April 1964, Cliff comments on the boys' interest in The Beatles: 'You've probably heard of The Beatles, I think they made a bit of a stir when they came back from America.' A little later on the same tape Andrew (who has been off school for two weeks and whose convalescence may have been a factor in this latest purchase) proudly announces that 'now we've got a television', and explains that 'television out here is like the BBC in England. We have *Mickey Mouse*, *Z-Cars* and *Sooty and Sweep*, *Steptoe and Son*.' For a 7-year-old these familiar programmes were a comfort amid the novelties of Australian life.[55]

Thirteen-year-old Robert was a shy teenager and was less talkative than his younger brother, but the descriptive and technical details in Robert's contributions – such as his opening piece on the first Christmas tape – are also revealing about what was noteworthy and significant: 'This is Robert here. In our garden there is eight taps with threads on them so you can connect the hose to them, and you have to leave sprinklers on the lawns all day to stop them drying up.' Robert's account, like Andrew's, was framed by comparison: 'Christmas seems about six months away here, because it's summer now and we're used to it being in the winter, getting quite cold, and now it's getting warmer.' On the tapes Robert was most guarded in his comments about the new high school, where 'some of the work's harder and some of it's easier'. Robert had struggled at school in England and his parents had hoped that a 'fresh start' in Australia would make a difference. Robert now agrees that in the long term the move to Australia was beneficial to his education and career, but at the time the transition to a new school was a painful process. Not long after arriving in Perth he had to take the end of year school exams and had *'absolutely* no idea what they were talking about'. The course content and teaching methods were utterly foreign and 'I remember failing spectacularly the end of that year'.

And feeling quite uncomfortable or dejected or whatever, that I was kept down and did first year again which was probably just as well. But it meant that anybody that I'd met and became any sort of relationship with was a year ahead of me then in school so I didn't — That sort of broke that, not that I can remember having too many friends at that school.[56]

Whereas Robert was silent on the tapes about his problems at school, Cliff was very frank about difficulties at work and the contrasts between working conditions in London and Perth, where he started a job with a local joinery firm. In the first tape he describes his work on a library extension in the beautiful grounds of the University of Western Australia: 'The work is very hard. I think I have worked harder here than I ever have in my life before. We get paid for it.' The wage of £30 per week was higher than Cliff's salary in England and was supplemented with weekend overtime, including one Sunday when he had to catch a taxi: 'It's quite an experience going to work in a taxi.' But the long hot hours making window and door frames with the heavy Jarrah timber were exhausting, and Gwen recalls that 'he would come home from work by bus carrying his tool box and his face would be grey from fatigue'.[57] In June 1964 Cliff spoke again about his work. 'The factory that I'm working in is rather old-fashioned. They've got old machinery which seems to be one of the things out here that the factories are old. You would think they would be new, but I think they want a bit of geeing up in that way.' Six months later Cliff at last found a job that suited him, as the coordinator of a shop-fitting business. By comparison with the very heavy and dirty hands-on work with the hard native timber, this job was cleaner and less tiring for Cliff, who had always liked drawing and preferred pushing a pen, 'so it suits me down to the ground, and I hope they don't get sick of me too soon'.

Cliff's ability as a craftsman is an important part of his personal identity, and one of his few disappointments in Australia – at least in those early years – was that employment did not provide the challenges and fulfilment which he had enjoyed as a skilled carpenter and joiner at the museum in London. Over the course of the two-year correspondence we can hear Cliff worrying about difficult and unexpected working conditions and trying to carve out a working life that would be both secure and satisfying.

Yet for Cliff in particular the sensual delights of the Australian outdoor life and environment were a great compensation. In the early tapes he shared his enthusiasm for 'the wonderful climate', described the countryside around Perth and recorded the thrill of learning to body surf: 'these waves they really come up really high, but once you get out and on to the breakers you just go up and down and if you can get on top of a wave and swim with it coming in you don't half sail in'. After the first year, in a Christmas tape recorded on 11 December 1964, Cliff concluded, 'Well, we've been here a year now and I think that we've had a happy year and we're certainly glad that we are out of the cold and damp and foggy atmosphere, especially of London'.

The Goods had bought a car so that it would be easier for Cliff to get to work, and the car 'opened up everything for us'. Each Sunday after church the family took an outing to the beach or up into the hills and beyond Perth – 'really I suppose to find out where we were' – and after just one year the car had clocked up over 5,000 miles. They bought a tent and travelled further afield on camping holidays. Andrew explains that these outings 'helped us to become Australians quite quickly', because they were learning about Australia in a more 'accelerated way than the locals'. Looking back on his migration, Cliff concludes that the main differences between their lives in England and in Australia were that they had a car 'and we could get around, and also we weren't so tied down to being indoors all the time'.[58] Camping, body surfing and nature photography were among the many pleasures which, for Cliff, confirmed the good sense of their move to a new life in a sunny outdoor country.

In the tapes to England Gwen Good was the primary spokesperson for the family and talked with great thoughtfulness about their migration experience. Her role as a commentator on migration expanded when, for a short time, she became a radio broadcaster. In March 1964 Gwen wrote to the ABC Women's Session detailing her first impressions of Perth. A few weeks later she was invited by presenter Erica Underwood to read her impressions on the show for a payment of £4. Over the next year she made another seven radio broadcasts, including 'Whose Decision' (about the decision to migrate), 'Strangers on the Shore' (on migrant problems) and 'Wish You Were Here' (a letter to an imaginary friend in England describing the family's first year in Australia).

In each case Gwen read from her own written script, which she often practised in advance on the tape to her parents.

Gwen Good's broadcasts – like her contributions to the family tapes – offered a perceptive account of migration from a woman's perspective, and discussed the difficulties as well as the pleasures of the experience. She wanted to explain why some discontented British migrants were returning home, and to challenge the 'hysterical' publicity of local newspapers. In 'Wish You Were Here' she noted that two migrant grievances – the inadequate information about Western Australia provided back in Britain, and inferior working conditions and the lack of apprenticeships – were sometimes justified, and cited Cliff's initial difficulties at work. Yet she concluded by asserting the success of her family's migration, and in so doing composed the Good migration story in terms of effort, determination and achievement, and suggested that theirs was both typical and exemplary as a story of postwar British migration: 'Nevertheless, the higher wages and kinder climate have made our migration worthwhile, and the children are growing up sturdy and sun-tanned. We have benefited too, by a heightened sense of perspective and appreciation of both our homeland and our new environment.'

This 'heightened sense of perspective and appreciation', and the constant process of comparison between past and present, here and there, was central to Gwen's articulation of her first years in Australia. For example, detailed comparison of British and Australian living standards was a recurring theme of Gwen's correspondence and broadcasts. She noted that comparative living standards were difficult to judge, but concluded that while Australian health and dental services did not match those of Britain's free National Health Service, and white goods were more pricey in Australia, in many other ways her family was better off in Australia. The quantity, quality and price of food was a central and recurring emblem of this improvement, and meat was the emblem of abundance, as it is in so many of the British migrants' narratives.[59]

Gwen had a sharp eye for the minutiae of cultural difference: barefoot children, flywire doors and laundry rooms, sand everywhere, shark warnings, letters in the mailbox at the gate, and hunting for the morning newspaper that has been tossed into the front garden. She delighted in the joy of pegging her washing outdoors on the rotary hoist clothesline and watching it 'spin round in the sunshine, instead of hanging limp and sad on the washing line on a typical English Monday morning'. The differences in seasonal rituals such as Christmas were especially marked for a regular churchgoer:

But Easter to me is even more strange. Spring chicks and Easter eggs decorate the shops but in the churches harvest festivals are celebrated and the notion of Spring being synonymous with Easter, a time of resurrection in nature as well as within the soul, is completely destroyed … I still have to stop and think what season we're having.

In her recordings Gwen dealt with this strangeness in a number of ways. Sometimes she compared the newness of Perth and Australia with the more established institutions and ways of England – for example, she celebrated the welcoming openness of the ABC – and described migrants like themselves as pioneers who were forging a new country: 'It's fun being in at the beginning of things though.' Occasionally she was surprised by the 'old-fashioned' aspects of Western Australian life such as septic sewerage and tin roofs, and she responded through an English suburban sensibility which expected indoor toilets and roof tiles.[60] Unlike some British migrants, Gwen rarely seemed to be bewildered or frustrated by the differences in her new life. The family tapes and radio broadcasts helped her to comprehend change, and in her recordings she noted continuities which rendered the superficial strangeness less threatening: 'The crescent moon may have looked the wrong way up and the gum trees and palms seemed strangely exotic, but the basic bond of understanding was there, and we knew we were with people who, although they lived on the other side of the earth, had the same outlook and set of values as ourselves.' And yet in this same broadcast in April 1964, 'Impressions of Perth', Gwen argued that the 'rain, fog and grey skies' of London made people 'more tense and somehow frustrated', and that in Perth 'the relaxed attitude and general friendliness of everyone is very noticeable to a Londoner'. Here, under the blue sky and in warm sun, 'people, like the flowers, open up and absorb some of the warmth and mellowness of the country itself'.

Gwen's mostly positive impressions of Perth and Western Australia were influenced by the comparative ease of her own family's immigration, and by the personal fulfilment and happiness she experienced in these first years in Australia, as she too began to 'open up and absorb some of the warmth and mellowness of the country'. In 'Strangers on the Shore', a broadcast about the difficulties faced by British immigrants, Gwen explained that once the 'honeymoon' of 'initial excitement and novelty' was over, the process of settlement could be facilitated by involvement in local organizations and the development of new friendships.[61] The Newcombe family provided invaluable practical support for the Goods, before they left London and in their initial months in Australia, and Gwen regarded Mrs Newcombe 'as my Australian mum': 'Well, she was just always there and if you went there she'd always ask you in and sit you down and she would tell me anything I needed to know and she was very wise, wise lady. And very *sensible*. And, yes, she was a *big* help to us.' Gwen made a conscious effort to learn about her new country and its ways, from Australian friends like Mrs Newcombe, but also from the local radio, including the 'Women's Session' and study broadcasts which were 'very useful in helping me to acquire the rudiments of Western Australia's history and geography'.[62]

Through Mrs Newcombe the Good family was introduced to the community of the Victoria Park Baptist Church. Apart from attendance at Sunday services and Sunday school, the Goods joined in church outings and fetes and other fund-raising activities, and Robert socialized at Baptist Youth Fellowship bowling nights and tennis parties. Cliff recalls that it was 'basically ... the church and our faith that helped us to settle', and with hindsight his sons realize that they benefited from diverse social interactions through the church by comparison with some English migrants who mixed mainly with other migrants and were less actively engaged with Australian society. Indeed, the Goods' religious practices were affected by the friendliness of Australian churchgoers, who 'were much more open about being Christians' and thus helped the Good family to 'develop spiritually'.

Though new friends and social networks helped the Good family to settle in their new home and neighbourhood, their immigration was not a straightforward or painless process of assimilation. The boys recall that there was never even a hint of return within their family. Cliff remarks, 'We came out with the intentions of staying and not with the intentions of, "Oh, if we don't like it we'll go back".' And yet, years later Andrew was very surprised when his mother commented that 'we couldn't afford to be unsettled'. There is a dogged determination, underpinned by prayer and faith, in Cliff and Gwen Good's migration story. In her radio broadcasts Gwen compared migration to marriage: 'If we embark on either with the idea that if we fail we can always be divorced, it's pretty certain we'll spend years of futility and dissatisfaction before returning to our former states.'[63] When she counselled other 'strangers on the shore' Gwen was speaking from the heart of her own experience:

Perhaps a sense of realism and brutal honesty are the best remedies for homesickness. When memories loom up and we picture ourselves among beloved friends in halcyon days it's necessary to take off those rose-coloured spectacles. Were all the days so sublime? All the friends so ever-loving? How about the bus queues and the drizzling rain? And those long, long afternoons? It helps sometimes to remember the original reasons for our migration. In the constant round of cooking, washing up, ironing and cleaning, it's easy to lose track of our ideals and to feel vaguely dissatisfied, when perhaps if we took time to examine just how far our ambitions have been realized, we could assess our progress and direct our lives towards the fulfilment of these ideals.[64]

Under the surface of this determination, and between the lines of Gwen's advice, there are signs of the inevitable pains and losses of migration. For Cliff it was difficult to reproduce the fulfilment of his British working life. Robert suffered in his first year at school, though he never regretted the move to Australia and now can't see himself 'as anything *other* than Australian'. Young Andrew's initial determination to become Australian was turned on its head in his teens, when he reverted to being 'proud to be English': 'You know, Perth's home, I don't want to go back to England or anything, but I'm English.'[65]

In many subtle ways, Good family life was still English. Cliff and Gwen spoke with the language and accent of their London home, and they sustained the manners and moral codes which had shaped the boys' upbringing in Northolt. British cultural influences of television and music were part of their everyday lives, and the foundation memories of the older members of the family came from another country and way of life. Even Malcolm, who only had second-hand memories of England from family stories and photographs, felt like an outsider as he grew up in Perth:

I felt that it was sort of me against the rest of the world in many respects and that I was different, and the other kids in the school were Australian, either Greek-Australian or Italian-Australian or Australian-Australian, and that there was something different about the way they acted and did things and the way we, we did things. And I saw a perception of that also in our church environment which was basically our social time outside of school. That the folk in the church were obviously very good to us in that they were befriending us as a family, but I think that Mum and Dad and ourselves saw that their culture was different to ours. I don't know whether we sort of made judgements on people or just found their characters a bit more brash than where we had come from. And so even I guess today, I don't actually consider that I think the same way, or look at things the same way as the average Australian would. And I think even humour I find different, and one thing I remember when I was a kid was listening to the *Goon Show*, which was a weekly event. And I know there was a programme on about Spike Milligan the other night and it sort of just brought back that memory of the *Goon Show*. And anything, any humour that I enjoy it does tend to be British. I've never felt Australian.

Each of the boys, in distinctive ways, had to make sense of difference and to deal with the double identity of the migrant child. Curiously Malcolm is the member of the family who has been least settled in Australia. As a young adult he married a Scottish migrant and they went to live in Scotland for several years. Perhaps it is significant that, as a migrant baby, Malcolm had no memory of family life in England; unlike his brothers and parents he could only draw upon a second-hand English identity and culture to help make sense of Australia. Malcolm felt like an outsider in Australia but he was also, in a sense, a foreigner in his own family. Paradoxically, a child with the least experience and memory of England could have the greatest difficulty in fashioning an identity for himself in Australia.

Gwen Good also felt 'different' in Australia. Though she never suffered from anti-English sentiment, her well-spoken English accent marked her out from the locals so that she felt a slightly uncomfortable undercurrent. It is only in the last year or so that she has begun to think, 'I'm Australian'.

Because I've lived here longer than I've lived in England. But before I never thought of myself as belonging anywhere.... It's funny really [laughs]. I don't really think, like you know you're supposed to talk with a sort of ocker accent, aren't you, and drink beer and, I don't do any of the right things ... But I *like* Australia. I wouldn't like to live anywhere else. But I think I came too late in life to really change enough. So I'm sort of neither one thing or the other.[66]

Despite the ongoing uncertainties of national identity, Gwen *is* quite clear that the three years in her first Australian home were 'some of the happiest of my life'.[67]

I felt really free. In England I felt like constraint as though people were expecting you to do certain things certain ways. I thought there in Australia when we came you were more free. There was more money to spend so you weren't worried about making it last the week so much because our whole aim in London was to make the money last the week. And it was pretty hard sometimes because we never went into debt. But in Australia it wasn't a strain, you could manage very well. And people were more relaxed I think. I think it's the climate, people are more relaxed and comfortable with it being warm. And there's not the tension and also there wasn't the class distinction. I didn't feel it, I think it is there, but I didn't feel it at the time. I just sort of felt more comfortable ... and people were very friendly and helpful.

The very fact of the family's success as an independent unit in a new country was a source of great pride. Gwen and Cliff agree that their marriage was 'cemented' by migration because they had to rely on each other and, with Cliff not wasting a couple of hours each day commuting, they had more time to spend together as a family. Significantly, Gwen's own self-esteem was strengthened by the success of her ABC radio broadcasts. She was pleased to be able to contribute to the family income, and justifiably proud of her own abilities as a writer and as an insightful commentator on the migration experience. In short, as her family thrived and she enjoyed her own successes on the radio, Gwen Good flourished in Australia.

Gwen's life changed again in 1965. She had written her radio scripts whilst baby Malcolm had a daytime sleep, but now that he was awake all day she decided to stop. Most importantly, in 1966 Gwen's parents arrived in Perth. Back in London the plan had been that Cliff and Gwen would set up home in Australia and that Gwen's parents, Walter and Nellie Edwards, would join them after Walter retired. This plan almost came unstuck when Nellie was diagnosed with tuberculosis and it seemed that she and her husband would not be allowed to come to Australia. As Gwen recalls, that would have been a 'tragedy' and would have forced the Good family to return to England. But prayers were answered and the TB cleared up 'miraculously'.

The Edwardses joined their 'Australian' family in the house in Swansea Street for a few months, until the two families bought three adjacent blocks in Gloucester Street, still in Victoria Park, and built two adjoining houses, one for each family, and moved in just before Christmas 1966. Though they were delighted to be together again, there were readjustments and tensions on both sides. The energetic Walter Edwards was restless in retirement until he created a new set of activities, and Nellie was beginning to show signs of the dementia that would require Gwen's care and support for the next decade. After three independent years Gwen and Cliff now had to deal with the responsibilities and inevitable intrusions of their extended family. Most significantly, the arrival of the Edwardses showed Gwen and Cliff that they had already become 'freer and more relaxed' through their experiences in Australia. Gwen 'found it very difficult' with her parents because 'I think we hadn't realized in those three years how *we'd* changed. And it was quite a shock, really.'

Eventually both sides of the family made the necessary adjustments, and Walter and Nellie Edwards enjoyed the warmth of Perth and were delighted to be near their grandsons. Nellie died ten years after her emigration and Walter lived for another ten years after that. He was a very active man who made the most of his Australian opportunities, and it almost seemed appropriate that he died after a heart attack whilst enjoying a driving holiday south west of Perth. Cliff and Gwen Good and their three married sons – along with their Australian grandchildren and great-grandchildren – are still living in Perth.

In many ways the Good family were fortunate immigrants. In Perth they were supported by the Baptist community and could afford to buy their own home and stock it with belongings shipped over from England. They arrived in Australia midway through the long postwar economic boom, so that even though Cliff was not entirely happy with Australian working conditions there was plenty of well-paid work for skilled tradesmen. In these ways the Good family's immigration was markedly different from that of British migrants who came to Australia with little more than their hand luggage, who did not have the capital to buy a house and escape from a migrant hostel, and who sometimes left Australia in despair. The enthusiastic ways in which the Good family interacted with Australian ways of life, and the positive sense they made of their new home, were shaped by this comparative good fortune.

And yet each member of the family – like all British migrants in Australia – had to comprehend and deal with a new physical and social environment, and the family tapes and memories offer vivid evidence about the thoughts and feelings of the recent immigrant. More than that, the tape recorded correspondence itself offered a valuable opportunity to think aloud about life in a new country, to make comparisons between old and new, and to begin to make comfortable sense of the strange and exhilarating experience of Australia.

Notes

1 Susan Jack written account US.
2 Little, *Letter to My Daughter*, p. 227; Jenkins, *We Came to Australia*, p. 107; Dickinson, 'Our Diary of Our Migration', pp. 51–2; Jolley, 'Who Would Throw Streamers and Sing to a Container?', in *Central Mischief*, pp. 61–2.
3 John Jordan interview US.
4 Jenkins, *We Came to Australia*, p. 109.
5 Tyas interview US; Shaw interview US; Jenkins, *We Came to Australia*, p. 112; Hart, *Pommie Migrant*, p. 37.
6 Cannon interview LU; Butts interview LU.
7 Preston, *Blowing My Own Trumpet*, p. 38.
8 Wright written account US.
9 Mavis Roberts written account US; Peter Barnes written account US.
10 Jolley interview, Battye Library, p. 50.
11 Ann Hawkins written account US. For comparable experiences see Francis interview US; Chris Gray interview US.
12 Vidler interview US. For contemporary letters of complaint about sponsors, see Joan Joynson, ' "Something You Like to Forget" '.
13 Edwards Crooks written account US; Hands (pseudonym) written account US.
14 Barber interview US; Stirling interview US.
15 Preston, *Blowing My Own Trumpet*, p. 38; Barber interview US; Barnes written account US; Roberts written account US.
16 Maggie Robinson (pseudonym) written account US; Black, 'Diary', 8 and 11 February 1949, Mitchell Library.
17 Jolley interview, Battye Library; Jolley interview, Mitchell Library, p. 3.
18 Scott, 'Changing Countries'. See also Scott, *Changing Countries*.
19 Cox written account US.
20 Ralph Price written account US.
21 Jordan interview US.
22 Dorothy Wright written account US.
23 Caesar, *Life Sentences*, pp. 2–3. Caesar's freed imagination is later troubled by the discovery that he is 'an intruder once again' on aboriginal land.
24 One other, perhaps more surprising concern related to the condition and treatment of Australian aborigines. It may be that changes in racial politics and attitudes to indigenous people over recent years have led migrants to emphasize their memories about aboriginal Australians, yet British immigrants seemed to be genuinely surprised and concerned about the conditions of aboriginal Australians in the 1950s and 1960s, in contrast with white Australians who often preferred to ignore the 'forgotten Australians'. See for example Ralph Price written account US; Casson written account US; Hawkins written account US.
25 Elizabeth Gray interview US. In her first telling of this incident Elizabeth self-censored the word 'bloody', but later she remembered that her sons had been amazed to hear their mother swear, and that the story had become a family legend.

26 Dickinson, 'Our Diary of Our Migration', pp. 54–5; Skowronski, *I Can't Think of a Title*, pp. 8 and 35.

27 Galletly written account US.

28 Liverani, *The Winter Sparrows*, p. 312.

29 Pat Brown (pseudonym) written account US.

30 Rooms interview US.

31 Patricia Barnes written account US; Hawkins written account US.

32 Galletly written account US.

33 Little, *Letter to My Daughter*, p. 231; Scott, 'Changing Countries', p. 13; Jenkins, *We Came to Australia*, p. 51.

34 Upton, *To the Undiscovered Ends*, p. 30.

35 McDermott interview US; Pickett interview US.

36 Chris Gray interview US.

37 Christina Daly interview US; Spencer interview US.

38 Hardie interview US. Migrants also recall with thanks the generosity of charitable organizations like the Red Cross and the Smith Family which loaned furniture and other household items.

39 Ralph Price written account US.

40 Daly interview US; Upton, *To the Undiscovered Ends*, p. 19.

41 Hill interview LU (Margaret Hill has amended this extract from the interview transcript to clarify her meaning).

42 Daly interview US.

43 Of course British migrants did not suffer anything like the institutional racism experienced by non-English-speaking migrants – yet the enmity directed at 'whingeing Poms' was quite extreme.

44 See Hassam, 'Whingeing Poms and New Australians'.

45 Stirling interview US; Robert and Margaret Smith interview US. See Bain, 'Post-war Scottish Immigration'.

46 Cliff Pester written account US.

47 Barbara Williams written account US.

48 Hawkins written account US; Benson written account US.

49 Jordan interview US.

50 Perfect written account US; Maile written account US; Jackie Smith interview LU.

51 Liverani, *The Winter Sparrows*, pp. 217–34 and 315–42.

52 Snuggs, *I Came a Migrant*, p. 50.

53 Pester written account US. See Zion, 'The Pop Music Scene in Australia'.

54 Good, 'Impressions of Perth', 1 April 1964. The sources for this case study include University of Sussex interviews with Gwen and Cliff Good; and with Robert, Andrew and Malcolm Good (unless otherwise noted, quotes are from the interviews); 'Autobiography of Gwendoline Ellen Good', undated; 'Autobiography of Clifford Edward Good', undated (copies in the University of Sussex collection); and thirteen audio letters from the Goods dated between Christmas 1963 and Christmas 1965, together with eight radio broadcasts made in 1964 and 1965 by Gwen Good for the Women's Session of ABC Radio Perth (Battye Library Oral History Collection, OH 1733).

55 Robert, Andrew and Malcolm Good interview US.

56 *Ibid.*

57 'Autobiography of Gwendoline Ellen Good', p. 35, US.

58 From both Good family interviews US.

59 'Wish You Were Here', 16 March 1965.

60 'Wish You Were Here'; 16 March 1965; 'Impressions of Perth', 1 April 1964.
61 'Strangers on the Shore', 1 July 1964.
62 *Ibid.*
63 'Wish You Were Here', 15 March 1965.
64 'Strangers on the Shore', 1 July 1964.
65 Robert, Andrew and Malcolm Good interview US.
66 Cliff and Gwen took out Australian citizenship 'when Gough came in' to ensure that they would not lose their right to live in Australia if they visited England.
67 'Autobiography of Gwendoline Ellen Good', pp. 35–6, US.

5

'Butlins without the laughs': life on the hostel

Australian migrant hostels, which were unique among the major countries of postwar immigration, have never enjoyed a good press. As the first points of residence for expectant migrants after a relatively luxurious cruise they were almost bound to provoke unfavourable comparisons. Often adapted from old army barracks or woolsheds, or hastily constructed and visually alarming Nissen huts, they were administered by officials keen to encourage rapid turnover, who deliberately erred on the side of providing minimal comfort. The austere structures could become cauldrons of seething discontent and do much to define migrants' attitudes to the new country.[1] Historians have highlighted the grim side of this unique phenomenon in Australia's postwar history for migrants of all backgrounds. Phrases such as 'Bonegilla: a place of no hope', 'something you like to forget, you know, a bit like the war', and 'definitely not the Ritz', encapsulate the overwhelming impression of disappointment and despair expressed by so many shocked migrants. For refugees, especially, the hostels recalled experiences of concentration and refugee camps they had only recently escaped. In some cases gender segregation continued the irksome arrangements of migrant ships.[2]

The general, and not unreasonable, presumption in historical accounts is that the British enjoyed a much more comfortable hostel experience than the rest. Indeed, some hostels were expressly reserved for British migrants, although pressure of numbers often forced authorities to mix Europeans with the British. Also, more British migrants actually gained access to hostels.[3] The differences were no doubt important, but still relative, and there was an outpouring of anguished complaints from British migrants, especially in the early years of makeshift buildings. The shock of substandard accommodation, poor food, lack of privacy, high rents which interfered with the ability to obtain independent housing, and tensions with fellow 'inmates', are seared into migrant memories, and typically remain part of family discussion and family history. The shock is captured by John Hardie's comment that 'I always say this, now I know what a refugee feels like', or Maureen Hands's recollection that her 'heart was breaking in two' as she cried herself to sleep on the first night at Adelaide's Pennington Hostel.[4]

But the hostels were also something more than this, both in migrant memories and in the ways in which their presence impacted on Australian opinion of the new arrivals. Complaints about hostels were among the first reasons for suspicious observers characterizing the British as 'whingeing Poms'; being readily articulate in the local language, the British were more likely to be heard than immigrants from other countries. But hostels housed large and shifting communities. Here important and often lasting alliances and friendships – as well as enmities – could be made, an active and vibrant social life might develop and protest activities could be initiated. At the same time, following the communality of the ship voyage, everyone had the opportunity to judge their neighbours, and these often sharply critical observations now loom large in migrant memories. Irene and Clifford Tyas's recollection of their hostel experience in the 1960s encapsulates many of these themes.

'We'd got a whole community': the hostel trials and tribulations of Irene and Clifford Tyas

Born in Nottingham in 1929 and 1931 respectively, Irene and Clifford Tyas grew up in battling working-class families shadowed by the Depression and unemployment. Both left school at 14, Irene to start at a clothes factory where she worked until she left for Australia twenty-one years later. Cliff followed his father and brothers into various factory jobs until he settled into plumbing – 'I took like duck to water' – and served a five-year plumber's apprenticeship followed by one year of national service in Germany. He and Irene met on a blind date. They married in 1951 and lived with Irene's parents for a year until a council house became available on an estate in Arnold on the outskirts of Nottingham, where their daughters Melody and Julie were born in 1954 and 1957. Irene and Cliff share very happy memories of their neighbours and neighbourhood during these first years together in Arnold. Always a very sociable man, Cliff relished his regular nights out playing darts and cards in the local pub, and Irene took on a second, part-time job in a fish and chip shop. Their joking banter about Irene's evening job paying for Cliff's evening socializing suggests an easy acceptance of their respective roles in a warm and supportive relationship.[5]

In the late 1950s Cliff's boss invited him to help set up a business in New Zealand. Cliff was tempted because he thought there would be opportunities to 'better myself', but Irene was adamant that she would not emigrate with two very young children. In 1965, with the girls a few years older, Irene changed her mind about emigration when a neighbour who was going to Australia told them about the migration scheme:

'Oh, fabulous. In Australia', he says ––– And his wife was an Arnold girl as well. And he said, 'Oh it's fantastic out there.' He says, 'And you as a plumber', he said, 'it's great. There'll be no problem about you getting a job out there.' ... So I thought to myself, well, we're going on in the same old way, and everything else. And I thought, well, let's take the plunge. You know, that's what I thought. I thought, we'll write up. And I've got all the letters and everything. And they wrote back, and we had an interview. Cliff was surprised, he came in one night, I said, 'I've got some letters, going to Australia, it's just ---' He said, 'You what?' So I said, 'Yes, I'm determined.'

Like many British migrant families in the 1960s the Tyases were not driven by economic need – 'we lived OK, there was no penny-pinching' – but were attracted by the sunny climate and outdoor image of Australia ('the girls loved swimming') and by the idea that 'we could better ourselves'. It was significant, however, that they had been unable to get a mortgage to buy their own house because they could not afford a deposit and because banks regarded Cliff's plumbing work as casual labour. At their migration interview the Australian official assured them that after a few weeks in a 'very nice' migrant hostel they would be allocated a flat of their own.

In June 1965 Cliff's father died (Irene's parents had died a few years previously) and now his widowed mother set herself against the emigration of her favourite son and his family, even though her other son, Bob, agreed to look after her. 'His mum said, "Well you're not going now are you, surely, with your dad died? That means that I've got five coming out the family, your dad and your four."' Cliff began to have second thoughts but Irene was determined not to give up: 'And I thought, oh, pressure's being to bear. So I said, "We want to start a new life, this is what you've said. We've gone all through with this."' Even when her own brother's wife died in December, Irene was not deterred; indeed she was encouraged by his continuing support for her Australian dream. On 16 January 1966, Irene's extended family was at Southampton wharf to wave goodbye. Cliff's mother, having decided that a dockside farewell would be too upsetting, changed her mind on the day, but reached Southampton after the boat had left: 'as we were sailing out … Cliff's words were, "It's all right for you, your family came; mine hasn't." And that was a bit of a guilt with me, that I lived with.'

The Tyas family was enthralled by the 'luxury cruise' on the *Canberra* – 'the service, the bars, the swimming, everything' – and they were enthusiastic tourists in exotic ports: 'It was all intriguing … Fascinating.' They had left England with Cliff's last week's wages and £10 from a house clearance sale, and arrived in Australia with £15. In Perth they resisted pressures to settle in Western Australia because their neighbour in Nottingham had emphasized that 'the best place is Melbourne'. Melbourne was a shock. The *Canberra* berthed in the middle of a heat wave and a dock strike and passengers could only collect their hand luggage. A taxi driver greeted the Tyas family with bemusement – 'I don't know about this, you've picked the hottest day, a strike

19 The Tyas family's passport photograph, taken shortly before they left Nottingham for Melbourne in 1966

at that, my goodness me!' – and Irene turned to Cliff and remarked, 'Is this a ruddy omen for us, coming here?'

Arrival at the hostel in the northern suburb of Preston is a vivid memory, as Irene relates:

He said, 'Where are you going then?' And we said, 'Preston Hostel.' He said, [in a dismal tone] 'Oh, right.' We thought, what do you mean by that, you know? [laughs] And then when we gets in the hostel … [Cliff: We thought it were an army camp. Just Nissen huts you see.] I thought, I thought, we're passing it. Actually I thought we was going to pass it, you know, and — and I'm looking for a flat, looking for flats you see. And when we went in there and we drove in there, I could have died. I said, 'This is Preston?' He says, 'Yes my duck, this is Preston Hostel.' I thought, oh my God! What have we come to?

Cliff continues the story:

The first thing we saw there, wasn't it, is, they'd got these great big hosepipes and they were hosing these Nissen huts down, and we couldn't make out what it was, could we? And anyway, they said, 'Oh they're cooling 'em down.' They were like ovens. They were only lined with hardboard, there were nothing else. Well they *was* ovens, weren't they?

Irene describes the accommodation:

Right, we reported to the office … and I remember this woman taking us down with the kids, and, I thought — Nissen. And we was at the end you see. But I didn't know that at the time. She opened the door for us, and I went in you see, and I thought, oh I'll go a bit further. I thought the whole Nissen hut was ours. And I went, and I said, 'Oh, is that wall — ?' There's a bed there, now — . And she said, 'This is yours.' And I said, 'Well there's only two rooms here.' So she said, '*Yes.*' I said, 'Well, there's only two beds. And where's the children sleeping?' She said, 'The children are in here, and you're here.' And I said, 'Where?' [Cliff: It were only a settee.] I said, '*Where?* Where's our — ?' And she said, 'Well you move your settee down.' I said, 'Well there's not going to be room.' And she said, 'Oh yes, there'll be.' She said, 'You don't need any food. You go to the dining-room, I'll take you to the dining-room now, and you'll be able to get something to eat; it's not quite the time but, we'll get you a sandwich or something.' And I thought, oh crying heart!

The walls were so thin they could hear every sound from the families who lived at the other end of the hut and on either side, and their own unit was so small that if the girls wanted to go to the toilet at night Irene and Cliff had to get up and move the bed-settee against the wall (when the packing crates arrived from the ship they had to squeeze a two by four foot crate into the corner). The public amenities – including the 'filthy' corrugated iron communal toilet and washing blocks – were no better. Irene and Cliff were appalled, but assumed that the hostel was only transit accommodation for a few weeks until they moved into their own flat. The next day these hopes were dashed when they were told there was a two-year waiting list for government housing, that local rented accommodation was scarce and expensive, and that many fellow residents were already saving to return to England.[6] Irene was devastated: 'I thought to myself, crike! We haven't got any money anyway, you know…. Really, that's really what disillusioned me…. But we stuck it.'

Determined not to be undone by this disappointment, on day two they began to take control of the situation. After several days searching for work Cliff walked into a big plumbing firm just up the road from the hostel, showed his papers, and was asked to start on Monday. Cliff's British plumbing tools were useless because they did not match Australian measurements; his work boots were in quarantine for six months; and he had to learn a range of new skills for Australian equipment and conditions, but he 'got on like a house on fire' with his workmates and 'had a happy life there, I did very well'. As soon as the girls were settled in the nearest state school Irene visited the local employment office and was directed to a cleaning job at a northern suburbs hospital. She had never been a cleaner before but was happy to have any job. Like Cliff she was worried about how she might be treated by her workmates – stories about Australian contempt for moaning hostel dwellers had already made a mark – and when she said that she lived at Preston Hostel 'you could see something in the impression that — "Can't you afford anything better than that?" ' But Irene's fears were soon allayed by the welcome from a senior medical officer:

'Mrs Tyas, anything you want at all, if we can help you in any way, you know, we will.' And, he says, 'I know you're on the hostel, and you're going to have it rough', he says, 'but, it doesn't matter here', he said, 'you're a team'. And he said, 'Consider yourself a team, you're keeping the department clean, and that's what it's all about.' And, I was fine.

Within a couple of weeks both Irene and Cliff had jobs that paid decent wages and which they enjoyed. Cliff's wage of just over $60 a week was more than double his English salary and they slowly began to save, buying what they needed – including 'a big Zephyr car' – in cash. The girls had made friends at the hostel and school and they 'really loved' the outdoor life, especially the local open-air swimming pool. When Melody moved up to high school in 1967 'she looked fantastic' in a new school uniform which was emblematic of the family's pride in its achievements – despite the disappointments – in that first year.

Although conditions in the hostel were pretty grim, the community that the Tyases found and made amongst the Nissen huts was an important and valued part of their new life, as Cliff recalls: 'But the life on there, it's like, you could — opposite you there was another door, and that was another family.... And you used to come out and sit on your step, or on the doorway step, on the threshold, and they'd be doing the same, and then, you'd be chatting. The comradeship and everything like that was fantastic.' Most of the 400 or so residents at Preston Hostel were British migrants (there were just a few Italian families) and Cliff took a lead in the vibrant social life of familiar British working-class pastimes. He had always been a sociable man, and now he helped organize a migrants' club which put on games and social events in the reception hall. He started a darts team, which joined a league and played against other hostels throughout Victoria; he organized a British football pools competition; and he drove the hostel children to basketball matches every Saturday. At Christmastime residents decorated the hostel restaurant and Cliff was the disc jockey at the Christmas party. Almost forty years on, Cliff and Irene recall the community spirit of Preston Hostel in an enthusiastic dialogue:

Cliff: The community was ...
Irene: What we were saying is —
Cliff: — was fantastic.
Irene: The hostel itself, the people that were there, we — whereas the conditions were bad, we made a lot of company and a lot of friends.

Cliff: And a lot of friends.

Irene: Friends, you know, that — because we were all in the same boat, in a sense, you know.

Cliff: Which it was.

Irene: And it was comradeship, let's say, more than anything, because we all understood one another.

Cliff: And everybody stuck together. And we started playing up about, they wanted to put the rent up, didn't they?

Irene: Yes, that's actually I think —

Cliff: That's where it all started.

In January 1967 Commonwealth Hostels Ltd announced rent increases for all migrant hostel tenants. For the Tyas family the rent rise was just under 15 per cent, from \$25.80 to \$29.10 a week, about half of Cliff's weekly wage.[7] Preston Hostel tenants, including Irene and Clifford Tyas, were incensed that the rent was going up despite the fact that the authorities had done nothing to improve conditions at the hostel. At a residents' meeting 'we were all up in arms' and many of the families agreed not to pay the additional rent and to campaign against the increase. At a second meeting with an official from Commonwealth Hostels, residents were told that if they did not pay they would be evicted. Irene recalls a heated exchange:

Because we kept our rent [increase] in a bank, we didn't use it at all. We said, 'We've not refused, but the conditions that we're living under, and that we have lived under, and the people before — '. Oh, and then they said, 'Well the people before you haven't complained, and it's just you making us the scapegoat', you see. And we said, 'Well, the people aren't us, and we're sticking together, that the people that are coming in after us want better conditions than we've got. Well we haven't refused to pay; we just want to take it further, and we're going to take it further.'

Irene and Clifford's friend and fellow-resident, Arthur Durrant, chaired a Preston Hostel Protest Committee which secured the support of Preston Labor councillor Carl Kirkwood, himself a recent Scottish migrant. In March, Commonwealth Hostels issued a court summons to the thirty-five Preston Hostel families, including the Tyas family, who had not paid the increased tariff. The rent strike was now big news and made front-page headlines in the Melbourne *Herald*. Arthur Durrant explained that 'the bailiff had no trouble handing out the 35 summonses … we sought him out. We want to take this matter to court. We want to fight it out there. It's the only way to bring the whole thing into the open.'[8]

British migrants at other Melbourne hostels held their own protest meetings and a state-wide campaign by the Combined Migrant Hostels Central Committee was supported by Labor politicians, trade unionists and other prominent Victorians, who raised funds to pay for a Queen's Counsel to defend the Preston Hostel rent strikers. The committee also printed a protest pamphlet about hostel conditions and agreed to send it to Britain where it would embarrass the Australian government and deter prospective migrants (see Figure 20). The four-page pamphlet – 'Who wants to live in a hostel – or be dragged before a court?' – included graphic photographs illustrating the crowding and neglect in the Commonwealth hostels and explained that the rent increase was unjustified and made it harder for migrants to save money to buy their own homes. British migrants did not ask for 'any special concessions or privileges, only the opportunity to reasonable transit hostel accommodation and the opportunity to make their own way into the mainstream of Australian life'. The pamphlet urged that 'housing loans should be available to ALL families in Australia' and thus made common cause between the plight of British migrants and that of Australian working-class families. It concluded that conditions in the hostels were causing many British migrants to return home and that the government was therefore 'squandering … millions of dollars of taxes imposed on all of us on attracting and transporting migrants to Australia'.[9]

On 3 April 1967 the case against Henry Hill, the first of the Preston rent strikers, was dismissed on a technicality; the Melbourne City Court judge ruled that the crown solicitor had not produced proof of federal government approval for the rent increase. Two hundred British migrants held a triumphant demonstration march past the court and up to Trades Hall, carrying banners which declared that 'Preston will not be pressed on'; 'To hell with C.H.L'; and 'They seek us here, they seek us there, then they dump us anywhere'. The *Herald* reported that 'women and children struck up the song "We Shall Not be Moved"' and shouted 'Up the Pommies' while men handed out copies of the protest leaflet.[10] Irene and Clifford Tyas were on the march and Irene recalls that there were slurs from some passers-by, who commented, '"You want to think yourself lucky that you're living on the hostel" and all this', but the residents were euphoric about this initial success.

By now the campaign was a *cause célèbre*. The left-wing *Tribune* newspaper sent a journalist to Preston Hostel and she reported 'concentration camp' conditions. The more mainstream *Australian Women's Weekly* also published a story about conditions at Preston, with a headline that urged 'Please, Australia, give us migrants better hostels'.[11] As Cliff recalls, 'It was a big high-up. I mean I was on ––– I was on television, in England!' But the success in court was only 'a stay of execution' and eventually the protesters lost in court and were forced to pay up or get out. In Irene's opinion, this was a victory of sorts.

But at the end of the day, what we did is, when we did pay, we said, 'Well at least it's brought it to the attention' [Cliff: Of everybody else.] ––– of the conditions and everything…. And funnily enough, when we moved off, I think it would be about six months or seven months, there were builders in there, six or seven months after we had moved on. So we had done some good, you know.

Who wants to live in a
hostel — or be dragged before a court?

DO NOT WANT SPECIAL PRIVILEGES

Migrants do not ask for any special concessions or privileges, only the opportunity to reasonable transit hostel accommodation and the opportunity to make their own way into the mainstream of Australian life.

British migrants accept the fact that their early days in Australia will be spent in hostels until they settle down and save enough to get a house.

They want to get out of the hostels, stand on their own feet and become part of the Australian suburban community.

WANT TO MOVE – CAN'T MOVE

Having tempted migrants to come out to Australia with glossy publicity and a $25 passage, the Government throws them into sub-standard hostels and increases the tariff to a point where a mere existence takes most of a migrant worker's wages.

Now for the fourth time in 40 months the Government has directed Commonwealth Hostels Ltd. to increase the charges for hostel accommodation.

GETTING SETTLED   SAVING FOR A HOUSE

To the prospective British migrant getting a house of his own is presented as a simple matter in Government publications attracting migrants to Australia.

But the facts are that buying or renting a house is not a simple matter.

Houses for rent are scarce and expensive, while buying a house requires a substantial deposit and long delays in obtaining a housing loan.

With little left in the family purse after paying a minimum of charges and family necessities, it is a heartbreaking effort to build up a bank account for a house deposit.

20 One of many clippings about the 1967 migrant rent strike retained by Irene and Clifford Tyas, 'Who wants to live in a hostel – or be dragged before a court?' was a leaflet produced by the Combined Migrant Hostels' Central Committee, with the support of a number of Victorian Trade Unions

Indeed, within a week of the first court case, the government announced that it would continue improvements to existing hostels while introducing new self-contained flats as alternative transit housing for migrant families.[12]

Though a small number of non-British migrants at Preston and other hostels participated in the protest, the rent strike was, overwhelmingly, a British affair, and was framed in terms of the racial identity of the protesters and by contradictory Australian attitudes to 'Britishness'. The hostel protesters represented themselves as respectable working-class families, lured away from their own comfortable houses in Britain by the Australian promise of a better quality of life, but now unable to save enough to buy into the Australian dream of home ownership because of the high rents charged for inferior hostel accommodation. The protesters and their supporters argued that British migrant families in particular should not have to suffer the squalor and frustration of the hostels. During the rent strike 'Disgusted' of Adelaide complained in a letter to a Melbourne newspaper:

Aussie hostels are more like POW camps and decent family life is impossible.... South Australia paid $1200 to bring my family out, but the feeling here is so anti-British that nobody worries whether we Pommies leave. The English explorers and pioneers, who went through so much hardship to open this land, would turn in their graves if they could see how South Australia is being sold out to the Yanks and Japs.[13]

By contrast, Australian critics of the hostel strikers derided them as whingeing Poms and compared them less favourably with their pioneer predecessors and with other non-English-speaking migrants who often coped with much worse conditions. At the bottom of the letter from 'Disgusted' of Adelaide the newspaper editor commented, 'Your fares were paid, you have a home and a job. You can't expect everything on a plate.' The federal government shifted uneasily between these two positions; when it did agree to invest in improvements to hostels and other forms of migrant transit accommodation the government was driven less by compassion and more by concern that the immigrant intake from Britain would be adversely affected by negative publicity.[14]

Towards the end of the rent protest, after a year and a half on the hostel, the estate agent parent of one of Melody's school friends found the Tyas family an unfurnished bungalow for rent in Thornbury, just up the road from the hostel. It was 'a lovely place' with a 'great big paddock' next door where Julie was able to keep a pony. Irene laughs when she recalls that they furnished the house from a second-hand store in Bell Street: 'If they'd have only seen us in England, you know, you'd left all your life's furniture and everything in England.... But it was heaven, it *really* was.' The only disadvantage of the new home was that they lost the regular social life and company of the hostel: 'People kept saying I wish we could meet more often, friends who had moved off the hostel.' This social isolation was exacerbated by the unwelcoming attitude of new neighbours. 'Australians were like we are with the blacks, then, talking now thirty years ago, that we didn't want one living next door to us, it degraded the area where you lived. Can you understand me? And they got the same kind of attitude to us, and we *felt*, we know how we felt, so we could understand how the coloured, the ethnics now, feel where they're living, and the whites don't want them or whatever.'

Irene and Cliff began to organize parties at their home in Thornbury for friends they had met at the hostel, 'and they got bigger and bigger and bigger', as Cliff recalls:

And I'd got a great big Grundig radiogram, and we had these singalongs. And then we'd finish off for the night, 'I belong to Glasgow' for the Scottish, and then, 'Hills all Around', Wales, you know. What's, something Harlech isn't it? And then, old 'Land of Hope and Glory', and, you know, all of 'em like, you know. And the Irish. And we used to sing all these like anthems.

The success of these parties inspired three couples who had become friends at Preston Hostel – Irene and Cliff, Gerry and Rosa Redmond, and Arthur and Rita Durrant – to form the committee of a Migrants' Reunion Club. They hired local halls for migrant reunion dances with a live band and a buffet prepared on Saturday afternoon at the Tyas house. Throughout 1968 and 1969 these dances were increasingly popular, and eventually Carl Kirkwood, now mayor of Preston, offered to loan Preston Town Hall for the migrant reunion dances and for pensioners' Christmas parties which the committee sponsored with their profits. The six committee members sold tickets to migrant friends and associates all over Melbourne and the local press promoted the events. On 18 September 1968 the *Preston Post* published a letter from Gerry Redmond which invited 'not only English, Scots, Welsh and Irish migrants. We find that we have more and more Australians coming. We are pleased with this, as it helps us all to mix. We have a six-piece Italian band and it's a real good night.'[15] Though the band was Italian, and Cliff explains that migrants from any ethnic background were welcome at the reunion dances, the main emphasis was upon reunion for British migrants. For these British migrants and their Australian friends the dances were, as Cliff recalls, hugely successful: 'And we finished up at the Town Hall, with a balcony. And 2,000 people near enough there. *Absolutely packed.*'

During this exciting period Irene and Cliff tried to put down roots in Australia but were dogged by ill-fortune when two opportunities to buy their own home fell through. Irene's guilt about leaving Cliff's widowed mother in England was rekindled when the old woman stopped writing letters (she did not have a telephone to receive calls of concern), and after an uncle offered them his house in Nottingham they decided to go back to England. We return in a later chapter to the challenges and disappointments of the Tyas family's English homecoming in 1970. Irene and Cliff now look back with some regret at opportunities they missed in Australia. And yet they also recall their experiences at Preston Hostel and in the Migrants' Reunion Club with pride, and as a time of great achievement in their lives. As Irene explained at the end of our interview: 'I've got to be honest now, if we hadn't have gone on the hostel, I don't think we'd have mingled as much, or had so many friends as we had. I also think that part of me, or part of us, got people together, which was another thing I did, in life, you know. So I've achieved that.'

Hostel horrors and delights

The Tyases' mixed hostel memories capture the ambivalence of so many who look back on their first Australian experiences. The well-known negative judgements about physical conditions, poor food, lack of privacy and objectionable neighbours coexist with enthusiastic recall of a positive introduction, the ease of making new friends, communal sociability, and even good food! The first negative impression could be enough to drive anxious new arrivals away promptly, at least if they had any savings to use. Maggie and Robert Smith, arriving in Adelaide in 1966, were horrified by the attitude of long-staying migrants with no ambition to move on and promptly dubbed the hostel, 'Butlins without the laughs'. Within days they left for Melbourne and found their own flat. Echoing a common complaint, their problem was not the hostel itself but the occupants. Maggie recalled, 'We ended up in this hostel where people ... just accepted living in a hostel and they were quite happy living in a hostel, no, but we thought ooh, oh don't like it here'. More commonly, once checked in and given the standard issue of 'the knife, fork and spoon, toilet roll, mug, and then shown where the toilet facilities were', bewildered new arrivals made the best of the austere facilities. But their mixed memories testify to a complex set of responses to a mostly unexpected episode in their new lives.[16]

Given the radical differences in standards between hostels, their gradual renovation over time and the huge variation in migrants' expectations and class backgrounds, the contradictory reactions are hardly surprising. The 'bloody awful' conditions, with prison-style food, that Albert and Anne Lougher remembered from their brief stay in a Brisbane hostel had much to do with the fact that the sex segregation they had endured on the voyage continued in the hostel. Yet for Wendy Jay, who had suffered appalling sickness on the ship with three young children, her brief stay in half a hut at the Melbourne Exhibition Buildings reception hostel was a comfortable relief, with food served by 'very pleasant women' from the Country Women's Associ-ation. Others describe an initial shock, but 'in the morning when we'd had a sleep it wasn't so bad as we imagined'. Dorothy Rooms was appalled by the grim facilities at Bathurst, especially the primitive outdoor toilets with canvas 'doors'. 'They'd no right to have brought us to places like that, they shouldn't have admitted anybody until they'd got it all organized.... It was terrible.' Yet Dorothy balances this negative memory with her enjoyment of the 'nicest porridge I ever tasted' and the campfires migrants lit outside the unheated huts each night for warmth. The campfires became instant centres of sociability: 'we'd sit round talking, you know, some people would come to ours and people would go to theirs … I really enjoyed it even though it was rough'. Irene Spencer, similarly, quickly recovered from shocked dismay at the basic facilities at Point Walter Hostel in Perth, and vividly recalls her spirits lifting once they gathered for a briefing, followed by 'a lovely meal laid on, nice cup of tea, very friendly atmosphere'. The hostel stay was short while the Spencers organized work and a rented house, but Irene recalled it as 'a wonderful stay there really because all the days were spent on the beach, our meals were cooked for us, *excellent* meals'. As if to underline her affection for Point Walter, she took work there as a waitress, and fondly remembers watching new migrants arrive, seeing them through the lens of her own positive outlook. 'And that was amazing wasn't it? I used to watch them come in all pale and apprehensive and I used to think, won't be long before you'll be like me, nice and brown.'[17]

Hostel residents of the mid-1960s, like Irene Spencer, could be bene-ficiaries of gradual improvements to hostel facilities made over two decades. But experiences and impressions varied from the start. Even in the mid-1950s Les and Joyce Dalley enjoyed the unusual privilege of their own kitchen in the half Nissen hut they were assigned at Gepps Cross Hostel in Adelaide. Most strikingly, those who moved between hostels were quick to make sharp comparisons. After Dorothy Rooms's grim start at Bathurst in the early 1950s, her family experienced two further hostels in Victoria, first at Yallourn and later at Williamstown. At Yallourn she remembered that 'we were treated like blinkin' DPs' by a dictatorial manager (see Figure 21). But Williamstown she regarded as 'wonderful, it was great'. The manager was 'marvellous', and they were able to swim in the nearby bay; but much of the difference had to do with the added amenity of a community hall 'where you could hold dances or concerts, whatever, or meetings. It was wonderful.' The impression of greater physical comforts was accentuated when they visited friends in the Brooklyn hostel, the former woolshed hated by its residents and notorious for power failures, 'so dismal and dark'. Dorothy's husband exclaimed on leaving, ' "By God!" he said, "I couldn't live there." … I said "No, neither could I … we're very lucky", because ours was nice and bright and clean' (see Figure 22).

21 In 1951 a neighbour at Yallourn Hostel drew this cartoon of the Rooms family's Nissen hut in Pauline Rooms's autograph book. Dorothy Rooms recalls that at Yallourn 'we were treated like blinkin' DPs' by the dictatorial manager Mr Ford

22 The Rooms family in the sitting room of their hut at Williamstown Hostel in 1953: 'Dorothy (junior) and Pauline standing, me and hubby and Albert junior seated. The fireplace was made by my husband which made it more homely. The room was heated by a single bar electric fire'

At another woolshed, Rosewater in Port Adelaide in 1951, John and Annabella Clark were shocked to find, after an initial stay at Bathurst, that 'Bathurst was a hotel compared to this'. But their frustration with the grim overcrowding, in tightly subdivided cubicles, was relieved within two months, when renovated units that were 'much more presentable' became available. While the frustrations of communal living and lack of privacy continued, John thought that for hard-pressed families the refurbished accommodation was reasonable.[18]

While physical conditions loom large in accounts of those primitive buildings, many of the more positive memories dwell on the sociability facilitated by crowded hostels. The community halls, the friendly campfires, solidarity induced by shared grievances, and simple neighbourliness, as we saw with the Tyas family, now make for powerful memories. Nicknames like 'pommie block' and 'little England' recall groups of close-knit British migrants who depended on each other for support and social life.[19] This was especially the case for women with children, who often spent their entire days in the hostel while husbands were out working or seeking work. At Finsbury Hostel in Adelaide Margaret Hill was at one point left alone with her five children while her husband worked at Maralinga. She became acutely conscious of the women's isolation from the outside world and craved even simple pleasures like window shopping. Close friendships formed, along with close-knit networks of women without the accustomed duties of housework and cooking. 'So we sat about in one or other of the flats with our knitting or sewing, drank tea and complained. The only way to get a change of scene was to go into a different flat, we did of course have our children to care for, but they seemed to play together well most of the time.' Vanessa Seymour, 7 years old at the Brooklyn hostel, recalls spending much time in the laundry, 'because we used to go and find our mums in the laundries, and I think the women used to talk in the laundries' (see Figures 23 and 24). The laundry networks proved to be a boon for Mary Clayton at Point Walter. When she broke her shoulder the other women promptly 'mucked around and got me help, got me help.... They did my washing for me, and no trouble.' For Mary the hostel experience was part of a 'big adventure', enriched by friendships and good times. Her husband, a 'big organizer' like Cliff Tyas, arranged a party at Christmastime, 'bought some little prizes, and we had little games and whatever, Christmas, lovely, it was lovely'.

If communal living naturally fostered close friendships and sociability, it could also provoke severe conflict. It is hardly surprising that such extensive mixing of classes, age groups and ethnic backgrounds produced tension. The most obvious clash, at least in ethnically mixed camps, was between the British and other nationalities, although accounts of these among our informants are few. In the early years there were undercurrents of British–German antagonism and stories of Hitler youth group remnants taunting the British, as Vanessa Seymour recalls, with slogans like 'we'll get you next time'.[20] But in mixed hostels close friendships between British and German couples were not uncommon.[21]

More importantly, perhaps, it was in their day-to-day observation of each other that the British began to define themselves as new migrants. Newcomers were quick to notice cliques of disenchanted hostel dwellers. Peggy Amor recalled, 'Somebody said to me once, "Don't listen!" She said: "All they do is complain here."' Such impressions provided ample opportunity for comparative self-evaluation, and the most common retrospective response for the critics was to define themselves as fundamentally different from the 'others'. This could be reinforced at the time by anti-social migrant behaviour, which aggravated the primitive living conditions. Theft was a common problem, and the victims, like Margaret Hill, were quick to connect a drop in standards to communal living.

To put it mildly, life on the hostel was rough, and made worse by certain people who forgot, or did not know, the basic decencies of communal living. Children ran riot without parental supervision. At mealtimes some children used the canteen as a playground, sending slices of toast zooming through the air, smearing jam and butter over chairs and tables, leaving barely touched plates of food all over the place, throwing salt cellars.... There was a lot of thieving; clothes went from the clothes line if left overnight, and cutlery, cups, trays, even plates of bread or other food disappeared off tables if left unattended (say you went back to the servery for something you had forgotten). A filthy mess was created as well. Floors were used instead of toilets. Toilets left unflushed. Used water left in baths.... Hostel management did their best, and the cleaners came around frequently, but at times in the hot weather the smell and flies made visits to the ablution blocks a nightmare for the more responsible tenants.[22]

The 'more responsible tenants' were quick to define their difference from others, but it is significant that while alien standards and habits were an irritant, the most emphatic complaint dwelt upon difference in 'attitude'. Years later this remains the major point of self-differentiation. In the Introduction we saw how John and Sylvia Cannon's alienation from 'whingeing Poms' – complainers with no intention to leave the hostel, simply sitting out their time before returning to Britain – reinforced a desire to find their own accommodation. These differences quickly became a central measure of identity for new migrants keen to get on, and it is no surprise that then and now an instinctive point of contrast coincides with the most prominent stereotype of British migrants – the 'whingeing Poms'. 'I never heard so many whingeing Pommies in my life', Peggy Amor declared, and Irene Spencer insisted that, grumbling as they arrived at the hostel, they 'give the Pommies a

23 Frances Akehurst in the laundry at Gepps Cross Hostel, South Australia, c. 1957. Hostel residents often complained about the communal laundries and washrooms, but for migrant women the laundries were also places of sociability and support

24 Frances and Carol Akehurst hang out the washing at Gepps Cross Hostel. Toddler Susan, born in Adelaide's Queen Elizabeth Hospital in 1956, stands in the laundry doorway

bad name, the whingeing Pommies'. 'Whingeing' in this sense is also code for other attitudes, as in Maureen Carter's family's prompt judgement that too many residents 'weren't trying to better themselves, they weren't trying to save to get off the hostel and rent accommodation. They were just languishing in this sort of welfare mentality, which my father didn't think was good.' Maureen and John Butts quickly dissociated themselves from apparently permanent residents at Preston. 'They amazed me, you know', Maureen commented. 'Did they expect to be given … a big house and job … and I think a lot of them did, I think they really thought the red carpet would have been put out for them and everything would have been laid on.' For those migrants who had left postwar Britain disillusioned about 'welfare mentalities' and loss of the work ethic, the 'whingers' symbolized the very British weaknesses they had hoped to escape.[23]

In practice, of course, the distinction between 'whingers' and 'non-whingers' was never clear cut, especially in the perceptions of migrants themselves. Dorothy Rooms, a passionate Mancunian, insisted that whingeing was determined by regional origin: 'it was mainly the southerners, it wasn't the northerners, didn't seem to complain as much, I don't know why. But it was. I mean the food was eatable. If it's eatable, why should you complain?' Yet Dorothy also admitted that she and her husband did their own share of grumbling and protesting; in Yallourn Albert Rooms led a successful protest about unfair 'rationing' of butter, and in 1952 the Rooms family joined a Melbourne protest march about hostel conditions. Margaret Hill, a long-term hostel stayer, stressed that she and her husband kept their grievances to themselves, but her husband was prone to 'letting off steam … I'd hear him with the other men, they were all having the same type of moan'. Her focus on male 'moaners' is intriguing in light of regular taunting of hostel women as whingers by hostel staff and outside shopkeepers. 'Almost anybody, anybody that thought you were complaining of anything, and even if it was a justifiable complaint, you were still a whingeing Pom.' Margaret also admitted that 'we did an awful lot of whingeing when we first came'.

The point of this is not to highlight contradictory memories, but to underline ways in which British complaining was rapidly stereotyped, even by the British themselves, into a largely British, more often English, ethnic characteristic. It is rare for migrants not to complain – to voice their shock at new and strange conditions, especially in the artificial and primitive state of postwar hostel living – but judgement of the 'whingers' provided a convenient label by which migrants might begin to define themselves. The stereotype of hostel whingers has also concealed – at the time and in popular memory and historical judgement – the validity of complaints about hostel conditions, and the continuum of ways in which hostel residents expressed their concern and challenged living conditions. From informal grumbling through formal complaints to outbursts of direct action such as the Preston rent strike in 1967, the concerns and activism of hostel dwellers deserve further research.[24]

Love on the hostel: illicit sex, adolescence and the ethnic mix

The conduct of sexual relationships in cramped hostel conditions is probably the most understated theme in migrant testimony. Frequent references to the chronic lack of privacy often mask embarrassment at the difficulty of conducting a normal intimate relationship beyond the hearing of others. The thin walls, Margaret Hill recalled, meant that 'if you wanted to have a row with your husband you had to go for a walk'. But sexual intimacy was not a matter to be resolved by going for a walk; it demanded restraint and discretion, with potential for marital tension. Despite the difficulties Margaret was aware of undercurrents of illicit sexual relationships in the hostel, and recalled her 'great shock' when she heard rumours of 'wife swapping'.[25]

If sexual awareness 'on the hostel' was normally suppressed, the presence of young 'foreign' single men could bring potential tensions to the surface in explosive ways. Mary Rose Liverani, who experienced hostel life as a 13-year-old Glaswegian, evokes these tensions vividly in her autobiography from an adolescent girl's perspective.[26] At 'Kershley', near 'Gullawobblong' (possibly an alias for Wollongong; the names are fictionalized), the British migrants were housed alongside seventy young single Italian men. Fears of sexual liaisons were rife, with British parents fearful about the young Italian men and their growing daughters (some men recalled their Italian wartime enemies as womanizers and rapists). Liverani's story extends to English and Dutch wives who fell in love with Italian men – so that fathers returned to England and Holland alone with their children. For Mary herself the threat became personal when she came home from school to find her mother teaching an Italian man English in their hut. In an awkward scene Mary berated her mother and told the man never to come again. Other British men lurked near the toilets waiting to assault young Italians suspected of wooing their wives.[27]

Awareness of illicit relationships was rarely far from the surface in Mary's family.

Margaret had given up counting those who passed her window at night. We watched them in silence from behind the curtain. My mother told us to keep our traps shut, but people knew just the same. Sometimes a couple would leave the hostel suddenly, the husband abruptly having decided to rent a house even if it was more than he could afford. Sometimes a single man left hurriedly, having exhorted a promise from a friend to send on the luggage.[28]

Liverani's account is entangled with her own adolescent fantasies and romantic images of the young Italian men, beautiful singers with strange manners and a passion for exotic foods. A high point in the hostel was a Christmas dance hosted by the Italian men who cooked Italian foods and presented each woman with a camellia, to the delight of the women and the glares of their husbands; the event was climaxed by a fierce marital row.[29] But despite its romantic gloss Liverani's account finds an echo in other testimony. Dorothy Roman noticed a marital break-up in the hostel when a young Yugoslav chef ran off with one of the wives, but she insisted that as hard-working parents they simply 'didn't have time for mischief at all!' At a Melbourne hostel Betty Richardson witnessed an episode in which British men, including her husband, beat up a group of young Italians, ostensibly for late night rowdiness. The aggravation had much to do with generational and cultural resentments sparked off by older British working males losing their sleep. But in Betty's case the episode was aggravated by a jealous husband. Mario, an 18-year-old Italian, was pursuing their eldest daughter (according to Betty he had 'no chance'), but a friend suggested to her husband that Mario was more interested in Betty. Jealous accusations and a serious quarrel ensued, and after reconciliation the family returned to England. The story lacks the romantic flavour of Liverani's prose, but conveys some of the simmering tensions around sexuality on the hostel.[30]

On the other hand Liverani's account misses the real potential for sexual danger for young women on the hostel. Threats came not just from hostel residents but from outsiders with easy access. In 1964 at Cabramatta 19-year-old Maureen Carter was acutely conscious of the risks. Local boys, many of them Italian, sought out young hostel girls, their menace and opportunity enhanced by car ownership, a thing unheard of in Maureen's rural Wales, and a hint of changes wrought in Australian suburban life by the 1960s compared to the 1950s.

I did not like the atmosphere there of the boys from the surrounding district coming onto the hostel in their cars, 'cause don't forget our boyfriends in Wales didn't have cars! There was, wasn't the money. And picking up girls, and — there were rapes. Girls were taken out to St Mary's. I mean, I didn't even know where St Mary's was. But in those days Cabramatta was very close to the country and, no, you know you had to sort of make it very clear as a young single female, that you were a good girl and you weren't like 'those girls'.

Being labelled a 'good girl' clearly affected Maureen's reputation among her hostel peers. 'I was called a "snob" again, because I wouldn't go off in the cars with the boys.' But for young women the risks were genuine.[31]

For young boys growing up the relationship with outsiders formed a very different kind of threat, but also a sinister challenge. In the early 1960s at

Bunnarong Hostel (near Matraville in south Sydney), Richard MacDonald saw very little of his parents, who worked long hours, and so for about five years, between the ages of 7 and 12, he spent most of his time outside school hours with his 'mates'. 'There was no sort of internal family thing ... I'd always eat with my mates, so that I'd never, you know, you'd never actually sit down as a family, or very few did.' Bunnarong was a predominantly British hostel, but close to a mixed European one, which provoked 'a lot of rivalry between the Australians, the British and the Europeans'. As Richard grew older he joined the 'gangs' which formed and ventured out on the 'quite serious gang fights that used to go on between them', retreating after external 'forays' to the protected 'compound' of the hostel. It was a 'pretty exciting' time for Richard. 'I mean, basically we'd congregate in groups of anything of up to a hundred kids and go on rampages.... And big "rumbles" in the park, and all that sort of stuff. Not very pleasant, ... but it used to happen.'[32]

Richard's youthful masculine hostel world could hardly be further removed from the nervous feminine one of Maureen Carter, the struggling times of Margaret Hill, the social life of the Tyas family or the fleeting experience of the Butts, who were so anxious to move on. Whatever the hostel dwellers' own personal experience, life on the hostel could be a critical stage for developing attitudes to Australia and forming an identity as British migrants. At the same time, once migrants left the hostel, they were to find a radically different world, with new challenges. Marjorie Foster, who spent only two weeks at Greylands Hostel in Perth, with her husband, was struck by the large numbers intending to return to Britain after two years on the hostel, and reflected on their failure to experience the 'real' Australia. 'And they went back. But, you see, it's really not Australia. It's a bit of no-man's-land; it's neither Britain nor Australia, so you can't judge the Australian way of life until you actually move off the hostel.'[33] In the following chapters we explore the varied ways in which, once 'off the hostel', British migrants confronted that 'Australian way of life'.

Notes

1 Joynson, '"Something You Like to Forget"', pp. 106– 26.
2 *Ibid.*; Sluga, *Bonegilla*; Peters, *Milk and Honey*, pp. 117– 21; Wilton and Bosworth, *Old Worlds and New Australia*, p. 109. By contrast, in 1966 James Jupp wrote that for British as well as non-English-speaking immigrants the Commonwealth hostels were 'a fraud and a disgrace' (*Arrivals and Departures*, p. 28).
3 Wilton and Bosworth, *Old Worlds and New Australia*, p. 114.
4 Hardie interview US; Hands (pseudonym) written account US.
5 Unless otherwise noted, all quotations in this section are from the interview with Irene and Clifford Tyas US.
6 On 3 March 1966 a letter to Cliff from the Victorian Housing Commission confirmed

that 'unfortunately, there is a large number of prior applications awaiting attention and a waiting period of somewhat lengthy duration may be involved' (Tyas file US).

7 The new and old tariffs were cited on the front page of the *Herald* (Melbourne), 4 March 1967.

8 *Ibid.*

9 'Who wants to live in a hostel – or be dragged before a court?', authorized by the Combined Migrant Hostels Central Committee, 'with the support of a number of Victorian trade unions', c. March 1967, copy in the Tyas file US.

10 *Herald* (Melbourne), 3 April 1967.

11 *Tribune*, 19 April 1967; *Australian Women's Weekly*, 10 May 1967.

12 *Australian*, 10 April 1967.

13 Unlabelled press clipping in the Tyas file US.

14 On government attitudes see Joynson, ' "Something You Like to Forget" '. For a personal account of an earlier rent strike, in Melbourne in 1952, see Rooms interview US.

15 *Preston Post*, 18 September 1968.

16 Maggie and Robert Smith interview US; Cannon interview LU.

17 Lougher interview LU; Jay interview LU; Farnfield interview US; Rooms interview US; Spencer interview US.

18 Dalley interview LU; Rooms interview US; Clark interview LU.

19 'Pommie block' was recalled by Jack Roscoe (interview US) in Darwin. Christina Daly (interview US) refers to a 'little England' mentality at the Annandale hostel in Sydney, and tightly knit liaisons with local English merchants, which she and her husband were keen to avoid.

20 Seymour interview LU; Clayton interview LU.

21 For example, Carruthers interview LU.

22 Amor interview LU; Hill, *Corrugated Castles*, p. 108, and interview LU; on theft see also interviews with Wall LU, Foster LU and Carter LU.

23 Amor interview LU; Spencer interview US; Carter interview LU; Butts interview LU; see also Chapter 2.

24 Rooms interview US; Hill interview LU.

25 Hill interview LU.

26 Liverani, *The Winter Sparrows*, pp. 195– 291.

27 *Ibid.*, pp. 235– 91.

28 *Ibid.*, p. 287.

29 *Ibid.*, pp. 259– 70.

30 Roman interview LU; interview US (confidentiality requested).

31 Carter interview LU.

32 MacDonald interview LU.

33 Foster interview LU.

6

An Australian working life

Many of us today take for granted that work is central to our identity, our sense of well being and usually our material welfare and success. This has invariably been the case for migrants, and not just for male breadwinners. In the search for a new life they are acutely conscious that their fortune in earning an income without delay could make or break the entire enterprise. For many postwar British migrants too – both men and women – the workforce was one of the main channels through which they came to know Australia and Australians. Working life, therefore, looms large in the ways migrants recount their stories, whether in terms of adapting to Australia, dazzling success, battling and survival or a sense of wounding failure.

On the surface this might seem to contradict the mindset of most people leaving Britain in the postwar years. We saw in the opening chapters that this was not a mass migration of the unemployed. For most people the availability of work in Britain was of small account in their decision to leave. Jobs were plentiful and factors like lack of opportunity for advancement, climate, future family prospects, adventure and the generalized promise of a 'good life' in the new country were the greater motivating factors. But once the umbilical cord with employment in Britain had been severed the prospect of work in Australia, and the course of subsequent careers, assumed pressing significance and could overshadow equally important priorities like housing, schools and family cohesion. Its importance is underlined by the frequent domination of 'job talk' in our interviews – particularly, but not exclusively, among men. How work was experienced varied considerably according to age, gender, class, time and place of arrival and other factors. In this chapter, with an eye on these different elements, we will examine ways in which migrants recall the quest for work and the meaning of their working life in Australia.

First encounters and fear of 'failure'

From the earliest years of the assisted passage scheme the pressing Australian labour shortage and a desire to privilege the British over continental Europeans dictated a virtually 'open door' approach to applicants' occupational backgrounds. Hence British men and women, the skilled and unskilled, white-collar, blue-collar and professional, all found it easy to obtain a passage. But not all of these were likely to find their preferred forms of employment upon arrival. Indeed, from the official perspective there were quite explicit preferences. Greg Humphries, one of the early selection officers posted to London in 1948, noted the desperate need for labour in key industrial projects like the Snowy River scheme and Bell Bay aluminium in Tasmania. 'We were basically looking for anybody who could make a contribution, particularly physically, towards the development of industries. People who didn't qualify were virtually the lame, the old and the blind. It was so easy, as open as that.'[1] Not surprisingly, among the mixture of British migrants disembarking in Australia, few were suited to heavy labour or engineering in the Snowy Mountains. Women in particular, but also the majority of British blue-collar and white-collar men, especially when married, gave little thought to such employment. The quest for the most suitable and best-paying work, therefore, became the most pressing issue upon arrival, even in an environment of labour shortage.

With boatloads of migrants regularly disembarking in the major cities there was no shortage of advice on how best to find that first job. Adaptability was the key message, and while jobs were invariably plentiful, except during brief periods of recession like the early 1960s, the accent was on finding any work in the short term as a stepping stone to more suitable positions.[2] Recruiting officers routinely gave this advice, regardless of the country or background of applicants.[3] Looking back in 1984 on her own family's experience, Janet Bloomefield encapsulated the common view: 'I think you have to be prepared to accept what you find.... Also in employment be prepared to do anything that comes along, not to be too proud and only go for the trade that you're trained for, because obviously financial standing is the first priority when you've got a family.'[4]

The enormous stress on making a good start, though, could place a huge burden on family breadwinners, usually male, to begin earning within days of arrival, so that anxiety levels began to rise from the moment of docking. Some migrants had already heard stories of making good from networks of friends or family members and were anxious to emulate them.[5] Optimistic talk among fellow migrants on the voyage about the chances of 'making a fortune' helped to raise expectations.[6] By the 1980s there were some rare examples of billionaires like Alan Bond, the erstwhile signwriter, to nurture inspiring myths of self-made British Australians – at least before Bond's uninspiring downfall.[7] But dramatic 'rags to riches' stories among British migrants were rare in the early years. Expectations were more likely to be kept at a high pitch by the general air of optimism and publicity pointing to the benefits of stable employment, better wages and a superior 'Australian way of life'.[8] But there were risks in this upbeat outlook. The seeming impossibility of return inclined ten pound migrants to anxious job seeking, as they realized, like Vera and

Bernard Makewell in 1954, that they had truly burnt their bridges.[9] With this 'make or break' psychology, difficulties encountered in the early stages of job searching might tarnish an individual's or family's outlook permanently.

Richard MacDonald's family story illustrates ways in which initial disappointment could provoke a downward cycle of under-employment and family misfortune. Richard was only 8 years old when his family emigrated from Glasgow to Sydney in 1961 during an Australian downturn in employment. His father had been a Glasgow fireman, and, along with his three brothers, all of them firemen, lived in a block of flats provided by the fire brigade. He also ran a small window-cleaning business and so was doing well when, in Richard's view, he was 'sucked in' by the Australian 'promotional campaign'. After emigration officers' assurances that he would easily find work in the Sydney Fire Brigade he was optimistic about moving his wife and three children to Australia. But within days of arrival these bright prospects were dashed when the Fire Brigade informed him that he was 'too light' to qualify as a fireman. With no fallback position in mind, he set out on a desperate search for any form of work which would at least cover the hostel rent. A series of short-term, ill-paid jobs, for which he was unqualified, followed. Limited transport from the hostel, first in rural Rooty Hill and later at Bunnarong in south Sydney, forced him to leave at two in the morning to travel to distant work, at one point as a waiter at the Coogee sports club. The experience was seared into family memory as the start of a downward cycle: 'I just remember from my dad, again, the rejection from the Fire Brigade sort of started off a chain rejection of, you know, jobs here and there and whatever he could get. That's why we were on there for such a long time.'[10]

The marginal income from poorly paid and intermittent work was inadequate to enable a move to independent housing, and so the MacDonalds seemed condemned to long-term hostel living. After five years of hostel existence, in desperation, Richard's father joined the army, and was given army housing, first on a small and remote army camp in Wallangarra, Queensland, and later at the Holsworthy military barracks west of Sydney. In both cases this subjected the family to further years of institutional life, often with the women and children alone, while Richard's father did two tours of duty in Vietnam. War trauma later saw him placed in a psychiatric institution for seventeen years; when he was finally discharged he took increasingly to drink and found it difficult to hold down any job. Despite long conflict the McDonald parents doggedly stuck together, although their youngest son, who regarded Richard as a father figure, failed to adjust to the world outside institutions and spent eighteen years in jail.

Richard recalled the lesson his father learned from the migrant experience: 'he said the old cliché to me that, you know, "You never really knew you had it all until you *left* it all!" [laugh] He never really got it back again!' The observation was apt. A man of drive and achievement in Scotland, he could reasonably have expected to make the best of things in Australia, rather than suffering half a lifetime of unstable employment, institutionalization and family dysfunction. Surprisingly, Mr McDonald never contemplated return: 'my dad always said that he made the decision, he'll stick to it and he'll never reverse it'. Richard could have become another victim of misfortune, like his brother, but he was determined to carve out a more successful career. Chafing at life on the army barracks and at quasi-parental duties with his brother, he left at 15 for King's Cross, was a father by 18, and then pursued his musical interests, becoming the owner-manager of a large company managing pop artists like Jimmy Barnes. Bankruptcy led him to shift into a catering career, but his employment has remained stable and, as an inner suburban home owner in Sydney in the 1990s, he later exemplified all the characteristics of the successful child migrant.

Such grim family stories are in the minority, even among returnees, but they do testify to the importance of the first encounter with the world of work. An early employment disaster could prompt return to Britain well before other processes of adaptation had set in.[11] On the other hand, a different version of the early disaster story connects it to the triumphal happy ending which is central to so many migrant narratives. Margaret Reardon's account of her family's calamitous sponsorship and employment letdown in remote New South Wales serves to underline their conquest of hardship and ultimate success.[12] Such stories are vindicating narratives which attach central importance to the early struggles to get ahead.

Urban priorities, rural realities

The Reardon story reminds us that not all the early occupations, and occasionally even longer-term careers, of postwar immigrants were located in the cities and towns. As the Australian authorities intended, most postwar migrants of all backgrounds found work in urban environments, or at least in remote heavy industry projects like the Snowy River scheme and mining projects. This feature distinguished postwar Australian immigration sharply from its earlier forms. Even between the wars the emphasis on importing a rural workforce and an incipient body of yeoman farmers had characterized immigration policy. The personal and social disasters of those 'settlement' schemes, which took urban workers from British industrial towns and expected them to start from scratch on remote and unsuitable land, are well known.[13] After the war the new and urgent priority of industrial development marked a dramatic shift, and one would have expected a British urban workforce to transfer readily to the Australian equivalent. Advice books recognized the highly urbanized nature of Australia, and worked hard to dispel bush myths about the country's society and character.[14] But the minority who moved to rural occupations were important exceptions; their stories remind us of ways in which the Australia they discovered was different from the old world, and of the kind of adventure, opportunity and open space which many migrants hoped to find.

There were a host of reasons why people came to risk the unknown challenges of rural work rather than the more familiar job in the city. The Reardons' short-lived skirmish with farm work stemmed from the accident of engaging with an unknown sponsor; they clearly exercised no informed choice and had no idea what to expect. Such cases were driven by immediate necessity and lack of information, and could make for a demoralizing start. But even the better informed could find the most testing conditions. Bridget Pluis was 11 when her widowed mother brought her five children to Sydney where she accepted the job of a cook on an isolated sheep station in southern New South Wales. Her mother was the genteel, well-spoken daughter of an Anglican clergyman; as one of the 'outside' staff, she was nicknamed the 'old Sheila' and treated with contempt and anti-English taunting by owners and the all-male staff alike. A first job like this was calculated to induce immediate plans to return, but Bridget thought her mother's refusal to accept defeat proved her resilience and set the stage for successful adaptation. The stakes were less momentous for young single sojourners, who could be much more light-hearted and short-term in their intentions; they often took readily to the well-trodden pathways of seasonal itinerant workers, from fruit picking to pig farming. Nigel Heath, a young single man who arrived in 1959, recalled that 'there was always work in the bush. They'd take anybody in the bush then.'[15]

The more unusual rural stories are those told by city dwellers who came determined to make a go of life on the land. Although a minority, these stories say much about what migration to Australia could represent to Britons in search of a fresh start, greater opportunity and, often, adventure. Alfred and Win Cook had every reason to be satisfied with their lifestyle in south west England when they sold up and moved to Tasmania in 1950.[16] Alf had acquired valuable radio technician experience in the air force, but after the war he continued his prewar administrative career with a petrol company, rising rapidly to the position of office manager. This supported a comfortable living for Alf and Win and their two young children, and soon after the war they bought their own house in Exeter. Photographic records from this time suggest a contented family life, with time devoted to family leisure activities. Neither felt any deep discontent and Alf was sure that 'if I'd stayed with the firm I could, well, would have retired at 60 and I would have had a pretty good pension'. But Alf and Win shared a feeling that this was not enough, either for themselves or for the children.

25 The Cook family at King's Park overlooking Perth in 1950. During the stop-over at Fremantle, migrants bound for the eastern states often visited King's Park and photographed themselves amidst the exotic splendour of the new land

26 The Cook family from Exeter could not afford their dream of a farming life in England, but through the assisted passage scheme and sponsorship from a sheep farmer in Tasmania the Cooks found 'Our first home in Tassie … there are acres of common land outside on which we will graze our cow when we get it!' In this photograph daughter Pauline plays with the neighbours' pony

Alf recalled that 'I sort of felt, well, I didn't want to be in an office for the rest of my life'. Living in medium-size towns in the south west had inspired dreams of moving on to the land; 'we'd always been outdoor people', Alf stressed, 'and I'd had several holidays on farms and I liked farm life'.

Financially, any prospect of the Cooks realizing their farming dream in England was unattainable. They had discussed the alternative of emigration

27 Win Cook took to the multitude of farm tasks with gusto. Here she spreads out the fleece from their pet sheep, 'Phillip', which has just been sheared by her husband Alf

since 1945 and insisted that the decision was entirely mutual, partly for future family welfare and partly out of a sense of adventure. Unusually, neither could remember who first thought of the idea of emigrating. Win's reflections hint at the strong sense of shared optimism which pervades their joint narrative: 'we just thought that, it was an adventure really, we, and it would be better for the kids, yes'. Their enthusiasms were facilitated by easy availability of the ten pound fare and direct contact through Australia House with a sponsor, a Tasmanian farmer.

The Cooks' powerful sense of optimism was sustained throughout the voyage on the *Asturias* and with their first contacts in Tasmania. Their sponsor, a sheep grazier near Ross, hired Alf as a jackeroo and provided a small cottage, a mile from the station (see Figure 26). The cottage had been furnished but was reminiscent of the kind of building which horrified others who were not prepared for relatively primitive rural conditions. But throughout the inter-view, and in the diary Alf kept from embarkation to settlement in Ross, there is no hint of disillusion or regret. After their first inspection of the cottage, Alf, with the budding farmer's eye, recorded:

The ground looks to be very good, a chocolate colour and quite heavy with a rather peaty consistency about it; it has been mostly dug over fairly recently and there is still a chicken run intact so we are hoping to get a few birds as soon as we move out. The chicken house is in poor shape but wood is very cheap here and easy to obtain so I shall soon be able to get that in order. The garden is more or less triangular in shape so it is hard to say just what size it is, but altogether we must have somewhere about five times the area of the back garden at Wimpole, – and then of course there are acres of common land outside on which we will graze our cow when we get it![17]

Alf's enthusiasm was shared by Win, who also took to the multitude of farm tasks with gusto, enjoying a steep learning curve, especially when she had to milk their new cow. 'Oh, when we left England I was just frightened of cows, I'd walk right round a field rather than touch a cow; the first thing I had to do was milk the cow, or else!' Early photographs reinforce the couple's insistence on their rapid adjustment; besides milking, Win shared in the process of shearing 'Phillip', the pet sheep, and preparing the fleece (see Figure 27). She also helped the grazier's wife, surprisingly teaching her the traditional rural skill of bottling fruit. On the *Taroona*, the Melbourne–Devonport ferry, Alf and Win had vowed to each other, 'Well, now we're Tasmanians'; as if to seal her determined adaptation, Win soon became an active member of the Country Women's Association. Here she found that her Englishness, far from being a liability, was regarded as a curiosity which assisted her acceptance.

After a year at Ross the Cooks were eager to try out the daunting challenge of farming life on their own. While they were able to buy 33 acres for a sheep run at Sidmouth on the Tamar, the problem of earning an adequate income off the land prevented their dream being fully realized. The sheep run at Sidmouth, a peach orchard and florist trade nearby at Legana and, later, Win's school lunch shop at Exeter (Tasmania), were inadequate to support the family, and the venture remained at what is now dubbed 'hobby farm' status. But they were close enough to Launceston for Alf to supplement the earnings with a steady income, first in office work and later in a succession of jobs in radio engineering. Eventually they sold off their rural enterprises, but only in retirement did they move to Lindisfarne, a suburb of Hobart.

While their original goal of becoming farmers foundered, the Cooks' working life satisfied their ambition of remaining close to rural conditions and communities, a preference confirmed for them over large cities during their brief sojourn in the more 'rushed' atmosphere of Melbourne after arrival. Alf's radio work continued to facilitate trips 'into the countryside … something that I was always keen on'. Most prominent in their memories now, underlined by the photographic and diary record, are the challenging times of their first year in that cramped farm cottage at Ross. Win insists that the entire venture was something they could never have attempted in England, and the Cooks underscored that sense of fulfilment in 2000 when, with a companion family from the *Asturias* in 1950, they brought their extended families together for a fiftieth anniversary celebration of their arrival.

Such positive stories invariably skate over the painful process of urbanites' adaptation to Australian rural life, especially for women. Mary and Leonard Thomas, a schoolteacher and artist respectively, who emigrated in 1952 from the outskirts of Edinburgh to Tasmania, were comparatively successful as dairy farmers. But Mary's most vivid recollections of the experience dwell upon the culture shock following her rapid transformation from a Scottish primary school teacher to a hard-worked farmer's wife. This was magnified by traditional rural male attitudes towards women, which did nothing to help her willing adjustment:

I can remember being rather resentful. There was a group of men, I think they shared jobs around the farms, you know, they, they'd come and help each other out, and I had to take morning tea or whatever out to these men, and they virtually ignored me, and that came very hard. I didn't, I didn't like it, I didn't show my resentment, but at the same time I thought it was a bit poor, yes.[18]

Mary's disapproval stemmed partly from a sense that she was a victim of bad manners, partly from the knowledge that she was an equal working partner in the family enterprise. Many women from the 1950s insist that they were reared on 'old-fashioned' attitudes to gender roles, but Mary's experience is a reminder that such attitudes did not reign supreme.

Uncertain beginnings: sponsors, hostels and employment

Rural success stories, alongside rural calamities, were undoubtedly minority experiences, although they do illuminate ways in which the search for new employment was linked to the imagining of Australia, and so often bound up with wider dreams of adventure and a new start. Most of these dreams were, of course, played out in government-targeted urban or industrial settings. Australian federal and state authorities were especially anxious to direct workers to areas of greatest need, often in unskilled or unpleasant jobs avoided by the native Australian workforce. For displaced persons, and for most assisted continental Europeans, the employment agreements with governments were unambiguous; they were required to work for two years where directed, and refusal could result in deportation.[19] For the British there was no such threat, although some who were sponsored by state governments believed they were bound by a virtual indentured labour contract. In general the freedom to work as desired meant that the British benefited from substantial positive discrimination compared to other Europeans; this makes for stark contrasts in British and other migrant stories about first jobs and initial work experience. Such contrasts in treatment prompted one historian to claim that the British were 'pampered' compared to others.[20] But conditions affecting the landing of the first job for the British still varied enormously, and could do much to shape subsequent experiences and attitudes. One of the most important differences was between those with prearranged jobs and housing through sponsors, and those who endured the uncertainty of job searching while resident in the government hostel.

The advantages of a preliminary arrangement with a sponsor employer could make a lasting difference to a family's outlook from the first day. As the rural stories illustrate, sponsorship could provide an immediate entry to earning capacity, thus eliminating those traumatic early days of the uncertain search for work. A fortunate few were met by employers or their representatives at the dock or airport, which added to the sense of security. Pat Drohan emigrated alone at 24 after arranging secretarial work in Ballarat through her former English employer, Villiers engineering. On her arrival in Melbourne on Boxing Day 1958, she was met by the manager, who drove her to Ballarat, where Villiers had her accommodation waiting. When she later heard about conditions in government hostels, Pat considered herself one of the favoured few. 'When I saw where some of them lived at, those Bonegilla camps, you know … what *horrific* places they were! I was just very fortunate to have somewhere to live.' In some cases the job offer could be finalized at the dockside. Les Dalley, a fitter and turner experienced in newspaper printing technology, met the Adelaide *News* chief engineer at Port Adelaide, who promptly closed the arrangement: ' "Okay, there's a job there for you, when do you want to start work?" And I said: "Well, give me a couple of days and I'll be in there," because I'd brought my tool boxes with me and everything.' The experience gave Les an instant and memorable introduction to more democratic work relations which contrasted starkly to those on English newspapers, where chief engineers remained remote from the workforce, shielded by commissionaires at the door.[21]

Employer sponsorship, though, did involve risks. While the meeting on arrival and ready-made housing smoothed the process, heightened expectations could be dashed when things went wrong. The O'Neill family, attracted by a sponsor's promise of a building trade job in Perth, left prosperous circumstances in the Midlands in 1970. By the time they arrived there was a recession in construction and the sponsor, unsympathetic to their anxiety, could offer them nothing. Within two months they returned to Britain, bitterly disappointed, at huge cost. Not all disappointments were so dramatic. George and Ray Bird were sponsored by the Melbourne Tramways Board in 1955, with immediate work as driver and conductress, and accommodation provided on arrival. Their enthusiasm for adventure and greater opportunity was dashed by early disillusionment, especially in the nature of the work. Ray – who had left a skilled job in accounts – felt she was 'absolutely hopeless' as a conductress, and tramways work seemed to offer none of the prospects they had anticipated. While some of their British workmates quickly discovered that the requirement to serve out a contract for two years was unenforceable, George and Ray stayed on, but their sense of disappointed ambition persisted and they returned in 1962.[22]

Many ten pound migrants, like John and Sylvia Cannon, landed their first job from a hostel. We have seen how hostel living could profoundly affect first impressions of Australia. The unfamiliar and institutional nature of hostel living itself, bound by rules and regulations which were traps for the unwary, also shaped and influenced the search for work. When it aggravated the obstacles of job seeking it could leave the most vivid memories of the challenges faced during those first anxious months. Stories abound of early morning queues to use the few available telephones in the hostel for prompt job enquiries; of men 'on the tramp' all day knocking on doors; and of unwilling wives taking work when their husbands' searches proved unsuccessful.[23]

A common hostel experience centred upon job interviews conducted with employers in the hostel office. Margaret Hill learned the hard way about the covert culture of the hostel job search when she and her husband, Jim, arrived at Adelaide's Finsbury Hostel in December 1956. Accommodation was rent-free until residents found their first job. The Hills arrived shortly before Christmas, and only later realized that most families were delaying earnest job hunts and interviews, thereby enjoying at least a month of rent-free living. Eager to get to work, Jim, a skilled house painter and decorator, took the first job offered, a relatively unskilled position as a factory maintenance painter. Although the work was unsatisfying, he was relieved to move straight into work, but had not calculated on the imminent three week Christmas shutdown with no pay. The mandatory hostel tariff quickly drove them into debt and made for a bad start for a family with three young children. Poor transportation and working conditions, the heat of an Adelaide summer, and the challenge for Margaret of managing her children, escalated the family stress. But the money was adequate, and Jim, imbued with a deep work ethic, later travelled to Maralinga and Woomera to earn a better income and wipe out their untimely debt.[24]

'Jobs galore': work practices in an era of full employment

The first job encounter was indeed crucial, but it could also recede in importance in conditions where most new arrivals had an impression of 'jobs galore'. During the long postwar economic boom years this was the predominant migrant experience in Australia. There were, of course, economic downturns during this period, when employment demand contracted. We have seen that sensitive industries such as the building sector could suffer sudden downturns, like that in the early 1970s, with disastrous consequences for those who arrived at the wrong time.[25] The sharpest downturn came in 1961–62, when the unemployment rate peaked at 3.2 per cent and almost unseated the Menzies government.[26] Migrants who emigrated twice, in the

1950s and early 1970s, stressed the greater difficulty of the job search by the later years.[27] But for the most part migrant memories from before the mid-1970s skim over the troughs in the economic cycle and recollect a rich array of multiple job choices, from unskilled to skilled and professional work, and for men and women. 'Never once', wrote Sydney Hart of his own 1950s experience, 'did I see in all Australia one single factory or works – except, of course, during an industrial dispute – with the discouraging sign, "No Vacancies".' He concluded that it was quite normal for workers to move readily between jobs. John Clark in Adelaide recalled the 1950s as the 'good days', when 'you could have a change of three different jobs in the one day … labour was … so short'. For women, the high demand for nurses, who could choose their hospitals on arrival, was legendary. Nurses, Grace Turnbull recalled, 'could go anywhere in the world'. But, as Grace discovered through her unskilled husband Alf, who 'could get a job anywhere', this was only the most obvious example of ease of employment for women and men across most occupations, virtually a trademark for two generations of postwar British migrants. Even those who suffered periodic bouts of unemployment maintained their optimistic outlook. Maurice Tomlin, a toolmaker who came alone in 1948, first to Queensland, then Tasmania and finally Western Australia, thought his frequent periods of unemployment in the 1950s stemmed partly from his strong views as a 'staunch trade unionist'. But he never doubted that another job would be available during an 'absolute glut of employment'.[28]

With unemployment a relatively minor issue, work grievances and anxieties tended to dwell on a range of obstructions. Some of the most common focus upon troubles encountered in finding the precise work of choice and past experience, together with challenges posed by rejected qualifications and different work practices. The very fact of frequent job changing could accentuate the remembered impact of working in alien occupations, although for some this was simply a brief stage along the way. For Ray Spencer, with mechanical experience but no formal qualifications, the need to take a job as a labourer in the Fremantle power station in 1966 is remembered as little more than a temporary irritant until he could find work for which he was qualified. But for others the quest to work in their own trade or profession could be a long and painful journey. In Chapter 9 we relate the experience of Janet Francis's father, plunged from his dispensing chemist work in England to 'grubbing out trees' in Victor Harbour because his English employment qualifications were not accepted in Australia. His story of failed expectations is among the most traumatic we have encountered, but it is echoed in men's and women's stories across the occupational spectrum. In 1969 Carol Brooks, hoping to save a faltering marriage, persuaded David, her thriving but heavy-drinking fisherman husband, to emigrate from Brighton to Perth. During the selection interview each had been told that they would find immediate work; fishermen were in high demand in Perth, as were trained hairdressers like Carol. Within days of arrival these expectations were dashed when David found it impossible to enter the fishing industry – 'we realized it was a very much closed shop like it is here with the fishermen. You just can't walk in.' Carol, too, had to retrain and take examinations to qualify for her hairdressing permit, and then endure a three-month waiting list. A difficult period of adjustment followed, as David retrained as a bus driver and Carol moved through a succession of unsatisfactory jobs before she finally requalified. For Carol those first two difficult years were a 'prison sentence', compounded by the inability to return home without refunding the passage money and some anti-English hostilities at work. But almost as soon as the two years were up her hairdressing fortunes turned the corner, she found her work more reward-ing and David eventually established a successful Artex business. For Carol these might have been the ingredients of a migrant success story, but other factors quite unconnected with work pushed her in a different direction. David's heavy drinking resumed in a more active social and outdoor life – she reflected on the irony of taking him to Australia to cure his drinking problem! – and in 1974 she flew home to escape the marriage and to raise her three-month-old baby with the support of her mother and family. Carol's attitude to her years in Australia is now bound up with that failed marriage, but when she reflects on her working experience and the rewarding lifestyle she concludes that 'to be quite honest if I'd been with the husband I'm with now I'd have probably been still over there'.[29]

The results of job changing dictated by immediate necessities were not always negative. John Clark emigrated to Adelaide in 1951 as a Scottish stone-mason. He had originally served his apprenticeship with his father and saw this occupational inheritance as a perfectly natural and lifelong commitment. In Adelaide he faced no technical obstructions, but the only suitable work involved an exhausting commuter's journey. John was attracted by job vacancies in a nearby sawmill, initially took an unskilled job, and later progressed to work as a band-sawyer. The change was made easier by rumours he had heard of silicosis among stonemasons, later confirmed when his brother, also a stonemason, died from the disease in the United States. John recalled his work of thirty-two years with the same sawmiller with pride, born of the benefits of old-fashioned workplace paternalism. His employer used his influence to obtain a house for John and his family; when they returned to Britain in 1958 after John experienced a period of unsettlement, only to return in 1960, his old job was waiting for him. 'And of course, I repaid my loyalty to him, that's the only job I ever had'. While this attitude was linked to other idealizations of the 'good days' of the 1950s, like greater personal safety and leaving the front door unlocked, John Clark's career change gave him a sense that 'we were more like pioneers then, in those days'.[30]

One of the most common, and perhaps predictable, causes of complaint was the controlling role of trade unions in hiring and work practices. When Kathleen Upton published an account of her family's tough two years in Brisbane and Perth the Australian problem of 'union rules' loomed large:

> There was a very strict Union rule: without a ticket it was impossible to obtain a job. Instead of weekly subscriptions, a whole year's payment had to be made before you could start work. In many ways this was unfair; work was hard to find and if anyone found a job in a different category, another year's Union money had to be paid.

From personal experience Upton was able to cite numerous examples of British and Dutch migrants defeated by union regulations. These included a hairdresser, an experienced engineer unable to work in the Kwinana oilfields in Western Australia, who then opened a grocery store in Tinton, and a London electrician who was forced to work as an electrician's mate, living with his family in poor accommodation while saving fares home.[31]

Upton's stories were not wholly inaccurate, although the picture was more complex than her illustrations suggest, and few of our informants report paying a year's dues in advance. Skill tests could certainly be required to gain entry into a trade, but for most skilled workers from Britain the closed shop was a familiar scene. Actual practice, though, varied across different industries and workplaces. John Hardie, a Scottish electrician, took care to bring his union card when he was hired in the mid-1960s by Australian Paper Mills at Morwell: 'if you didn't join the union you didn't have a job, simple as that'. Maurice Tomlin, a dedicated unionist and trained toolmaker in England, who had worked mainly as a turner since his arrival in 1948, applied for a tool-maker's job in 1965, only to be 'laughed at by the Union man ... who denied the credibility of the certificates'. The rebuff challenged Maurice to upgrade his qualifications, which then led him into a series of advanced education courses and eventual promotion to management positions. On the other hand, George McLanaghan, whose work in the Scottish building industry was unskilled, managed to obtain a Carpenters' and Joiners' ticket in Melbourne in 1956 simply by sending his wife into the union office – he had feared being asked questions which might betray his meagre training. A payment of 10s. and recent arrival 'from the old country' was enough to earn him membership, and he found this was common for joiners and bricklayers, although not for electricians and plumbers, who were subject to more stringent testing.[32]

One of the more general emphases in recollections of unions and industrial relations is a sense of greater flexibility in the application of workplace rules, and of work culture more generally, in Australia compared to Britain. Joan Britton's husband had served a seven-year printer's apprenticeship in London, but was shocked to find his Perth employer ignoring the rules: 'he took people off the street, gave them a month's training, and gave them their papers; they were printers. You couldn't do that in England, you … had to show your indentures.' Some interpret this flexibility as a time of greater workplace freedom before increasing union control 'spoiled' the more relaxed relations between workers and bosses. Cliff Good fondly remembered his early days as a carpenter in Perth for the 'nice atmosphere amongst the blokes' and the easy relationship with bosses, who would routinely offer extra bonuses for completing a job before the weekend. Les Dalley, a fitter and turner with the Adelaide *News* in the 1950s, was similarly impressed with the caring and 'hands on' attitude of proprietor Rupert Murdoch, who was frequently on the shop floor and sent out for food when the men worked late.[33]

A window on Australian society: workplace culture and ethnic relations

The appreciation of a more relaxed workplace atmosphere often extends to commentary on Australian culture and identity more generally, and for some British immigrants it pinpoints what they found most surprising and different about working in Australia. A routine shock greeted conscientious workers, like Robert Smith, a fitter and turner in Melbourne, who was admonished by union members for working too quickly. John Hardie was astonished to find that when his electricians' union called a local strike it was taken as an immediate cue to retire to the beach: 'you finished up on the beach fishing, you had the union meeting on the beach and the fishing rods were out'. John thought that the 'laid back' Australian attitude extended to avoiding positions of responsibility and explained the national stereotype of Scottish and English workers as shop stewards as well as foremen.[34]

This impression of a more 'laid back' attitude amongst Australian workers illuminates some complex responses to different working experiences. Comparison of egalitarian Australian work relations with stiffer and more hierarchical conditions in Britain was a common response, but it could also be misleading. Joan Pickett had worked in the typing pool for British Railways in Manchester, and in retrospect thought she had been 'regimented in the old-fashioned way, you know, very sort of dedicated to work'. By contrast, when she joined the ABC in Adelaide in the early 1960s she was surprised at the 'more casual' work relations, where the bosses would join the workers for tea and lunch; the strangest custom of all was being sent home at three o'clock when the temperature hit 100°. 'You didn't know who were bosses and who were servants if you like, in Australia, it was much more relaxed.' Yet this common response was challenged later when she worked in a typing pool in Hobart for the state public service, where work relations and authority were more reminiscent of the stiffness of the railways environment in Manchester.[35] The contrast suggests that differences which were readily perceived to be national and cultural might have had as much to do with the nature of different workplaces and subtle variations in relations of production.

Material conditions of work in themselves often made for a rude shock in the first job, particularly in the first postwar decade when new industrial development in Australia was slow to take off. In Maryborough, Queensland, Maurice Tomlin was astonished to find himself working as a turner on a lathe 'on a couple of big wooden blocks and a dirt floor', a stark contrast to what he had known in 'the spotless tool-rooms of Birmingham'. As a carpenter who had done highly skilled work at the Wellcome Institute Museum in London, Cliff Good was shocked when confronted with primitive working conditions and machinery in Perth. 'The machinery was pretty old. We used to say it came out of the ark! [laughs].' Cliff shared his surprise at these conditions with his British co-workers, who outnumbered the Australians, and, perhaps fortuitously, frankness about old and new world contrasts occasioned no resentment. But among a predominantly Australian workforce the outcomes of comparison could be quite different. Albert Lougher had been trained as a watchmaker and in 1954 brought demanding standards of workmanship to his job in Sydney with a jewellery firm. He was quick to notice more lax standards during his induction test and on the job, and the difference soon provoked trouble when his fastidiousness slowed down productivity. Albert explained the contrast in terms of national character: 'The Aussie when he works he's after the dough, if he can get eight straight jobs he'd go for it, but if you got to make a part, it's got to be worth while, you know, I mean and not only that they didn't want to make parts, they'd buy it from the --- .' When the manager asked Albert to do some high-precision repair work for extra money this prompted workmates' hostility to the upstart intruder. 'Of course this caused a bit of revelation, "you bloody poms come out here making" ... and I got a bit of flak.' Anti-British discrimination was not, of course, restricted to those who might display superior skills, but it was never far from the surface when migrants pointed to differences compared to 'the old country'.[36]

Whether or not provoked by comparisons with British practices, the workplace was one of the most common sites where migrants were likely to have their first experience of anti-British prejudice. Most newcomers to a male-dominated workplace experience some degree of teasing and initiation testing, but for migrants cultural difference, national stereotypes and deeply embedded native fears of 'job stealing' could provoke more explicit taunting.

By the postwar years there were ready-made clichés about the British which could make for an uncomfortable start. Les Dalley, one of the few Britons on the News Limited shopfloor in Adelaide, had to learn quickly how to keep quiet to avoid the 'whingeing Pom' charge; tensions heightened when Australian and British cricket or rugby teams were competing. 'Well, I'd shut up and get out of harm's way, because it got a bit heavy.' Elizabeth Gray became a matron in a school for delinquent girls in Melbourne, and discovered promptly that 'what mattered was … you didn't moan'. Routine complaints about the weather, she thought, were part of British culture, 'they don't mean I hate it here. But the Australians, of course, hated this. They thought it meant they didn't like it there.' Against this we need to remember that, especially during the 1950s, discrimination based on religious sectarianism between Protestants and Roman Catholics could easily eclipse Australian–British and other ethnic tensions. Albert and Anne Lougher each faced 'terrible' probing questions about their religious background when applying for jobs in Sydney and were astonished to discover the political equation between Labor and Catholic, Liberal and Protestant.[37]

Memories of anti-British taunting at first sight seem to be all of a piece, drawing on a long Australian tradition of 'Pommie' stereotypes and sensitivity to criticism. But experiences varied dramatically across different workplaces. Sylvia Cannon's first experience of being 'frozen out' by resentful typists at a Ford office in Geelong, to the point of feeling threatened, was never repeated in later employment. Building sites, too, could be quite unpredictable in their social climate, often depending on the predominant make-up of the workforce. David Bailey, who came from London to Sydney in 1968, was acutely conscious of 'Pommie bashing', but found that the taunting tended to subside if there were relatively large numbers of British on the site. When, as often happened, British workers outnumbered Australians, he reflected, 'It's funny how when they're outnumbered, suddenly they've got relatives coming out of the wood-work. It's amazing, like, you know. "Oh yes, I've got an uncle in England, oh my mum comes from —" But normally they wouldn't admit it, if it was on the other foot.'[38]

Over time, British workers in large workplaces tended to become just one migrant group among many in an ethnically mixed workforce, often finding themselves supplanted as the main butt of hostility by Italians, Greeks or others. For some Britons not previously exposed to foreigners the adjustment could be difficult. George McLanaghan, from an Ayrshire village background, found it 'really hard to fit in' to a Melbourne screen printing firm in the mid-1960s because a mixture of nationalities 'spoke more among themselves, you know, their own language'. More commonly, though, workplace solidarity seems to have overshadowed ethnic difference. John Hardie, who also encountered non-Scottish workmates for the first time in the Latrobe Valley, looks back on a mostly harmonious workplace in which British, Italian and Greek electricians were united by a common investment in the work ethic. Ethnic hostilities were only likely to emerge, temporarily, when the crew was under intense pressure to complete a job on time and one mistake might put the entire project, together with bonuses, in jeopardy. 'That was the one time I would say where the nationalities seemed to separate a wee bit, you became protective if you like of your own.'[39]

John Hardie came to Australia in 1964, and his tentative tolerance gives some hints of the more worldly attitude of a new generation of British migrants after the early 1960s, for whom 'foreigners' were ceasing to represent, automatically, a strange or threatening difference. Keith Whittle remembered a Burmese charge hand and Italian and Croat workmates in Perth in the late 1960s: 'Yes, I mean, there was quite a varied selection, I mean different places we went to, we even had some Aborigines, worked with them. Yes, I mean I got along with most people.'[40] These attitudes may have been slow to spread among British migrants, but they contributed to a changed setting in the 1960s which encouraged a more liberal approach to cultural difference in the workplace. There were some early seeds here, perhaps, of grassroots multi-culturalism, which was to become a more public ethos in the 1970s and 1980s. Young migrants of the late 1960s and 1970s seemed increasingly to take the differences for granted, even across starkly different workplaces. David Bailey has always been sensitive to 'Pommie bashing' on building sites, but he stresses that he was never worried by the regular presence of Italian workmates. It is difficult now to disentangle these views from the effects of more recent years of multicultural promotion. But Kate Rowe, a 20-year-old single Londoner who came to Sydney in 1970, speaks enthusiastically for that new generation: 'Everywhere I've been, there's always been, I mean I worked at SBS! ... The ethnic mix, I loved the ethnic mix! I was, I just think it, it's, everyone contributes their own flavour, so to speak!'[41]

The 'men's story': pride in a working life

These glimpses into individuals' working lives chart a range of challenges and shifting attitudes, from the depths of alienation to rapid accommodation to new conditions. Despite the severity of some of the more negative experiences it was rare for work-related problems to be the sole reason for returnees to leave the country. In the few cases where employment issues are remembered as a motive they are likely to be mixed with more general concerns about economic security, like lack of national insurance and a national health scheme.[42] Much more common in the way migrants describe their work is a sense of achievement, often against the odds, crowning a long struggle. While this is evident in both men's and women's working stories, men are more likely to put career at the centre of the story. Their accounts tend to spring into life during recollections of times at work, evoking memories of pleasure, camaraderie and achievement. A sense of enjoyment and pride is most evident in men's vivid work memories, where they relish the opportunity to speak at length about technical complexities of the job, their skill and adaptability, union business, work friendships and even the qualities and faults of bosses. Keith Whittle became most animated when talking about his succession of labouring jobs in Perth in the 1960s, especially his achievements in improving health and safety rules as a shop steward. Proud, self-defining aphorisms – like Les Dalley's 'the biggest learning curve I had' and Cliff Tyas's 'I could adapt myself to anything' – punctuate men's recall of their early job experiences. This perception of the central importance of work in men's life histories is often evident in wives' and children's memories of their husbands and fathers. Maureen Carter spoke positively of her father's pleasure in his new Australian occupation, a home television repair service: 'He loved it, he loved it.... Never a chore, he absolutely loved it.'[43]

Pride in the achievements and details of a long working life is not confined to migrants, but it often reinforces a conviction that the act of migration, whether permanent or temporary, was well justified. Patricia Wall's story of her father's mission to contribute to the building of Australia illustrates a more serious dimension of pride and patriotism attached to migration and career ambitions.[44] In October 1949 her family, at that time parents and two children, left Aberdeen for Canberra on the *Georgic*. Her father, James Hardie, a carpenter, had been sponsored by Peak Constructions, along with twenty-four other workers with their families, to support the intensive building projects then underway in Canberra. James later explained to Patricia that the move was motivated by a quest for greater opportunity: 'There are more opportunities in a new society for you to do whatever you want to do.' But there were other considerations. The family, her mother especially, suffered long-lasting war trauma when their house was bombed in 1944. In 1947 the Hardies lost a baby daughter, and James determined to give his wife a fresh start; the decision, as so often, was bound up with intimate family dynamics, including the mother's alienation from her sister. Beyond that, though, James seems to have approached his migration as though it were a sacred mission, convinced by the recruitment officers that he and the entire family were coming to 'build the new national capital'. Before the Hardies even landed that mission was put to the test.

As the *Georgic* approached Melbourne early in November the children among those twenty-five families suddenly became aware of agitation among the parents. Patricia recalls the event vividly:

All of a sudden on board ship life became a bit hectic, because parents were running round like scared cats, or there was something wrong. And it wasn't until we reached Melbourne that the children were actually told that we were not welcome in this new land, that we had to find our way back to the UK as there were no jobs, no accommodation, nobody wanted us.

The cause of the commotion was the news that Peak Constructions had gone bankrupt, and although the families had emigrated under the government ten pound scheme, they were told initially that they must return to Britain. Before the ship docked James took a leading role in a 'sit in' in the ship's saloon, where the twenty-five families declared their refusal to leave the ship until new arrangements were made for their employment in Canberra. There they reiterated James's determination: 'Right, we were contracted to come to build the national capital in Australia.' Hasty negotiations resulted in the families being transferred to a holding camp in Albert Park. Patricia recalled the family's shock on seeing the bleak compound. 'When they took us there … by bus, the adults, I can recall them saying, "Why has it got barbed wire?" And they said, "That will be removed." It was never removed.' Teenagers soon learned to defy the night curfews by cutting the barbed wire, but the Hardies had to undergo three months in the camp until misunderstandings about their status were resolved and all the families were allowed to remain in Australia.

In time some of these *Georgic* families took work and found accommodation in Melbourne. But the Hardies refused to leave the camp, following James's vow to settle nowhere but the national capital where he could realize his mission. He did, though, seek work, while the rest of the family attempted to return to a degree of normality and the children attended Prahran Primary School. After investigating an offer in Werribee he reported that, although he could see a future there, 'it wasn't the national capital, and he was determined, he had a promise from the government, with his migration officer, that he was coming to build the national capital and build it he would!' A job with Jennings Constructions in Melbourne turned the tide. Discussions with the union about his ambitions resulted in a high profile interview with the recently defeated prime minister, Ben Chifley, which was reported in the Melbourne press. Just three months after their unpropitious arrival the Hardies were on their way to Canberra through a transfer with Jennings.

James Hardie came to take enormous pride in the capital he had helped to build: the Academy of Science, the Space Tracking Station, the Canberra Centre, foreign embassies, and promotion to the position of project manager, were just a few of his claims to achievement. In later years, when James and his wife became active with church and community groups, his proud guided tours around 'his' national capital were the highlight. The pride was inseparable from the future he felt he had given his children. Patricia reflects:

I think, on returning to the UK, I can see what he meant by a better life. We had the freedom, we had the ability to say what we want, when we want it, we have the ability to *do* something about constructing the type of society that we want to live in, and I'm very proud that he, he took the step! Very proud! Unfortunately his parents never saw the profit of his work here.

James Hardie would have taken deep pride in his work if he had never left Aberdeen, but from 1949 his work identity was bound up with his awareness of being a migrant. A deeply religious Presbyterian who '*lived* his religion', according to Patricia 'he considered it an honour to be a carpenter, because he felt that there was only one very, very famous carpenter'. He was equally attached to his Scottish heritage, and to freemasonry in both Aberdeen and Canberra, where he set up a new lodge. He regularly wore his kilt at lodge meetings and, with his wife, conducted Scottish dancing classes on their front lawn at Narrabundah. But none of this was inconsistent with a parallel pride in deep commitment to Australia and a sense of social obligation which was evident in his work for the Good Neighbour Council helping European immigrants in Canberra to find employment; many of his later friends were new immigrants. His only reservation about Australians stemmed from familiar British scepticism about working standards: ' "Don't worry about it mate, it'll be right!" Dad, no, it has to be right, first time or no.' His exacting standards on the job were, in effect, all of a piece with his identity as Scottish migrant, devout Christian and committed Australian.

James Hardie's story is unusual, even for 1949, in evoking a powerful streak of idealism beyond individual ambition. But it also belongs firmly to the first generation of postwar migrants' stories, with its commitment to unrelenting struggle and pride in 'workmanship', essentially a form of respectability tied to self-respect. By the 1960s, while the migrants' search for greater opportunity continued, the contrast between British and Australian employment opportunities and conditions had diminished. Migrants' stories from this later generation were less likely to be couched in terms of idealism and more likely to reflect on calculated comparisons between material and working conditions in both countries.[45]

The 'women's story': pride, work and home

Almost unthinkingly we tend to associate stories of pride in work with men. For most of our period the common attitude in Britain and Australia to married life was based firmly on separate spheres, with men as breadwinners and women full time mothers and 'homemakers'. This is reflected in many stories from women across different class backgrounds, who underline their primary commitment to being at home, at least with young children, and often speak of taking paid employment in the early years in Australia as an unfortunate necessity.[46] But this is far from being the whole story. The acute financial pressures of migration, the need to get established immediately, sometimes before husbands began to earn, put women with children under great pressure to take paid work. While this could pose huge problems at home, many of the stories which emerge from those experiences also provide evidence that, even in the 1950s, some migrant women resisted the mainstream expectations of the time. The generation of women who grew up before the war, who mostly left school early with ideas of working until marriage, and who unexpectedly faced difficult years in the workforce during wartime, may well have been more open to adjusting their ideas during a second upheaval in a new country. It is difficult to know how far these migrant women may have been a spur for change, but in effect they paved the way for their daughters, who demanded a freer choice from the start.

From all that we know of the pressures of migration it should come as no surprise to find that British married women, like other women migrants, took up paid work at a higher rate than did non-migrants in both Britain and Australia. In the early 1960s Reg Appleyard's demographic data showed that migrant wives from Britain were taking employment at a greater rate than were

28 After arriving in Australia in 1954, Anne Lougher never doubted that she should remain at home with her children. But like many women migrants, during a family financial crisis she immediately sought employment, though she was careful to find work – including a stint as a barmaid in Sydney – that fitted in with childcare

Australian-born wives. Furthermore, Appleyard's longitudinal survey pointed to an increase in married women's employment intentions from 38 per cent while still in Britain to 62 per cent after arrival in Australia.[47] These statistics coincide with much individual testimony, where the migrant wife's working history, together with strenuous childcare strategies, is often in conflict with a stated preference to stay at home with young children. Anne Lougher, for example, never doubted that she should remain at home with her children, but during a family financial crisis she immediately sought employment; she was then careful to find work – at one stage in a pub – that was consistent with childcare: 'I had to do something at night so that I could look after the children during the day' (see Figure 28). Moreover, when couples arrived without children, like the Cannons in 1961, it was common for both to work long hours, often while saving for a house, until the birth of children, then for the wife to withdraw from the workforce. But it was also possible that circumstances or personal preference might draw mothers back into the workforce, and to adopt what is commonly regarded as a more 'modern' pattern, despite their strong convictions. Sylvia Cannon's youngest son was only 4 when she returned – tentatively – to the workforce, and ended the 'chapter of my life' devoted to full-time child rearing.[48]

For a large proportion of working-class women the necessity to earn an income in unskilled or semi-skilled occupations before and after marriage had been taken for granted for generations, and even in the 1950s many women adhered to this practice despite prevailing ideological prescriptions. Dot Hallas, who came to Melbourne from Huddersfield in 1952, would have liked to spend time at home with her two children, and would have been supported by her husband, who 'didn't believe in women working, after they had children'. But these sentiments, in both countries, had to give way to financial imperatives. The choice in Melbourne was made easier for Dot in part because she was able to hire a neighbour as childminder, but it was hardly out of the ordinary for her. Summing up her ideas in retrospect, she recalled the assumption she grew up with: 'You just *had* to work ... part of your life, you *had* to work!' Over time this stark necessity could evolve into discretionary preference. In retrospect Ethel Ledgett, a working-class Londoner, thought that her work at Grace Brothers in Sydney from 1956, despite the difficulties, gave her invaluable 'independence' and self-reliance compared to her friends. For Anne Barkas, who came with her family to Newcastle from South Shields in 1960, heavy evening cleaning work to help the family get established soon evolved into a matter of choice, 'well, to try and get on, you know, 'cause we wanted a car and a television'. These patterns were not confined to working-class women. Former Conservative Party agent Betty Preston, whose determination to work led to a second political career in South Australia, was determined from the start that she should contribute to the family welfare.[49]

Whether driven by need, traditional attitudes, or, as some women assert, simply for 'something to do',[50] the actual experience in the workforce could be emphatically positive and recollected as a matter of pride. Pat Drohan, a medical secretary, captures the sentiments of many enthusiasts in recollecting her early workplace as a 'second home'. Within days of arriving in the hostel some women promptly took paid work with no sense of grievance. As it did for men, work could provide an instant opportunity to make friends and to gain acceptance in an otherwise strange environment. Dorothy Floyd noted that 'I've worked ever since I came here and I enjoyed working, otherwise I wouldn't be working in the office … you know it's something that keeps you in touch with other people'. Other hostel women often seized the opportunity to work in the hostel itself, which facilitated childcare arrangements. For Dorothy Rooms, work at the Williamstown Hostel in 1952, cleaning and making tea, was a 'smashing job' which enabled her to buy 'extras' for the children.[51]

While many of these women seem to have been ahead of their time in their frequent employment and attitudes to paid work, the challenges they faced throughout the 1950s and 1960s in combining work with childcare were more stark than those faced by today's working mothers. Institutional child-care was virtually unknown, social attitudes mostly disapproving, and at home an unsupportive husband could handicap the search for work and render the resulting 'dual role' intolerable. On the other hand altered circumstances, as well as a second income, could bring husbands to a more cooperative stance. Alf Floyd admitted that he had grown up with the idea 'that the woman's place was in the home, and barefoot, pregnant and in the kitchen style', but claimed that wartime exposure to the Women's Royal Naval Service, Dorothy's work in munitions and the need for her income in Melbourne after 1952 gradually modified his ideas. His eventual view that 'if a woman wants to work she's as much entitled to work as a man' seems to have been forged through long experience and negotiation.[52]

Women with professional nursing qualifications, even when they left work after marriage, were well placed to resume work out of need or preference. Official views, in Victoria for example, barring the employment of married nurses, were being widely ignored in practice by the 1950s. Betty Simmons tells a story of a nursing career which indicates some of the directions women's careers could take in the 1960s and thereafter. Betty came from a middle-class background in Wales; her father was a school headmaster and her mother a nurse who had worked throughout her marriage, a fact which Betty recalls brought local status and 'high esteem' to the family.[53] Her mother's example seemed to inspire Betty with enthusiasm for her own nursing career in London, and after she married Clifford, a 'coach body builder', he was initially happy for her to work. But while still in England, and after she had withdrawn from work when her children were born, he 'assumed the chauvinistic attitude. It really bugged me.' During the Suez crisis Clifford's hours were cut back and Betty concluded that the only solution to their critical cash shortage was for her to go back to work. '"You wouldn't dare", he said. He was such a damned fool, he was still saying "you wouldn't dare" when I walked out the door in uniform to go to work.' This did not resolve the tensions, since the careful balancing of mutual shiftwork arrangements to allow for childcare failed to meet Betty's expectations. 'His idea of looking after the children was going down to his mother's and watching the telly.'

The Simmonses' English experience influenced their adjustment when they emigrated to Adelaide in 1958, with four children. Faced by a difficult living situation with their sponsor, they were desperate to earn enough to be independent and buy their own home, a goal which had eluded them in England. The new conditions brought a further change of attitude in Clifford. 'Well he was real dead keen when I got here.' But part-time weekend nursing jobs were scarce, and it was ten months before Betty finally found a suitable job, involving long periods of travel; 'this is the joke, Clifford found it in the paper'. But for Betty the old domestic complications continued, particularly when Clifford was in charge of the children on weekends. 'Before very long Clifford had got Carol cooking the tea, and she was only 10 or 11. And I didn't approve of that. He was supposed to be looking after them. He didn't do it to my satisfaction.'

While Betty's long determination to work had a material motive – even a simple project to furnish their living-room took two years of intense saving – there were other benefits. Looking back she saw weekend work as a crucial element in her adjustment during the stress and isolation of the early years. 'I do think that going out to work is a big help.… Yes, I mean when you're stuck in the house and you've got no outlets.' Although she had to suppress the temptation to compare working methods with those in English hospitals, she accumulated lifelong friends at work. In later years she pursued adult education and creative writing, 'which I don't think I would have had the nerve to do in England'. She also supported a range of feminist causes. Today she watches her daughters still struggling to balance work, childcare and marriage, 'and they spend all their time arguing about the distribution of domestic chores'. Betty's strong views stem in part from her early experience, which she now shares with her daughters: 'Well, it's like what I said about our marriage; whilst I was working we had absolute equality, but once I became dependent I was treated like a dependant.'

Betty Simmons's resolute combination of her professional career with marriage and motherhood contrasts sharply with the varied tactics of those married women who sought out unskilled or semi-skilled jobs to make ends meet. But all these migrant women had in common a willingness to adopt strategies – often desperate family survival strategies – in the face of continuing disapproval of married women's work. Their enthusiasm for what was often a trying ordeal underlines the positive role that work played in the migrant family economy and in their own adaptation. Like men, women could discover a wider world at work, and make lasting friends. As Wendy Jay recalled, 'I think I adjusted more quickly because I had to work with Australians, and mix with … Australians'. Others who stayed at home could be acutely conscious of what they were missing. Gill Whittle's loneliness with three children in an isolated Perth suburb was magnified for her by the knowledge of her husband's convivial times with his workmates.[54] In the next chapter we will see that not all women who stayed at home with young children suffered in this way. But women's work was a central element in the British migrant experience.

Self-made migrants and the next generation

Reg Appleyard's survey for 1959-60 showed that, while British assisted migrants to Australia were above the norm of British workers generally in terms of skills, their ambitions to get ahead rarely extended to entrepreneurial goals.[55] That is, few expected to lift their socio-economic status, though most aimed to improve their conditions in the same occupations. Many of the stories told here confirm Appleyard's findings. Satisfaction almost invariably meant achieving a better life in similar occupations to those pursued in Britain. Single-minded pursuit of wealth and status through business ventures, which is common among the success stories of some non-English-speaking migrants in Australia, is unusual among the postwar generation of British assisted migrants.

There are, of course, important exceptions and variations on this theme. Some migrants did indeed make dramatic occupational gains well beyond their expectations. The trajectory from the shop floor to management was the most obvious pathway for skilled workers. We saw Les Dalley move from a shop floor newspaper office as a fitter and turner to a prestigious management position, a success he attributed to a lucky break. Others, like Albert and Anne Lougher, tried their hands at family businesses with modest success, or sometimes near bankruptcy and risks of marital breakdown. By contrast we saw in the Introduction how John and Sylvia Cannon ultimately changed both their occupational status and their social status by gaining tertiary education and becoming marriage counsellors. For John in particular this was a long journey from his car salesman's career. But this was a rare course for assisted migrants to take, and, significantly, John was not from a skilled blue-collar trade, from which men were more reluctant to move.[56]

It is hardly surprising to find that the children of adult migrants were more likely than their parents to make dramatic career progress. Even the most notorious example of British entrepreneurial success, Alan Bond, came to Perth as a young child and was soon eager to escape school for wider horizons.[57] Many children of the first generation of postwar migrants were less scarred by the caution-inducing experiences of the Depression and had better opportunities to extend their education beyond the age of 14 or to start their own businesses. Ron Benson was 14 when he came with his parents from Durham to Perth in 1959.[58] Because the move thwarted his ambition to become a professional soccer player he was a reluctant migrant; he could not adjust to his school in Midland and left within a year. A succession of unsatisfying white-collar jobs led him to sales positions in electronics companies, and ultimately a partnership, an achievement far beyond his father's own goals in 1959 of modest prosperity in white-collar work. Ron was acutely conscious of the dramatic generational difference this represented, noting that he had also moved far politically from his father's socialist roots to membership of the Liberal Party. He reflected that his career would have vindicated his parents' thinking in 1959 that emigration would provide greater opportunity for their children. But he confessed to the younger generation's scepticism, adding that 'I could have achieved similar goals in England', as could his own children, who were all university graduates, not unlike their English relatives. These views identify a substantial shift in opportunity and attitude among the children of the postwar migrant generation, and foreshadow the greater mobility of youth, in which the more 'globalized' migrants from developed countries around the end of the twentieth century see minimal differences between countries in terms of work opportunities.[59] These attitudes were most pronounced among single sojourners, whose commitment to work and place was rarely enduring, and we will see more of this in Chapter 8.

John Howell, who in 1958 came from London to Melbourne at 14 with his widowed mother, illustrates a rather different story of dramatic success in a traditional trade.[60] Within months of arrival he was apprenticed as a carpenter. Once he was qualified, a succession of work moves took him to Apollo Bay, a Victorian coastal town, where eventually he set up as a builder, bought a farm from a local landowner, and soon after married the landowner's daughter. Over forty years after arrival he and his wife run a major building business, a farm and holiday cabins. John was motivated by a strong work ethic, and attributes his success to hard work and application. But his values have as much to do with close-knit community belonging in a small town as with financial success.

I can show you houses we've built, dozens or hundreds of houses round the place, and I've employed lots of people in the town. And I have a great respect for all the people that've worked for us, and … I regard them all as my friends. But … I don't regard making a million dollars as being an accomplishment as much as just being involved in the society.

Few migrants of John's parents' generation achieved his kind of success, but his commitment to community echoed the same close-knit English neighbour-hood he recalled in Croydon before leaving for Australia. Reflecting on his career success, like most men in our study he returned to family themes, counting it a great success that his sister had come to settle with them: 'I suppose, accomplishing all what we've got here around us, where we live, and having the family still all around us.' His sentiments remind us that the world of work was never far removed from the world of family and community, and we will see more of these links in the next chapter on migrant family lives.

Notes

1 Martin, *Angels and Arrogant Gods*, p. 15.
2 The rate of assisted migration was geared to employment prospects. Note, for example, the decline in assisted British admissions during the 1961–62 recession to 27,178 compared to 35,063 in 1960–61 and 41,833 in 1962–63. Appleyard, *The Ten Pound Immigrants*, p. 160.
3 Martin, *Angels and Arrogant Gods*, p. 22.
4 Bloomefield interview, Battye Library, quoted with permission.
5 Makewell interview LU; Margaret Hill interview LU.
6 Lougher interview LU.
7 Barry, *The Rise and Fall of Alan Bond*.
8 White, *Inventing Australia*; Murphy, *Imagining the Fifties*.
9 Makewell interview LU. See Chapter 7 below on the Makewells' 'nesting narrative'.
10 MacDonald interview LU.
11 See Chapter 9 and Crooks written account US.
12 Reardon interview and written account LU. See discussion of the Reardon story in chapters 2, 7 and 11.
13 Roe, *Australia, Britain and Migration*.
14 For example Tribe, *Postmark Australia*, p. 2.
15 Pluis interview LU; Laycock written account US; Heath interview US.
16 Cook interview LU.
17 Cook, 'The Cook Family Voyage', LU.
18 Thomas interview LU.
19 Dutch migrants from the earliest days enjoyed similar leniency to the British. Peters, *Milk and Honey*, pp. 175–6.
20 Bosworth, 'Australia and Assisted Immigration from Britain', pp. 187–200.
21 Drohan interview LU; Dalley interview LU.
22 O'Neill interview US (see Chapter 9 for fuller details of the O'Neill story); Bird interview US.
23 Bloomefield interview, Battye Library, quoted with permission.
24 Hill interview LU; Hill, *Corrugated Castles*, pp. 97–8.
25 See above, and O'Neill interview US.
26 Bolton, *The Oxford History of Australia: 1942–1995*, pp. 90, 146, 187, 213–14.

27 See Roscoe interview US; Heath interview US.
28 Hart, *Pommie Migrant*, pp. 45 and 165; Clark interview LU; Grace Turnbull interview LU; Tomlin interview LU; Tomlin letter to BBC, 2 January 1997. See also Roman interview LU.
29 Spencer interview US; Francis interview US; Brooks interview US. Hairdressers were particularly bitter about their inability to resume their previous occupations without interruption. See, for example, Davis interview LU; Blackmore interview LU.
30 Clark interview LU.
31 Upton, *To the Undiscovered Ends*, pp. 49, 74 and 118.
32 Hardie interview US; Tomlin letter to BBC, 2 January 1997, LU; McLanaghan interview US.
33 Britton interview LU; Gwen and Cliff Good interview US; Dalley interview LU.
34 Maggie and Robert Smith interview US; Hardie interview US. See also Stirling interview US.
35 Pickett interview US.
36 Tomlin interview LU; Tomlin letter to BBC, 2 January 1997, LU; Gwen and Cliff Good interview US; Lougher interview LU.
37 Dalley interview LU; Elizabeth Gray interview US; Lougher interview LU. Les Dalley experienced similar religious discrimination among printers in Adelaide: Dalley interview LU.
38 Cannon interview LU; Bailey interview LU.
39 McLanaghan interview US; Hardie interview US.
40 Whittle interview US; see also the interview with Robert Stirling, a left-wing shop steward who supported his Greek and Italian workmates in a Melbourne shoe factory (US).
41 Bailey interview LU; Rowe interview LU.
42 See Rooms interview US; Elizabeth Gray interview US.
43 Whittle interview US; Dalley interview LU; Tyas interview US ; Carter interview LU; see also Barrand interview LU.
44 Wall interview LU.
45 For example *Daily Sketch*, London, 25 October 1966, p. 8; Bailey interview LU.
46 For example, Makewell interview LU.
47 Appleyard, *British Emigration to Australia*, pp. 183–4.
48 Lougher interview LU. See also Blackmore interview LU; Cannon interview LU.
49 Hallas interview LU; Ledgett interview LU; Barkas interview LU; Preston, *Blowing My Own Trumpet*, p. 40; Preston, *Destination Australia*.
50 See for example, interviews with Mary Clayton, Veronica Anderson, Maureen Carter and Eileen and John Fairbairn, LU.
51 Drohan interview LU; Rooms interview US. See also Spencer interview US.
52 Floyd interview LU.
53 Betty Simmons (pseudonym) interview LU.
54 Whittle interview US.
55 Appleyard, *Ten Pound Immigrants*, p. 61.
56 Dalley interview LU; Lougher interview LU.
57 Barry, *The Rise and Fall of Alan Bond*, pp. 10–53.
58 Benson interview LU. See also Bailey interview LU. The social and economic trajectories of the children of postwar British immigrants deserve further comparative research.
59 See Hammerton, 'Epic Stories and the Mobility of Modernity'.
60 Howell interview LU.

7

Suburban dreams and family realities: making a home in Australia

Although we still love the grey, crowded city of our birth, we're glad we came to Perth, the loneliest city in the world, and we know now that this is the place to make our home and bring up our children.[1]

Gwen Good's enthusiastic if ambivalent comments about her family's comfortable adjustment in Perth, less than a year after their arrival in 1963 from London, expressed the desires of thousand of British migrant families. The quest for improved living conditions and good financial prospects was frequently reduced to the pursuit of 'a good place to bring up children' and to assure their futures. 'Making a home' involved a search for decent housing beyond what had been experienced in Britain, the accumulation of a widening range of household possessions and settlement in a usually suburban, congenial, like-minded community. These goals were designed to cultivate a more fulfilling family life and a good marriage. They were goals common to postwar generations living in both Britain and Australia, but were articulated more pointedly by migrants who often felt that their move put their families' futures at risk. Years later the stories they tell still focus powerfully on those dreams and the complex ways in which each family struggled to realize them.

As we saw in Chapter 1, Australia's preference for British immigrants was closely connected to a desire for fertile young couples who would easily adapt to the 'Australian way of life' in the suburbs.[2] Migrants' fixation on the 'Australian dream' of suburban life with male breadwinners and female homemakers was thus a happy coincidence. We know that, in physical location at least, these ambitious goals were largely fulfilled for the bulk of British migrants, who settled across a range of middle and outer suburbs.[3] Unlike the first generation of postwar continental European migrants, who gravitated towards initial concentrations of their own ethnic groups in cheap housing in the inner suburbs,[4] the British mostly moved in a short time into newer suburban districts. But these broad trends give a misleading impression of the process of settlement and adjustment for British migrants. The journey to successful suburban settlement involved a daunting series of challenges, any one of which could threaten the success of the venture for the whole family. In this respect the British migrant experience differed only marginally from that of other migrants. Housing itself, which was in chronic shortage in

Australia as well as Britain in the immediate postwar years, posed the first and major difficulty for the new family; significant adjustments in standards of living could be required in new suburbs with minimal infrastructure like plumbing, and the greater comforts of new amenities and appliances associated with the 'Australian dream' could be hard won; the process of settling into a new community, establishing friendship networks and adjusting to new modes of social life, even with the asset of a common language, could be daunting; above all the process of settlement could imperil the harmony of marital and family relationships. Most of these factors affected migrants differently over time, influenced by the dramatic changes affecting urban life in Australia between the late 1940s and the early 1970s, but they dominate the stories told by migrants. These accounts are a revealing window into the turbulent process of British–Australian suburban settlement.

The rental mindset

We have seen in earlier chapters that while finding employment was rarely a problem for the first generation of postwar migrants, housing was a different matter; sad stories of the housing shortage often echoed similar tales told about Britain before departure. Long stays in hostels or with sponsors could drag on when the most basic rental accommodation proved to be elusive. The story of the Tyas family in 1966 – forced to remain in Preston Hostel because of the long waiting list for a Housing Commission flat and with rental accommodation virtually unobtainable – typified the dispiriting start for families desperate to get established on their own from the first week. For all but a few with ready capital the first urgent priority was the search for rental housing. Rental is often remembered as an interim measure before realization of the ultimate dream of home ownership; perhaps this underlines the degree to which this element of the 'Australian way of life' influenced the aspirations of a generation for whom renting had been taken for granted in Britain. But for some from the first wave of postwar migrants the long tradition of a working-class rental mindset never faded. George Bird recalled that while he and Ray were influenced by their friends' vague ambition to buy a block of land, 'we just didn't get round to it.... we were quite content to rent, we'd never owned anything in our life before anyway so we were just content to work and rent'. Rosemary Hurst's parents, similarly, never entertained buying a house in Hobart, although gradual prosperity spurred her father to buy 32 acres of rural property, with a shed, which he used as a virtual hobby farm, selling his vegetable produce door to door each summer. Dorothy Rooms's family lived in a succession of hostels in New South Wales and Victoria in the early 1950s, always convinced that they could never afford to buy land or a house, nor find affordable rented accommodation. Dorothy recalled that her husband Albert quickly adopted a fixed attitude about Australian housing: ' "People keep telling me to buy a plot of land here," he said, "but the only plot of land I'd get," he said, "is six foot by three". That was his attitude … no way that we were going to get a house.' When, after three years, they returned to Manchester, convinced they could never obtain decent housing or get ahead, their easy acquisition of a new council flat vindicated Albert's bleak view of the possibility of affordable housing in Australia. Yet during their three years in Australia they saved enough for return fares for a family of five, which, if they chose, might have freed them from hostel living. For the immediate postwar generation the old rental mindset died hard when confronted with the vagaries of the Australian housing market.[5]

For the larger numbers who did gain access to the rental market the impression must have been one of utter chaos, as migrants of various nationalities competed with each other in efforts to find any scarce space with a roof; old garages, caravans, outhouses and crowded rooming houses were often the first ports of call. Annie Barkas and her family experienced life in both a converted garage and a caravan in Newcastle before renting a small house. Bill and Catherine Bradley, newly arrived in Fremantle from Glasgow in 1952, recalled a general confusion of migrants calling desperately door to door in search of rooms or garages for rent. Catherine and her two daughters spent their days this way to the point where the girls incorporated the experience into their play-acting, one taking the role of the 'lady', the other playing the would-be tenant, chanting, 'Do you have any rooms?' In Perth there were ubiquitous stories of spartan rooming houses for migrants in Hay Street. In 1954 Joan and Clifford Britton occupied a small room in Hay Street with a double bed; they paid an extra pound to put in a single bed for their 7–year-old, used metered power to boil the kettle and were bemused by the chip heater for bath water. 'Oh I thought Australia was crude! Very crude, I did! But, we settled in.'[6]

The desperation to find independent housing could be closely bound up with circumstances only recently left behind in Britain. Tom and Beryl Walker arrived in Perth in 1953 from a history of struggling to break free of family domination on both sides. In Weymouth Beryl's mother had forced them out of their caravan to live with her when Beryl was pregnant.[7] Tom's work, too, was plagued by dependence on his mother's and sister's grocery shop in Bristol, for which he had only received 'spending money'. With this background Tom and Beryl's eagerness to find independent housing for themselves and their baby was hardly surprising. But the Perth rental market was bewildering. Having paid a deposit in advance for a small house in Cottesloe, they had been confident of smooth access to a rented house after arrival.

'So we did have visions of having a home of our own once we'd left Tom's mother, it was just a question of getting around there and organizing it.' Unfortunately the ten pound deposit exerted no leverage, and after an angry scene they left with the owner's taunts ringing in their ears. 'And they said, no, there was lots of Australian soldiers that didn't have homes and they would be buggered if the Poms were going to have them.' This was not the last of their failed and costly ventures to find the much desired 'place of our own'. A brief period renting two rooms from a woman who domineered over Beryl did little to satisfy their desire for independence. 'She was a bit of a dragon. I couldn't bath the baby because she thought he might make a mess, I couldn't boil the kettle because I was using electricity. Tom was out all day at work so I pushed a pram all day to keep out the way, but it was wintertime now, and Tom also had to service her car and do all the gardening.' Finally the Walkers' persistence paid off, when, after first being turned away, they obtained a sparsely furnished house in Scarborough. Years later, after several moves, they were still in Scarborough, eventually buying their own house, initially shared with tenants to help pay the mortgage. Beryl suffered bouts of severe homesickness in the isolated suburb, but reflecting on how the long struggle affected their marriage she was emphatically positive:

No, I should think if anything it brought us closer together. We both agreed that we really wanted to get out of the situation we were in – even if we got another caravan – leaving Tom's mother. And even if we got another caravan we just both felt that we'd be better on our own, we thought we could make – we'd be happier if we lived on our own. That was what we always felt.

The story told by the Walkers is one of success and achievement; but it is built on an epic account of struggle, in which the battle to define themselves apart from domineering family members is inseparable from the realities of housing shortages, in both Britain and Australia, and the vagaries of employment opportunity. For Tom the later story of proud achievement and vindication, marked by the successes of their children and grandchildren, was all the more potent because of perilous wartime experiences during the Normandy landing. For Beryl it was a turnaround from early years when she was desperate to return and contemplated leaving the marriage. Their story is a reminder of how the vividly recalled early years of struggle to find the most elementary standard of housing could be a prelude to more comfortable suburban life.

Simple access to self-contained rented housing of the kind found by the Walkers was sheer delight to many after even a few weeks of communal sharing. Ray and Irene Spencer were part of the later migrant generation, arriving in Perth by plane in 1966, but their housing experiences were not unlike those of their predecessors. After a spell in Point Walter Hostel they shared a nearby house with a Romanian refugee, but while Ray was away working in the north west Irene leapt at an opportunity to rent a house by themselves. 'So it was nice for me to have a door I could lock, entirely on our own, and this was next–door to our Australian friends. And they've turned out to be *wonderful* friends, the ones we still write to today.' On his return Ray heartily approved of the move, and when they were offered a Housing Commission home at Medina, which had a reputation as an English ghetto, they promptly turned it down. Ray's delight in this modest house – 'asbestos … on stilts' – was linked to his poor upbringing in the cramped terrace of a Welsh mining village and a history of inadequate rented housing. 'No way I was going to move from there, beautiful garden, vine, tree and all the rest of it. It was an ideal spot, the sort of place I would love to have owned…. Always lived in caravans, accommo-dation, lived with my parents, I was up to here with it. I wanted a place of my own.'[8]

In fact the rental mindset could keep newcomers content with the life of tenants when conditions were an improvement on what they had left behind. In 1959 Elizabeth Gray went from one floor of a council house in Chingford, Essex, to a larger rented house on 2 acres of ground near Nunawading, and despite the hard work and muddy walks to school for the children she found it exhilarating and healthy. For the later generation more modern housing itself, together with appliances, could add to the sense of improvement. Carol Brooks and her husband David left Brighton in 1969 for Perth and soon found a modern flat which highlighted the contrast between old and new. 'Oh, it was lovely. Well, we'd had an *old* flat in Brighton and this was like a modern flat with built-in wardrobes, built-in fridge and cooker and everything, all nice worktops. It was lovely. Neither of us had had anything like that before. It was all old what we'd had in England.'[9]

The 'nesting narrative' of Vera and Bernard Makewell

While ingrained British working-class habits of renting died hard, the most earnest ambitions of the great majority of young migrants were focused on buying or building their own home. Vera and Bernard Makewell place this quest for housing at the centre of their story, and illustrate the power of the 'nesting narrative' for sustaining a positive attitude to migrant identity.[10] The Makewells, both from working-class backgrounds, came to Sydney from London with two young children in 1954. Both had limited formal education, but Bernard's communication engineering experience with the air force during the war set him on a successful career in telephony which he pursued in Sydney. In later years in Australia he left this work to go into business as an independent builder and cabinet maker, mainly from experience he had acquired while he and Vera built their own houses in Sydney. One might expect that Bernard's career success would be the focus of their proud story, and there were indeed overtones of this in his commitment to the work ethic. He stressed that 'the attitude' towards work in England was one motivation for him to leave – the limitations on advancement, the lack of recognition for hard work and general devaluation of the work ethic. But his career trajectory was not at the centre of their life story. Instead it was structured around a shared account of the struggle to establish their living space: the 'culture shock', the early difficulties with sponsorship and the long drawn-out struggles during the building of two houses. This was indeed a nesting narrative, for which the very bricks and mortar where we conducted an interview stood as the ultimate vindication.

The owner of Vera and Bernard's first Australian home was their friendly Australian sponsor, Marjorie, who had persuaded them to emigrate while she was visiting London. Marjorie was a matron in a Sydney hospital who spent little time at her remote rural home near Stanwell Park, about half way between Sydney and Wollongong. The isolated location dictated a three and a half mile walk, along the railway line, to both the station and the nearest primary school. Bernard was at work in Sydney for most of the day and Vera, who felt strongly about staying home to care for her children, was on her own and faced the daily walk to school carrying her 3-year-old along terrain too rough for a pram and infested with black snakes. She soon discovered that most of the children went to school on horseback. While Vera now insists that she enjoyed the house and location, the practical difficulties forced them to look elsewhere, and Marjorie found them a house in the nearby village of Otford, opposite the lone-teacher school, where they shared with an elderly widower, an ex-gold-miner. The widower expected Vera to feed him, to light the fire and do general housekeeping, all of which she took on without complaint. But the elderly widower was also excessively 'amorous': 'I went into the laundry, he puts his arms round me and, and I couldn't move!' While this went no further, Vera began to fear him: 'I wouldn't leave the children with him, and I just felt that I, that wasn't the right thing to do'. Combined with continuing transport difficulties, and a rat-infested house, this was enough to spur the Makewells, within two months of arrival, to seek housing closer to Sydney.

The fact that Vera and Bernard had owned their house in Newbury Park, London, for seven years before their migration, gave them an advantage over the majority of migrants who had to seek scarce rental accommodation. But still their choice involved relentless struggle. Lacking sufficient capital for a suitable house, they jumped at the chance to buy a large block of land with a garage in the south Sydney suburb of Revesby. Without hesitation they chose to live in the garage while building one room at a time, on weekends, with Bernard as builder and Vera as self-defined 'labourer'. Floods and storms, blown-off roofs and leaking walls regularly disrupted their efforts. Vera describes cooking in the garage in her gumboots in several inches of floodwater, carrying food and dishes back and forth between the one newly finished room and the garage. It took eight years of such labour before the house was completed to their satisfaction, but, as they said, almost in unison, 'we just accepted it'. Moreover, as if to register the triumph of their labours, and perhaps to mark their upward mobility, in 1967, soon after they were comfortably settled in Revesby, they sold the house and began the process all over again; their new home was in the more fashionable northern Sydney suburb of Newport, on a steep hill overlooking the Pittwater inlet. Not content with the existing building, they began again to recreate the house of their dreams.

Reflecting on their story, replete with family pride and enjoyment of grandchildren, both Vera and Bernard insisted that they had regularly agreed on the big decisions, from choosing to emigrate, to housing, work and childcare. Sharing the labour of their joint enterprise also gave each a joint investment in the success of their long struggles, which served to distance them from others with less determination. When asked how they saw their migration experience, Bernard's reply invoked a comparison between themselves and the general run of British migrants: 'We found there was a tendency among our Australian people to introduce us to English people. They always thought that we would want to meet English people.... But frankly, after we met a few of them, all they did was whinge, and we didn't want to meet them.... I think we made an effort.' Their account – a kind of battlers' tale – served to vindicate their migration decision by contrast with those of their contemporaries who lacked what Bernard called 'backbone', the 'whingers' who expected Australian prosperity to fall into their laps on arrival. The same 'whingers', they insisted, had dogged their heels during their voyage on the *Orion* in 1954, and the Makewells had determined to stay away from them, finding their friends in Australia among the native-born and those of other nationalities. The interview was regularly punctuated by assertions of their determination, which distinguished them from what they felt was the general character of British migrants. 'When we came out,' Vera remarked, 'we said we've got to make a go of it because we can't afford to go back, and we aimed, we worked for that.' Incorporated into this self-vindicating narrative was the proud assertion of their Australian citizenship, again in contrast to others who had clung to their British nationality. Moreover, migration and home-building were experiences each could share, whereas their employment history was almost exclusively Bernard's, since he remained the sole breadwinner until their children were out of school.

Buying and building the Australian dream

The Makewells' story is a telling example of how the housing quest could command shared sacrifice and determination for years after arrival. In Chapter 2 we noted that in 1959 British immigrants brought a median of £289 to Australia, barely enough to furnish let alone buy a new home. Only the most fortunate, who had sold homes in Britain and brought sufficient capital for a deposit in Australia – like the Good family in Perth – were able to buy their own homes within weeks or even months of arrival. Several chapters of Thomas Jenkins's autobiographical guidebook, *We Came to Australia*, focus on buying and establishing a home in Australia, and attest to the momentous significance of the venture and to the advantage of their comparative afflu-ence. The Jenkins family had sold an 'above average' semi-detached house in Walton-Upon-Thames for £6,250. Arriving in Perth in 1965 they rented a family home while they scoured the new outer-suburban subdivisions for a block of land upon which to build their new home: nothing 'less than a brand-new house would do for a brand-new life'. Nine miles out of town, in Ross-moyne, they chose a plot upon a ridge of pines: 'Perhaps memory, of pines in Scotland standing beside brown water or high on snowy hills, pulled us.' After endless tours of show homes they selected their dream home, but the next few months 'drove us to despair, to quarrelling and to incoherent bewilderment', as builders haggled over prices and fittings and the Jenkins struggled with byzantine planning rules as well as septic tank sewerage and other Australian 'strangenesses'. Eventually, about six months after arrival, they moved into a light and airy home with roof timbers that creaked with the rise and fall of the heat of an Australian day; 'you get to like the sound of the house talking'. The block had cost £2,000, the house £5,088, and after paying a substantial deposit the Jenkins had a mortgage for £4,500 at 6.25 per cent. Thomas Jenkins warned the migrant seeking his dream home about the risk of financial 'over-extension' and that he would 'need all his money and most of his courage and patience to raise the wind for a home in Australia.'[11]

The struggle to save up and buy your own home was not always success-ful. In 1949 Lancashire man Sydney Hart and his bride Betty started married life in a caravan – 'purchased at great expense' for £400 – which they towed to a 'perfect setting' on a slope overlooking the sea on the south coast of New South Wales. 'From our plateau we had everything our hearts could desire.' But the torment of insects and floods, and the arrival of a new baby, forced the Harts to seek a house. Sydney calculated that he could buy a home for about £2,500, including a £700 deposit, and that this was just about affordable with his savings and a weekly wage of £15, though he worried about the quality of Australian housing.

You might even believe you could get a brick bungalow in return for the outlay of that sum of money, or at least an up-to-date elaborate weather-proof wooden bungalow. So much for the dream! What you get in return for the considerable outlay is a four-roomed wooden dwelling with a corrugated-iron roof.

With no pavements and no roads, the need for several gallons of paint each year, and high insurance on inflammable dwellings, the last straw for Hart was lack of a proper hot water system. And, looking ahead, 'think of the condition in which those timber walls would be by the time the mortgage was paid off!' An alternative plan to enlist mates to help build a home on a plot of land fell through because roofing materials were unavailable for six months, at which point the Harts gave up and instead spent their savings on return to England, with Sydney concluding that, 'I think the answer of ninety per cent of returning emigrants – certainly my own – would be found in the Australian newspapers under the heading, "Houses for Sale"'.[12]

But for most enthusiasts, reservations about the quality of Australian housing were unlikely to thwart the temptation of home ownership. Gwen Good likened the primitive tin roof of her first home in Perth to that of a backyard shed and feared what her parents might think, but this was of relatively minor account in the family's drive to settle in the new home.[13] Indeed, building or buying the first house is often the most vividly remembered story of the early years in Australia. Fondly recalled struggles to attain the first home form something of a recurring motif in the migrant life story, reminiscent of pioneer narratives, eclipsing negative experiences and regrets. The vividness of the memory is palpable in details of novel building processes as well as the adventure and excitement of do-it-yourself construction and living rough. Dot Hallas, for example, was a classic reluctant migrant in Melbourne in the early 1950s; she had acquiesced in her husband's determination to emigrate, essentially to maintain marital harmony, and 'cried every night for twelve months.... I didn't care about England, I wanted me mum!' But after escaping difficult sponsorship conditions in East Brunswick to a block of land in outer Glen Waverley, Dot took to the new adventure of amateur building with great verve. Her story is punctuated with hilarious memories of encounters with the building inspector at the outdoor toilet, desperate measures to conceal the fact that her family of three were living illegally in a primitive shed, and the 'fun' of communal building. With a preschool daughter, Dot had to make complicated childcare arrangements in order to work as a cleaner in a pub, and, with no savings, each stage of building had to wait until they had cash in hand. But Dot and her husband soon entered into the spirit of joint enterprise, with mutual help from neighbours who shared water and loaned equipment.

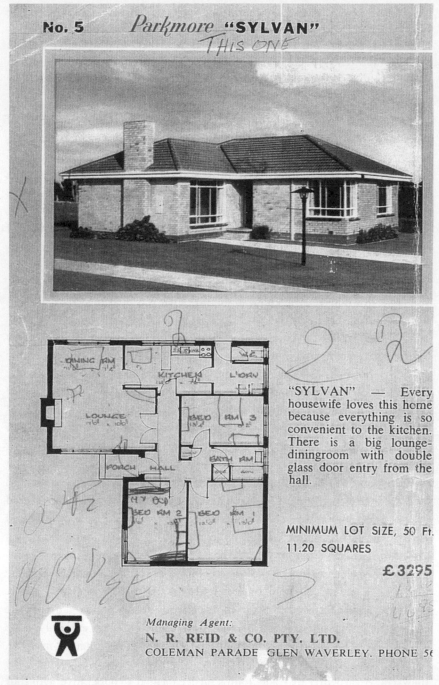

29 In 1960 the Forrest family from Dunbartonshire in Scotland, who had spent two years in a hostel and then a shared rented home, chose their new dream home, 'Sylvan', in the Melbourne outer suburb of Glen Waverley. One of the Forrest children proudly scrawled 'This one – our house' on the plans in the Parkmore Homes brochure

Oh! But we were happy! … We got the house to a certain stage, we finished one bedroom. And Doug was a plasterer so he plastered it for us. And John made his kitchen cupboards. You know, it was things like that. And he put a catwalk through the kitchen, to get to that bedroom, so we pulled the partition down in the shed, put the beds in the bedroom…. And in that little room, I think it's 10 by 11, we had a double bed, a single bed and a cot.[14]

Dot's story returns regularly to the pride of achievement and enjoyment of neighbourly sharing. The house grew as the money became available, reinforcing their sense of independence. 'We used to put so much away every week, till we had enough for the stumps, and then the bearers, and then the walls, and then the windows and then the roof! And that's how we built the house! We never owed money. Because we couldn't get a loan! So, when it were finished it were finished, and it was ours!' Dot's fond recollection of working alongside neighbours, who invited the Hallases to use their bathroom, perhaps best encapsulates the transformation all this effected in her attitude to her migration: 'He had his bathroom fixed. And they said: "Oh, you come down here", you know, so we did. That was hilarious! We had some fun. Mm. And that never dies ---.'

At their most extreme, shared building practices became voluntary building societies of like-minded British migrants, a rare expression of ethnic solidarity normally associated with non-English-speaking migrants. In the mid-1950s Betty Tilley and her husband joined forces with eleven other families from England, Scotland and Ireland to build their houses on twelve-quarter-acre blocks on three streets in the barely settled outer suburb of Yokine, Western Australia. All the men were skilled tradesmen, including carpenters, plumbers, electricians, a painter and a roof tiler. Each of them took turns as chair of the 'building society'; they drew lots for the blocks and built the houses in groups of four, also chosen by ballot. The men took rostered weekends off and apparently completed the entire enterprise promptly and with no serious disputes. While this formed the potential foundation for a close-knit British community, Betty insists that once the building was complete the dispersed nature of the housing blocks encouraged them to socialize with Australian and other migrant neighbours, so that the apparent ethnic solidarity was short-lived. Similar cooperative ventures occurred across the country, although not always with the comfortable outcome enjoyed by the Tilleys. John Jordan's father brought his family to Wollongong in 1950, having already purchased a block of land on an idyllic spot overlooking Lake Illawarra. A carpenter by trade, John's father formed a cooperative with four English tradesmen he had met on the ship and they agreed to build their houses on adjoining blocks. The group followed familiar practices, living in hastily constructed garages, 'like living in a big caravan', while the building proceeded. 'What a *lot* of people seemed to do is that they built the garage [near] to the house and moved into the garage. And that's precisely what we did.' But as the other migrants completed their houses, John's mother found the primitive living conditions on an unserviced block intolerable, and the family's homesickness drove them back to England, with their house never built. Ironically they later re-emigrated to Australia, this time to live in public housing, only to return again when the two sons settled in England. But for John that final return remains a matter of regret, and he retains vivid memories of the building venture – of the excitement, for example, when electricity poles came closer 'until one wonderful day we had actual electricity'.[15]

Australia could be identified with home ownership ideals well before departure. For John Jordan's parents the prior purchase of land in Wollongong said much about the identification of Australia with property-owning family life. Many postwar British migrants rapidly adjusted their rental mindset to one in which home ownership was central to their vision of a family future. The readiness of our interviewees to respond to questions about family life with vivid details of house building and buying, the strangeness of Australian houses and the joys of modern appliances in the new family home, attests to ways in which they quickly absorbed the 'Australian dream'. Other researchers of Australian suburban families have noticed how home ownership, with all the trappings, was inseparable from ideas of family, that 'family life is entered via home ownership'.[16] While for British migrants these ideas may have acquired greater importance over their lifetime in Australia, the vivid recall of those early years does suggest a rapid and willing adjustment to Australian norms.

Many British migrant stories of home acquisition are memories of marital, family and community solidarity, which cemented commitment to the new country and underlined the success of the migration. But it is hardly surprising that such a momentous decision as buying or building the first house easily provoked conflict. The tendency for some women to be prime movers in pushing home ownership, often reflecting their initiation of the migration decision, carries interesting implications about gender relations in the postwar years. Maureen Carter's stepmother took the initiative to arrange a loan and choose a house in the west Sydney suburb of Campsie over her husband's certainty that such things 'were not for the likes of us'.[17] Maureen recalls that in later years, after the purchase proved to be a great success, her father took credit for the whole idea! For Margaret Reardon's father, a 'reluctant migrant' who clung to the prospect of returning to Scotland, the ultimate gesture of resistance to 'finality' in the family's settlement was to refuse the purchase of a home. After several years living in a Housing Commission house in the Canberra suburb of Deakin – 'a lovely suburb', according to her mother – they were offered the opportunity to buy. By this time the likelihood of return was remote, but for father the prospect of home ownership was the final symbolic step he refused to take.

My mother wanted to buy that house.... I think it was 11,000 pounds you could buy it for, or dollars, and he refused. He said, 'I'm not buying anything here because I'm eventually going home', and that was it. He still had it in his mind that he would eventually end up in Edinburgh.... My mother had committed herself well and truly and wanted to buy that house more than anything.... They never bought it. And it was [later] valued at $98,000 or something, yes.[18]

'It brought us together': the fortunes of marriage and family in Australia

Tensions over the crucial decisions of home ownership remind us that the pressures of migration could subject marriage and family life to deep and lasting stresses. For a minority these stresses were ultimately insurmountable, resulting in family breakdowns which could in turn lead to a further 'new life' in Australia. But questions about how a marriage fared under the pressures of settlement and struggle commonly elicit, rather, the response that 'it brought us closer together'. Very few British couples settled among supportive groups from their own British background, and most had lost their extended family networks and thus were acutely conscious of the need for mutual support. 'It brought us together, greatly, greatly,' Josephine Blackmore insisted, 'because you've only got each other.' Cliff and Gwen Good agreed that 'If anything it cemented it.... We relied on one another more.'[19] As John and Sylvia Cannon's case history showed, these general statements of solidarity are rarely enough to encapsulate the ups and downs of an entire marriage and family life, but couples who now celebrate their long and successful partnership are most emphatic about asserting their loyalty under pressure.

One of the first, and often most testing, decisions facing couples with children after arrival, with real implications for the nature of their family life, was whether the wife should seek paid work. In Chapter 6 we saw how important it could be for migrant wives to find some form of employment, even during early years of child rearing. Necessity and past practice meant that British wives and mothers took employment at a greater rate than their Australian-born counterparts. This of course was at odds with the suburban separate spheres ideal widely publicized in postwar years as being integral to the 'Australian way of life'.[20] There is very little evidence that our informants were at all critical of this ideal; indeed, their enthusiasm for suburban home ownership underlines their eagerness to enjoy its benefits. Preference for staying at home with young children was a frequently asserted sentiment, and when the husband's income was adequate women usually opted for full-time childcare, at least with young infants. Kathleen Barrand in Geelong recalled that during the 1950s she had been 'just a housewife ... totally dedicated to the children ... totally happy, I felt very fulfilled'.[21] Although in later years she began to express some regret that she had missed out on more diverse experiences by being out of the workforce, there is no hint that she felt such misgivings at the time. This was probably enhanced by her closeness to a streetful of supportive women in the same situation, some of them British migrants.

While there is no doubt about the overwhelming commitment of the British to these traditional domestic arrangements in a suburban setting, what is most striking is the flexible attitude of aspiring British suburbanites towards their means of achieving the ideal. When necessity dictated, women were adept at moving in and out of the workforce, sometimes with regrets but often resorting to ingenious forms of childcare. The need to work was never far removed from fundamental family ideals. George and Connie Adam were committed to Connie remaining a full-time mother in Perth, but when they were unable to manage without her income Connie's justification for taking a succession of jobs and running small businesses rested on their bedrock family goals. She explained, 'we did all the things we wanted to do for the kids; that was really what we came out for'.[22]

Maureen and John Butts's varied careers in Australia exemplify the flexible approach to family and work arrangements that could be dictated by the material circumstances of migration, but which accompanied gradual adaptation to Australian suburban living. In 1959 they left St Helens, Lancashire, for Melbourne, with one child, after disappointment with their attempts to build a house.[23] For John the move was also motivated by dissatisfaction with his work as a toolmaker; for Maureen it was in part pushed by intrusive pressures from her mother, who she felt had neglected her during a wartime childhood. A new country offered escape from the intrusion but also an opportunity for Maureen to give her children a different upbringing, in effect a generational break with her parents. 'My feelings were that I would not treat my children like I was treated.' For both of them the move offered an opportunity for home ownership, which had been thwarted in England, along with a better life for their children.

Within a day of arriving at Preston Hostel John obtained work, and, faced with inactivity, Maureen organized a dancing class for hostel children. Soon afterwards they rented a small house in the carefully chosen location of Black Rock; 'we wanted to be near the beach', Maureen recalled. She then promptly found work in an office, a vital step for their home-buying ambitions, but also something she had always taken for granted. 'I think I was probably a little bit like my mother in that way ... back to work, you know, after the children.... I mean, I wanted to be there for the children, but I didn't hesitate if there was a job that I could fit around them, you know.' A friendly neighbour eased the 'fitting' by taking Sue to kindergarten in the mornings and caring for her in the afternoons.

The Butts's goal approached realization with the purchase of a block of land in Frankston, but after three years in Black Rock, on the spur of the moment and recalling their delight with the west on a brief stop-over during the voyage, they resolved to move to Perth. Here Maureen's second child was born, she moved in and out of the workforce, and they finally realized their home-ownership ambitions, trading up over the next three decades from Leederville to South Perth, Carine, Safety Bay and finally to Waikiki. With a vigilant eye on accommodating childcare to employment, they bought a news-agency and post office in Safety Bay, where Maureen continued to work, often part time, even after selling the business. For John, too, Perth brought dramatic changes, finally freeing him from his trade. He began by selling insurance, moved into retail work and became a wine company sales representative. An evening job with a health club inspired his interest in community recreation, which led him to enrol in a diploma course, later a university degree, and local council work as a recreation officer. By 1985 he was deeply involved in local affairs and was elected to Rockingham council, the start of a long career in local government service.

On the surface this is a classic story of migrant success in material terms, of self-improvement, successful working careers and increasing prosperity. John acknowledges its force in his proud recollection of achievement and service, of never being unemployed, advancing his education and contributing to community welfare. But for both Maureen and John their story runs much deeper, into accounts of family well being and hesitant integration into sub-urban life. Soon after the Butts's arrival in Melbourne John turned to his old enthusiasm for athletics, and this provided their main social outlet in the early days, together with the company of an English couple from the ship. Time allowed for only minimal socializing: 'we were so intent on working and trying to get started', Maureen recalled. John added that their tendency to see only English friends reflected their initial distance from any neighbourhood attach-ments. 'We hadn't made any Australian friends because we'd never kind of become community, attached to a community, I suppose.' In Perth this changed, as John's athletics networks and Maureen's tennis club spawned further Australian and British friendships. Even so, close neighbourhood intimacy of the kind Maureen had known in St Helens remained elusive. 'That was the difference between England and Australia, really, I found, because that doesn't happen here.' The obstacle on most occasions turned out to be an alien drinking culture among both neighbours and athletics clubs. Neighbours' invitations, even on a Sunday morning, turned out to be demanding drinking occasions. In Leederville they quickly discovered 'we'd been labelled as, we just weren't their kind, because we didn't drink'.

For this reason John and Maureen maintained a respectful distance from neighbours while enjoying a growing network of family-friendly contacts and frequent 'social outings'. Once the children were at school the opportunity for wider community involvement and friendships expanded. Their ultimate commitment to a familiar Australian 'way of life' was the building of a beach house, which occupied every free weekend until the children became old enough to protest. Reflecting on the years since arrival, Maureen stresses their agreement on the fundamentals of family life, especially of child discipline. Neither of them ever questioned their traditional division of labour, in which Maureen did the lion's share of domestic work and household management, with John's occasional help and heavy work in the garden. Maureen's sense of achievement ultimately had little to do with her working life. Australian remoteness from England enabled them to escape intrusion from parents, but the greatest result of their migration was 'staying together and having a happy family. There's not many of them about! [laughs] ... and we've been very fortunate, you know, in the fact that we've ... had a really good marriage, and we're proud of our children.'

Variations on the Butts's suburban 'happy families' story reverberate through our interviews. The high retrospective valuation placed on successful raising of a family in Australia is perhaps unsurprising from women, but men's reflections are strikingly similar, even when, as with John Butts, their careers are a matter of pride. Grahame Manoy told an engaging story about his 'struggle', forging a career in Perth, initially in the clothing trade, and later in a family business eventually taken over by his daughter. But the struggle was essentially a family story, with difficulties along the way: 'I'm not going to say that we have sailed through to the happiness that we've got now without problems'. For Grahame this required the sacrifice of affluence for 'living life' and close intimacy; 'we couldn't be closer', he commented about his children and his marriage.[24]

Many of these stories also complicate our traditional impressions of the household division of labour in the 1950s and 1960s. Not surprisingly, women assumed the major burden of housework, whether or not they went out to work. But it is significant how often couples departed from the strict division. Most interviewees recall a traditional arrangement in their parents' marriage in which men retained responsibility for well-defined domestic duties like regularly cleaning and repairing shoes for the whole family.[25] These practices were breaking down in the postwar years, and the change may have been hastened by migration. But in other respects migrant household practices display a remarkable flexibility, with men routinely taking on, or at least helping with, cooking, cleaning and childcare tasks. Betty Tilley in Perth described her sharing of tasks with her husband as 'one and a half jobs each', in sharp contrast to her parents. Mary Clayton thought such sharing extended to patterns of authority, insisting that 'there was no boss in our house, no boss'.[26]

For men there are two intertwined themes which inform the regular celebration of family and domestic life. One is about successful marriages, often recalled during a contented retirement together; another is about close relationships with children, implying a superior model of fatherhood compared to that represented by their fathers. The sense of change is captured in Albert Lougher's memorable quip that on the eve of their emigration they were pioneers of a 'new generation, not like my dad'.[27] Recent scholarship exploring postwar fatherhood has underlined ways in which British working-class men's memories incorporate rejection of old models of fathering alongside the class-ridden values of their parents' generation; migration presented an ideal opportunity to assert these differences. Mark Peel notes that working-class men abandoned the past represented by Britain with a 'particular passion' and that their newfound loyalty to Australia rested on their ability to become more successful providers, 'better men than their own fathers', and better fathers themselves in the new country. Though British migrant fathers retained the traditional role as family breadwinner, relationships within the home were changing in subtle but significant ways.[28]

'When things settle he'll change': migration and family breakdown

The stories of John and Maureen Butts or Vera and Bernard Makewell speak for the large body of migrants who associate contented marriages and family harmony with their adaptation in comfortable suburbs. The wider realities, of course, were rarely quite so simple. Submissive women, in particular, rapidly acquired new skills of assertiveness and independence under the challenges of relocation and employment, as Maureen Butts recalled when she reflected on her 'timidity' at the time of migration compared to her later self-reliance.

Margaret Hill's story of a reluctant emigration, an unhappy marriage and divorce some years after arrival illustrates the ways in which migration could foster sharp changes in marital dynamics.[29] Her account of her marriage is a painful one, but, like most marriages when deeply probed, it reveals complex threads of shifting power balances and fluctuating stages of companionship. On leaving Merseyside for Adelaide in 1956, for example, she was to all intents and purposes the classic reluctant migrant; she was tired, the mother of three young children, pregnant (she was to bear five more children in Australia) and pushed by her husband to leave in a way which gave her no choice. Margaret's recall of their departure vividly portrays dependence on her husband and her reluctance and exhaustion; yet she also admits that after two bad winters in a damp house with flu epidemics and sick children she had been persuaded by a doctor that they would be better off in a warmer climate. Her portrayal of a frequently dominating husband, too, makes concessions to his domestication. A caring father, he routinely 'baked, he cooked, he cleaned' and bathed the children; when sex segregation on the *Otranto* prevented fathers from bathing and dressing young children ('one of the main complaints of the women'), 'I found Jim didn't care. He wasn't allowed in the ladies bathroom so he couldn't bath the children there, so he bathed them in the wash trough in the laundry. He didn't let that stop him bathing the children.' Most dramatically, though, Margaret contrasts the one-sided mode of their migration decision with the longer-term results: 'once I'd got here and I settled, in the long run, I settled and made myself a life here, and he is still bitter and unsettled and discontented'.

For several turbulent years after arrival the Hills' lives were not suburban at all. The Finsbury migrant hostel became home for two years as their growing family presented an obstacle to finding rental accommodation. In desperation Jim forsook his trade as a painter and decorator for work as a lighthouse keeper, 'a job with a house', first at Kingston, later on Neptune Island in the Spencer Gulf. In Kingston Margaret found her 'first taste of how life could be in Australia'; the children thrived and she made close friends. The posting to Neptune Island promptly terminated her promising social network and replaced it with correspondence schooling, water shortages, shipping emergencies, and, crucially, social isolation. When Jim resigned in anger after a row with the authorities the family found themselves once again homeless in Adelaide and, against the normal regulations prohibiting readmission, were forced back into the Finsbury hostel for a further nine months.

Help from the South Australian Housing Trust finally located a remote 'temporary' four-room fibro house 'on stilts' in Oaklands Park, and after two years another rented house in Mitchell Park. Here Margaret began to make a new life for herself, more especially when Jim was away working for several months at a time at Woomera and Maralinga. Finding herself frequently with 'a kitchen full of kids', she became involved with the children's school and helped to organize a local youth club. But this also marked a deterioration in the marriage:

I had developed a network of friends ... I had got myself involved in the kindergarten and the school group and the Red Cross and the Salvation Army and these things so I had developed a network, but he didn't.... And when he came home it was a different story ... we just found life was different when he came

home. And when he stopped going away to work which coincided with the time
that I had my last child … and he was home all the time and he just didn't like me
being out at these meetings and going to these places, so … he'd ring up and if I
wasn't there, he'd come home and say, 'You were out in the middle of the day', and
then he cut off the housekeeping money, he did all the shopping, it just went
worse from there.

Margaret recalls telling herself that her deteriorating marriage was simply
a temporary aberration due to the upheavals caused by migration and frequent disruption. Just as she had hoped when in England that Australia would
change Jim, 'I kept thinking he'll change.… And so when I was here I kept
thinking when things settle he'll change, but of course he didn't, he just got
worse.' When domination escalated to domestic violence Margaret finally left
the marriage, initially without her children. She went to Melbourne and faced
a long, ultimately successful, child custody battle. In Melbourne she returned
to her old trade as a bookbinder, worked hard at single motherhood and found
herself a new community, first in Sandringham, then in a succession of
eastern suburbs. Looking back now she reflects that Australia fundamentally
affected her marriage by enabling her to become independent: 'finding my
feet and being able to do things, and being able to apply myself to problems
and solve them and cope with them. Yes … I think he would have preferred
me to stay dependent.' But her independence was mostly forged, in both
Adelaide and Melbourne, through close involvement in suburban life, in
fostering and sustaining local organizations, often in defiance of her husband.
In the suburbs she gradually progressed from the hapless migrant woman
caught in classic embarrassments – like turning up with an empty plate when
asked to 'bring a plate' – to a prominent local figure, as president, for example,
of the Chelsea 'Life Activities Group'. Compared to what she describes still as
an 'insular' and 'hide-bound' life in England she now celebrates her successful
settlement in Australia, and proudly writes successive volumes of autobiography.[30] 'You can see I've done well here. I mean notwithstanding I walked
out of my marriage with nothing. So in forty years this is me. In the meantime
I've married my daughters … and helped all my kids get a start, 'cause father's
been useless.'

Alongside those marriages which fractured among the stresses and
changes of migration, there were others which soldiered on in some form of
dogged companionship, often 'for the sake of the children'. After arrival in
Sydney Ethel Ledgett 'knighted' her husband 'sir bloody Andy Capp' for his
capacity to evade housework by sneaking off to the pub, and she admitted
casually that 'we had fisticuffs'.[31] Yet Ethel never considered leaving, judging
such tension to be perfectly normal over forty years of marriage. Vanessa
Seymour's mother underlined her long endurance in what Vanessa styled a

'totally dysfunctional' family, taken to Tasmania without consultation, by divorcing her controlling husband only when the children had left home, after twenty-eight years of marriage. Her comment to Vanessa about her experience of migration was simply that 'I would have liked Australia much better if your father had been a better husband'.[32]

Child migrants like Vanessa bring a uniquely critical perspective to the ways in which their family lives were disrupted for years by the upheaval of migration. Adolescent daughters, in particular, were themselves prone to resent having to leave home, and were acutely sensitive to any worsening in their family life. Margaret Reardon, for example, admits that, much to her mother's chagrin, she was her father's stalwart ally in opposition to the move and did little to smooth the early difficulties. Jackie Smith was a characteristically rebellious 13-year-old when she and her parents left a rich south London network of working-class neighbours and extended family in 1959 for Adelaide. Her desolation was captured in a lament for the loss of family Christmas in the bleak dustbowl of Elizabeth: 'Christmas, that was the end of Christmas … In England I had this family Christmas where, you know, everybody got together and it was a real celebration. We went to Australia, there was no more family Christmas. There was no more family, no more family Christmas.'[33] For these young discontents the suburbs could resemble a 'desert,' representing the negation of everything to do with thriving family, community and social life. Ironically, it was precisely the promise of a better family and social life which had driven the great bulk of British families to settle in new Australian suburbs.

Living the 'dream': migrant families in Australian suburbs

Historians of Australian suburbia have long had to grapple with conflicting attitudes to suburban life. After the war developers urged the need to expand the boundaries of 'the good life' without hindrance, conservationists warned of the costs of rampant destruction and social critics equated suburbia with cultural sterility. The 'suburban pioneers', mostly Australian born, who built their houses in new suburbs in the 1940s and 1950s were usually oblivious to such polemics. In their recollection it was experiences of 'privation and insecurity' which shaped their dreams of the 'good life'. The hardships of raising children while building or buying on the bush fringe and living without services and facilities were common for much of this generation, and memories of that pioneering now loom large in their life histories.[34] British migrants joined this movement with great enthusiasm, sharing its hardships and benefits, but they also brought to it the migrant's more complex burden of cultural and family baggage, so that every experience, every privation and every delight was magnified by the strangeness of a new land and customs. This is as true for the long period of adaptation to suburban living as it is for the difficult phase of home building and acquisition.

Adult migrants' recollections overwhelmingly focus on the 'delights' of these years, and recall excitement and fulfilment, as they built new lives around their children's futures. Similar themes recur here to those promised in migration propaganda, particularly the revelling in a more outdoor life, the greater social informality and freedom from convention and class division. Most parents, at least, insist that they did find a better place to bring up their children. If some of the changes initially incurred shocked disapproval – like Gwen Good's alarm at children running wild without shoes, even to school – in retrospect the reservations become objects of humour and fade into insignificance beside celebration of the positives.[35]

Once settled, migrants were quick to make the most of the attractions of a warm climate by cultivating the much-touted 'outdoor life', often a passport to a freer form of social life. We saw in Chapter 4 how, for Cliff and Gwen Good, swimming at the beach and camping in the bush served as a regular reminder of their good fortune in Perth compared to the 'bus queues and the drizzling rain' they had left behind. 'Outdoor life' was, of course, experienced in a wide variety of ways, from John Hardie's fishing trips, the Jordans' prawn catching and Frank Kemp's father's rabbiting (a great improvement on Scotland, where the practice would have risked arrest for poaching!) to Grace Turnbull's tennis.[36] It also varied in degree according to climate, with the warmer states of Queensland, Western Australia and New South Wales enjoying a better reputation for the 'blue skies' and virtual year-round outdoor socializing.

Social life required the cultivation of friendship networks, and while these were often dictated by location, they did much to shape the nature of migrants' adaptation, bringing them face to face with people from backgrounds often radically different from their own. Neighbours might include recent British or European migrants, but most found themselves in predominantly Australian neighbourhoods. Assertions about helpful and considerate neighbours far outweigh complaints of anti-British sentiments. Wendy Jay had 'never met such friendliness' as that she encountered in Tasmania when, with three young children, they confronted the primitive 'shack' they bought outside Hobart.[37] Their most helpful neighbour was a Polish builder who converted their shack and remained a lifelong friend. Pat Drohan's Ballarat neighbours, all Australian, made up a tight little self-help group, bringing in each other's washing in the rain and caring for sick children. This was not, of course, an uncomplicated story, and could vary according to location, age, class and temperament. When Pat moved she found herself among 'aloof' neighbours, also Australian. Margaret Reardon's mother from Edinburgh was a deeply committed migrant, eager to assimilate in Canberra, but Margaret thought the mixed-class composition of the suburb of Deakin inhibited the extent of neighbourliness, which remained at arm's length. Maureen Carr, who emigrated with her mother and grandparents, found that her grandparents, unlike herself and her mother, instinctively gravitated towards elderly English friends, who were plentiful in the Sydney suburb of Greenacre. 'Keeping ourselves to ourselves', a time-worn English formulation of household privacy and reserve, could also limit socializing. Children of migrants, too, might be more critical than were their parents of the depth of Australian neigh-bourliness. Maureen Carter, conscious of the close-knit Welsh village of her childhood, noticed the limited nature of her parents' friendships. They were rarely close to more than one or two neighbours, 'not like in Wales, where you knew the whole street. And you could leave your kids with anybody in the street.'[38]

While the neighbourhood was an important influence in the adaptation process, the more dramatic paths to a sense of belonging were a myriad of local institutions and organizations. The most common experience was engage-ment with children's schooling, which for women especially could be the most important introduction to Australian networks. Valerie Proverbs, who adopted children in Launceston, reflected that having children was important 'because you get to know people'. In Perth Maurice Tomlin and his wife remained on the school parents' and children's committee for twenty-five years, driven by Maurice's determination that his children's education should be better than his own. After six years as president he was thoroughly integrated into the local Midland community. The process was boosted by close involvement with church activities, Sunday schools, church camps and regular meetings which drew them into the community. For Maurice, who experienced a profound religious conversion a few years after arrival, these were central to his daily life. Indeed, church involvements could be another point of entry into social life, as they were for Cliff and Gwen Good, although many of our respondents described themselves as 'lapsed' adherents.[39]

Church and school engagement could encourage the enterprising not just to join but to initiate local institutions. The 'pioneers' who threw themselves into these activities did much to shape communities which were in embryonic formation, often with limited services and facilities. From their early days in Elizabeth, Joyce and Les Dalley sought out local involvement; Joyce especially had 'always been involved in Girls' Brigade and pre-school and Scripture, in the Schools, I've always done that'.[40] But remarkably she also started the Girls' Brigade and, with Les, set up the Baptist church in Elizabeth. Years later, when they moved to Raymond Terrace in New South Wales, she again set up a local Girls' Brigade. Joyce, indeed, was among those energetic migrant women in Elizabeth who, Mark Peel has noted, 'managed' public institutions in their families' interest.[41] But parents did not have a monopoly on local innovation. Rosemary Hurst was 16 when she arrived in 1950 with her parents in New Norfolk, near Hobart.[42] Missing the Girl Guides she had enjoyed in Worcestershire, she agitated the local scoutmaster until he helped her to organize a Guides branch, where she remains known locally as the 'captain'.

Most local organizations were gender-specific, and offered seemingly familiar places of contact. For women on the rural fringe or in country towns the Country Women's Association was an ardent welcoming and coopting agency, as Sylvia Cannon discovered when she was recruited to bake cakes and make jam. Virginia Anderson's mother threw herself into CWA activities in suburban Caversham, near Perth, in the early 1950s, and soon afterwards was caught up in voluntary sewing work with the women's auxiliary for the local hospital. One result was a wide circle of mostly Australian-born local friends. But it was unusual for women to find all their contacts simply from one local organization. In East Doncaster Grace Turnbull belonged to a mothers' club and, aware of few outlets for teenagers, organized a youth group. But her friends were also drawn from a diverse range of sources: her nursing colleagues; her tennis playing; the Methodist church; her children's school; her husband's workmates; and, most interestingly, Alf's Masonic network, which generated familiar forms of socializing. 'I was drawn into Alf's circle, it was his friends that I, like the Masonic, we'd … have the meetings here, and their wives would come and I'd entertain them while the men got on with their business, and things like that.'[43]

The Turnbulls' joint engagement with the Masons is a reminder that the lodge provided a comfortable friendship network for some men, often those who had had nothing to do with the Masons in Britain. Normally this was an anti–domestic influence, and, despite the mixed socializing, Grace Turnbull recognized this in her critical assessment that it was 'a male thing, it expected the women to work and not to join in. I was always against that; I called it a schoolboy thing.' Some men were also critical, in retrospect, of their Masonic days, recalling the tendency to sectarian and anti-Catholic influence, but significantly, in an echo of the long rules of secrecy, they preferred to keep these views anonymous. There were also more mixed recollections. In Sydney Albert Lougher resisted joining because of his firm view that in Britain the Masons were an exclusive middle-class organization, with no place for working-class men, but he was persuaded that in Australia they were less socially exclusive. Once he did join he remained critical of the ritual emphasis, the sectarianism and 'political side', but enjoyed the benevolent work. But because membership was dependent on invitation it more likely reflected the fact that men had already integrated socially by the time they joined, evident in Alf Floyd's and Graham Manoy's proud status as 'Past Masters'. Both men became Masons several years after their arrival.[44]

For sport-minded men involvement in soccer clubs could do far more to draw them into the community than other outlets, an influence that could also be appreciated by women. Predictably, soccer, as a participant rather than a spectator sport, was likely to appeal mainly to young men and child migrants, eager to bring their well-honed skills to new territory. And while soccer was still dwarfed in Australian culture by other mainstream sports – Australian Rules, rugby and cricket – the keen players usually found a way to indulge their passion. Among the British, the enthusiasm for soccer was particularly marked amongst Scottish migrants. Robert Smith, who had been an accomplished player in Edinburgh, came newly married to Melbourne in 1966. Within weeks, new soccer contacts invited him to train, and he promptly found himself playing for Juventus, the top Melbourne team. The well-known 'ethnic' character of Australian soccer at the time meant that the team had a predominantly Italian and Scottish make-up, and the young couple entered into the unusual social mix with enthusiasm. Maggie, at least until her baby was born – within eighteen months of arrival – saw the new contacts as an utterly novel experience. 'So you learnt from everybody you met about their kind of life. It's a *very* good learner … we got to know a lot of Italians because of Robert's football.' The Smiths' heady experiences came to an abrupt halt when Robert broke his leg just after the baby was born, which eventually drove them to return to Scotland. Robert Stirling, another Scot, who flew to Melbourne from Kilmarnock in 1965, actually emigrated in part to join his soccer friends. After a leg injury he spent many years as a part-time soccer trainer, making particular friends with Ukrainians. Bill Bradley, from Glasgow, had similar experiences in Fremantle in the early 1950s. After adjusting to the shock of playing in Perth heat waves, an injury – and fear of being incapacitated for work without insurance – brought Bill's playing career to an end, but he and Catherine continued to build a social life around the small soccer community.[45]

Soccer, and sport more generally, was not of course a universal guarantee of social integration. Some men resented the assumption that they would automatically bring sporting skills or enthusiasms with them; this could be a social handicap in a society preoccupied with sport. When a neighbour in Tasmania asked Winifred Cook if her husband played football her negative response elicited the abrupt reply, 'Oh well, you're no good to us then.' The same assumptions could govern migrant organizations, as John Hardie found in his first approach from the Traralgon Caledonian Society, asking whether he could play football and the bagpipes. Determined to resist, he refused to admit that he could do both. 'I could play the bagpipes and I could play football but I wasnae to get involved.' Child migrants, too, did not automatically take to the sporting field, and shared with some Australian children the experience of never being wanted on the team. The three sons of Cliff and Gwen Good joked about their lack of sporting prowess; Robert recalled that 'the only thing I remember about footie was not having any skill in it at all. I couldn't kick the rotten thing.' On the other hand, for boys who did bring skill and enthusiasm the experience could shape their adjustment quite dramatically. Chris Gray's family suffered a traumatic introduction to Melbourne in 1956, but once in Brisbane at his first job, still only 14, Chris found his soccer skills to be a passport to inclusion. In England he had been a 'nobody', an average Sunday player, but in Brisbane he and his brother were elevated to top players, their migrant background a key to wider acceptance. The soccer club became 'like a family club', the biggest part of their lives. Chris's description illustrates the prominent role played by soccer clubs in family and community life, and the way in which sport could be shaped by migrant influences and identities.

I used to play for the team called Bardon near Paddington ... because everybody used to come on a Saturday, you know, the mums and dads, and, it was, like there was a charity event, it was like that every Saturday. And at night-time they used to have dances and that, and you know, sing-alongs in the clubhouse and that.... We were football fanatics then. Because we realized that we was good players there, which we wasn't in England ... you wasn't struggling to get a game, you'd certainly get a game, because you're English, you know.[46]

For the great bulk of migrants who insisted that they emigrated to Australia to provide a better life for their children this sport-driven pathway to integration was no doubt gratifying. But for the children themselves the process could be a less straightforward success story. Ron Benson, who came from Durham to Perth with his parents and three siblings in 1959 at the age of 14, was in no doubt about his parents' motivation: 'they wanted a better life for us, as children'.[47] Their arrival was cushioned by the supportive and enthusiastic sponsorship of his mother's sister, a successful war bride. After some initial difficulty for his father in finding work in business administration, the family quickly adapted in the suburb of Bassendean, the parents made friends in the neighbourhood without difficulty and they became more active members of the local Anglican church than they had been in England. On the surface theirs was an ideal settlement, not handicapped by Father's conservative reluctance to buy a house. The purchase of a car – a classic rite of passage into the postwar good life – enabled regular weekend trips to the beach at Rockingham.

But Ron experienced the move as a grave step backwards, and was a deeply reluctant adolescent emigrant. In England his overweening ambition to play professional soccer came to a dramatic halt: 'I was working towards that, in terms of the teams that I had played for and the trials that I'd had just prior to coming to Australia.' On top of this his good record at school, with prospects of going to university, was severely compromised. Initially placed in a technical stream well behind his level in England, he was alienated from the Perth school experience, and at 16, with no opposition from his parents, left to join the workforce. At this stage Ron was, unlike his parents, a chronically disaffected migrant, routinely comparing English and Australian ways, a self-confessed 'whinger'. Yet his recollections tell a further story, dominated by the familiar lubricant of the sporting field. Ron, too, found that his soccer prowess was more highly valued in Australia. Even at school, still 14, he played for the senior side in the first state school boys' team, and he later excelled at cricket. Both at school and afterwards his soccer enthusiasm opened up a range of enduring multi-ethnic friendships and associations, with British migrants and Australians as well as Croations, Serbs, Maltese, Italians and Dutch. 'In the mid sixties I actually went to play professionally for a team … in the Swan Valley, Swan Athletic. And they were very good to me, and I enjoyed my time playing on the Swan, and I still go up there occasionally and see the guys that I played with.' At the same time a varied career, in the Public Service, sales and audio-engineering, led ultimately to prosperity in his own business. Looking back on his life since arrival, though, sport still looms large. 'I've been a member of a political party in Australia, and … I've been a member of service clubs, you know, I've been involved in soccer at playing level, coaching level, and administration level, so you know I've, I've been community-minded in Western Australia.' At the same time, unlike his parents, but like some of his own generation, he remains ambivalent about whether migration was the best thing for him, noting that some of his English friends did indeed become professional footballers and did well at university.

Parenting and inter-generational tensions in Australia

Migrants' cultural baggage, bound up so closely with aspirations for their children, brought a diverse array of attitudes towards parenting, and the combination of migration and changing times, notably in youth culture, prompted rapid changes in family life and parenting practices. Most commonly, the view that migration would bring families closer together sustained both early years and later recollections. For example, Brian and Connie Ward were determined not to replicate their own upbringing in dislocated wartime families. 'Our children have always come first, and we always put them first. I mean, we've built our lives round our children, so they've had a totally different upbringing to what we have had.'[48] But the deep commitment to family togetherness, acted out countless times in iconic beach weekends and holidays in the new family car, soon came into conflict with the very 'openness' and 'freedom' which was so often prized in Australian life, and posed dilemmas for parenting.

At their most extreme, the parenting problems faced by British migrants were indistinguishable from those experienced by postwar western parents generally, when generational rebellion took on more dramatic forms. But migrants invariably tell these stories through the lens of migrant experience, in which adjustment, for example, to a seemingly radical new youth culture presented one more of many cultural challenges, potentially unsettling their conviction that migration was good for the children. Maurice Tomlin worked hard to shield his children from what he saw as a more permissive drinking culture in Perth by never allowing alcohol in the house 'until the last one was an adult'. But his careful attempts to shield his children from the apparent excesses of Australian culture were put to the test when his youngest daughter 'got involved with these Bodgies' and asked, 'Would it be all right if I went and stayed with this bloke for the night?'[49]

For most children and adolescents migration offered opportunities for greater freedom than they had known before. The notion of 'running wild', especially in outer suburbs and rural districts, pervades much of their testimony, and is common to both sexes. Rosemary Hurst, 16 on arrival, recalled a happy childhood in 1940s England, but insisted that 'I don't think that we got as much out of life as we did when we came to Australia. You know, we were able to do whatever we wanted.' Michael Siberry, on the outer fringes of Hobart in the 1950s, recalls the new pleasures of open space and easy movement among friends' houses, 'a very happy time for us kids ... it was just more open, a more active kind of, you felt you had more space'. Vanessa Seymour, also in Tasmania, thought that her carefree childhood contrasted with the difficult adjustments faced by her parents, and stemmed in part from parental neglect: 'We used to run wild. In Nubeena we used to row boats and fish and swim ... Yes, no. I had a great childhood.'[50]

Margaret Reardon's memory of her mother's supervision offers one of the strongest statements about how parents too could gradually adapt to new standards of parenting. The eldest daughter, with three sisters, Margaret had been accustomed to strict control, especially by her mother, a devout Catholic, before emigrating at the age of 16. The careful surveillance continued in Australia, but gradually Margaret perceived a change, as her sisters grew up and they 'were allowed to do so much that I hadn't been allowed to do'. Margaret's description of her mother's gradual relaxation of parental control allows a unique insight into ways in which deeply traditional attitudes, previously sustained by extended family and community surveillance, could yield to new conditions.

Yes, the sheltering started to fall away. Mum took to the easy-going way of life. Incredibly, I couldn't believe it, this religious woman who was straight down the line and had laws that governed us and protected us from just about everything. Here's this woman suddenly enjoying the freedom, being less restricted. She could actually accept new ideas and Australian customs without too much shock horror, you know, to see my sisters being allowed to go out to parties and all this sort of thing, you know, without the restrictions of, we'll pick you up and we'll drop you and all this sort of thing. I used to stand back in amazement and just watch my sisters getting dressed for this party and that party.[51]

Parental control of girls, of course, was traditionally more rigorous, and slower to change. For boys the customary early teenage shift from school to workforce signified greater independence, even when they stayed at home, while for girls like Margaret entry to the workforce made only marginal difference to the close supervision of their school years. The difference, though, was relative. Sheila Vidler described her parents as 'quite strict' and controlling of all their children, and upset when her older brother began going out in Sydney 'and coming back when he felt like it'. But it is hardly surprising that in the new country the 'freedom' of a more 'easy-going' culture often came to be experienced as freedom from family. Maureen Carr's close-knit extended family in London, with a 'very possessive' grandmother and mother, could not survive their move to Sydney, even during her schooldays, as she immediately exploited the intangible shift, 'the freedom of it'. 'You were stuck with the family in England, you couldn't, living where you are you can't get away, you can't do things, but here you just seem to "I'm going out now" and that's it, you were gone. But you never did that in England, no it was different.' Later, with her own children, Maureen consciously modelled her parenting against her English experience: 'they have their own life. They go, they do what they want to do.'[52] In these ways that postwar generation of British migrants who came to Australia 'for the sake of the children' and who were often determined to build their lives around their children, were in for a surprise. The new 'freedoms' of a different country and changing western standards could challenge the very family closeness which they hoped would be sustained by migration. This is one of the most striking measures of the different ways in which migration was experienced by older and younger generations, yet continued to change all of them. In the next chapter we will see how the younger generation of single 'sojourners' came deliberately to exploit migration as one of the new postwar freedoms they appropriated for themselves.

Notes

1 Good, 'Impressions of Perth', 1 April 1964, Battye Library.
2 Paul, *Whitewashing Britain*, pp. 25–63; Murphy, *Imagining the Fifties*.
3 Jupp, *Immigration*, pp. 96–7.
4 Wilton and Bosworth, *Old Worlds and New Australia*, pp. 127–9.
5 Bird interview US; Hurst interview LU; Rooms interview US.
6 Barkas interview LU; also Jordan interview US; Bradley interview LU; Britton interview LU.
7 See above, Chapter 2; Walker interview LU.
8 Spencer interview US.
9 Elizabeth Gray interview US; Brooks interview US.
10 Makewell interview LU.
11 Jenkins, *We Came to Australia*, pp. 128–48.
12 Hart, *Pommie Migrant*, pp. 219–20.
13 Gwen and Cliff Good interview US.
14 Hallas interview LU.
15 Tilley interview LU; Jordan interview US.
16 Richards, *Nobody's Home*, p. 117.
17 Carter interview LU.
18 Reardon interview LU.
19 Blackmore interview LU; Gwen and Cliff Good interview US. For similar comments see Walker interview quoted above, LU; Cannon interview LU.
20 White, *Inventing Australia*; Murphy, *Imagining the Fifties*, pp. 70–1.
21 Barrand interview LU.
22 Adam interview LU.
23 Butts interview LU.
24 Manoy interview LU.
25 For example Adam interview LU; Hajinakitas interview LU; Seymour interview LU.
26 Tilley interview LU. See also Proverbs interview LU; Kemp interview LU; Clayton interview LU.
27 Lougher interview LU.
28 Peel, 'Dislocated Men'.
29 Hill interview LU. Margaret Hill has made some minor amendments to these extracts from the interview transcripts, to clarify her meaning.
30 Hill, *Corrugated Castles*; Hill, 'Water Under the Bridge', LU.
31 Ledgett interview LU.
32 Seymour interview LU.
33 Smith interview LU.
34 Davison and Davison, 'Suburban Pioneers'.
35 Gwen and Cliff Good interview US.
36 Hardie interview US; Jordan interview US; Kemp interview LU; Grace Turnbull interview LU.
37 Jay interview LU.
38 Carter interview LU.
39 Proverbs interview LU; Tomlin interview LU; Gwen and Cliff Good interview US. Out of 119 surveyed La Trobe interviewees, 36 described their religious practice at the time of migration as 'lapsed', 'nominal', 'non-practi sing' or 'intermittent'. Eight described themselves as having no religion.
40 Dalley interview LU.

41 Peel, *Good Times, Hard Times*, pp. 129–30.
42 Hurst interview LU.
43 Cannon interview LU. See Introduction; Anderson interview LU; Grace Turnbull interview LU. See also Weisinger interview LU, who recalled that even in Broken Hill the Mothers' Club was 'how we started to make friends'.
44 Grace Turnbull interview LU; Lougher interview LU; Floyd interview LU; Manoy interview LU.
45 Maggie and Robert Smith interview US; Stirling interview US; Bradley interview LU. See also other Scots: Carruthers interview LU; Ivor Miller interview LU.
46 Cook interview LU; Hardie interview US; Robert, Andrew and Michael Good interview US; Chris Gray interview US.
47 Benson interview LU.
48 Ward interview LU.
49 Tomlin interview LU.
50 Hurst interview LU; Siberry interview US; Seymour interview LU.
51 Reardon interview LU. Margaret Reardon has made some minor amendments to this extract from the interview transcript to clarify her meaning.
52 Vidler interview US; Carr interview LU.

8

Ten pound pioneers of the backpacking generation

Sojourners

In September 1965, exactly five years after she had taken up the ten pound passage to Australia, 31-year-old Joan Pickett – a medical secretary from Manchester – wrote an anniversary letter from Ocean Island in the central Pacific to her parents back home. She recalled 'waiting glumly' in London with her friend Jean for the boat train to Tilbury and wondering 'what on earth we were doing there in the first place'.

I know now that I was on the threshold of a whole new world of people, places, sights, sounds, thoughts and experiences, although I sometimes regret that to achieve this I've had to be away from you all for such a long time…. I sometimes begin to think, generally in bed at night, of the many many people and places I've come to know since leaving home … I can sail down the west australian coast, cross the Nullarbor plain, jog in a jeep along outback roads, attend opening nights at a Melbourne Theatre, splash around coral pools of the Barrier Reef, join the throng at the Royal Sydney Show or the Cairns Race Meeting, or if I really can't sleep I can always get up and listen to 'The Voice of Washington' or 'Radio Solomons' on my new radiogram…. Although I might spare a few thoughts for that 7th September, 1960, as we steamed up the Thames and out to sea – I think I have seen just a bit of what lies beyond and, strange enough seem to have learned more about my own country from further away, and surely a bit more about myself. (Back to normal next letter) Love Joan.[1]

Joan Pickett was one of several hundred thousand young single Britons who travelled to Australia on the ten pound scheme.[2] Some planned to settle; many were enjoying an open-ended working holiday; most were, like Joan Pickett, transformed by the experience. Between the late 1940s and the early 1970s they pioneered the backpacking, gap year working holidays of the late twentieth century.

Migration historians have generally associated 'sojourners' (usually defined as temporary residents) with return migration, and have mostly assumed that sojourners were ambitious young men, such as the eighteenth-century Scots who travelled to Jamaica and the Chesapeake 'to earn a fortune as quickly as possible and return home with it'.[3] In Australian history the term 'sojourner' is virtually synonymous with single Chinese and Italian men who sent earnings back to their families and intended eventually to return home. But regardless of provenance and gender, these sojourners have often been excluded from studies of migration.[4]

In fact, women along with men figure substantially as sojourners in British migration history. Even in the nineteenth century, large-scale assisted female emigration schemes attracted a minority of adventurous women – from governesses to domestic servants – who used facilities of subsidy and protection to enjoy what were essentially working holidays, moving from country to country, usually but not always within the Empire.[5] These youthful travellers sought a temporary livelihood or fortune, but increasingly, into the twentieth century, they were alert to adventure, wider horizons and, by the postwar years, something they often came to call self-discovery. But before the war the concept of a 'working holiday' in Australia was almost unimaginable, and was certainly unaffordable, for most working-class Britons. The ten pound scheme enabled a generation of young Britons to imagine and afford a new type of international travel.

Migration theorists argue that 'being a migrant is not a matter of moving a certain distance for a certain length of time. It also involves an attitude of mind – the concept of intention.'[6] Young British postwar travellers certainly seized on the opportunity of the ten pound passage, but when they left home they often did not regard themselves as 'migrants'. Indeed, their return rate of about 50 per cent was at least twice as high as the return rate for British migrant families.[7] Immigration officials were well aware that not all the single men and women who took the subsidy would settle in Australia, but they anticipated that a significant proportion would be tempted to stay on, and that those who returned to Britain would have made a valuable contribution during their two or more years in Australia; they might even encourage family and friends to emigrate.[8]

We have already seen how the Australian experience of these sojourners was very different to that of migrant families. Single migrants could move readily between job opportunities around Australia and found it comparatively easy to save money for their travels and return fare, or to invest in a life in Australia. Single migrants were expected to find their own accommodation and most moved easily between lodging houses, flats and shared houses. Like all new arrivals from Britain they encountered the strangeness and familiarity of Australia, not always successfully, but they were less bound by financial and family constraints and more able to lead the life they wanted.

In this chapter we use four short case studies to exemplify themes in the sojourner experience, to show how that experience might differ over time and for men by comparison with women, and to illuminate its profound impact upon the single men and women who took up the ten pound passage. The case studies offer a taster of issues for further research.

'Australia made me': Archie Shaw and Daphne Knights

Archie Shaw was born in 1927 into an extended working-class Manchester family.[9] In 1941 Archie's father – who had been in and out of work throughout the 1930s, and who 'always liked a pint' – joined the Royal Navy. As a lone parent through the war years Amy Shaw worked hard in her job as a French polisher to keep Archie and his younger sister, and during these years a close bond developed between mother and son. Archie loved his schooling and was an enthusiastic reader of adventure and travel stories, but like most working-class boys of the time had no choice but to leave school and find a job when he turned 14. With no father to help him join a trade, he started as a lift-boy with the Manchester *Daily Mail*. Upon turning 18 Archie tried to enlist in the navy – he had savoured the seafaring stories of two uncles who had been in the navy long before the war – but was turned down because he wore glasses, and instead joined the army in 1946 and enjoyed two and half years of national service in Britain and Ireland.

Archie returned home in 1948 to find his father 'back to his old ways': 'He liked his booze you see, that was the trouble with my dad.' At the *Daily Mail*, demobbed ex-servicemen had returned to their prewar jobs, and Archie was forced into shift work as an editorial messenger boy. He hated the 'upside down' life of shift work and 'couldn't imagine myself wandering round that editorial department for the rest of my flippin' life'. Archie does not recall a precise moment when he decided to go to Australia: 'All I can say is that somewhere along the line I read about this free passage scheme, thought I'd have a go at it, applied, and was accepted. And it was as simple as that really.' He had 'itchy feet' after his time in the army, and was excited by the prospect of discovering the places he had imagined in his reading and through his uncles' stories, but poor prospects in England were his main motivation for emigration. 'It was a blank end as far as I could see. So, and I thought, this is an opportunity, I'll go and see what I can do somewhere else, you know.' Though Archie was sad leaving home 'because it meant leaving my mum behind of course and my sister', he assumed that he was leaving Manchester for good: 'it never really entered my mind that I would be coming home again, I just thought I was going to stop'. He worried that he was deserting his mother in her difficult domestic situation but accepted her blessing at face value ('she said, "You go and make what you can of your life, while you've got the chance"') – and even imagined that if he succeeded in his new life he might be able to bring her out to Australia.

Emigration to Australia was everything that Archie Shaw had hoped for. The *Esperance Bay* left Tilbury in 1949 and was packed with emigrating ex-servicemen and women, mostly in their twenties. Archie had a 'great trip', teaming up with two cabin mates and then travelling with them to Bundaberg, where they worked on a sugarcane plantation. He relished the outdoor life and the camaraderie amongst the workers and families living on the plantation: 'Oh it was great, it was great. It was a *completely*, absolutely different life altogether to what I'd known.' The three mates moved on after the wet season set in and ended up in Newcastle, where they found work at sea and Archie started as a trimmer on the *Ulooloo*. For the next couple of years he worked on various ships ferrying merchandise around Australia, with Newcastle as his home port: 'I enjoyed every minute of it. It was great, it was … my lifetime dream had come true, hadn't it? I always wanted to go to sea, and, here I was, free, gratis and for nothing, it was great.' He admired the wider outlook of the Australians he met (which he contrasted with the 'blinkered sort of society' he had grown up in), was too busy and interested in his life to get homesick, and had no thoughts of return to England.

Early in 1952 a letter arrived from Manchester which was 'just a complete shock out of the blue':

It wasn't off my father or anything, it was off one of my aunts, my mother's sister, and the first lines I read was, 'I suppose by now you'll have heard of your mum's passing away.' And that was the first I heard of it. And it was an absolute complete shock. I'd --- I'd --- [sighs] Oh! I don't know, I just, I felt as though I'd betrayed her in a way. And the first thing that come in my mind was to try and get home. I don't know what I could do when I got home, but it just --- it just overpowered me really, I just --- I just had to get home for some reason or other.

Even today this is an achingly painful memory and Archie struggles to explain his actions. In 1952 he didn't know anybody in England who had a telephone so he could not use the phone to discuss the situation with his family. The funeral was long past and it was too late to join the rituals of mourning. He just felt 'seized' by powerful feelings of responsibility and guilt for deserting his mother: 'I don't know why I should have *felt* guilty, but I just did. I think it was because maybe the sad life she'd led over the years, and, it was all coming back now.'

Archie signed off the ship as quickly as possible and used his savings to book a return passage to England, fully intending to come back to Australia. He sought leave of absence from the Seaman's Union and hung up his union book in the Melbourne office so that it would be there on his return. Back in Manchester his relatives would not tell him about his mother's death and it wasn't until years later that one his aunts 'finally told me that she'd got that desperate and down in the dumps that she'd seen herself off. Which made it even worse, you know. Oh dear. I really felt as though I'd deserted her then.' There were tensions within the family. Archie's sister was recently married and his father 'hadn't changed very much', and 'in a way I was glad I was going back to Australia'. In the meantime he went to live with his grand-mother in another part of town, and found a job in a cable-making factory to earn a living until the date of his return passage in 1953.

Romance changes the story. Archie met Joan through a family friend, and they got on well and started going out together. Joan had no intention of leaving her mother and travelling to Australia, so they decided that Archie would take up his return passage so that he could work and save enough money in Australia to return to marry and buy a house in Manchester. This type of scheme – a recurring motif in nineteenth-century migration stories – was very unusual amongst the postwar ten pound migrants; in Archie's case it was driven by love. He was, in effect, transforming his aspirations from one ideal of manhood, the migrant adventurer, to another, the family man. 'I was getting to the age now where, I'd been and done a few things and I'd been and

30 In November 1954 Archie Shaw sent this card from Geelong back to his girlfriend in Manchester: 'Taken in the cabin, sitting on my bunk, notice yours, June's and Stephen's photo's on the bulkhead'

seen a few things, and, I thought it was about coming time to put down your roots and make a go of things.' The difficult family life of Archie's childhood perhaps reinforced the domestic ideal: 'I've always been a home-loving man in a way, and so I — that was my aim, I thought, a nice home, kids, settle down in a reasonable job, and that would do me then, you know. A bit, a bit wimpish, but still, nevertheless — [laughs]'.

Back in Melbourne Archie collected his union book and returned to the sea. Again he enjoyed seafaring adventure and camaraderie – including a vividly recalled voyage to the Antarctic – but with the help of one particular friend, 'who wouldn't let me go boozing or owt like that', 'slowly but surely the old bank balance rose'. By 1955 he had saved 1,200 Australian pounds, which was equivalent to the 1,000 English pounds he figured would set him up with a house and furniture in Manchester. With 'really mixed feelings' – 'I was sad to be going, and leaving all the friends I had behind, but I was happy at the fact that I was making another new step' – he sailed to England. He and Joan married and used his savings to pay a deposit of half the value of a small semi-detached house in the Manchester suburb of Heaton Park. The Australian connection also helped Archie into a new career after a visit to the labour exchange:

And they said, 'What was your last job?' So I said, 'Well I was in the engine room crowd on board ship.' So he said, 'Ah, engineering that. Would you fancy training as a plant fitter?' So I thought, well, why not? So I said, 'Aye.' So, I went on a government scheme you see, plant fitting. So, again, it put me on the right track didn't it, the Aussie adventure, put me on the right track again.

Archie finished up working for a Manchester firm for thirty-one years as a plant fitter, bonus administrator and work study coordinator: 'Considering I started as a lift lad at the *Daily Mail*, I think I've not done too badly really.' He and Joan had one son, who trained as a teacher, and in retrospect Archie concludes that his life 'really started taking off' when he made the decision to go to Australia, and that Australia 'made me all I am today in a way': 'It got me into a new job, it got me into a new life, it put money in my pockets; it made it so that when I finally came back to England I could put money down to buy a house, and buy furniture, and get married. So, I've got a lot, I owe a lot to Australia, and the fact that I went there, I must admit. [laughs]'

Archie Shaw typifies young single men of the first generation of ten pound migrants. They often assumed that they would settle in Australia, and they saw their emigration as a bright opportunity to carve out a new life and career; if they travelled around Australia they were seeking employment more than sightseeing and self-discovery. And, as the circumstances of Archie's anguished bereavement attest, in the 1940s and 1950s Australia and Britain could still feel agonizingly distant.

The story of Daphne Knights, another Australian sojourner from the 1950s, echoes aspects of Archie Shaw's experience whilst hinting at the rather different constraints and opportunities for young single women at this time. Daphne was a Londoner, born in 1933 into a working-class family that lived in a rented flat just behind Kings Cross Station. She had one other sibling, a sister who was eight years older, and apart from several happy years of war-time evacuation with cousins in East Anglia, Daphne recalls a shy and rather lonely childhood. Her father had a mixed experience of itinerant work and unemployment during the Depression but after the war found secure employ-ment as a supervisor with the Metropolitan Police Food Service. Daphne's mother, who had been in service as a young woman, continued to work through her married life, 'charring' in other people's houses. Neither parent had more than the basic education, but Daphne's father was a 'thoughtful man' who encouraged his daughter's education. She passed the scholarship exam for secondary school and matriculated at 17, but the family could not afford her dream of university and instead she studied commercial courses and started work as a secretary.

I got a really good job at a professional institution called the British Institution of Radio Engineers and got a good grounding, in everything, working there and I was coming up for 21 and the usual, you know, you get a bit: 'Oh well, there's more to life than this, surely', still didn't have a lot of friends, still very shy, believe it or not! [laughter] …. I remember my twenty-first birthday, I was depressed! …. I had people saying to me: 'But you're so lucky, you've got, you know, good parents, you've got this, that….' but the, you know, it's a bit like that song: 'Surely there's more to life than this!' But I felt I had to find it – thank God I did! … One of my feelings of why I went, if I put it in a nutshell, was, that I had the goal of getting through school, getting my exams, getting the job, conquering the job, and because I didn't get married or that side didn't happen: 'What else do I do?' I had no money.[10]

Daphne knew about the ten pound migration scheme because several relatives had already gone to Australia, and when a married friend of the family who was also about to emigrate came to stay and offered to sponsor Daphne, this seemed to offer the opportunity she had been seeking. Describing herself as still chronically shy when she left England in 1956, Daphne insists that she treated her voyage on the *Strathnaver* as a deliberate exercise in identity change.

I don't know *how* I ever went, but I went, and I thought: 'Well, this is me, I'm Daphne Knights from nowhere, from London, make something of yourself!' And I did, I came out of my shell, and, anyone wanted me to join in I joined in…. And it was a ratio of six men to every woman! So, from having no boyfriends, no experience, it was wonderful! … And I took to it, I loved it, and entered into it and got involved with the ship's concerts, not in the performing but in the, helping. I had my sewing machine [laughter] on board, they got it up for me and I was doing the costumes.... And so by the time I got off the ship, you know, I was a totally different person. I was outgoing, raring for anything.... I feel that if I'd have stayed in England, I'd have been the typical spinster that stayed at home, you know, looking after parents and things, which, I never had to, they let me go, which was the most wonderful thing my parents ever did.

Daphne's parents supported her decision, but like many others they worried about a young woman travelling alone to the other side of the world; such concerns were appeased by the possibility of return after two years. In the first two decades after the war daughters were still expected to live at home with their parents until they married or perhaps went to college – though this latter option was rarely available to working-class teenagers. The ten pound scheme offered an alternative to marriage for women who wanted

31 'Mum – left to right, two friends, me, Bob, in a barbecue, Daphne xx (recognise my jeans – the green ones I made!)' When Daphne Knights returned to London after four years of work and travel around Australia her mother did not recognise the 'very poised young lady' from the 'shy, retiring girl' who had left home in 1956. Daphne recalls, 'I think that going to Australia took me out of myself'

to leave the parental home and create their own independent life, and thus enabled young working-class women to transcend the social expectations of the time.[11] Daphne viewed the ten pound passage as a godsend, recalling that 'for ten pounds I could have a new life'.

Daphne survived the start of her 'new life' on the voyage. When leaving England, young men and especially women left behind the restraints of family and community and were exposed to new opportunities and challenges. Daphne recalls the constraints and risks of female sexuality in these years before the Pill. As she put it, 'I'd had all this high time on the ship and luckily, kept my head, shall we say! [laughter] Arrived intact, as they say [laughter].' Once in Sydney she settled into the life of a single working woman, at first sharing with an older woman who gave her mature 'sisterly advice', later living on her own, and moving homes and jobs between Sydney, Brisbane and Launceston. She took up tennis, dancing and bush-walking, and used her annual holidays to see more of the country. Before long her peripatetic habits became essential to her self identity, as she adapted to her surroundings like a chameleon; this extended even to her religious attachments, moving from an early mixture of Methodism and Anglicanism to Baptist and Catholic observance depending on her friendships. 'Oh, I've tried everything,' she commented, 'at the end of the day I was interested in what other people thought'.

Daphne's life was not, though, all a 'bed of roses'. Like Archie Shaw, two years into her stay she suffered the death of a parent and was unable to return for the funeral. Her account is symbolic of the isolated world of the migrant from the nineteenth century and onwards until at least the late 1960s.

I was very aware of how *young* Australia was, and that you were on the edge of the world, I can quite see why they thought they reached the edge of the world. You were a long way away. My father died, and I didn't know until a week later … I just got a letter from home and I opened it when I first saw it, I remember, and I read it, and he was dead and buried.

It was another two years before Daphne returned to England. She left Australia in tears but had decided that she should get back to her widowed mother, who was 'getting on a bit'. Daphne's mother and sister did not recognize the 'very poised young lady' from the 'shy, retiring' girl who had left them four years earlier. But within two years she emigrated again, this time to the United States, then to Canada briefly (more 'civilized' than Australia), and returned before going again for a short working sojourn in the United States, and some years later a further visit to Australia. In England she stayed in touch with her travel mentality – 'this wanderlust in my blood' – by working for a travel agent. But she still dates her personal transformation from the original move. 'I think that going to Australia took me out of myself…. I know I'm an extrovert now, I'm not an introvert, and I have been for an awful long time.'

Daphne Knights shared with others in the 1940s and 1950s a disillusion with postwar Britain, and was prepared to contemplate a permanent move: 'we wanted to escape, but we were prepared to do our bit. I mean I, I wanted to work, I didn't just want to go and use it as a, a wonderful holiday, I intended to stay for ever.' Unlike Archie Shaw, she did not define her migration or travel in terms of career development. As we saw in Chapter 2, single women emigrants of the initial postwar generation were less influenced than single men by career expectations. But in other respects Daphne Knights and Archie Shaw shared common features of the first sojourner generation of the 1940s to mid-1960s: acutely conscious of the unbridgeable distance from home; traumatized by the pain of being unable to return home to mourn the death of a parent; focused on work as central to the experience of sojourning; and placing the migration experience at the heart of a life-transforming process which still defines personal identity. We associate these features with accounts of migration common to both nineteenth- and twentieth-century experience, from women and men.

But in their relaxed attitude to travel and work, the generation of Daphne Knights and other single women, in particular, bears some resemblance to the sojourning mentality of today's highly mobile backpackers. Eunice Gardner chronicled her adventures in an aptly titled volume, *The World at Our Feet: The Story of Two Women Who Adventured Halfway Across the Globe*, published in 1957. Leaving Kent alone on the ten pound passage in the early 1950s, Eunice, a hairdresser, soon met her English companion, Diana Williams. The pair hitch-hiked around Australia, complete with Union Jacks on their rucksacks, and encountered a succession of like-minded single British itinerants. Their adventures continued on the overland journey home through India, Afghanistan, Persia, Iraq, Turkey and Europe, the increasingly popular itinerary of budget-conscious young travellers. Eunice and her companion had never contemplated permanent migration; her travels were motivated by what she described as 'the wander bug', a notion which set her apart from her friends at home. But Eunice and Diana were to be followed by another generation of sojourners for whom their book-worthy adventures of the 1950s became a routine rite of passage.[12]

By the mid-1960s sociologists were beginning to draw attention to significant changes in attitudes to migration and travel. These relate obviously to the dawning and consolidation of the jet age, which would eventually transform a momentous and mostly irreversible journey across the world into an investment in recreational globetrotting. In 1967 the Canadian migration sociologist Anthony Richmond defined a new type of migrants as 'transilients'; they reflected the changing nature of modern urban industrial societies 'whose populations are increasingly mobile, both geographically and socially'. Their movements, he argued, implied no inadequacy on the part of either country since there was an international market for their skills. These modern sojourners 'enjoy travel for its own sake, they find little difficulty making friends wherever they go, and they lack strong family or community ties that might compel them to become sedentary'.[13] The shifts are evident among the stories told by our sojourners, and mark what has now become taken for granted by most of us but represents one of the most significant historical changes in attitudes to travel and migration in modern times.

32 Young Yorkshireman Michael Laycock travelled to Australia in 1964, fully intending to use the ten pound passage as a passport to travel the world. In 1966 he was employed – on one of many itinerant jobs – to survey the land depicted in this photograph for a proposed tea plantation near Tully in north Queensland

A new generation of travellers: Michael Laycock and Janet Wrigley

The narrative structures embodied in stories told by two different generations of sojourners point to this shifting orientation towards 'transilience'. From stories focused on the working life, new lifelong friends and the emotional wrench of absence from family, many single sojourners from the late 1960s and 1970s represent themselves more as outside observers, consumers of experience, in effect tourist creators of a travelogue embracing the British and wider world. The trends are common to both sexes, although they are more pronounced in the stories of footloose lone male travellers, perhaps more prone to risk-taking travel in remote areas.

In 1964, at 22, Michael Laycock left Skipton, Yorkshire for Brisbane on the ten pound scheme, not remotely conscious of being a 'migrant'.[14] A brief stint in the merchant navy had whetted his appetite for further travel, though he travelled with others whose experience still had more in common with migrants of the 1850s. He was struck by the other-worldly background of a young male companion on the plane who had just crossed for the first time from Skye to mainland Scotland, and was now emigrating to Queensland. An itinerant sojourner in every sense, Michael proudly related his long list of jobs and impressions. These included an outback sawmill camp in western Queensland, the Whyalla blast furnace, mission supply boats from Broome to Groote Eylandt, supply work for the Yirrkala Mission on Gove Peninsula, working on a prawn trawler and towing a Chinese junk. By 1970, fresh from a working stint in New Zealand, he was in Darwin awaiting papers for the overland trip across Asia; out of idleness he began to record impressions in his journal, giving a measure of the way that backpacking hippy culture by now dominated some key cities and had become a significant aspect of the sojourner experience.

Since arriving back here from New Zealand I've noticed a lot more travellers here. Some having just arrived from Indonesia or Singapore and others from the southern states waiting for visas, permits, what have you, ready to do what's become a well worn track – the overland trip to Europe. The Singapore authorities are trying to make things difficult by refusing admission to anyone with long hair (on head or chin!) and as a lot of the travellers are of this type, I feel it is not going to be easy. They are all classed as Hippies and by the number of beads, bells, beards and batiks, it is justified to some extent....

Sitting in Rocky's Place under the tree where he died about three years ago. He was an old Darwin character who used to live beneath the tree. One morning he was found dead. I faintly remember it as it was then. He wouldn't know the place now. Open air cafe serving fish and chips, hamburgers and soft drinks. It's a meeting place for travellers now and perhaps in a way Rocky would sympathize with some of the people here who are stepping out of society as he preferred to.

Michael's journal also made sympathetic references to the plight of aborigines and ended when he embarked on the overland trip, first working in West Irian and then cycling from Singapore. Finally settling in Scotland in the early 1970s, he enjoyed people's envy of his Australian experiences and remembers the country 'with great fondness'. Jet plane or overland travel and the hippy counterculture mark a significant difference between the Australian experiences of young men like Archie Shaw in the 1950s and Michael Laycock's generation fifteen years on.

Janet Wrigley's story illustrates the rather different ways in which women might take advantage of easier modern 'transilience'. A secretary living with her parents in Bayswater, her interest was sparked in 1968 by a neighbourhood house full of young Australians, New Zealanders and South Africans sojourning in London. Janet explains her move as a characteristic late 1960s drive for change, though even in 1968 the ten pound scheme still offered young women a way of leaving the parental home. 'I was 25 years of age and still living at home and still in my first job. After seven years with the same company I was looking for a change of direction, either work wise and or location wise, but where do I go to earn approximately the same amount of money as in London – Australia!'[15]

With a like-minded friend, Janet signed on for the ten pound passage and in 1968 embarked on a Greek liner, bound for Melbourne, where an Australian couple they had met in London had agreed to sponsor them. Janet's observations from the start focused on the mix of people and relationships: the sex-starved Greek crew on the voyage; the nightly goings-on of young people thrown together in a confined space; the British couple who separated when the wife became pregnant by a Greek crew member. In Melbourne, comfortably settled in a South Yarra flat and promptly employed as a secretary by an international company, she took to the frenetic social life of the expatriate single. While her friend eventually married and settled in Melbourne, Janet was clear that she hadn't come to Australia 'looking for a husband'. She was quick to form opinions of Australian men, who 'were keen to wine and dine you and then wanted sex straight away in return and if you refused you were never asked out again or even worse, [they] attempted rape'. Disliking most Australian men – 'very immature but also chauvinistic' – she concluded that Australian married women were insecure and suspicious of single women like her. At the end of her two years and much internal travel Janet leapt at an offer from her company of a similar two-year position in Holland. While not remotely homesick, and though she had been contemplating a move to Sydney, the offer was too good to refuse and afforded a free visit to her family in London.

In retrospect Janet regards her Australian years as the start of a sojourning identity, and the stimulus for some years of a classic backpacking existence in her late twenties.

I worked in Holland until the summer of 1972 after 18 months with the Hague office. I took all my belongings back to my parent's place in London, strapped a back-pack to me and off I went again, travelling around Europe, Turkey, Syria, Lebanon and back to Greece, where I met a wonderful man, took him back to London late August 1973 and married him in September 1973. He just happened to be born in Australia but he is the most unlikely Australian ever to be found who has no desire at all to ever live in Australia, but enjoys going back to see his family from time to time.

Attached now to an Australian with a similar degree of 'wanderlust', Janet has enjoyed overland trips across Asia, worked again in Australia, where she finally enjoyed her long-awaited round–Australia trip, and has gone 'back and forth like a ping-pong about three times'. 'Perhaps it was Australia that gave me even more itchy feet than I already had and the courage to travel on my own to see more of the world. Our 'long' stint travelling days are over, but we do still go back now and then for a quick visit to see our Australian side of the family.'

Reflecting on the meaning of her travels, Janet articulates the sojourner's common understanding of temporary migration as a transformative life event, an episode in which she learnt skills that others usually imbibed closer to home, but which with easier mobility were now increasingly being played out on a more global scale with richer dividends.

It all worked out wonderfully well, and I thoroughly enjoyed my two years out in Australia. It was a tremendous experience, one which taught me to become independent in many ways. I had to do so many 'firsts'. I left home for the first time. I had to find somewhere to live for the first time. I had to learn to try and cook for the first time (I'm still not very accomplished at this though). I had to do housework for the first time and I had to be a responsible adult for the first time in my life. I had many rich experiences, mostly good, and it was a learning curve I wish everyone could have had. I felt very fortunate to have had the opportunity of going to Australia – who knows, I might still have been there if it wasn't for that company with whom I took my first job.

Several themes emerge from these sojourner life stories, and most of them relate closely to issues of identity. Nigel Heath emigrated to Australia twice, first as a single nomad, later with his English wife; he captured the life-transforming theme in his reflection that 'I was not to know that I was embarking on the experience of my life and would make it my reference point in the years that followed'.[16] For young single men and women a ten pound investment paid for a rite of passage and, in many cases, a dramatic coming-of-age. It took them away from extended families and community networks and offered an exciting, temporary alternative to marriage and career. As Joan

Pickett explained to her parents, she was introduced to 'a whole new world of people, places, sights, sounds, thoughts and experiences'. Through their travels, sojourners like Joan learnt 'just a bit of what lies beyond and ... more about my own country from further away'. Perhaps most importantly, by leaving home and creating their own life in a different country, many, like Joan, learnt 'surely a bit more about myself' and were transformed by this learning.

With travel an opportunity for personal self-discovery, the erstwhile itinerants of the 1960s and 1970s were more likely to shy away from a robust national identity of any variety, preferring to define themselves through the distinctive features of their travel history. Janet Wrigley's boast of 'a learning curve I wish everyone could have had' best expresses the sense of difference from those lesser mortals who lack the broadening experience of travel and itinerancy.[17] These sojourners also tend to understate their distinctively British (or English, Scottish and Welsh) attachments, since they often describe their transilient identity in transnational terms, something above national loyalties. 'Hybrid' identities were a common result of sojourning. After moving on from Australia to New Zealand in 1967, Joan Pickett wrote to her parents of her 'triple identity' as an Australian, New Zealander and Mancunian English-woman.[18] The young sojourners of the late 1960s and 1970s, infected to some degree by the idealistic youth culture of the time, were often suspicious of all forms of patriotism and staunch national identity. They were emphatically not joiners of loyalty organizations such as the UK Settlers' Association or the Victoria League. Maggie Campbell, an Oxford middle-class nurse who left for what she thought would be a two year stint in Australia in 1969, admitted that she 'never felt particularly British,' and thirty years later happily voted for an Australian republic. Kate Rowe, moving alone to Sydney in 1970, similarly admitted to having 'no sense of identity [in Britain] at all, none'.[19] The transnational 'mobility of modernity' and identity of this second generation of postwar sojourners was beginning to transcend its old British contours and identities, and in that respect it foreshadows the more routine attitude to travel stimulated by the age of the jumbo jet.

Sojourners distinguished themselves from the much larger body of family migrants, and in many respects they constitute a quite distinct group of postwar British 'invisible migrants', deserving of separate study. In this brief chapter we have sketched just some of the contours of their different history. From the beginning their outlook and experience was differentiated by gender. The career orientation of Archie Shaw contrasted markedly with Daphne Knights's ambivalent aspirations for a 'new life', but both sought escape and both suffered from traumas of family separation. Soon afterwards, the younger generation of Michael Laycock and Janet Wrigley, more open to flexible travel possibilities, pioneered the highly mobile features of late twentieth century 'transilience' and transformed 'wanderlust' into a way of life quite distinct from that intended by Australian immigration authorities. These sojourners shaped the ten pound migration programme to their individual purposes, and in so doing not only transformed their own life histories but also blazed the trail for the backpackers of today.

Notes

1 Joan Pickett letter to Mr and Mrs H. Pickett, Ocean Island, 7 September 1965, US.
2 Appleyard, *British Emigration to Australia*, pp. 118–22, calculated that from 1955 to 1960 16 per cent of postwar assisted migrants were unaccompanied men and women.
3 Karras, *Sojourners in the Sun*, pp. 1–3. See also Bodnar, *The Transplanted*, pp. 52–3.
4 Karras, *Sojourners in the Sun*, p. 4; Chan, 'European and Asian Immigration into the United States in Comparative Perspective', pp. 37–8.
5 Hammerton, *Emigrant Gentlewomen*, p. 135. See also Gothard, *Blue China*, pp. 203–8. On the reverse movement of women from Australia to London see Woollacott, *To Try Her Fortune in London*.
6 Champion and Fielding, *Migration Processes and Patterns*, p. 83.
7 Richardson, *British Immigrants and Australia*, pp. 57–61.
8 Martin, *Angels and Arrogant Gods*, p. 14.
9 Shaw interview US.
10 Knights interview LU.
11 On this theme see also Pickett interview and letters, US.
12 Gardner and Williams, *The World at Our Feet*.
13 Richmond, *Post-War Immigrants in Canada*, p. 252.
14 Laycock written account US.
15 Wrigley (pseudonym) written account US.
16 Heath written account US.
17 Wrigley (pseudonym) written account US.
18 Letter from Joan Pickett to Mr and Mrs H. Pickett, Wellington, 12 March 1967, US.
19 Campbell interview LU; Rowe interview LU.

9

'My wayward heart': the British exodus from Australia

Return migrants: invisible twice over

In 1962 Mary Holmes emigrated from Newport to Australia with her farmer husband and five children. In 1963 – and five years before they eventually returned to Wales – she wrote a poem, 'The Migrant's Dilemma':

> Oft I toss and turn at night, sleep troubled & uneasy.
> Back and forth my thoughts they dance, in a maddening crazy frenzy.
> The land is good, full of chance, the people kind & friendly.
> So tell me why my wayward heart is always homeward turning.[1]

Return migrants are voices we rarely hear in Australian history.[2] Migration histories often neglect the experiences of the returnees, focusing instead on the struggles and successes of the migrants who stay on. This type of historical amnesia is especially true of migrant nations like Australia or the United States. In Australia, migration is a central element in the story of the making of a nation, from the federation nation of pioneering settlers and their descendants to the multicultural millennium nation forged by migrants from many lands who have a sought a safe and prosperous home in the new world. The British return migrants are invisible twice over.

In fact, return is a common feature of most migration schemes and movements. A surprisingly high proportion of the great wave of migrants who travelled from Europe to North America in the late nineteenth century returned across the Atlantic, and it has been estimated that the return rate for British emigrants to all destinations in the period between 1870 and 1914 was a staggering 40 per cent.[3] For the postwar British who journeyed to Australia estimates of return vary but average at just over 25 per cent – more than enough to earn nicknames such as 'boomerang migrants' and the 'to and froms' which were ascribed to British return migrants.[4] Reg Appleyard calculated a 29 percent return rate for his survey of British migrants from the late 1950s; while Alan Richardson concluded that the return rate for these migrants in the period 1959 to 1967 was 24 per cent for married couples and just over 50 per cent for single men and women. More recently, Graeme Hugo has noted an increase in the return rate of British migrants as they reach retirement age.[5] These figures highlight the extent of return migration but also the difficulties of statistical analysis: return rates change over time and they vary for different types of migrants; the statistics struggle to deal with return migrants who re-emigrated to Australia (Appleyard estimated that between a third and a half of his sample of British returnees went back to Australia) and are flummoxed by the serial returnees who move back and forth between the two countries. And of course these statistics do not include the British migrants who were desperate to return but were prevented from doing so by financial or personal circumstances. Sandra O'Neill, who 'escaped' from Perth back to England after six terrible weeks in 1970, recalls that a common saying of the time was 'if they could build a road back to England, it would be full of people walking back, because, so many were trapped'.[6]

So why did so many of the postwar British migrants decide to leave Australia and return 'home'? At the time the tabloid press in the two countries offered starkly polarized explanations. In Britain, newspapers picked up the stories of return migrants like Sandra O'Neill, and blamed the Australian government for misleading advertisements which attracted the assisted passage migrants to a country unable to deliver on its promises, and for the insecure labour market and the appalling conditions of migrant hostels. In 1962 a Reading man, recently returned from Australia, wrote to his local newspaper to inform readers that Australian immigration publicity ignored the acute housing shortage, widespread unemployment caused by an economic slump, and inadequate social service benefits:

Australia is no longer the land of opportunities and progress for the average working man. Yet Australia House still endeavours to give people the impression that it is. Consequently, when British people arrive here and discover the truth they become frustrated and resent the deception that persuaded them to give up their homes and jobs and come here, in most cases to find that they had jumped out of the frying pan into the fire.[7]

In Australia, the popular press – and indeed popular opinion – blamed the 'whingeing Poms' who had enjoyed favoured status by comparison with non-English-speaking immigrants and yet were not able to stick it out through the tough times and make the most of the 'land of opportunities'. In their book promoting emigration to Australia, Elizabeth and Derek Tribe argued that the criticisms of return migrants like the man from Reading were unfair and misleading, and that the 'vast majority' of the postwar British migrants 'have been happy and are now pleased to regard Australia as their home. Unfortunately there will always be some men and women who are misfits. Unfortunately too, these are usually the people who make the most noise.'[8] In a series of 'Women's Session' radio programmes broadcast by the ABC in Perth during 1964 and 1965, London emigrant Gwen Good spoke to an imaginary friend in Britain about the shock of seeing 'some parts of the

Western Australian press counter-attack with sarcastic comment and acrid cartoons, rather like a touchy teenager':

Did I tell you about the group of dissatisfied migrants who returned home last year? There were only about eleven families in all, but how the newspapers jumped on it. Some of the publicity was quite hysterical. In fact some people at Fremantle booed the ship as the migrants left Australia. Thank heavens you didn't treat us that way when we left England.[9]

Not surprisingly, the Australian government was concerned about the high return rate amongst British immigrants. The express preference of the government's postwar immigration scheme had been for migrants of British stock, and it had been assumed that such migrants would readily settle in a nation of British character, language and institutions. British immigrants enjoyed comparatively favourable conditions and were heavily subsidized through the assisted passage scheme, but their high rate of return represented a poor yield on a substantial investment. In 1957 this prompted the federal government to fund research by Reg Appleyard about British immigrants and to commission an official enquiry into the problem of return.

Throughout the late 1950s and 1960s commentators advanced a range of explanations for return. Appleyard's research concluded that while the assisted passage scheme was crucial for the competitiveness of migration to Australia, the high rate of return amongst the British immigrants was in part due to the relative ease of their selection, passage and return. Most returnees had been better off in Australia than before leaving Britain, and financial concern was not a primary motivation for return. Appleyard emphasized the character and sociability of the migrants, and the extent of their cultural assimilation within Australia – or homesickness for Britain – as significant factors in the equation of return, whilst also noting the importance of family pressures and obligations. Research by social-psychologist Alan Richardson also suggested that a degree of 'acculturation' was an important influence for settlement. The 1967 Report of the Immigration Advisory Committee (investigating return migrants from different countries of origin, including Britain) argued that employment and other economic forces were less significant motivators for return than personal and psychological factors. The report concluded that many British migrants returned because they had taken the initial emigration decision too lightly, or because they did not have the necessary character to become successful immigrants.[10]

These conclusions highlight some important causes of return, but are underpinned by the assimilationist ideals of the period. They tend to accept a rather simplistic model of migrant character – the tough will survive while weak 'misfits' return with their tails between their legs – and assume that successful settlement is a neat linear process of assimilation through which migrants gradually take on the culture of their adopted home and become contented Australians. There is a fine line between the scholarly and official explanations of return and complaints by the Australian media at the time. At the opposite extreme were British contemporary newspapers that down-played the ways in which return migrants contributed to their own fate and emphasized the importance of external forces and conditions in Australia.

British migrant life histories offer a rather different perspective on return, and suggest alternatives to these simplistic and polarized explanations. Janet Francis's life story points the way.

Janet Francis: 'I'm not the alien any more'

Janet Francis was born in Bristol in 1938, the first child of Betty and Edward Dungey. Janet's mother had a very difficult upbringing; with an alcoholic step-father and a mother struggling to raise her four children, she only had a limited education and then worked in a shop and as an usherette until she married in 1936 at the age of 19 'for a bit of peace and security'.[11] As a young man Edward Dungey worked in a chemist shop in the village of Shirehamp-ton just outside Bristol. The chemist took him 'under his wing' and sent him to night school, where he qualified as a dispensing chemist – his profession for twenty-five years before the family emigrated – and then as a chiropodist. In 1939 the young Dungey family bought a house in Shirehampton, just before Edward Dungey was called up at the start of the war. For a time he was stationed in Wales and his wife and daughter came to live with him, but when Janet started to speak Welsh they sent her back to Bristol to live with her paternal grandparents, with whom she developed a very close relationship. At the end of the war the family home in Shirehampton was occupied by tenants and it was another two years before the house became vacant and Janet went back to live with her parents, and with two new sisters, Maisie and Trish, born in 1944 and 1945 respectively.

Growing up in wartime England had a significant effect upon Janet's emerging national identity; she vividly recalls the numerous parties, flags and patriotic songs at the war's end: 'I think this is why I hold England so dear now because I know what the boys fought for, you know, to give us the right to live in freedom and in this green and pleasant land and that's why I think I was a bad candidate for Australia, because England means *absolutely everything* to me.' Janet has 'lovely memories' of growing up in postwar, semi-rural Shire-hampton. Though she failed the 11–plus exam and spent 18 months at the local secondary modern school, she took an exam and won a half scholarship to a private school in Bristol; 'that was the making of me because that gave me the savoir-faire and gave me the ... the grounding that I needed I think'. At about this time her parents decided to buy a business and sold the house in Shirehampton; after two false starts they bought an off licence in the Bristol suburb of St Pauls which Betty managed while Edward continued his day job. Janet had failed her end of school exams ('I was a *terrible* examination candidate') but a 'terribly boring' job as a laboratory technician persuaded her to go back to school, paying her own fees. This time she passed, got a job with an insurance company and earned a place in a teacher training college in Coventry: 'But then my parents got this *hair-raising* idea about going to Australia and of course that, it was all wiped out.'

Janet struggles to understand her parents' decision to emigrate; even though she was working and contributing to the family income she was not part of the decision-making. Betty Dungey had met an Australian Battle of Britain pilot, Mr Thorpe, who had an English wife and two adopted children, and she used to help Mrs Thorpe with housework and babysitting.[12] When the Thorpes returned to Australia, where his family had a farm near Victor Harbour in South Australia, they offered to sponsor the Dungey family and provide them with a house on the farm, free produce and £12 a week, for which Edward would work on the farm while Betty helped to look after the Thorpe children. Janet thinks that they were tempted by this offer 'because Australia was such a young country and because it seemed to have so much to offer and they had three girls, I think they couldn't see any headway'. Added to this, young Maisie had bronchitis and a doctor advised that a warmer climate would be better for her health. Janet also recalls that their inner-city Bristol neighbourhood of St Pauls was beginning to change with the arrival of Caribbean immigrants in the 1950s: 'the dark people were just arriving and one day one came into the shop and came behind the counter and helped himself to the things he needed, you know, like a self-service and that was it. I think that was the time they sort of thought, right this is it we're going, and it was all systems on go then.'

Betty Dungey was particularly keen to emigrate and Janet is still not quite sure why this was so. Perhaps Betty hoped to make the family fortune and return; when things went wrong in Australia she would claim that she had only intended to go for two years. By contrast with Betty, Edward Dungey was very close to his family and according to Janet 'I don't think he really in his heart wanted to leave his family but to keep our family together I think he had to go for her sake'. Eleven-year-old Maisie had already moved five times in her short life and this was 'just another one', though she also felt 'quite excited as it was the topic of conversation at school and in the "Off Licence" we ran'.[13] But Janet was horrified by her mother's plans:

Well my favourite age was 17 and I had *just* started to live, I had started to make a few friends and go dancing and I had a couple of special friends that I used to go to dances with and ——— [long pause] I think that is one of the reasons I didn't want to go to Australia because I was beginning to live and I just, I couldn't bear the thought of it.... I mean I *hated* Australia with a passion even before I left England.

Janet had started to live her own life and had developed relationships outside her immediate family – with boys as well as girls – that she did not want to lose. Most memorably, she wrote to the minister of agriculture and fisheries to see if she could take her pet dog to Australia, but was told she must leave it behind. Though her father's mother had died in 1948, she was particularly close to her paternal grandfather, who was 'heartbroken, couldn't realize why they wanted to go to the end of the earth'. None of her father's family came to wave them off at Bristol's Temple Meads Station: 'they weren't in agreement with it and I don't think they wanted to see us go'. Two weeks after the Dungeys arrived in Adelaide, and just after he had been notified of their safe arrival, Edward's father died from a heart attack.

Janet has mixed memories of her voyage to Australia on the *Otranto* in April 1956. The old ship was on her second last voyage and 'she creaked and groaned': 'I remember standing on the deck waving to England thinking oh when will I see it again and feeling absolutely shattered and heartbroken'. And yet like many other migrants Janet enjoyed the entertainments and adventure of an ocean liner. She befriended a girl called Margaret and they each fell in love with a waiter. In retrospect she realizes that she was looking for love on the rebound, but at the time she imagined returning with her waiter to England; she even travelled up from Victor to stay with Margaret in Adelaide and meet up with him when the ship stopped off on its way back to England: 'as soon as the ship got back to Tilbury he sent me a "dear John" so that was the end of that romance [laughs]'.

Mr Thorpe met the Dungeys at Outer Harbour and drove them through the bush to the farm, which was in a valley 12 miles out of Victor Harbour. Janet sustained her resentment: 'I remember him saying, "See all the sheep in the paddocks", and I sort of, "Don't look like sheep to me, looks like maggots on some green meat", I was trying to be as derogatory as I could about Australia.' Arrival was a terrible shock. There were two houses on the property and it seems that Mr Thorpe had told the immigration authorities that the Dungeys would be living in the comfortable farmhouse that he was actually building for his own family, and had all along intended to put the Dungeys in a tin shed up the road.

When eventually we got there it was just heartbreaking. We had no fly screens, we had no screen doors, we had no running water, we had a bucket under the kitchen sink, we had no electricity, we had *nothing*, and I thought is this Australia?

I thought it was the end of the earth, never mind Australia. I thought it was dreadful, and I couldn't bear the smell, you know, if it rained a few spots you could smell this dust. It was, outside was all brown. I mean the grass was that high and it was all brown, it was *horrible*.

The property wasn't cleared and instead of living off the land as they had imagined, the Dungeys had to buy all their food. At 42 Edward Dungey was totally unsuited to the hard physical labour of grubbing out trees, but when he tried to get a job as a chemist in Adelaide they refused to accept his British qualifications. He started to drink at night and came out in carbuncles on his legs, a reaction that Janet thinks was stress-related: 'drinking wouldn't have helped but it was a way of putting yourself into oblivion to forget your troubles'. The domestic conditions were appalling and Betty was desperately unhappy from the start. Even young Maisie, who was initially excited by the new life, recalls the primitive housing and terrible problems with mosquitoes and that 'it was hell' for her parents.[14]

Janet's own frustrations continued when she was told that in order to train as a teacher she would have to go back to school for another year. At 18 she had no intention of returning to school and instead started work as a telephonist in Victor Harbour. Through the job she began to make some friends and even attended local dances but she suffered terrible homesickness, and whenever she heard a British accent on the telephone 'I would just hone in on them'. The problem was exacerbated by Australian criticisms of 'whingeing Poms': 'they'd laugh when they said it and that was the thing, you had to laugh ... I stood so much of it and inside I would be crying, I would be laughing outside but crying inside and I got to the stage where I couldn't take it any more, and I think perhaps mum felt like that too'. Though she had to pay her mother for board and repay her father for the motorbike she rode to work, for 18 months Janet saved £5 of her £8 weekly salary and schemed about getting back to England.

After 18 months the Dungeys left the farm and moved into a house just outside Victor Harbour, and Edward started work as a medical orderly in a rehabilitation centre. Soon after the move he came home one day and announced that they had used up their savings and didn't have enough funds to return to England. His wife was already in despair and this shocking announcement triggered her nervous breakdown: 'I guess it started with her not wanting to mix and not being involved in anything and then she was trembling, she couldn't put a cup to her mouth without it shaking and she just got herself into such a state and she had to go into hospital and ... they were going to give her shock treatment but they didn't.' Janet had to take over the mothering alongside her own job, and though Betty was only hospitalized for a few weeks Maisie recalls that at this point 'my childhood ended and stark reality took over'.[15] After their mother came out of hospital the Dungeys moved to Adelaide. Betty got a job as a cook and Edward started a chiropody practice. Eventually they bought a house in Hazelwood Park and Betty began to accept her Australian fate. 'She'd sort of settled down *somewhat* by this time; I think her heart was still in England but her family was there, and by this time two of us were married, so I think she sort of had to cut her losses and just settle to the best of her ability.' One consequence of the family's migration – and of the loss of their extended family – was that the Dungeys became and remained very close-knit: 'we always recognized any birthday, we would all go to the house of whose birthday it was and make a big thing of it because there were only the five of us. We had nobody else so we tended to stick very close together.'

Before moving to Adelaide Janet had met Alan Francis through a contact at the Victor Harbour telephone exchange. They started to go to dances together and she stopped saving and scheming for return. Alan's family was not entirely happy with the relationship, in part because Janet was three years older than Alan but also because 'I was English. Once Alan and I started going together that was it, we were forbidden to see each other, we used to meet each other in secret.... They resented English people, they didn't want Alan to marry me 'cause I was a Pom.' Despite these family tensions, Alan and Janet married in 1962, settled in Adelaide and had two sons, Paul and Roger. For Janet the period of her early married life and childraising was a second and very different phase in her history. She recalls the demanding activity of being a working mother, busy with the children, running the home, socializing, so that 'I didn't have time to be homesick'. Deeply in love with Alan, she adapted to a comfortable lifestyle: 'we had a good life and we both had a car each and we had lovely holidays together and a lovely family and I settled down, my life, my family was, you know, the most important thing in my life'.

And yet, just occasionally, Janet's feelings about England would re-emerge. During Alan's periodic work absences the homesickness would revive, fuelled by her loud playing of 'Land of Hope and Glory'. A neighbour, she remembers, 'would say the next day, "were we feeling a bit nostalgic last night?" [laughs]'.

I guess it's always been there the homesickness but I was able to overcome it, I mean it wasn't first and foremost in my mind in that second middle phase.... And I used to play Vera Lynn, 'There'll Always be an England' and all the war songs, I'm very partial to all her songs 'cause that's my memories, that's what I grew up with. Mmm.

In 1979, four years after the death of their father, Maisie took her mother on a holiday visit to England. This was the first of several trips Betty enjoyed before she died: 'she loved them, she always said if she had enough money and her family went, she wouldn't think twice about going home, but I mean it wasn't possible'. As Janet's sons now grew up and left home the settled pattern of her own married life began to feel less complete and her homesickness worsened. She made her first trips 'home', in 1985 with Maisie, and then in 1988 with Alan, and she recalls how these trips reinforced a sense of not belonging in Australia and planted the seeds of return:

I mean here's me, absolutely homesick, been homesick for the last ten years and what are we doing here, this is ridiculous, and you know I didn't come back for a holiday until I'd been in Australia for twenty-nine years, and people used to say to me out there, 'It's not what you left, it won't be what you think', and okay it had changed a little, I mean when I went out there we didn't have motorways or anything but basically where I went down to Shirehampton where I was brought up the village is still the same, double decker buses still go down past each other and you sort of step back on the pavement like this, hadn't changed at all. And I knew that, even after twenty-nine years, I knew that this was home and this was where I really wanted to be.

In 1993 Janet's eldest son Paul took a working holiday in England, and stayed on after marrying an English woman and buying a house. The second son, Roger, was already married with two young children, but couldn't find permanent work in recession-hit Australia; he and his family decided to get one way tickets to Paul's wedding and then find work in Britain. Both sons settled in England, finding employment more easily than they had in Australia. Janet's dream of return seemed much closer now, but she didn't believe it was possible until she read about a 75-year-old woman who had come from England to live with her daughter-in-law in Adelaide, and spoke with this woman on the phone:

And she said to me, 'You do it', she said, 'you're still young', she said, 'if you want to do it, you do it'. And I said, 'I'm so frightened', I said, 'I know it's my country and I know they speak English; but', I said, 'and I understand my parents, what they must have felt when they went out to a strange country *with three kids in tow* not knowing a soul, only the sponsors'.

Janet still worried about asking Alan to leave his parents, but he responded firmly, 'My boys are my life' and became 'the main stalwart ... he was just like the Rock of Gibraltar'. Despite all Janet's anxieties about money and insecurity, Alan reassured her: 'You've been talking about it for years, we are going to do it'.

They pulled down their big old rambling house in Adelaide and built two duplexes, planning to use the proceeds of the sale for their retirement in England. In the late 1990s the housing market collapsed, they were forced to delay their departure and the sale produced less capital than they had hoped to

33 Janet Francis returned to England in 1997, forty-one years after being taken to Australia with her family as a reluctant teenager. At her new home in Sussex, with her Australian husband Alan, Janet finally found 'this sense of belonging, that you know I'm one of them now, I'm not the alien any more, I'm not the foreigner.' Janet died in Sussex in February 2004. Her ashes are scattered in England and Australia

take to England. In one final, paradoxical twist, Janet took out Australian citizenship shortly before leaving to ensure that if her sons came back to Australia she would not be trapped in England, but on the condition that she would not relinquish her British citizenship and would not have to make a public display of loyalty to Australia: 'I said to the boys, I said, "Well, I'll have to have half my brain removed to become an Australian citizen", no offence [laughs]. So of course they laughed and I said, "But I'm *not* telling anybody, now this is a big secret, I'm not telling anybody", and I said, "I'm not going up on the stage, I'm *not* doing it in front of people".' In November 1997 Janet, now aged 59, returned with Alan to live in England after forty-one years in Australia.

Return is never easy and places of the heart rarely stay the same. At first Janet and Alan tried to settle in Bristol, where Alan found a job in a factory. They rented a flat just outside the city and near to the kennels where Janet's Australian dog was in quarantine – she had determined not to leave another dog behind. But drugs and crime seemed to be rife and the neighbourhood was *'absolutely the pits, it was dreadful.* And you know the element that was there was absolutely *disgusting'*. A car accident rocked Janet's confidence and she began to think about giving up and going back to Australia, but 'Alan said "No bloody fear," he says, "we're not, we haven't tried it long enough"'.

Roger and his wife Karen brought them to live with their family in Surrey and helped them to find a house not far away on the edge of a small town in Sussex. Just as they were about to buy the house Janet suffered one more shocking blow, with a diagnosis of breast cancer. Again her sons rallied around to sort out her healthcare needs and finalize the house purchase.

Nine months after arrival, while Janet was in the midst of chemotherapy following a mastectomy, she and Alan moved into a new home which looks out over a small cottage garden into the green fields of her English dreams. The house is not as large as the one they had in Adelaide, but 'for the first time in my life I am happy'.[16]

I think it's that sense of belonging, when I walk around and I see some sort of layabouts or sheer poverty I think — but that is part of England and I don't like some of the things, but all the trees and I look at the sky and last night we were having a pot of tea out in the garden … at half past nine and it's so quiet around here, and it was so lovely and peaceful. And I said to Alan, 'This house, I love the house, it's nice and by English standards it's quite large' … and I think this sense of belonging, that you know I'm *one* of them now, I'm not the alien any more, I'm not the foreigner, Alan is now, I've been the foreigner for forty-one years because I *never* felt accepted as a true Australian while I was out there.

Janet inducted Alan in British ways of life, including afternoon tea at Buckingham Palace (after their names were drawn out of a barrel at Australia House) and the Millennium Proms in the Royal Albert Hall: 'to see Alan standing there as an Australian waving the Union Jack singing "Land of Hope and Glory", I thought I'd never see that [laughs]. It was a sight to behold.'

In 1999 Maisie and her husband also retired to England (the youngest sister, Trish, remains in Adelaide with her family), and in May 2000 Maisie's son arrived in England on a one way ticket 'to start a new life in his mother's homeland'.[17] These members of the Dungey family have come full circle, and feel that their migration story has ended. And yet their future remains uncertain. At the conclusion of our interview Janet captured this tension when asked if this is where she thought they would spend the rest of their lives:

Absolutely, wild horses wouldn't get me away now. I went before because I had to, I would never, *never*, unless circumstances changed. If say my boys went back and I could see no more future here well then I guess I would go back with my tail between my legs but it wouldn't be by choice. I'm home now and this is where I belong and where I want to stay, for ever, for as long as I've got.

Postscript: Janet Francis died in Sussex on 6 February 2004, after a courageous battle with cancer, just as work on this book was completed. Her ashes have been scattered in England and Australia.

Understanding return

Janet Francis's life story highlights the long-term influences which lie behind more superficial explanations of migration and return. Family dynamics, for example, are part of most return stories, but they are usually deep-rooted and complicated, and we only begin to understand their effects through the long span of a life history. Thus to comprehend the Dungeys' emigration we need to know more about how Betty's early life contributed to a long-term frustration with England and her idealized hopes for an Australian future, and about her relationship with the Thorpe family. To understand Janet's resistance to emigration and her youthful scheming to return it helps to know about her close relationship with her grandparents and the crushing of her teenage aspirations. And we can only explain her eventual return after forty-one years when we know about her sons' decisions to live in England, and Alan's devotion to his sons and to the achievement of Janet's dream.

Similarly, though tangible economic factors are significant within most stories of migration and return – for example the Dungeys' expectation of improved opportunities for their daughters and the brutal reality of their initial years in Australia – these economic forces and their impact upon migrant decision-making can only be understood in relation to migrant subjectivity. By 'subjectivity' we mean the aspirations and emotions which are underpinned by a person's sense of identity: who she is, what she comes from, and what she wants to become. We can understand the emotional resonance of Janet's dream of returning to England, for example, when she talks about her wartime childhood in rural Somerset and how it engendered a potent English identity, evoked by patriotic songs and symbolized by a pastoral idyll of the English countryside.

The story of Janet Francis and her family spotlights many of the factors which caused migrants to return to Britain, including economic difficulties, homesickness and family reunion. Most importantly, it shows how these factors interweave within a migrant family history. To help assess the relative importance of the different factors which influence return we have quantified in Table 4 the explanations which members of our panel of over 200 return migrants cite in their written accounts as making a significant contribution to their decision to return from Australia. (Motivations for return differed according to family status; the family statuses represented on this panel are indicated in Table 3.) Of course this is a very rough numerical breakdown – we know from our interviews that the written accounts we have received from migrants sometimes only provide a partial explanation for return by comparison with our in-depth interviews – but the survey provides an invaluable overview. It confirms some of our hunches, suggests directions for analysis and challenges some of the more simplistic explanations of return.

First, a significant minority (just under a quarter) of our respondents cite economic and job-related factors as contributing to their return, though very few returned primarily because of unemployment or desperate financial difficulties. Only a very small minority cite housing difficulties as contributing to return, and conditions in migrant hostels barely rate as a reason for return. Accidents and illness – and a resulting concern about long-term security in Australia and the comparative costs of healthcare – are mentioned slightly more frequently than problems with accommodation. A number of returns were influenced by aspects of Australian lifestyle, the character of its people and the climate, though very few reported that negative Australian attitudes to British migrants (the so-called 'whingeing Poms') were influential. Only a handful returned because they 'hated Australia', and these are outnumbered by many more return migrants who rather liked – and even 'loved' – Australia, and for whom Australia itself was not a reason for return. Though feelings about Australia and Australians were not particularly significant, homesickness for people, places and ways of life in Britain, or a sense of not feeling 'at home' in Australia, did influence the return of a very significant minority of our respondents (well over a third). Most important of all – influencing at least half of our return migrants – were the complicated responsibilities, needs, desires and tensions of family relationships, which pulled people back to Britain and then often kept them there despite a personal preference for Australia. Families loom large in the stories of migration and return.

If we now consider each of these factors in turn we can understand how they contributed in complex and interconnected ways to what was often a painful and difficult decision. From migrant stories we can develop a rich, multidimensional picture of return.

Table 3 Family status of return migrants

Family status	
Families with children	114
Couples without children	20
Single adults	73
Children who returned as adults	13
Total returns in sample	220

Source: written accounts by return migrants received by the University of Sussex project in 2000.

Table 4 Factors cited as influencing return to Britain

	Families	Couples	Singles	Child	Total
Never wanted to emigrate	1			2	3
Work offer in Britain or Europe	4	1	2	1	8
Unemployment	5	1	1		7
Employment-related problems	19	3	2		24
Financial difficulties	14	1			15
Ill-health	21	3	4		28
Australian health and welfare provision	6				6
Educational opportunities in Britain	4				4
Hostel conditions	5				5
Housing conditions	5	1			6
Housing availability or cost	8	1			9
Marital tensions or breakdown	12	2	3	1	18
Extended family tensions in Australia	3			1	4
Pregnancy or birth of children	11	4	1		16
Family care responsibilities in Britain	17	2	13		32
Return to be with family in Britain	10	3	14	1	28
Return for love or marriage	1		8	4	13
Left Australia to see the world				4	4
Returned as planned at the outset	1	2	20		23
'Trapped' on return visit to Britain	4	3	17		24
Homesick	36	10	5	1	52
Lonely	5				5
Hated Australia	4		1	1	6
Australian attitudes to British migrants	3			1	4
Australian character	5		5		10
Australian environment and wildlife	13		1		14
Australian society and way of life	4	1	5	2	12
Never felt 'Australian' – too 'British'	5		3	1	9
Too far from Europe	2		1		3
Wanted to grow old & die in Britain	4		1	2	7
Miscellaneous factors	6	2	4		12
Total	238	40	111	22	411

Note: from our panel of 257 British migrants who wrote to the University of Sussex project about their return from Australia, we have identified factors contributing to 220 'returns' (members of the same returning family have only been counted once). 'Child' denotes those who emigrated under the age of 21 as members of families and returned as single adults. Migrants who returned twice (14) and offer two separate explanations have been counted twice. Several multiple returnees are counted for each time they offer separate explanations. Respondents who were members of family groups which returned together have only been counted once, and we have excluded respondents for whom it was impossible to identify explanations for return. The survey does not include returnees who resettled permanently in Australia – though many wrote that they would have returned if they could have done so.

A migration paradox: the assisted passage scheme and return

One important preliminary qualification concerns the timing of return and the ways in which the assisted passage migration scheme itself affected patterns of return. For some migrants return was always part of the plan, or at least a strong option. A significant minority in our sample, almost invariably single people, had always intended to return.[18] It was not uncommon for young single migrants, or young couples without children, to think of the ten pound passage as a cheap rate for a working holiday. As we saw in Chapter 8, some of these young sojourners had expected to return after the two years; many settled after enjoying Australian life and work and perhaps marrying; others decided to return and settle in Britain or were called back by family responsibilities. Only very occasionally did families emigrate with the idea of return. The 'itchy feet' which inspired Dorothy Wright to emigrate with her husband and small baby suited her husband's desire to gain engineering management experience outside Britain. Five years later, as they had planned, similar 'itchy feet' brought them back home. Dorothy insisted theirs was not a 'migration experience' but was invaluable nonetheless. The Wrights were 'freed from a social code that had (in my case anyway) kept me in a rather rigid and conventional way of life. In a way the experience liberated me.'[19]

Of course back in Britain and in retrospect it was easier to emphasize an original intention to return, even though different circumstances might very easily have led to settlement in Australia. But most migrant families (unlike single sojourners) assumed that they were going to settle in Australia, and return was rarely planned from the outset. More often, return was a consequence of a decision too lightly taken or of unreal expectations shattered by daunting experience. The cheap passage and the easy approval processes did little to deter applicants acting on a whim or with unstated ambivalence, and the glowing publicity certainly raised expectations. Some migrants recall thinking that if the dream didn't work out, then you could always come home.

Very few returnees explain return in terms of their own failings or ambivalence, but the more astute migrants offer an incisive commentary. The hostel stories we explored in Chapter 5 include some of the most critical judgements made by migrants about fellow residents unwilling to give the new country a chance. John Williams, in a Brisbane hostel in 1965, criticized migrants who were 'disgruntled' because Australia could not provide a 'quick fix' for all their problems.[20] Ralph Price was a 10-year-old only child when he left Liverpool for Perth with his parents in 1951. Though the family seemed to be better off in Perth and Ralph himself had no desire to see England again, the family returned in 1955 and whenever Ralph asked his parents for an explanation 'each would say it was for the sake of the other!' In later life, Ralph reflects upon his parents' migration and return:

I think the whole enterprise was in a way not taken sufficiently seriously. Not sufficiently informed or planned, and I wonder what made relatively conservative and sensible people do that. Perhaps the upheavals and terrors of war had made people in a way somewhat reckless. Perhaps the idea that they were going to a predominantly 'British' culture led people to under-estimate the extent of the adjustments they were going to have to make. There was no language barrier.... Probably the fact that it was virtually free suggested an approach that said, 'Well if it doesn't work out we can always come back.' The very fact that so many others were doing the same legitimized and normalized it, making it appear less risky, with lower stakes than there actually were.

On the other hand, there was I believe a huge, and perhaps unrealistic expectation of success, both in the minds of the immigrants and the receiving community. This fed an understandable feeling of failure and indeed guilt. I think they were somehow perceived by others and/or themselves as not having 'what it takes'. Strength, independence, commitment, balance, courage, fortitude, flexibility, guts....

These underlying feelings are I think suggested in both of my parents' extreme defensiveness about taking responsibility for the decision to return. Indeed their inability to acknowledge or explain what it was all about for them.[21]

The two-year 'probation' period – requiring assisted migrants who returned within two years to repay the balance of outward fares in addition to return fares – had a significant effect upon potential returnees. Less than 10 per cent of the returnees in our sample came back within the first two years (see Table 5). Very few migrants could afford to return within the two-year period, and those who could only did so when they were desperate. Marion Kells had been enjoying a new life in Sydney with her husband Colin in 1966, when an unexpected pregnancy made her desperately homesick. Her parents loaned her money so that she could return within the two-year period and have her baby in England.[22]

In some cases the financial difficulty of early return had the effect anticipated by the immigration authorities. Chris Gray recalls that his Manchester family had a miserable start in Australia. A sponsoring uncle housed them in an isolated and primitive shack in the wintry hills outside Melbourne, and each night the parents and three sons would sit around the open fire, 'crying, because we thought, what we've come all this way for, into a place like this; we was expecting it to be, you know, lovely sunshine and everything's rosy. And we just, every night we sat round the fire, and we'd be talking about England, and we'd all be crying, all of us, my dad and all, and saying, "We've made a mistake".... If we could have come back home, we would have done there and

Table 5 Returnees' length of stay in Australia

	Families	Couples	Singles	Child	Total
Less than 2 years	11	2	4	1	18
2–3 years	41	12	39	2	94
3–10 years	50	4	21	3	78
More than 10 years	12	2	9	7	30
Total	114	20	73	13	220

Note: see Tables 3 and 4 for details about the sample from which this table is derived.

then." But return was not an option: 'my dad just said, "Well, we've got to give it a try, you know, we're stuck here for two years, because we can't afford to pay the fare home straight away", so he said, "we've got to get some money to get some fare to get back home anyway". And that's what persuaded him then to, my uncle Jack said it's a lot better in Queensland, to try up there, and come up there and give it a go up there.' Though the Grays were homesick for two years, the climate in Brisbane was good, there was plenty of bricklaying work for father, and the boys joined soccer clubs and began to feel more settled.[23]

But while the two-year probation forced some migrants to buckle down and make the most of their new life, for others it caused acute pain and festering resentment. Catherine Barber emigrated with her parents, siblings and grandmother from Scotland in 1964 and returned when the two years was up, mainly because her nan could not stand the heat in Perth. She recalls that once her parents had decided to return they became more negative about Australia and 'began to see the problems'.[24] For Carol Brooks the two-year period was like 'a prison sentence'. She hated the flies, the heat and rudeness of the Western Australians and was unsettled by other unhappy British migrants. But as soon as the two years were up and she knew that she could come home, she started thinking, 'Well it's not so bad really'. 'All that time you have that two years hanging over your head you felt, well as I say like a bit of a prison sentence, but as soon as you knew you could *come* home it felt completely different. Strange really.'[25] In fact, just under half of our sample of returnees went home during their third year in Australia. By this time they had to pay only their return fares and had decided that Australia was not for them, that they were needed back home, or that the two-year working holiday was over.

The economics of despair

Economic factors contributed to the return of about a quarter of the British migrants in our sample, though financial hardship in Australia was rarely a primary cause of return; household expenditure – and the cost of living in Australia – was almost never reported as a problem. That astute migrant commentator Gwen Good noted that comparative living standards were difficult to judge, but concluded that although medical services, white goods and electronic equipment were more expensive in Australia, most other items – and especially food – were cheaper.[26] There were unexpected expenses (the Farnfield family from Sussex had not realized that they would need a car in Australia for Don to get to work, and were annoyed at the cost of school books for their three boys) but on the whole family income went at least as far if not further in Australia.[27]

Most migrants also recall that wages were higher in Australia, and – as we saw in Chapter 6 – it was usually easy to find work and to move between jobs. Only a handful of our respondents ascribe their return to unemployment or difficulties in attaining work. Most of these were unlucky to arrive in Australia during an economic downturn in their particular trade, such as the O'Neills, who went home to England after only six weeks after their building company sponsor withdrew a job offer because of a downturn in the industry.[28]

A rather different but equally small group of 'economic' returnees are those who were offered a better job or who sought enhanced career opportunities back in Britain or in Europe or the United States. These tended to be single migrants or male breadwinners in professional occupations with an international corporate structure; Dorothy Wright's husband, Mike, tired of factory management for Nestlés in Victoria and wanted head office experience, and so brought his family back to England in 1965 after five years.[29] Professionals who traversed international career structures can be compared with some single migrants, mainly working-class men, who tired of an itinerant working life on the frontiers of Australia's mining, manufacturing and pastoral industries and had not found the right relationship or job in Australia; they returned to Britain hoping to make a more settled domestic and working life. In 1959, 23-year-old Nigel Heath left a dead-end job in London and took the assisted passage to Australia, where he enjoyed travelling the country, playing sport and taking odd jobs in the city and out in the bush. Working as a fettler in north Queensland, he suddenly decided that he didn't want to end up like workmates who had little to show for their lives other than great yarns and effects of heavy drinking; he was lonely, and decided to overland back to Britain and a new life: 'That was the big thing, to be, someone to share your life with. And I'd been there for four years and I was drifting, there was not going to be much chance of finding someone I don't think, not when you're a drifter.'[30]

Though finding a job was not usually a problem for British migrants, a range of issues related to employment – mostly experienced by men who were the main family breadwinners – did influence a significant number of returns.

Some migrants who had brought grown-up families to Australia were told that they were too old to get a job in their own trade, and had to accept inferior work and the humiliating recognition that wives, sons or daughters might be the main family breadwinners. Others had been assured that they would find a job in their trade and were disappointed when they were forced to accept unskilled work. As we saw in Chapter 6, some – like Edward Dungey – were appalled when their British qualifications were not accepted by Australian employers, unions or professional associations, and were forced to take unsuitable and less well paid employment.

The men who were worst affected by these indignities rarely tell their own story but wives and children offer poignant accounts of husbands and fathers who were all but destroyed by their Australian experience. Elizabeth Gray recalls that after their arrival in 1959 her husband Harry could find little work as a plasterer in Queensland, where most of the houses were timber. He worried about job security and that there was no Australian equivalent to the British national insurance scheme, he became unwell and developed a facial tick, and he grew obsessed with return. Despite the fact that Elizabeth and their three sons were very happy in Australia, the Gray family returned to Essex in 1961. In 1951 Alvyn and Bruce Bates emigrated with their parents and sister to Brisbane, where their father took up a sponsored job as a saw doctor in a timber mill. One of the brothers who owned the mill resented their father and was critical of his work; Alvyn recalls that 'as a consequence he became very unsettled, unhappy and effectively had a nervous breakdown. Towards the end of his time in Australia he began to look very haggard', and after little more than a year his old employer in England paid for the family's return.[31]

These are tragic stories about the aspirations of working-class craftsmen and the destruction of their masculine identity in Australia. They were proud working-class men whose identity was primarily bound up in their professional craft and an ability to provide for the family, and who found, to their humiliation, that they were unable to sustain this identity in Australia. Barely able to admit failure, their bodies and nerves cracked up, and their only, desperate hope was return.

The acute problems of housing in Australia, which we explored in Chapter 7, contributed to the difficulties of British migrants. Several of the families in our sample were shocked by the state of accommodation in sponsored or rented housing, or in the migrant hostels, and this persuaded them to return home. And yet by contrast with contemporary controversies about housing the number who returned because of the poor state of accommodation in Australia is comparatively low, and in most cases there were other contributory factors. In 1951 Fred Ford, a fitter and turner from Salford, found that he had been completely misled by rosy descriptions of first-class hostel accommodation and the ease of obtaining housing loans in Sydney. Conditions in the migrant hostel were 'atrocious' and 'life was unbearable for my wife with two small babies…. We felt like European refugees.' But while these conditions and the difficulty of buying a house led to deep disillusion, the decision to return was driven as much by anti-English taunting and prejudice which Fred suffered at work.[32]

As the example of the Ford family suggests, at least as important as the actual conditions of accommodation was the prospect of renting, or ideally buying, a home. We have seen how home ownership was part of the dream of emigration to Australia, and was actively promoted in migration publicity and sustained by those struggling house builders who became part of the 'pioneer' legend of successful British migrants. But the dream could equally be a potent frustration – as we saw in Chapter 7 with the example of Sydney Hart. Ray Spencer grew up in poverty in a coal mining village in South Wales during the Depression. His determination to one day buy his own house was a large part of the motivation which drew Ray, his wife Irene and son Alan to Australia in 1966. In Perth they found spacious rented accommodation – with a lemon tree in the back yard! Ray and Irene both worked and began to save, and they all loved the outdoor Australian lifestyle. With a thousand dollars in the bank they found a house they wanted to buy for $3,000, but the bank refused a loan for the balance because they had no collateral:

I was the most disappointed man in Australia…. A place of our own, this is one of the reasons we went to Australia to get a place of our own 'cause there was so much property going up in those days…. So I got a little bit despondent from that. I can't remember exactly when that was. But it must have been about a year or eighteen months before we actually came home. And I think that started to set the rot in.

The frustration of Ray's lifelong dream of a family home (and the news that they could get a mortgage for a house back in Bridgend) was a major factor in the Spencers' return in 1970, but as was so often the case there were other important factors. Irene had an accident and was off work for three months, and began to worry that if anything serious happened to her and Ray there would be no family to look after Alan. She also wanted to see her family and tell them about her Australian adventures. Back in Bridgend Ray was delighted to buy his own home, but Irene soon regretted their return to 'dreary old Wales'.[33]

'The Australian way of life wasn't for me'

Though many British migrants had minor gripes about aspects of Australian society, lifestyle and character, few report these as important reasons for return. Yet those few who did return at least in part because they disliked

Australia often record that dislike in vivid, even virulent, detail. Kenneth Dixon and his family paid their own way back to England after only two months in Melbourne and blamed an appalling Australian experience on the false advertising, the terrible heat and barbaric schooling of the children.[34] A few found the Australians rude and boorish, and were, like Fred Ford or Janet Francis, upset by anti-English attitudes and comments. Some were appalled by the macho drinking culture with its sexism and rigid gender separations, or by the superficiality and materialism of the Australian lifestyle, as described by young English mother Anne Cox:

I hope this is not being read by a Western Australian but a more belligerent, rude, uncouth, money orientated unfriendly race of people I have yet to meet. We were invited to other English people's houses that seemed to have adopted the same mentality. Their social life consisted of meeting other English people at each other's houses, consuming vast quantities of charred meat (I developed a life long aversion to barbecues and still avoid them whenever possible), jumping in and out of small pools, discussing how big their next pool or car would be and convincing themselves that life was so wonderful.[35]

Probably of greater significance for return was the Australian environment and especially the hot climate.[36] Many migrants, particularly those in the north or outback, were also irritated by Australia's insect life, and for a few like Kathleen Upton insects were the last straw. With her husband Ron and 3 year old daughter she had a tough two years in Australia during the mid-1950s; with Ron initially unable to find the work he wanted, they moved between various primitive houses in Queensland, Perth and the bush, and Kathleen suffered terrible homesickness. They tried to build 'half a house' just outside Perth but Kathleen's enthusiasm was drained by record summer heat and plagues of mosquitoes, and finally broken by a grasshopper which got under her skirt:

I danced a fandango all down the road, slapping at my thigh, trying to dislodge the creature and feeling its legs pricking my flesh. Indoors I did a strip-tease in record time and was left holding my pants with the remains of its long legs waving at me while its body was squashed all over my thigh. Ugh! I made up my mind that the Australian way of life wasn't for me and they could keep their great outdoors and all the horrid things that went with it! At the end of two years we would go home.[37]

Homesickness

Yet hot weather, insects and other elements of Australian life and society influenced only a very small minority of the return migrants. Homesickness – potent feelings about the places, way of life and above all people in Britain – was far more significant in decisions about return. 'Homesickness' is a troublesome term. It has often been used – by migration officials and contemporary commentators, by historians and indeed by migrants themselves – as a shorthand explanation which simplifies or even conceals a complex experience. It is sometimes dismissed as a not particularly important or long-lasting feeling, as something you grow out of or which eases with time. It carries particular cultural meanings – for example the British migrant association with 'whingeing Poms' – and is commonly explained away as a female problem, signifying women's particular bonds to place and people or their emotional vulnerability and weakness. Migrant stories confront these assumptions and require us to consider homesickness in both intimate detail and general terms.

We have already seen – in Janet Francis's account of her mother's breakdown and of her own re-emerging homesickness, or in Chris Gray's story of his recently arrived family weeping beside the fire of the dismal house provided for them in the hills outside Melbourne – that homesickness could be a potent aspect of the British migrant experience. John Williams's story highlights the diverse ways in which homesickness was experienced, as well as its dramatic effects. John was an electrician who emigrated from Swindon to Queensland in 1965 with his wife Esther and two young children. They built a beautiful house on a block of land outside Brisbane – 'Savernake represented the realisation of all our hopes and dreams' – and two more children were born in Australia. Homesickness set in for John after the house was finished and they were happy and well settled, 'but something was very wrong':

I began to feel vaguely ill from time to time and could discover no reason for it. Then one day, Esther's mother sent us a calendar showing pictures of England. As soon as I saw it my heart sank and I felt very miserable. Hardly crediting it, I began to consider the possibility that I was homesick, a thing which I had always roundly condemned everyone else for! Little by little, I began to notice other things which caused a similar reaction, such as watching an English comedy on TV.

One late afternoon as the heat of the day began to abate, the time of day I loved on the land, I was outside popping-up stumps when I heard a jet high above. I looked up, and what a picture it made! The deep blue sky framed by eucalyptus trees and, far above, the vapour trail and shiny body of a jet, obviously a passenger Boeing 707. Then, as I realized that the aircraft was probably on its way to England (at least, it was heading in the right direction), the now familiar lurch of the stomach hit me, and my eyes welled full of tears. 'How stupid!' I thought, angrily.

As time went by, this feeling became all too familiar and something obviously had to be done about it, but I had no idea what. By now, my sleep was regularly disturbed with dreams of England. The things I yearned for most were not, strangely enough, the people, but little peeps of England such as church steeples set in the centre of clustering villages and gently rolling hills. Most powerful of all was the image of myself sitting on an old Cotswold stone wall![38]

Though Esther and the two older children were much opposed to leaving Australia, as John became more dejected and ill they reluctantly agreed to return to England.

John's account highlights a number of points about homesickness. It shows how homesickness can be a constant, everyday experience, or can be triggered at particular moments through poignant memory association and disturbance, such as the calendar with pictures of England or the aeroplane flying overhead. In many migrant stories sound is a potent trigger, and songs – for Janet Francis 'Land of Hope and Glory' and 'There'll Always Be an England' – recall another time and place and evoke a sense of loss through their lyrics and emotive music. Events such as Christmas were poignant reminders of the absence of family and friends, and the stark differences between the two countries were highlighted by rituals which seemed hollow in an upside down world. Kathleen Upton spent her first Australian Christmas Eve at Fremantle Docks farewelling another migrant who was returning to Britain and felt 'very subdued'. On Christmas morning the sound of Bing Crosby singing 'Silent Night' provoked her to tears:

'Switch it off. I can't stand it,' I cried. The thought of those at home, playing games round the fire, roasting chestnuts, eating turkey and mince pies, the tree with all the lights and small gifts was just too much to bear. We had no special dinner, cold corned beef and tomatoes was all that our budget allowed. I couldn't wait for the day to end.[39]

For migrants like John Williams and Kathleen Upton this emotional disturbance extended into their most intimate dreams.[40] But homesickness might also be fostered and reinforced in social settings. Many return migrants describe the unsettling effects of mixing with disgruntled ten pound Poms, either in the hostels or at recreational events. Chris Gray recalls this effect when his family moved to Brisbane:

And, all the people we knew, my mum and dad knew, and even the lads I played football with, said, 'Oh, as soon as we save enough money, you know, we're going to go back to England' and that. And for the first two years I thought, well, I agree with them, I thought, I did miss England a little bit, and Australia wasn't quite as adventurous as I thought it was. And they used to have plenty of parties between all the English people, and they was always saying, 'Oh, wait till we get back to, oh we can't wait to get back to England', you know.

Homesickness was experienced in terms of the absence or loss of differ-ent aspects of 'home'. John Williams's longing was for place; the physical environment had always been important to his sense of identity and belong-ing, and in Australia he missed an idealized pastoral English landscape – just as he would later miss the Australian bush. Similarly, Janet Francis missed the fields and country buses of her formative west-country childhood, and a sense of British patriotism which had been forged in wartime. Elizabeth and Derek Tribe, a university couple who emigrated in 1956 and wrote a guidebook for professional migrants, asked fellow migrants what they most missed of life in Britain. One of the 'more serious answers' was the English countryside. They warned readers that 'if you want to spend your Sunday afternoon pleasantly strolling over Downs, along tow paths and through primrose woods, following well-worn tracks and climbing well-worn stiles, then Australia is a dead loss'.[41]

This longing for pastoral England is fascinating in a number of ways. Firstly, the rural England that is missed is usually the very specific landscape of the southern English home counties. Secondly, most of the postwar immigrants who missed this rural England had come from cities and suburbs. Their Australian longing for pastoral England seems to be an overseas manifestation of the twentieth-century cultural phenomenon by which the English middle and working classes located their national identity within rural England. Outside London, the urban British were never far from the countryside, and the train and then the motor car had contributed to a rural tourism which was encouraged by advertising and by a prolific cultural industry of ruralist writers and painters. From the vantage point of city slums and smoking factories the English countryside was – after the industrial revolution – perceived as paradise indeed, and working-class emigrants carried this longing in their cultural baggage.[42] The stark and sunburnt Australian countryside may have fuelled a longing for a green pastoral England, but the cultural origins of this particular homesickness were located back home. Significantly, a pastoral idyll does not seem to be a significant part of the homesickness of immigrants from urban Scotland, whereas urban and rural Welsh immigrants describe powerful feelings of 'hiraeth' (homesickness) for the valleys and hills which are such a resonant part of Welsh identity. Maureen Carter was 19 when she left Neath in South Wales:

There must have been hundreds of people on that railway station, all singing 'We'll Keep a Welcome in the Hillside'! It brings tears to my eyes now! And one of the lines is, 'We'll kiss away each hour of hiraeth, when you come home again to Wales'! And I, I, I still crack up when I think of it. And I just had that feeling for so long, well it seemed like so long, when I first came.[43]

Memories of place were enmeshed with nostalgia for particular ways of life, as the young Worthing mother Anne Cox – who so vehemently disliked the rude Western Australians and their superficial lifestyle – recalls of her own homesickness in Perth during the early 1970s: 'I missed the public library, the swimming baths, going to the pub with friends, the green of the downs, the public transport system.' Migrants from the north of England, and especially women, often recall that they missed the socializing in local pubs, and thus evoke one form of urban homesickness as a counterpoint to the more typical ruralism.

Most of all, homesick migrants missed people; a significant proportion of our sample of return migrants went home so that they could be closer to their family and friends. Dot Hallas had never really wanted to leave her close extended family in Yorkshire but her mother had said that she should follow her husband to Australia, where she 'cried every night for 12 months! ... I didn't care about England, I wanted me mum!'[44] In 1960, 19-year-old Terry Stephens had been thrilled by the prospect of adventure in Australia with her new husband Ian, but after their first child was born she became lonely and isolated in suburban Melbourne. She missed the cultural life she had previously enjoyed in Brighton, but above all she desperately missed the five brothers and sisters who had been so important in her English life: 'My sister played the piano and every time I heard, I mean we liked a lot of classical music but any time I heard the piano I would just cry.'[45]

Though homesickness involves a sense of loss or absence from another place and time, it is fundamentally about the here and now. Homesickness grows out of how you feel about where you are, about the life you're leading and the actual or prospective achievement of aspirations. For British migrants homesickness was as much about their lives in Australia as it was about their 'home' in Britain. Part of the evidence for this argument lies in the stories of migrants who were not homesick, or for whom momentary pangs of longing were offset by the positive challenge and excitement of their Australian lives. These are men and women who had taken a grip on their new lives, who were living the life they had imagined or were actively working – maybe even struggling – towards their migration goals. Though Ray and Irene Spencer's migration came unstuck when they could not buy a house in Perth, neither of them experienced homesickness:

We only phoned home once didn't we? That's all, to say we were all right and things like that but no, never really missed the family. But we were so busy all the time, I mean, I was working, Ray was working, Alan was out all the time with his friends. We didn't really have a lot of time to miss the family. There was so much to do.

Even Janet Francis, who experienced terrible homesickness when she first arrived in Australia and again later in life, recalls that when she was busy and content with a young family of her own she 'didn't have time to be homesick'.[46]

By contrast, a closer look at the material circumstances of British homesickness in Australia helps us understand the malady. For example, homesickness was often particularly acute for women who were expecting a baby (especially a first child), or who were at home with young children while father was working long hours away from home. These women wanted the practical and emotional support of mothers and the extended family back in Britain, and while husbands made new friends at work young mothers were often lonely and isolated. Contemporary commentators – and many of the migrants themselves – argued that women were more prone to homesickness than men; in our sample women returnees recalled significant episodes of homesickness six times more often than men. It is likely that the significance for women of social and family networks is part of the explanation.

Yet there is also a hidden form of male homesickness. It is rarely labelled as such – perhaps because of the stereotype of female weakness – but there are abundant clues in reports by wives and children of the physical and emotional breakdown of their menfolk. These are the men – like Harry Gray, Edward Dungey or Bruce and Alvyn Bates's father – whose masculine identity had been crushed by their problems at work or their inability to sustain their bread-winner role. They became desperate to return, even obsessed, and though they might not have labelled themselves homesick they had all the symptoms.[47] Even for men like John Williams, who explains his homesickness in terms of a longing for pastoral England, we can see other explanations within their Australian lives. At about the time he began to yearn for the villages and rolling hills of the Cotswolds, John Williams had resigned from a steady electrician's job with Frigidaire and tried to make a living selling his artwork; it was a disastrous failure. One dream was deflated, and the other – of building his own home in the Australian bush – had been achieved, and John was thus at a point in his life where homesickness could easily take root.[48]

These case studies also confront simplistic models which explain home-sickness as a passing phase – which you get over or grow out of – or as a con-stant emotion which festers and deepens over time. Homesickness comes and goes with the phases and events of life. For example, government records show that in recent years there has been an increase in the return rate of older British migrants. Janet Francis's experiences exemplify this trend of 'retire-ment migration' by men and women who, in later life, feel a resurgence of homesickness and a growing desire to live out their lives in Britain.[49] At the other extreme are the young men and women who came to Australia as children with their migrant parents, who enjoyed growing up in Australia, and yet in early adulthood were drawn back to their country of origin. In Chapter 4 we saw this pattern in the story of Malcolm Good, who had come with his parents to Perth as a baby. Michael Siberry was 6 in 1963 when he left Bournemouth with his parents and older siblings for Tasmania, where his father worked as a GP. They lived in a lovely house in Hobart alongside a sprawling patch of bush and Michael relished the outdoor lifestyle. After training at drama school in Sydney he had three successful years as an actor with the South Australian State Theatre Company, but something was missing:

I always remained curious about my dad's brothers, my mum's family and I just wanted to get back. And all through being in Australia I'd sort of, through watching television and through letters and magazines, built up this image of this place here, and always felt I would go back whether I was an actor or not. I sort of thought maybe I'll go to college in England because it was part of the outside world, a bigger outside world.

On returning to England in 1979 I actually wrote in a diary 'I feel complete'.... I felt ... maybe an outsider as far as Tasmania was concerned, and I felt actually I *belong* where my parents came from, and that was my initial feeling.[50]

Some British immigrants believed that a short visit back home might cure homesickness. In the 1950s a British holiday was not affordable for most migrants, though by the 1960s some among the earliest immigrant wave had amassed sufficient savings to afford such a trip, and the reduced cost and comparative ease of jet travel made the return visit a more realistic option. As early as 1963, Elizabeth and Derek Tribe noted that 'many of our friends, particularly the wives, tell us that, after a trip home, they have returned to settle much more contentedly in Australia'.[51] Ivy Skowronski emigrated from Bournemouth with her Polish refugee husband and their children in 1959, and they settled in the South Australian townships of Whyalla and Salisbury. For many years Ivy endured 'bouts of homesickness': she missed 'the sweet freshness of the English countryside, or twilight evenings watching the sea', and she 'longed to see her mother and brother, plus umpteen cousins, not to mention friends ... on the other side of the world. No longer could I hop on the bus to visit them for the day.' In 1971 her family urged her go home to see her 90-year-old mother, and to take up the new cheap rates offered by 'Group Travel' organizations to British migrants who wanted to visit 'the old country'. Ivy enjoyed the reunion with her mother and other relatives, but England had changed:

it was all grumble, grumble, about high prices, the government, the Common Market, the trouble in Ireland. It was all very depressing.... Yes, there were marked changes in England and I had not grown with these differences, that was why they were so noticeable. I too had changed in my ways and outlook on life and because the last twelve years had been spent away, I was now able to make a comparison.

Ivy flew back to Australia 'with my homesickness for England cured for ever'.[52]

Some migrants who returned to live in Britain later wished that they had only come home for a brief visit to meet relatives and assuage homesickness.

Irene Spencer realized too late that a short visit was all she had really needed and she deeply regretted selling up in Australia and resettling in Wales. But for others a return visit had the opposite effect on homesickness. For Janet Francis and her sister Maisie McDonald holiday trips to England intensified the dream of a permanent return. Phillip Maile's mother 'had' to travel back to England on a regular basis to visit her family, but 'even after thirty-seven years, the homesickness ache remains, especially for Mum'. Phillip married an English woman who herself made several trips back home:

Each time she returned to Australia very emotional and homesick for a week or two, and tried so hard to explain how and why she missed England so much. Her Mother was obvious, but also the quiet beauty of the place, the genteel way of life, the villages, the history, the culture her roots her memories. Where had I heard these words before, I wonder?[53]

The contrasting examples of Phillip Maile's family and Ivy Skowronski confirm that while homesickness is deeply felt in terms of absence and loss, it is generated by feelings about the life migrants lead in the here and now. Home visits might help the homesick British immigrant to recognize the positive features of his or her Australian life, but they are just as likely to engender a sense of inadequacy and incompleteness, and a hankering for 'home'.

The family dynamics of return

Australia wanted young immigrant families, and these families arrived in a period of postwar history when a traditional model of separate roles in the nuclear family prevailed and yet was beginning to break down. Family relationships were a factor in at least half of the returns by British migrants. The specific causes are diverse and complex, complicated by intergenerational and transnational responsibilities, demands and desires, and can best be explained in terms of the stages of family life.

For some migrants, marital breakdown resulted in one partner – more often the woman – going home to seek support from the extended family. As we saw in Chapter 7 with Carol Brooks taking her fisherman husband to Australia to cure his drinking problem, some couples migrated in an attempt to shore up a troubled relationship and to make a new start, only to find that moving to the other side of the world accentuated their problems and led to return and separation.[54] In some cases the pressures of migration contributed to family breakdown. At 21, Patricia Barnes married a former merchant seaman who had loved the Australian climate and way of life and now planned to emigrate under the ten pound scheme. Patricia never wanted to leave her London family, and had a nervous breakdown over the decision, but agreed to go because she loved her husband. In Australia he enjoyed a hectic work and social life and they bought an impressive brick bungalow in the Brisbane suburbs. But within a couple of years Patricia, who was at home with two children, 'needed to go back home to my family, I felt so alone'. Her father-in-law paid for boat tickets for herself and the children, and they hoped that 'Pat would miss us so much that he would return to England himself later, but that didn't happen'.[55] Our archives include many poignant stories of families torn apart by conflicting attitudes to migration and return.

Failing marriages did not necessarily fracture along faultlines created by the traditional gender roles of the sociable working man and the isolated woman at home. As we have seen in earlier chapters, economic circumstances forced some migrant wives and mothers to join the paid workforce so that they could contribute to family goals of economic independence and home ownership. Sometimes migrant wives relished a newfound freedom while husbands were troubled by changing roles. Gloria Rennison married her first husband in 1959 when she was 16 and he was 26. In 1965 they emigrated, with two young children, from the West Midlands to Wollongong, where he worked as a lathe engineer with BHP. They were appalled by conditions in the migrant hostel and moved to Sydney, where they shared a house with another migrant family and both Gloria and her husband found jobs. But in 1969 they returned to England: 'I loved Sydney and didn't want to go back to the UK but my husband did, as I was getting too independent so he started saving to get us back home.'[56]

In other families where one partner went home the other would sometimes follow, hoping to restore a failed marriage, or because he (only occasionally she) could not bear to be parted from his children. Phillip Maile explains that after 15 years his marriage broke down,

and my very homesick wife and my three lovely young children returned to England for good, and even though we were finished I just had to migrate back to England just so that I could see and be near the children. So that's why I came back, not because the green hills or my roots were calling … because I loved and still do Australia, the lifestyle and people.… BUT England and my new life here has pleasantly surprised me.[57]

The connection between marriage and return is not always negative. A number of British migrants returned for love, perhaps to marry a childhood sweetheart, or in pursuit of a boyfriend or girlfriend who had moved to the other side of the world and whom they could not persuade to live in Australia. John Jordan emigrated to Australia with his parents and returned to Merseyside as a young man, hoping to persuade a childhood girlfriend to join him in Australia:

When it became obvious that I was not going to entice Barbara back to Australia, I had to then reconcile my thinking to the fact that that this is where I was going to be.... It wasn't difficult because once you fall in love with somebody then that takes precedence over every aspect of your life.... So I had to then think, no, this is what I have to do, this is the future, and reconcile my thinking to it. And as I say it's only in reflective moments like these that I look back and say what might have been, but my life has taken a different path.[58]

Making a better life for the children was a primary aim for migrant families, but children sometimes became part of the problem and a cause of return. In some ways migration was much more difficult with the added costs and needs of children; childless migrant couples often behaved more like the single migrants who were able to work and travel around Australia with little restraint. Once a couple had children, or even as they prepared to have children, the dynamics of family life and migrant decision-making were transformed. A significant number of our sample of return migrants came home either when a prospective mother became pregnant or soon after the birth, and many more returned because of the additional pressures of raising young children. Young mothers like Terry Stephens or Carol Brooks felt an almost primal need for the emotional and practical support of their own mothers or siblings, and the social isolation and loneliness which often accompanies motherhood in conventional marriages was particularly acute for migrant women.[59]

Christina Daly's story highlights the potent effect of motherhood on the female migrant. In 1973 Londoners Christina and her husband John took up the ten pound scheme as the cheapest way to travel and escape the miserable English weather. They settled in Sydney, travelled frequently, worked hard, bought a beautiful house with a swimming pool, and enjoyed the outdoor waterside lifestyle and the exciting social and political changes of Australia in the 1970s. In 1981 they took out citizenship and began to think of themselves as Australian. But Christina's sense of herself as settled in Australia had begun to be disturbed when John took up a work posting in Switzerland at the end of the 1970s and they spent eighteen months in Europe; she remembered that she enjoyed the changing seasons and the ways in which winter and summer created very different ways of living ('I missed that being able to hibernate away for three months of the year'). The birth of the first of two children in 1984 had a more dramatic impact, in several ways. Opportunities for regular travel, in Australia and to Europe, were curtailed. Christina gave up work – not wanting to repeat the pattern of her own lonely childhood with both parents at work – but in so doing lost touch with her friendship network: 'All the friends that I had were at work, and I was just becoming more and more isolated and actually getting very depressed.' In all her years in Australia she had avoided Christmas because the summer festivities didn't seem right and made her homesick, but 'when we had our son and of course you have Christmas with children and everything, that was when I actually started to think long term'. She also wanted the children to know their grandparents in England. John had no particular desire to return ('he flatly refused to ship himself back') and discussions about their future went on over two years until John was offered a five-year contract in Holland; they agreed on a European compromise, which eventually led them to settle back in Britain.[60]

Most often migrant children followed the decisions of their parents and had little choice or influence in emigration or return. Ralph Price, a teenager who returned to Liverpool after four years in Australia with his parents, recalls, 'There was scant regard for children, who were just dragged along as luggage.'[61] But parents sometimes made return decisions based at least in part upon the needs of their children. Some, like Christina Daly, worried that children would miss the important bonds with grandparents and other family members. A few felt their children might receive a better education in Britain. Other parents, who sensed that the family might eventually return, decided to do so while their children were still young and before they reached an age when their loyalties would be tested by strong ties in Australia.[62] Just occasionally, parents returned to Britain because one of their children was miserable in Australia. Sussex family Don and Dorothy Farnfield and their three sons flew to Perth from London in 1966. Don worked as a painter and decorator with the State Housing, Dorothy found part-time work as a home help, and they made new friends and enjoyed the outdoor life. All the signs pointed to a contented settlement in Perth. But the eldest son, Keith, who had settled well at school, became unhappy once he started white-collar work at the Railways. He hated work, was 'very very despondent' after a rejection from the Australian navy, and announced that he wanted to return to live with his grandmother and apply to the British navy. Don and Dorothy reminded themselves that the boys' future was their main aim – as Don recalls, 'Oh well that was the reason that we went out in the first place, it wasn't so much for us, for our sakes' – and after a family meeting they agreed they would all return. Dorothy explains that it was not an easy decision: 'I wanted to come back and I didn't want to come back, I wanted to make Keith happy because he was unhappy.'[63] This story shows how emotional issues between parents and their offspring – often most acute as teenagers prepared to leave home – could be magnified by migration and result in painful dilemmas for migrant families.

Concerns about the welfare of children were also part of the reason why accidents and ill-health contributed to a significant number of returns. An accident at work or the serious illness of a parent accentuated a sense of insecurity within a migrant family and reminded them that in Australia they could not usually fall back on the extended family for support. Some migrants also craved the 'cradle to grave' security offered by the British National Health Service. By the 1950s the NHS was already deeply entrenched and revered in the consciousness of British working-class people, who recalled the poor service and high costs of prewar treatment and were wary of the private insurance schemes available in Australia. Anne and George McLanaghan emigrated from Ayr in Scotland to Melbourne in 1955 with their son Douglas, found work and began to make friends through their local Baptist church. When Anne was diagnosed with tuberculosis and placed in a sanatorium for ten months (she suspects that her immune system was weakened by the stress of migration and homesickness), the Baptist congregation helped George to look after Douglas while he juggled work commitments. But after Anne came out of hospital they decided to go back to Scotland, where they knew they could rely on family and community support. As George explains: 'At home I knew, when you took ill at home, anyone, a neighbour or anyone would have looked after Douglas, and that's what hit me. I knew I could sleep anywhere, under a hedge or anything; but with Douglas, it was different.'[64]

In the decision to return, the health of family members back in Britain was even more significant than the health of the migrant family in Australia. A significant proportion of migrants – about one in seven in our sample – returned to Britain because they needed to care for relatives, most often ageing parents. Single migrants often returned because of a family duty of care – they had no competing responsibility for children in Australia – but families which were well established in Australia were also pulled home by these bonds of loyalty and need. Some returned too late, after the death of a parent, driven by guilt and remorse and shocked out of a settled life in Australia. Others simply returned because they knew that increasingly elderly and frail parents depended upon them. Many hoped to get back to Australia but found themselves 'trapped' in Britain by family commitments and financial constraints.

Some migrants had avoided this pull back to Britain by emigrating with grandparents or bringing them out once the family had settled. In Chapter 4 we saw how the emigration of Gwen and Cliff Good and their three sons was only possible because Gwen's parents agreed to follow them to Perth. If, as was feared at one point, Gwen's mother had been prevented by illness from coming to Australia, then the whole family would have been forced to return to England. For other extended families, emigration with a grandparent caused more problems than it solved. The Vidlers had to leave their grandmother in Australia when they went back to England because she was not well enough to travel, and Catherine Barber's nan hated the heat in Australia and was one cause of her family's return.[65]

More often, British family emigration only involved the nuclear family of parents and children. In this regard British migrants sometimes thought they were different to what they perceived to be the more extended immigrant families from other countries. Keith and Gill Whittle emigrated to Australia on an

Italian ship and have vivid memories of the Italian migrant families: 'And *they* always came as a family unit, but a *huge* family unit, wasn't there? There were brothers, sisters, aunties, uncles, grandads, grandmas.'[66] The nuclear families of British migrants were forced to become more self-reliant in Australia, and some relished their independence. But in times of crisis and need the distance from an extended family might be deeply felt, and was a cause of many returns.

At a later stage in family life, when migrant parents themselves grow old, questions about 'home' and return are posed in rather different ways. The example of Janet Francis shows how, in retirement and freed of work and family responsibilities, migrants could think anew about the future and decide to come 'home' to live, and die, in Britain. Sometimes the strongest desire is to be reunited with surviving family members; sometimes there is a resurgent longing for the landscapes and lifestyles of youth; often these feelings are underpinned by a strong feeling that Britain is still 'home'; it is the place where you feel most comfortable and content and would like to end your days.[67]

Of course, just as family ties could draw migrants back to Britain, such ties could also prevent retired migrants from fulfilling a dream of return. John and Sylvia Cannon, whose story we related in the Introduction, remain divided about their preferences. While Sylvia doubts she could ever live with the 'grey skies' and 'claustrophobic' attitudes of England, John's re-emerging love for his homeland forces him to live with frustrated desire: 'If it were not for my children being here, I think I would move back to England.'[68]

The experiences of John and Sylvia Cannon – and of Janet Francis – remind us that migration never ends and return is always a possibility. In the next chapter we will see that coming home is never easy, and that return is rarely conclusive.

Notes

1   Holmes written account US.
2   Loretta Baldassar explores the Italian return experience in *Visits Home*.
3   Richards, 'Annals of the Australian Immigrant', p. 16; Baines, *Migration in a Mature Economy*, p. 279.
4   See Williams written account US; Bruce Bates written account US.
5   Appleyard, *The Ten Pound Immigrants*, p. 103; Richardson, *British Immigrants and Australia*, pp. 57–61; Hugo, 'Migration Between Australia and Britain', p. 53.
6   O'Neill interview US.
7   Quoted in Tribe, *Postmark Australia*, p. 94.
8   *Ibid.*, pp. 95–6.
9   Gwen Good, 'Strangers on the Shore', and 'Wish You Were Here', 1 July 1964 and 16 March 1965, Battye Library.
10 See Richardson, *British Immigrants and Australia*, pp. 31–73; Appleyard, *The Ten Pound Immigrants*, pp. 79–108; Commonwealth Immigration Advisory Council, *The Departure of Settlers from Australia*.

11 Unless otherwise stated, all quotations in this section are from the interview with Janet Francis US.
12 'Thorpe' is a pseudonym.
13 Maisie McDonald written account US.
14 *Ibid.*, p. 2.
15 *Ibid.*
16 Francis written account US.
17 Maisie McDonald written account US.
18 In our sample these 'sojourners' are just slightly outnumbered by those (twenty-four) who never intended to return but who found themselves 'trapped' in Britain after they returned for a visit.
19 Wright written account US.
20 Williams written account US.
21 Ralph Price written account US.
22 Kells interview US.
23 Chris Gray interview US.
24 Barber interview US.
25 Brooks interview US.
26 Good, 'Wish You Were Here', 1 July 1964, Battye Library.
27 Farnfield interview US.
28 O'Neill interview US.
29 Wright written account US.
30 Heath interview US.
31 Elizabeth Gray interview US; Alvyn and Bruce Bates written accounts US; see also written accounts by Edward Crooks and Barbara Williams US.
32 Ford written account US. See also Dorothy Rooms interview US.
33 Spencer interview US.
34 Dixon written account US.
35 Cox written account US.
36 For example Barber interview US; Roscoe interview US.
37 Upton, *To the Undiscovered Ends*, pp. 76–7.
38 John Williams written account US.
39 Upton, *To the Undiscovered Ends*, p. 71.
40 Williams written account US; Upton, *To the Undiscovered Ends*, p. 82.
41 Tribe, *Postmark Australia*, p. 14.
42 Wiener, *English Culture and the Decline of the Industrial Spirit*; Matless, *Landscape and Englishness*.
43 Carter interview LU. See Mary Holmes written account US.
44 Cox written account US; Hallas interview LU.
45 Stephens written account.
46 Spencer interview US; Francis interview US.
47 Appleyard (*The Ten Pound Immigrants*, p. 99) notes that returnees back in Britain often blamed their return on the wife's homesickness. Both Sandra O'Neill and Dorothy Rooms were furious when their husbands blamed return on their homesick wives; in both cases the real problem was the husband's discontent (interviews with Sandra O'Neill US and Dorothy Rooms US). According to the sociologist F. Davis (*Yearning for Yesteryear*, p. 56), men faced with major life discontinuities such as retirement or unemployment are especially likely to suffer from nostalgia or, in the case of migrants, homesickness.
48 John Williams written account US.

49 Hugo, 'Migration Between Australia and Britain', p. 53. See also written accounts by Jean Pritchett US; John Robinson US; and Christine Watkins US.

50 Siberry interview and written account US. Michael Siberry's feeling of 'completeness' in England was shortlived: 'My return only served to deepen a sense of confusion and isolation. Within six months I felt that I didn't belong anywhere. The England that I kept in my head didn't exist.' For a comparable experience (one of four like this in our archive) see the written account by Cliff Pester US.

51 Tribe, *Postmark Australia*, p. 11.

52 Skowronski, *I Can't Think of a Title*, pp. 55–65.

53 Maile written account US.

54 Brooks interview US; see also interviews with O'Neill US and Kells US.

55 Patricia Barnes written account US.

56 Rennison written account US.

57 Maile written account US.

58 Jordan interview US.

59 See interviews (all US) with Stephens, Brooks, Kells, Adams, Bird and Hardie.

60 Daly interview US.

61 Ralph Price written account US.

62 See Smurthwaite interview US.

63 Farnfield interview US.

64 McLanaghan interview US.

65 Good, 'Autobiography', US; Gwen and Cliff Good interview US; Vidler interview US; Barber interview US.

66 Whittle interview US.

67 See written accounts by Christine Watkins US; Jean Pritchett US; Joyce Webb US.

68 Cannon interview LU.

Part III

Migration, memory and identity

10

Coming 'home'

The poignant economics of return

Return was a costly business. The outward journey had been heavily subsidized, but to get back to Britain return migrants had to pay every penny, and for a family this could be a lot of money. A fortunate few were able to draw upon savings or the income from the sale of an Australian home, but then found that they had very little left for starting again back in Britain. Some relied on loans, usually from a family member back in Britain, sometimes from an unexpected source. After his father's nervous breakdown, Bruce Bates recalls a 'true miracle' and 'the extraordinary astonishment and relief that he and my mother expressed when, literally "out of the blue", he received a telegram from England. It was from his previous employer, John Hickman and Son, begging him to return', and offering to pay the return fares for the family of five and to reimburse the government because they were leaving within the two-year probationary period. Less fortunate returnees scrimped and saved for the fares. Marjorie Adams squirreled away her family allowance every week, and John Hardie recalls working 'twenty-five hours a day' for nine months whilst Margaret 'tightened the belt up a little' at home. Before returning in 1964 Terry Stephens used to buy a whole lamb's fry (lamb liver) for 1s. 6d. and she and Ian 'used to live on lamb's fry for half the time' while they saved their £416 boat fare – which Ian estimates would be about £8,000 in today's money. In 1972 the total cost of the O'Neill family's return to the West Midlands, including air fares and the costs of shipping furniture and other belongings, was £5,000.[1]

The economics of return trapped many migrants in Australia. Sheila Vidler's parents could only manage to save fares for themselves and 13-year-old Sheila, and asked her 19-year-old stepbrother to raise his own return fare. He decided to stay in Australia and 'disowned' the family. After a desperate few months in Australia the Crooks family sold the furniture they had brought from England and borrowed money from in-laws to pay their two sets of fares, but even then there was only enough for the parents and 13-year-old Barbara. Her older siblings Peter and Mary agreed to stay in Australia, and the eldest son Ted paid his own return fare plus another £110 (the outstanding balance on the fare for the outward journey) 'to get my freedom back'. Almost every account we have received from a return migrant tells the pitiful stories of others who could not afford to return. Dorothy Farnfield estimates that 50 per cent of their English migrant friends wanted to come back. John Hardie's wife Margaret had been terribly homesick in Gippsland and he was shocked into taking her home after he chanced upon a group of Scottish women who had been hospitalized with severe depression. A hospital official explained to John that 'The only thing we can do is put them on a train, or a plane or a boat back, that's the only cure [but] 90 percent of who you see here won't do it' because 'they've got themselves into such a financial hole and owed so much money they would never ever get out of Australia unless someone from the UK could come forward and say, "There's your fare"'.[2]

The returning ships became a potent symbol of frustration and hope for British migrants who felt trapped in Australia, or who were saving up for return. Catherine Barber recalls that it became a family ritual on Sundays to go down to Fremantle to see all the ships, and 'you got to walk around the ships and, you know, it was "Which ship will we go back on?"' John Williams remembers the sadness of Brisbane hostel dwellers who were longing to go home:

Other people I felt very sorry for were those unhappy souls whose main joy in life was watching the Brisbane River for ships arriving from, and departing for, England. When one such ship appeared, steaming majestically up (or down) the river, and crowded with people on deck, they would wave and cheer with all their might and then burst into hysterical sobbing. Clearly, some people's hearts must have been absolutely broken by the migration experience.[3]

Travelling home: 'migration' becomes an 'adventure'

Departure could be just as painful for those on board. If leaving Britain was marked by excitement and trepidation, leaving Australia was scored by a more troubling mix of emotions: relief, disappointment, regret and uncertainty. Dorothy Farnfield – who probably would have stayed in Australia if her eldest son had not been so unhappy – recalls that 'it was sadder coming back than it was going'. Teenager Ralph Price, who never really knew why his parents decided to go home and who had relished his four years in Western Australia, recalls the huge crowd that gathered to farewell the *Orontes* in 1955 (see figure 34):

I mean you could hardly get any more on the quay. People swarmed aboard to say their farewells, and when they were ordered ashore, we caught streamers thrown up from them, to hold on to until they broke as the ship moved away, in probably the most chokingly emotional public scene I have ever experienced. In fact my eyes are brimming up as I recall it.[4]

The voyage home was experienced and has been remembered in several rather different ways. For some the return voyage is a muted memory, in part because there was not the excitement and anticipation that had marked the voyage to Australia, and perhaps because returnees were emotionally numbed by their difficult experiences in Australia and a sense of anticlimax or even failure. Sheila Vidler was 13 when she sailed back to England with her parents after two years in Sydney and Brisbane: 'It was quite a long voyage. I don't remember an awful lot about it, not really, not as much as I did coming out. You know, I think like that was a big adventure and I think that stuck in my mind more than going home really.'[5]

Some returnees experienced the voyage home as a huge relief. When the Gray family left Australia in 1961 most of their fellow passengers on the *Fairsky* were also British return migrants:

it was really a big party of English people, or Poms, all coming back together on the one boat, and the majority of them was all happy because they was leaving, because they were on the way, they thought, back to paradise in reverse, reverse way isn't it, coming back to England, thought everything was going to be great back here again, you know, after leaving Australia. So everybody was full of theirselves really.

Five years later, when Chris Gray and his brother David sailed back to England after a second stint in Australia, this mood of relief and revelry was darkened

34 The Gray family left Brisbane to return to Manchester in 1961, and in this photograph are farewelled by three British relatives – marked with crosses towards the back on the right – who had decided to stay on. Another return migrant, Ralph Price, recalls of his own departure from Fremantle in 1955 that 'we caught streamers thrown up from them, to hold onto until they broke as the ship moved away, in probably the most chokingly emotional public scene I have ever experienced'

by tensions between the English returnees and a group of Australians who were heading for Europe:

there was a lot of clash between the Australians and the English; the English that were coming home because they didn't like Australia, they were calling the place, and the Australians would stick up for their own country. And I think nearly every night on the boat there was fights.... And they were throwing them in the jail on board the ship. You know, the captain even appealed to them to stop all this fighting, stop all the bitterness between the English and Australians.[6]

Other returnees who had struggled to raise their return fares and could only afford the cheapest available passage contrast this economy voyage with the comparative luxury of the subsidized voyage to Australia. Teenager Barbara Williams compares the 'absolutely fantastic' journey out on the *Canberra* in 1963 with her family's return a few months later: 'We found a passage home on a Greek ship – not exactly the *Canberra* – which took us as far as Piraeus. We then took a ferry to Brindisi and finished the trip back to England overland by train. It was a very, very long journey home.' Her brother Ted Crooks recalls that while Barbara and their mother had a cabin he and Father were bunked in steerage with forty Greek men. Stanley Crooks was on the verge of a nervous breakdown so they paid a bit extra from their 'very limited funds' to move into a cabin with the women of the family, only to find that the cabin was 'alive with cockroaches'.[7]

In striking contrast are those return migrants who decided to make the most of the homebound voyage, and to enjoy a special holiday and a new adventure. Some who had emigrated by boat flew home so that they could experience a new mode of transport; others who had flown to Australia took the ship home so that they could see something of the world. Many returnees who had come out via the Mediterranean and Suez went home across the Pacific and through the Panama Canal so that they could say they had sailed around the world. Some spent the last of their savings on the voyage of a lifetime. A Melbourne-based Scottish couple, Bobby and Margaret Stirling, had to make a decision about their future when Bobby's mother was taken ill in Scotland in 1970: 'it was just one day we sat down and talked about it, were we going to buy a house with furniture and live out there, or should we have the trip of a lifetime? And we decided that we would sail back, and we came back with the *Fairstar*, and we sailed from Melbourne to Sydney, to Tahiti, through the Panama Canal, into Barbados, up to Lisbon, to Southampton.'[8]

Some return migrants paid extra to ensure that this luxury cruise would be better than their outward voyage as immigrants. Irene and Clifford Tyas had false hopes that an uncle in England would provide them with a house when they got home in 1970, and spent £2,000 of the £3,000 they had saved in Australia on a 'luxury cruise' with 'an upstairs cabin outside with windows' that took them the other way round the world, through Panama and the exotic ports of Curaçao and Tahiti. Ray and Irene Spencer had flown to Australia with their son Alan in 1966 because they wanted to get there as quickly as possible, and Ray recalls that they 'decided to see a bit of the world on the way back' in 1970. They still enjoy the memory of the 'little bit of excitement' of touring Singapore and Rome in style. Fred Ford recalls, quite simply, that the 'superb voyage' with P&O was 'the best part of the three years away'.[9]

The migrants who made the most of their return trip wanted to enjoy a holiday of pleasure and adventure after difficult times in Australia and before the serious challenges of their return. At a time when overseas holidays were still unusual for working-class Britons, some assumed they would never again have such an extraordinary opportunity. Others wanted to be able to say that they had circumnavigated the globe. These returnees were transforming their Australian sojourn into an adventure, and the return voyage began a process – which would be confirmed in family stories and personal memories – of reinventing an unsuccessful 'migration' as an adventure that would be the 'experience of a lifetime'.

Coming home is grey or green

Coming home is harder than you imagine. The return to Britain evoked a range of emotions, sometimes sharply defined but often confused and even contra-dictory. Marion Kells 'just felt a great overwhelming relief' that she was back home and could have her baby in England. The heavily pregnant Sandra O'Neill 'kissed the ground' when she landed in England with her family: 'really the thing that sticks out in my mind was when my little girl, who ran up straight to my mum and she said, "I've missed you Nanny." She said, "Don't like Australia, flies in Australia."' Carol Brooks had very mixed feelings when she flew into Heathrow with her young baby in 1974 after five years in Australia, and with her husband remaining in Perth:

Yes, it was *raining*, it was one of those really drab days, you know. And I looked around and thought, oh my God have I done the right thing? You know, as you do. And we got on the train and came down to Brighton and my uncle was waiting at the station as well, my mother's brother with his wife, and as soon as we walked out of the station into Brighton I thought, Yes, I've done the right thing. I knew. I just felt, yes I'm back on my home ground again, I can cope, you know, yes. And I *did*, very much so. I moved on, yes.[10]

Some returnees felt special because of their time in Australia. When the Whittle family came home to Brighton 'everybody wanted to speak to us, didn't they, they all wanted to ask us questions about Australia. "Why have you come back?" We were famous, weren't we?' But more often the return migrants felt that family and friends back home were not interested in hearing about their Australian experience, or that the question, 'Why have you come back?' was an implied criticism. Sydney Hart arrived in Australia in 1949, left in 1951 when he and his wife could not afford to buy a house, and wrote insightfully about their experiences in 1957:

It is quite common to hear, both in England and Australia, that the returned emigrants are not of the same calibre as the old settlers. 'They can't take it!' is a commonly-used expression about them. Maybe it was so in my own case, maybe I just wasn't the right type, but were the old pioneers satisfied with just four wooden walls and a small block of earth some 60 feet by 100 feet, and a lifetime's mortgage to pay off? They wanted more than that, and they could see a way clear to get it by their own efforts. And believe me when I say that it takes as much courage, if not more, to be an emigrant returning to his home town or village as to be an outward-bounder with an unknown future ahead.[11]

It is not surprising that return migrants – stung by criticism – sometimes blamed conditions in Australia for their return. After a recession in the Western Australian building trade forced the O'Neill family to return home to the Midlands in 1970, Sandra O'Neill wrote a letter to the Birmingham *Evening Mail* saying that Australia 'wasn't as wonderful as was being painted'. Researcher Reg Appleyard, who accompanied return migrants on a voyage back to Britain, noted that they often devised 'a "story" of life in Australia so compelling that it could be seen that return was their only option'. Yet this need for an external source of blame very often coexisted with internal feelings of disappointment and failure. Sandra O'Neill felt 'a little bit cheated that you didn't have the opportunity at that time', but she also felt 'as if you've failed as a person going over there'.[12] Personal disappointment was expressed in terms of coming 'back to square one' or coming 'full circle' and having to 'start again'. Cliff Tyas had felt 'elated' at his first sight of the coastline of England but his wife Irene 'just felt, I've got to start again.... I had a lot of disappointments when I came back. So, in a way, I thought to myself, serves you right. You've probably had things more out there than here.' After over-landing from Australia in 1964, Nigel Heath came into Dover on a 'nice crisp autumn morning' and walked up the high street:

And to see the milk on the step and the money on top of the milk bottle. They were little impressions of England which were soon blown away, all that. Nobody leaves their money on top of the milk bottle now, it'd get nicked. I was glad to be back I suppose. It was a good time *to* be back, in autumn. But reality set in pretty quick. I mean the first job I had when I got back I was labouring again ... So I hadn't made any progress in that direction whatsoever.[13]

Personal disappointment could be entangled with disillusion with Britain, which did not always live up to idealized memories or to comparisons with Australia. On the train back to Scotland in 1966, Catherine Barber remembers thinking 'how dismal and dreary everything looked' after Australia, where 'everything's very modern and spanking new. And then you're suddenly seeing all these old crumbling buildings, and old tenements and things.' Another teenager, Alvyn Bates, had not wanted to come back to England with his family, and was not impressed when they returned to Wolverhampton in 1952:

My overriding feeling at being back in England was of being in the middle of a termite heap. After the wonderful open spaces and airiness of Australia I was back in a noisy, crowded place. I later came to think of England as being a place of class-consciousness, snobbery, and hypocrisy. To that rather naive, adolescent seventeen year old the wonderful openness of the skies and the countryside seemed reflected in the Australian character, hard, even crude, but honest and unequivocal.[14]

Of course impressions of Britain depended upon the circumstances of return and upon the length of absence and extent of change. Returning to England in 1964, Nigel Heath thought that some of the class barriers which had been 'holding things back' in Britain had been 'blown out the window' while he was away: 'It had been blown away, in four years I was away it had virtually gone. It was quite amazing the contrast. I suppose it was something to do with The Beatles, I don't know.... Yes the class barriers were down, definitely. Lads like myself, lower middle-class lads, were beginning to push themselves up.' In 1963 13-year-old Barbara Crooks was also excited by her return: 'The sixties were just about to start swinging and I was extremely glad to be back in the UK!'[15]

The return migrants were particularly struck by the very different physical environment and climate of Britain, and their feelings about return – just like their emotions about leaving Britain in the first place – are often expressed in the contrasting colour metaphors of green and grey. Returning in 1964 from Melbourne, where she had been terribly homesick, Terry Stephens recalls that 'it was almost as if we hadn't seen the colour green for three years'.

And when we came back here we just couldn't drink in that greenness enough and we appreciate it even now just looking out there.... I'm quite serious when I say I daily give thanks for my environment because I just think we're so lucky to live in this wonderful beautiful place. And Australia didn't seem beautiful, it seemed — different. It was beautiful in many ways but it was so dry and so hard compared with this country.

The Jordan family had also been acutely homesick and had tired of living in the garage they were converting into a home on a hill outside Wollongong, but teenager John Jordan was shocked when they landed at Tilbury in 1954: 'my first impression was everything was dull and drab. And the houses were grey and the sky was grey and the people were grey, and there was no pleasant bright cheerful wonderful atmosphere so my first impression was, *my God what have I done? ...* how have I found myself now back in this *dump*?' The colour of return, and the emotions it evoked, even varied within families. Whereas Ray Spencer – who had been so disappointed when he could not get a mortgage in Australia – was delighted to buy his own home in Bridgend and enjoyed the 'greenery and the old pub life', Irene soon realized that she had made a great mistake:

And as soon as I got off the plane, on to the train and looked at all the backs of the houses coming out of Cardiff.... 'What have I done?' [in a whisper], I just thought, what have I done?.... there was still the excitement of meeting the family but it wasn't long after I'd come back that I was sorry I'd left all what we'd left behind. This place? [sighs] — back to the same old thing — back to the same weather, dreary, I'm going to say this, dreary England, Wales [laughs]. Nothing ever happens to you.[16]

While first impressions delighted some returnees and troubled others, the practical difficulties of resettlement could turn doubt into despair. Getting a job was not the main problem, especially for migrants returning in the comparatively prosperous years before the mid-1970s. Many working-class tradesmen recall with pride as well as relief that they were 'snapped up' by their old employers when they got home, though they also noticed that wages were often lower in Britain. John Hardie remembers that in 1967 'I was paying more in tax in Australia when I was working these long hours than what I was earning at home for a month and that frightened me, I'll be honest'.[17] Some return migrants – particularly those who had been in Australia long enough to save more than the return fares – came home with sufficient capital to buy their own home and settle down in some comfort.

More often, returnees were worse off than when they left Britain, and some were practically destitute. Housing was their greatest concern. There were no hostels for return migrants, who now found themselves at the bottom of waiting lists for council houses. With no money for a deposit on their own home, many returnees were forced to move in with relatives, often with disastrous results. In 1963 Marjorie Adams's homesickness had caused her family to return to Bristol, where they were unable to get a council house for a year and the two oldest boys had to live with family friends and relatives whilst Marjorie, Bert and the three youngest children lodged with her mother. Marjorie 'nearly had a nervous breakdown that year' and still blames herself for the effects on the children and for the loss of their Australian opportunity: 'it all comes out in later life, they tell you about it.... And I said to Bert, "What did I do to them, really, it was not fair to them what I did really".'[18]

Perhaps inevitably, family tensions festered as return migrants squeezed into their relatives' small houses and then often overstayed their welcome. Return migrants who were forced to live with their parents – and who had often become more self-reliant and independent in Australia – found that they were treated like children. After eight years travelling around Australia and the Pacific, Joan Pickett only managed at home for six months before getting a flat on her own: 'I found that a bit difficult, getting back to being, you know, going to work and coming home, and Mother wanting to know why you're late, or, you know, what you're doing, and — I found *that* was a bit of a struggle, settling back at home.' Elizabeth Gray's father had written to say the returning family could stay with them until they got their own home, but her mother didn't really want three boys in the house:

So we arrived and I could see she was hostile, my mother. The atmosphere with her was dreadful.... The atmosphere made my life a misery. And Harry also when he found that the houses were a thousand pounds dearer, his nerves started again [laughs]. And he wouldn't buy a house. Every house I looked at he found something wrong with it. Anyway we'd been home a couple of months and I said, I couldn't even work [her mother insisted she stay at home to cater for the extended family] and the money was going, and I said, 'Look, I can't stand this Harry, you've got to make up your mind, you either buy a house or we go back to Australia, I can't stand this.' 'Oh we'll go back to Australia,' he said. So back we went.[19]

Unsettled and uncertain

Migration researcher Reg Appleyard estimated that between a third and half of the British emigrants who returned to Britain subsequently re-emigrated to Australia.[20] Though this is almost impossible to quantify, our research confirms that a significant minority of the British returnees did go back to Australia, or wanted to go back but were prevented from doing so. As we have seen in the case of Elizabeth Gray and her family, some only stayed in Britain for a very short time because of difficult domestic circumstances. For John Jordan and his parents, 'It had been a real shock to see what they perceived England to be was not what England was at all. A rosy glow painted round England from a distance and then the reality of what England really was. That came home to us all, the grey, the horrible drab, all of these factors, that came home to us all at the time.' It was 'intolerable' living with relatives and the money they had brought back from Australia was rapidly diminishing because John's father was earning much less in England. John recalls that his father had brought a big American Chevrolet back from Australia – 'whether he was doing it to show what a success he'd been and to rub the noses into the dirt of the people that he'd known and saying, "Look at this", but damn me that's what he did' – but had to lock it away in a garage because he couldn't afford to run it. John was unable to contribute to the family income because, aged only 18, he was due to start British National Service in a few months' time. No employer would take him on, and he was delighted when his mother announced, 'Right, well let's get out of it and get back to Australia.' John's older brother – who had not emigrated with the family – worked for a shipping line and arranged a special deal on a passage (the car went with them!). Back in Wollongong they were 'literally penniless' and were amazed at the generosity of the bank manager who gave them a loan to get started again. The local newspaper picked up the story and did a feature headlined 'Migrants Long for their Australian Home'. John and his father both 'dropped into a job quite easily'. Best of all, the Jordans were drawn out first in a ballot for a Housing Commission home (John has a hunch that the ballot was 'influenced'). After just a few months staying with a friend they moved into a house in Unanderra that was a far cry from the garage on a hill which John's mother had so hated their first time out.

Proper house, bungalow, nice, everything about it, had everything that you wanted in a nice spot, well nice enough spot. Gardens, all the rest of it. Different thing entirely. Different concept. Very happy. Very happy to be there. Dad and I playing golf whenever we could.... And it was a *wonderful*, wonderful lifestyle. Plenty of money. Working when you wanted to do, out in the sun all day, what could be better? Brilliant, wonderful.[21]

While some returnees were rapidly disillusioned and went back to Australia as soon as possible, others did so when circumstances changed in their lives and made the return possible. The teenager Chris Gray had never wanted to return from Brisbane with his parents in 1960: 'I always said I wanted to go back, and, it kept playing on my mind all the time, I want to go back, because I enjoyed it so much, you know, and, as I say, like the weather was terrific.' When he turned 18 he made enquiries about returning to Australia and was told that because he had been a child when the family came out on the ten pound scheme he could use the scheme once more, as an adult. In 1965 Chris and his brother David returned to Brisbane, where they had regular well-paid work and loved the outdoor sporting life. 'Me and my brother was on our own for the first time, which was different, and we enjoyed it, you know, we did our own thing'. However, they were unable to persuade their parents to rejoin them in Australia, and when in 1968 their father wrote to say that Chris's and David's names had come through for season tickets at Manchester United, they decided to return to Manchester. 'And that was, that was the only reason we came home, nothing, not because we didn't like Australia, loved the place.'[22]

Even returnees who had made a clear decision to remain in Britain could find themselves pulled between the two countries and the very different lives they offered. Intrepid travelling secretary Joan Pickett returned to Manchester when her father died and was 'absorbed' into Mancunian life after starting a temporary job which lasted for twenty-three years. At one level Joan thought she had got travelling out of her system and was determined not to leave her family again. But her dreams suggest a deeper psychological ambivalence:

it was sort of events that forced my hands in a way, but I was quite happy to stay home, I — I'd got it out of my system then, you know, and I thought, well, if I go back, if I go back to Australia, it'll be for good, it'll have to be, I can't keep going backwards and forwards. And for years I kept having this recurring dream, I was either in Australia and I wanted to be at home, or I was [in] England and I wanted to go back to Australia. And it obviously worried me for years. But I ... settled back home. And I don't think I could have left my brother and all my family again, so —[23]

For some returned migrants, family circumstances mean that return, like migration itself, is never conclusive. Janet Francis acknowledged that although 'wild horses wouldn't get me away now', if circumstances changed and her sons went back to Australia 'I guess I would go back with my tail between my legs'.[24] Others describe family histories which twist and turn as different members move between the two countries, torn between family relationships in each country and unable to settle in one place or the other. Doug Benson emigrated to Australia with his parents and five siblings in 1961, returned to England and travelled the world as a young man in 1965 and 1966, and then came back to South Australia with his Scottish girlfriend to marry in 1967. They were both homesick and in 1969 went back to Britain, where they raised a family and settled in Somerset. Doug describes the unsettled histories of his extended family – and the consequences of transnational family life – in bewildering detail:

Several members of the large family that originally emigrated in 1961 have subsequently been somewhat unsettled. My parents, brothers and sister have all moved around a lot. My middle brother went back to Britain in 1970; he returned to Australia a few years later, has been back here again for a couple of years but is now resident in South Australia. My sister married a Scotsman in Australia, then they went to live in Scotland in 1970. They divorced in 1982; she returned to Australia for a couple of years around ten years ago, but returned again to Scotland where she still lives. My parents and two youngest brothers returned to England in 1971, but my parents could not settle and went back to Australia with my youngest brother after two years. They returned to Britain again three years later, but went back to Australia again in 1979. My father died the following year and my mother, usually accompanied by one of her sons, has lived on and off in both Australia and Britain ever since. At the age of 83, she is now living in England but hoping to return to Australia, where she has three sons and four grandchildren, at the end of this year.

As for my own feelings about emigration to Australia, I can say that overall I view it as a positive experience, in fact a turning point of my life. If we had not gone to Australia as a family, our lives would no doubt have turned out completely differently. It started a fascinating journey and travel experience. There are pros and cons in any actions we take; the biggest negative result is that as a family we are spread between Britain and Australia and have not seen very much of each other, especially the youngest generation.[25]

While some British migrants are unable to settle in either country, a few have tried to create a life that includes both countries. Norma Palin emigrated with her husband and children in 1956, and now describes herself as a 'commuting Pom'. She has a granny flat on her daughter's property in Queensland and a house in Liverpool which she shares with a childhood sweetheart she married in 1981 after divorcing her first husband: 'we spend each year commuting. We count ourselves very lucky to be able to do so.' In 1971, 18-year-old Christine Leach and her husband emigrated from the north of England to Perth. Complicated family responsibilities and breakdowns have taken her between the two countries almost a dozen times, often stopping for several years at a time. Now, writing from England but 'going back at the end of this month!', she has 'the best of both worlds with a house here and there I bought when my children were growing up with an excellent job with Telecom Australia':

Everyone was excited to see me, the first time, but now they say oh its you again you go to Australia like we go to Scotland! I have a lot of friends in both places some are as bad as me and some worse for returning home. I have met most of my friends when I have been working here or there, and we write to each other or now it's easy with the emails. They like my accent as it changes depending on where I am. Some are very judgmental but I think they are just envious.[26]

In interviews, some return migrants comment that they would like to spend half the year in each country, but few can afford to do so. Indeed, many return migrants who wanted to go back to Australia found themselves 'trapped' in Britain and unable to return. About six months after their family's unhappy return to Bristol, Marjorie and Bert Adams applied to re-emigrate to Australia, but were told that although most of the children could go free they would have to pay full fares for each parent and for Deborah, who had been born in Australia. On these terms, return was just not an option.[27] When the Australian government put the British on an equal footing with other migrants in the 1970s, some returnees who wanted to go back to Australia were frustrated by their lack of Australian citizenship and by the new point system. Ralph

Price had spent four years in Australia with his parents in the early 1950s and then re-emigrated as a young man in 1962. In an attempt to save a faltering marriage he followed his wife back to Britain in 1970. Several years later, with the marriage over, Australia 'tugged more strongly again at my heart' and he made enquiries about return, assuming that with 'Resident of Australia' stamped in his (British) passport he would have no problems:

So it was a terrible shock when the officer told me that, after I think it was three years without returning, you forgo your rights, and must then get to the back of the queue with would-be immigrants who are given permits on the basis of the system of points given for skill need, close family, etc. We in Britain had turned away from the Anzacs – cynically in my view, and the special relationship no longer existed, and Australia's need for immigrants had dwindled along with their wider throw of the net, meant that I had little or no chance of getting back. So I reluctantly set about trying to build a life in England, but my heart was never really in it.[28]

Reflecting on a similar experience, Irene Spencer regrets the oversight of never taking out Australian citizenship and lives with the 'dull ache' of home-sickness for Australia and the life she lost: 'To be honest with you I've never ever left Australia [long pause]. This isn't my home any more, Australia is.'[29] Almost inevitably, migration and life in two different countries unsettles national identity and the sense of belonging. Some return migrants manage to hold together aspects of their Australian and British identities, in complex ways and varying proportions, ranging from Janet Francis's resolute assertion of Britishness to Irene Spencer's frustrated ache for Australia. A privileged few commute between their different homes and identities; many still journey to Australia in their imagination.

Bringing Australia home

Many return migrants believe that the Australian sojourn has had a lasting effect upon their character and outlook. Travelling around the world and then trying to make a new life in a different country widened personal horizons and generated a sense of possibilities in life. Jack Roscoe, for example, contrasts his learning experience with the inertia of friends who had never left Manchester. 'Well, as you meet up with old friends and everything, you have the feeling you've been and kind of seen different places, been half way round the world, seen different people and all that, but they haven't, they're still in the same routine as they were when you left.' Even the most disappointing migration experiences could teach useful lessons. Fred Ford is bitter and angry when he looks back on his family's three years in Australia, 'but it was very interesting and I learnt a lot, especially from the sea voyages'.[30]

Our 'sojourner' stories in Chapter 8 showed that young men and women who were forced to be self-reliant in Australia often returned to Britain with greater confidence in their own abilities, and a newfound independence. This was particularly marked in relation to parents and extended families unprepared for the transformation. John Hardie reckons that 'three years in Australia I grew up ten, attitude wise, and the way I looked at people, the way I treated people, the way I expected to be treated *by* people ... aye I think it did change my outlook on life definitely'. Margaret Hardie agrees that 'it made me independent and I really could stand on my own feet'. One of the reasons they had left Scotland as a young family was that they felt 'hemmed in' by their parents, but now they had 'broken out of the whole barrier', as John explains:

before we went we were frightened to say anything in case we offended, in these days I think that was a big thing, you never offended, if your mother says you look after your daughter this way, you looked after your daughter that way. I think when we came back it was a matter, if you don't mind we'll do it our way, you know, we grew up, you took command of your own lives and that was nae bad thing.[31]

Paradoxically, while parents and other relatives exerted a powerful pull back to Britain, in some cases the independence and even separateness of the nuclear family was consolidated through migration and return. Catherine Barber had grown up in a close-knit Glasgow working-class extended family; but when they came back to Scotland after two years in Australia her immediate family moved with their father's work to the new town of Livingston and relations with the wider family were different: 'I suspect that the sort of nuclear family became more important when we were in Australia, and I think to a large extent when we came back, you know, that continued. You know, they didn't get sort of drawn back in with the, you know, sort of the aunts and uncles again.'

Like some other return migrants, Catherine Barber's family had also been influenced by Australian ways of living which they brought back to Britain:

they had a different kind of life, you know, a different kind of social life. But having said that, I think, because they had had that life, they actually managed to sort of plant that life here, and they had a more Australian type life here. We used to get up and go away, we had the car, we used to go away at the weekends, and go for long runs, and, well it wasn't barbecues, but you know, the picnics would be there.... Mum and Dad, they went out, they had never been in the habit of going out, you know, so they would go out for a meal or something, and they would drink or some — which they had never done before.[32]

By contrast, George Bird explains that he and his wife Ray had to 'change back again and become Brits' when they came back from Melbourne to Hove in 1962:

Yes so we *had* changed, I think we had, not thinking about it. But I think, yes, maybe we felt more tied, hemmed in, you know, there's none of this let's go off to Wagga Wagga today or something, for a drive and get out for the day. Always felt we wanted to do that and we did. We had the time, we had the car didn't we, and of course it was cheap to do it, car, petrol and things were much cheaper there. But then coming back I suppose we had to change and feel this closed in feeling again and working for a living, paying more taxes, didn't get so much of your money out of it did you over here.[33]

Migrants were also influenced by Australian ideas about the physical environment; some created a British house and garden which reflected Australian attitudes and associations. Phillip Maile had emigrated to Melbourne at the age of 5 and when he returned thirty-five years later – to be near his children after his ex-wife had taken them back to England – he looked 'for a property that gave me my sense of space, and consider myself very fortunate enough to find it and afford it'. When the British nurse Avis McDermott brought her new Australian husband back to England in 1961 they used a plan from the Australian *Women's Weekly* to build an open-plan bungalow with large glass windows lighting up the living spaces and linking them to the back yard. Over the years they have filled the house with Australian paintings and curios, creating an Australian sanctuary amongst the crowded terraces of Nottingham. The house is proudly named 'Digger's Rest' in acknowledgement of their labours of creation, but also after the small Victorian country town of the same name. By giving their British houses an Australian name return migrants indicate the continuing resonance of Australia in their everyday lives. Shelagh Worsell's house in Dorset is called 'Warrandyte'; Ray and Irene Spencer named their house in Bridgend 'Noalimba' after a migrant hostel in Perth; Ralph Price's parents lived at 'Banksia' in High Wycombe (Ralph wonders, 'Why is it that people seek to remind themselves of places they've tried so hard to get away from!').[34]

John Williams had built an Australian bush house for his family on a 10-acre block outside Brisbane, but was drawn back to Britain in 1971 by what proved to be a superficial homesickness for an English rural idyll:

One of the first things I did when we arrived back in England was to make straight for an old Cotswold stone wall. I sat on it and immediately thought, 'Huh! What's so great about this?' It was cold and wet; the stone was uncomfortable and it kept rocking about; it was slimy and covered with moss; and cars were continuously passing by. I was cured within minutes! But there was no hope of an early return because we had sold up everything, spent much of the money on fares and, most important of all, it just wasn't fair on the family, who had not wanted to leave Queensland in the first place. I was very unpopular at that time, and they still blame me, even now!

In the 1980s the Williamses applied to emigrate again but their successful application was deferred when recession began to bite in Australia. Resigned to a life in Britain, John has created a little Australia at his home in Malvern:

So now, back in England, we live in a bungalow which reminds me of a low-set Queensland home. Among the plants in our garden are three young eucalyptus trees, an Australian tree fern, a stag-horn fern, several tea-trees and a bottle-brush shrub. We intend to go again sometime, to see Brisbane properly, and perhaps visit Savernake, to get our feet once more on that ten-acre block of land which still means so much to us. Also, we want to see again those marvellously majestic North Queensland tree-ferns, so tall, thin and graceful. In the meantime, I continue to dream.[35]

Australia is an important holiday destination for British return migrants who have retired and who can now afford a temporary visit. Many meet up with friends and relatives in Australia, including family members who did not come back; others feel some compensation for the frustration of their desire to live in Australia; most relish the opportunity to 'walk backwards in the past'[36] and feel a poignant mix of pleasure and pain as they revisit hostels which are now housing estates or see how the trees they planted in a suburban garden have flourished and grown. Ray and Irene Spencer 'took the second option' in 1992 and enjoyed a 'wonderful welcome' from their Western Australian friends. For Irene it was 'just like going home': 'I fell in love with Australia and to me that was my home, that's the only way I can explain it. It's an extra-ordinary feeling.' When John Williams finally revisited Queensland he walked out of the doors at Brisbane airport and 'The welcoming, fragrant warmth enfolded me and I had not exaggerated the feeling at all. It was a great welcome "home".'

Other return migrants are still saving for that trip, though for some it is now an impossible dream, and yet even they enjoy a virtual identification with Australia on the television and in other media. In interviews they describe the pleasure they take in the Australian accents of *Neighbours* or *Home and Away*, or upon meeting Australians in the street (some commented favourably on Al's faded Australian accent or Lani's much stronger and more recent Queens-land voice).[37] We conducted our interviews with return migrants around the time of the Sydney Olympics, and several interviewees said they had relished the images of Australia which were beamed into their living rooms every day; they expressed vicarious pride in an Australian achievement. Chris Gray commented, 'It was fantastic what they put on, the Aussies. I think, I thought, well this is one time the Yanks have been beaten by somebody who can do something better.... Everything about it, you know, not just the opening ceremony, the Games, where they were held, and, they made Sydney look fantastic. And it is, you know what I mean.'[38]

'The time of my life': remembering the Australian sojourn

The ways in which return migrants now remember their Australian sojourn highlight the personal meanings and significance of their abortive migration experience. When we started to collect accounts by former ten pound migrants living back in Britain we anticipated that their memories of the years in Australia might be negative, soured by sadness, regret or a sense of failure. This turned out to be true for a small minority of return migrants. There are some whose remembering is still seared by the tragedy of families damaged and torn apart through migration and return. Londoner Peggy Kirby emigrated to Perth with her husband and daughter in 1963 but hated the heat and the loneliness and brought the family back in 1966: 'my husband never forgave me'. Another Londoner, Patricia Barnes, was achingly homesick in Brisbane and when she came home with her sons after two years she hoped her husband would follow. He never did, and one son subsequently went to live in Australia:

I look back on my migration experience with sadness, and wonder how my sons and my life would have been if we had not gone, or if we had not come home.... 'Australia' has split my family.... Looking back on my years in Brisbane, there were many good times, and I met some good friends, but to me, family is every-thing. I do not know if I was right to return or not.... If only we had a crystal ball??[39]

There is a sense of relief in the memories of migrants like Janet Francis – who returned after forty-one years – or Sandra O'Neill, who returned after only six weeks and contrasts her own subsequent good fortune with compatriots who were trapped in Australia. Relief is sometimes underpinned by anger or disappointment at the ways in which migrant families were treated by Australian immigration authorities and others who were supposed to support their migration. For a very few return migrants anger is the primary emotion and theme of remembering. Salford fitter and turner Fred Ford feels that he was lured to Australia by false promises of a better life for his children, and that his 'dream of a different country and a different life' was ruined by the terrible conditions in the Commonwealth Hostel, the difficulties of buy-ing a house, and the 'intimidation, aggression and insulting behaviour of the Australia male': 'When I look back on my experience it is with disillusionment and disappointment. I was very angry and bitter.'[40]

These return migrants are often aware of the reputation of the 'whingeing Poms', and their recollections are refracted through and against the stereotype as they recognize something of themselves but also resist the derogatory implication of personal inadequacy. Financial worries and concerns about ill-ness and long-term security drove John Moore and his family back to London after four years. He has many sad memories of their time in Australia and is critical of Australian migration officials who sent them to a hopelessly inappropriate destination, but he is also pleased that their experiences are of historical interest and wants to assure us that 'a lot of us did try, even with events being against us'. Ann Cox writes of an appalling year in Perth and Sydney as a homesick young mum in the recession years of the early 1970s: 'it was an overwhelming experience, a financial disaster which we never recovered from but I don't regret going which is a strange feeling'. She concludes: 'Having read this through I sound a typical "whingeing Pom" but that is how it was.'[41]

Much more common than anger or bitterness in the memories of return migrants, particularly amongst those who were unable to get back to Australia and felt trapped in Britain, are feelings of regret and a poignant sense of missed opportunity. Regret frames the memories of the Tyas family. Cliff and Irene Tyas ran a country pub after they came back from Melbourne in 1970, but that was 'killed off' by Cliff's arthritis and the decline in the rural pub business, and they now live in a small council house near Nottingham. Cliff reflects upon the opportunities in his life and regrets not taking up two work opportunities in Australia that might have offered a very different life: 'As I say, I've had two opportunities – well three, I took one, which was Irene, that were a blind date. And, the other two things is, not taking those two opportunities I had in Australia. And the one I've got here I took the opportunity to do, and it wasn't a success.'[42] These stories of migration and return are entangled with larger life histories about personal hopes and life regrets. The ways in which we remember past experiences shape our sense of who we are, and migration memories are potent ingredients in return migrant identity.

Though regret is a common theme in the memories of return migrants, just as many conclude that they have no regrets about going to Australia or about coming back to Britain. And regardless of whether these memories are tinged with regret or not, the single most common way of remembering the years in Australia – amongst migrants of every age and status – is that it was the 'time of my life'. David Casson spent nine years of his childhood in the 1950s roving around south-eastern Australia as his parents moved between jobs and towns, and 'Looking back in retrospect, my "adventure" to Australia was probably the best nine years of my life'. Young Scotsman Wallace Shirreffs loved the outdoor life in Sydney and Port Macquarie and although he had to return to Scotland when his mother took ill, going to Australia 'was the best thing I ever did and wouldn't have missed it for anything'. Cyril Williams's family left Perth after two years because they had never really felt at home in Australia, but 'it was an adventure we would not have missed. GOOD ON YOU COBBER.'[43]

Though many return migrants only spent a few years of their lives in Australia, that time in their life is often remembered in vivid detail and the memories of these years have a disproportionate significance. Cliff and Irene Tyas regret their missed opportunities during four years in Australia but they also relish retelling their Australian stories and are delighted to illustrate them with copious newspaper cuttings and family photographs. Their leading role in the Melbourne hostel rent strike which made headlines in 1967, and in the development of hugely popular migrant dances, are sources of great pride. At the conclusion of an interview, Al asked Cliff and Irene how, after thirty years, they look back on their migration:

Cliff: Fantastic.
Irene: Yes, really.
Cliff: Fantastic. I couldn't pull it down. Australia were my second home, let's put it that way.
Irene: But — Yes, it really — yes, it was something in your lifetime that probably other people — You can go through life, you can be married and go through life, and just do the same old thing, and you can get a bit of money together and you can do all this and that and the other, but at the end of the day, we can sit here, we haven't got anything, but we've lived.[44]

Jack Roscoe remembers his migration in similar terms. Jack had gone twice to Australia, once for two years as a young single man in 1959, and then again in 1972 with his wife and daughters. They returned because Jane Roscoe was unhappy in Australia – Jack liked the climate and lifestyle but put his family first – and settled back in Manchester, where Jack worked as an electrical engineer with Kelloggs for twenty-two years until retirement. In the interview Jack explains how he looks back on his two times in Australia:

When I started work at Kelloggs, there was people there who had been there since they left school. This Les Higgy, he's, well, Les Higgins his name, he's just finished now, retired, but, he's been there over forty years, just there. And I think, oh, you know, I've kind of done all this. What's the alternative? Start work, stay working at a place for forty-odd years, or do what I did, a job here, a job there, meeting people, moving around. And I *much* prefer, even though he gets a bigger pension than me, I much prefer what I did. Because my father once said to me, he says, as he was getting older, he says, 'You know, I live on my memories'. And it's true. As you get older, you've got your memories behind you. If I'd have just stopped round here, working, some engineering places round here, I wouldn't have had many memories would I? But kind of, going out there, I've got a lot of memories, and fond memories. Places, people I've met. Yes, it was good, really good.[45]

What comes across in the remembering of so many return migrants is this sense that going to Australia was a great achievement – for some the most important in their lives – and that these memories are particularly special.

There are several ways to explain this phenomenon. Regardless of the end result, in going to Australia these men and women did something extraordinary in their lives. By comparison with their 'stay-at-home' workmates and relatives, they wrested their life out of its ordinary pattern, out of the rut, and created a dramatically different life. They saw the world beyond the terraces of their home town, and they experienced migration as a remarkable adventure. In Irene Tyas's evocative words, 'we haven't got anything, but we've lived'.

Indeed, this process of transforming the migration experience into an adventure story is given shape and substance in the remembering of return migrants, as they recall their circumnavigation of the globe, the strange new ways and places of Australia, their travels and their tribulations, and their return with a new knowledge of the world and new understandings of themselves. The return migrant's adventure story narrates a rite of passage, and in many cases – most obviously for the many migrants in their teens and twenties – also defines the Australian experience as a coming of age, a time of self-discovery when the boy became a man, the girl a woman, or the young family gained strength and independence. For many return migrants, the time in Australia was a profoundly formative period, and it is remembered in those terms; indeed, personal growth through adventure – the time of my life – becomes the main way in which the Australian experienced is remembered, and the Australian sojourn thus occupies a central place in the identities of ten pound migrants who settled back in Britain.

Other features of the process of remembering help explain why Australia figures centrally in the memories of so many return migrants. For most of these men and women the period of migration was relatively short and is clearly signposted in memory, with a neat beginning and end. By comparison with other periods of life – for example the routine years of the workplace – the time in Australia is brightly lit in memory precisely because so much was new and different, exciting or traumatic. Distinctive events and experiences are often sharply recalled. They also make good stories, and migration stories thus figure significantly in the collection of life stories with which return migrants entertain, amuse or educate family members and friends.

Not all return migrants have been able to share the stories of their Australian experience. We have already seen that some returnees were disappointed that people were not interested in their migration stories and saddened as their Australian life became a missing piece in the puzzle of their relationships with friends and family. For a few, the Australian migration was so traumatic that it could barely be talked about. Twenty-three-year-old Lynda Higgins went to Australia with a female friend in 1969 and despite very negative experiences in work and amongst the Australians she stayed on after marrying another migrant and starting a family. The marriage deteriorated and her father supported the return of Lynda and her two sons, but back in England Lynda's family – which had never approved of her emigration – refused to speak of it, and the memory was a silent but continuing pain.[46] Another twenty-three-year-old, Diana Worth, also went to Australia against the wishes of her family. She hated Australia, was terribly homesick and required medical attention when she returned after a few months: 'it is only now that writing has not upset me!!'[47]

Some of our respondents explain that writing about their migration for our project has been a cathartic experience, in which important memories that have been bottled up are recognized and affirmed as significant in their own lives and for the historical record. Ralph Price, who emigrated as a child with his parents in 1955 and then again by himself as a young adult in 1962, was profoundly affected by the invitation to write about these episodes in his life:

When I spotted the item in the *Brighton and Hove Leader* 31.3.00 – headed 'Search on for "ten pound Poms"' – I just thought 'Hmm, that's me!' The Project leaders make some thought-provoking observations. A million people moving from one country to just one other country is a very significant historical event about which we hear virtually nothing. It is an event of some significance to Britain, and must have had a formative impact on Australia. I think the population of Australia at the time was only about ten million, and that of a very young nation. Clearly there is a job to do here, and the more I thought about it, the more excited I became about doing it. In the first couple of pages of notes I became aware of an almost cathartic effect it was having on me as I went through the issues that have had an effect on my identity and my life ever since, just as they have on Australia's.[48]

Many return migrants took great pleasure in writing for us about their Australian lives. Most were keen to be interviewed and those we did get to see were delighted by the opportunity to talk with us about this important time in their life. Their eyes lit up as they brought out well-thumbed photo albums and migration miscellanea such as ship's menus, tourist brochures and letters of commendation from Australian employers. Before beginning their interviews, Al and Lani wondered how their own Australian nationality might influence the stories they would hear, and feared that their presence might unleash repressed anger about Australia and Australians. In fact, as noted in the Introduction, for the most part their nationality had the opposite effect. Interviewees were delighted that Al or Lani knew the places that had become so special in their memories and could identify with aspects of Australian life that they had found, in Susan Jack's words, 'very familiar and awfully strange'.[49] It is possible that a British interviewer might have drawn out more critical accounts, but on the whole we were impressed by the frankness of the life stories we were told and by the enthusiasm of the telling. As in many oral history projects, the interviews provided a valued opportunity for people to share their story of an event of great personal significance with an interested and informed listener.

Events are scored in memory when they make a good story and when there is a receptive audience for telling and retelling. In recent years, some of these return migrants have found – and made – an audience for their Australian stories. Several have produced memoirs so that their children and grand-children can enjoy the Australian adventure; others write about their experi-ences in parish newsletters or local newspapers; the most confident give talks to the local Women's Institute or the University of the Third Age about their journey to the other side of the world. In these very public tellings the migration story is often fashioned and consolidated into an exciting and entertaining account of adventure in a strange south land.[50]

Memories sustain a sense of identity, and in old age memories are especi-ally important for sustaining a positive sense of self. As Jack Roscoe's father noted, we live on our memories. Old photographs and documents, and life stories themselves, become increasingly valued when our most affirming experiences are in the past. Joan Pickett enjoyed the time of her life travelling and working her way around Australia and the Pacific for eight years in the 1960s (see Figures 35 and 36), and now speaks with great insight about her Australian memories:

Well they seem to be more vivid than other memories somehow. Because there were so many of them, and they were all such new experiences. And as I say, if I can't sleep at night, only occasionally, you know, I can go back to Ocean Island, and I can start walking round or driving round, and everything is still so vivid. Or I can go in Hobart, and I can climb up the road to Mount Wellington. I can see it all, it's still there. And I've got loads of lovely slides of course, I must get them collated one of these days. But, no, it's all so vivid, because it was, it was something so completely different. The other was sort of normal, and this was abnormal, and it stuck out in your memory. And it's still very — And of course, if anybody finds out, if I mention it occasionally, I don't bring it up in the conversation, but if anybody finds out, and they want to know all about it, so I have to keep bringing these memories out, so of course, I never get a chance to forget anything. And if I do, it's all written down there of course [in letters to her parents which they kept for her]. But you know, things that I may have done in my earlier life, before that, those weren't documented. So I've probably forgotten a lot of things I did before that. But this was *so* different, and so out of the ordinary, that, that it stays fresh all the time. Mm…. Yes, it's something different that people keep asking you about. You don't get a chance to forget in other words. Yes.[51]

Joan Pickett's thoughtful reflections about the nature and significance of her memories highlight many of the patterns of return migrant remembering. Joan explains that her Australian sojourn looms large in her memory because it was a special or 'abnormal' time of 'vivid' experiences. She shows how the

35 Joan Pickett (centre) and her friends Jean and Pat landing at Aden in 1960, en route to Australia. Joan recalls that 'the young people' on the *Oronsay* had their own active social life and 'didn't have a lot to do with the families who were going out'

36 Joan Pickett, interviewed in 2000 at her home in Manchester, holds photographs of her Australian 'sojourn' and recalls of her eight years in Australasia that 'they seem to be more vivid than other memories somehow, because there were so many of them, and they were all such new experiences'

eight years of travel are clearly signposted in her memory and thus readily recalled. She explains how her Australian slides and letters provide a source of reference that sustains her memory, and she notes that she is often asked to tell the story about her years in Australia, 'so I have to keep bringing these memories out'. The memories help Joan to get to sleep, but they also serve as a profoundly significant record of achievement and contribute to Joan's very positive sense of identity and of a life well lived.

In short, far from being a negative or bitter memory, for most return migrants the years in Australia are remembered and told as the 'time of my life'. Even when the Australia sojourn was a great struggle it has, more often than not, become a positive memory and a rich resource in later life. Though most return migrants left Australia many years ago, Australia remains an important part of their lives and identities.

Notes

1 Bates written account US; Marjorie Adams interview US; Hardie interview US; O'Neill interview US.
2 Crooks written account US; Farnfield interview US; Hardie interview US.
3 Barber interview US; John Williams written account US.
4 Farnfield interview US; Ralph Price interview US.
5 Vidler interview US.
6 Chris Gray interview US. Chris Gray's experience confirms Reg Appleyard's argument that fraternization among shiploads of returning British migrants increased their disaffection with Australia. Appleyard, *The Ten Pound Immigrants*, p. 100.
7 Barbara Williams written account US; Crooks written account US.
8 Stirling interview US.
9 Tyas interview US; Spencer interview US; Ford written account US.
10 Kells interview US; O'Neill interview US; Brooks interview US.
11 Whittle interview US; Hart, *Pommie Migrant*, pp. 223–4.
12 O'Neill interview US; Appleyard, *The Ten Pound Immigrants*, p. 100. Appleyard also noted that six months after coming home, when some return migrants were beginning to have second thoughts, they were more likely to cite homesickness or family responsibilities as reasons for return.
13 Tyas interview US; Heath interview US.
14 Catherine Barber interview US; Alvyn Bates written account US.
15 Heath interview US; Barbara Williams written account US.
16 Stephens interview US; Jordan interview US; Spencer interview US.
17 Hardie interview US.
18 Adams interview US.
19 Pickett interview US; Elizabeth Gray interview US.
20 Appleyard, *The Ten Pound Immigrants*, p. 103.
21 Jordan interview US.
22 Chris Gray interview US.
23 Pickett interview US.
24 Francis interview US.

25 Douglas Benson written account US.
26 Palin written account US; Leach written account US.
27 Adams interview US.
28 Ralph Price written account US. See also McGarrity written account US; John Williams written account US.
29 Spencer interview US.
30 Roscoe interview US; Ford written account US.
31 Hardie interview US; see also Margaret and Robert Smith interview US; Pickett interview US.
32 Barber interview US.
33 Bird interview US.
34 Maile written account US; McDermott interview US; Spencer interview US; Worsell written account US; Ralph Price written account US.
35 John Williams written account US.
36 This phrase comes from a taped account by Frances Akehurst US.
37 Frank Warner (written account US) visits local Australian theme pubs for their congenial atmosphere and accents; see also Casson written account US.
38 Chris Gray interview US.
39 Kirby written account US; Patricia Barnes written account US.
40 Ford written account US. See Enoch written account US; Dixon written account US.
41 John M. (Moore is a pseudonym) written account US; Cox written account US.
42 Tyas interview US.
43 Casson written account US; Shirreffs written account US; Cyril Williams written account US.
44 Tyas interview US.
45 Roscoe interview US.
46 Higgins (pseudonym) written account US.
47 Worth written account US.
40 Ralph Price written account US.
49 Jack written account US.
50 For examples of memoirs see note 11 in the Introduction.
51 Pickett interview US.

11

British Australians: migration, nationality and identity

National identity in Australia has, for some time now, been intensely 'problematic', a regular preoccupation of scholars and of old and new Australians as they struggle to define themselves against a colonial past and an ongoing diverse 'settler' present.[1] The British have rarely shared the same obsession, although in recent years the impact of immigration and pressures for Scottish and Welsh devolution have brought a similar degree of introspection, especially on vexed debates around 'Englishness'.[2] For British migrants in Australia issues of national identity have often been secondary to perceptions of their individual sense of struggle and accomplishment, an awareness heightened by the act of migration. The 'battler' identity of some migrants is shared widely, and is in tune with the more general Australian attraction to a mythology of 'struggle, courage, and survival, amidst pain, tragedy and loss'.[3] But the reflections of British migrants on their attachments and longings underline the diverse ways in which they seek to make sense of their life histories. While the issues of national belonging are rarely settled and final for them, the varied ways in which they deal with conflicting loyalties, family relationships and unresolved separation are the common properties of a migrant identity, and not a simple matter of an old British or new Australian patriotism. In this chapter we explore some of the ways in which the postwar British Australians have managed their evolving sense of belonging during two generations of migrant lives, and how their migration stories express complex personal identities.

The British-Australian loyalties of Ron Penn

On Australia Day, 1986, Ron Penn was awarded the OAM, the Medal of the Order of Australia, for service to the community.[4] For Ron the unexpected honour was one in a succession of distinctions and awards which crowned a long career in Australia since his arrival in 1947. In 1953, as Chief Petty Officer, he had headed the Sea Cadet Corps Honour Guard for the Sydney Coronation Pageant; he had a leading role in Australian scouting, which took him to Nagoya, Japan, to forge a new scouting partnership alongside a sister city arrangement with Sydney; he was a prominent leader in the NSW Presbyterian Church, worked with the Korean and Cook Islands churches and was made an 'honorary Cook Islander'; and in 1959 he became a Justice of the Peace. In 1977 and 1978 he shared platforms with Neville Wran and Gough Whitlam at citizenship ceremonies, where he spoke about the Australian flag. His medal led to further recognition when he was invited to a royal garden party at Buckingham Palace during a visit to London in 1988. For Ron, a proud but modest man, these distinctions signified the greater opportunities and enhanced career he had enjoyed through his move to Australia, which 'would not have been available to me if I'd have stayed in England'. His pride in Australian citizenship is matched by continuing loyalty to Britain and deep, if ambivalent, patriotic emotions. The very ambivalence of Ron's attachment to both Britain and Australia hints at the uncertainty and mutability which continues to shape the national identity of British Australians years after their arrival.

Ron's life story mirrors so many of the migrant histories we have recounted in this book, but again its representativeness is qualified by its uniqueness. Born in 1927, he was brought up in Chiswick and Twickenham, by parents from poor struggling backgrounds but upwardly mobile, imbued with a powerful work ethic and presiding over a close-knit family. His father was proud of his forty-four years of loyal service to the local Chiswick Products company, where he had progressed from manual labour to managerial status. 'He was a very proud man and proud of his job, but I don't think he ever really felt himself any better than any other man.' His mother gave up her wartime employment upon her marriage but continued to do fine needlework and clothes design from home for modest payment. His parents' blend of drive and humility did much to mould Ron's character. Though he was of the inter-war generation and class that routinely left school at 14, Ron won a scholarship in 1938 to the Thames Valley County School, a site vulnerable to air raids, where schooling was regularly disrupted. Within three years he decided that the Thames Valley schooling, oriented to white-collar work, was not his bent, and he transferred to a technical college, aiming for work 'as a toolmaker or a draughtsman or something like that'. This soon evolved into an interest in science, and by 1943 he had found work as a laboratory assistant in his father's company.

For Ron, though, his youth is recollected just as powerfully for his determination to contribute to the war effort. Even in 1938, at the age of 11, he volunteered as an air raid precautions messenger, the youngest in the county, and was actively occupied during the Blitz. At the same time he joined the school's army cadet corps and the Twickenham air scout group – possibly the first ever formed. After the 1944 D–Day invasion, at the age of 17, Ron 'decided the war was going to end without me getting into the armed services and that wasn't something I wanted to happen'. His prompt enlistment in the 'Boy

Service' of the Royal Navy was circumscribed by limited eyesight, but before the war ended he worked in the naval canteen service, stationed at HMS Westcliffe in Essex and later at Dover.

As the war drew to its end Ron's naval career took an unexpected turn through a journey which was to shape the rest of his life. In July 1945, well before his ninteenth birthday, he was ordered to join an escort carrier bound for Sydney. In Sydney by September, limited berthing allowed Ron and five shipmates to rent a small flat in Bellevue Hill where 'we bought ourselves civilian clothes and lived in comparative luxury'. His somewhat lonely life as a young sailor adrift was short-lived; it came to an abrupt end on 1 October when he joined a picnic in Hyde Park arranged by student teachers eager to invite 'some lonely British sailors' to join them. For Ron the rest now seems to have been inevitable: 'of course, one of those who went on the picnic was Betty, who is now my wife and after that we were pretty constant companions'. By the following July Ron and Betty were deeply in love and Ron had begun to overcome her parents' suspicions against having 'an ex-Royal Navy sailor as a prospective son-in-law … a migrant and an ex-sailor and all the rest of that'; but, with demobilization looming, all the dreams were suspended when he was ordered to return to England on the *HMS Indefatigable*. Suddenly a bright future became uncertain. Their parting 'was quite distressful, but I made no promise to return because at that time I just didn't know how I could achieve it, so there was no point in making a promise'.

Back in England in 1946, and demobilized, Ron told his anxious parents about his determination to return to Australia, but, with no easy way to do so, of necessity he turned his mind to work. A position as a laboratory assistant in the Physiology Department at the London School of Medicine offered new career promise, but Ron's thoughts were fixed on Sydney. In March 1947 he saw an advertisement inviting ex-service people of selected trades to apply for assisted migration to Australia. A prompt response brought an interview in May, and in June he boarded the *Orion*, bound for Sydney, one of the early voyages in the new migration venture.

Preoccupied with Sydney, Ron had little regard for those painful rites of passage which colour most migrant memories of leaving. For a 20-year-old his departure – likely to be permanent – from a close-knit family would be understandably distressing, but Ron admits that this was overshadowed by his eagerness to join Betty. The family managed to travel to Tilbury to see him off, but the event was more emotional for them than for Ron. His mother, he knew, after 'heart to heart talks', had supported his resolve to return, even though it must have 'broken her heart almost to — persuade me to send a cable to Betty'. Like those other youthful migrants who left with little regard for their parents' feelings, Ron was imbued with the excitement of anticipation, but like them, too, he was storing up reserves of guilt for future reflection. 'I was feeling the joy of coming back, but to them, I'm sure at the time I didn't realize just how traumatic it probably was.' Only forty-one years later, during a return visit and long talks to his sister, did he begin to realize how upsetting his move had been for his parents and that the trauma may have been partly responsible for his father's early death at the age of 62.

The six week voyage was a 'very happy one', with many young single companions, particularly fifty men bound for work with Tasmanian Hydro and eleven young Scottish women sponsored by an Adelaide appliance factory. Recently liberated from the hardships of wartime service, they revelled in the luxuries of the refitted emigrant ship. Yet they were surprised at the time, and later, to discover that some British passengers had complained volubly about food and conditions on board. Ron carefully preserved a news cutting reporting the letter of complaint signed by a hundred angry passengers, which seemed unbelievable to his friends when they joined for a reunion many years later – a reminder, too, that not all British migrants shared his positive outlook. The excitement of the voyage was crowned during a stop-over at Melbourne, when the passengers were given a Lord Mayor's civic reception at the town hall, a celebration of the second official arrival of British migrants. By this time the excitement and camaraderie among the young passengers had built strong friendships, central markers in longer-term memories of their migration. Fifty years later Ron conducted a search for surviving passengers, and formed the 'Orion JJ47' group ('JJ' signifying June and July), with an occasional newsletter and a reunion of some members. While Ron found the contacts difficult to sustain after a few years, his enthusiasm marks the enduring importance of the event for him.

Most observers would regard Ron's subsequent migrant story as a dream-run, the envy of those who struggled for years in hostels, primitive housing and ill-suited employment. Ron himself acknowledges his painless adjustment, which made it easy to distance himself from other migrants, in a letter written after the interview. Unlike his fellow passengers, he recalled, 'I had been to Australia before, I had private accommodation ready for me to move into, and I had a good chance of getting a good job with plenty of advancement possibilities. I really didn't need to cling to the other British migrant type people'.[5] His good fortune was enhanced by the ability of former friends, property owners, to provide a rented room for him in North Bondi, where the young couple lived briefly after their marriage in January 1949. By 1955 they were able to build a permanent home in Revesby, where they brought up three children and have lived ever since. In his career, too, Ron took advantage of the numerous 'advancement possibilities' he had anticipated when he found a laboratory technician's position in the Veterinary Physiology Department at

the University of Sydney. During a forty-year career he completed seven
years of part-time study, progressed to laboratory manager, wrote scientific
papers, travelled on overseas study tours, became president of the Professional Officers' Association, and in his spare time lectured on animal care at
the Sydney Technical College. Alongside his publicly recognized achievements in community service, this gave ample grounds for Ron to celebrate the
opportunities and good fortune he enjoyed in Australia.

With such a positive story it is hardly surprising that Ron came to take
patriotic pride in his attachment to Australia and his contribution to national
welfare. But it is a complex patriotism influenced by a continuing attachment
to Britain, a theme traceable to his earliest years after migration. Recalling his
strong identification as British in 1947, he explained that moving to Australia
posed no problem, simply because 'I felt I was moving to another part of
Britain'. This was sustained by many of his experiences at university and in
community work. In the early years his supervisor and half of his work
colleagues were English, and much of his public activity, like scouting, had an
international dimension. Although it was 1983 before he took out Australian
citizenship, this had a complex family dimension, since he had been reluctant
to upset his mother; it was important to her that he should not, as she saw it,
'renounce' his British citizenship, and he felt bound by that filial obligation
until she died. In 1953 he wrote an information piece on Australia for the in-
house magazine of Chiswick Products Ltd, his former English employer. The
article contained useful facts and impressions of Australian life in the 1950s –
on Americanized language, architecture, transport, wage levels, beach and
bush life, rabbits, 'corrugated roads' susceptible to flooding and 'curious place
names'. His impressions coincided with those presented by emigration
promoters, 'a grand country, inhabited by grand people'. Significantly, the
accompanying illustration was a newspaper image of the Coronation Pageant
at the Sydney Showground, with Ron, 'our contributor', marked by an arrow
(see figure 37).[6]

Before long, though, Ron's dual loyalties were put to the test. Soon after
arrival he joined the 'ex-Imperial Sub-Branch' of the Returned Services
League, a branch expressly formed for British ex-servicemen. His membership was short-lived after he found an excessive tendency to sustain a British
'conclave'. 'I think I felt that I shouldn't isolate myself in that way.... I think I
had a fairly strong feeling that you shouldn't lock yourself into a, an ethnic
group if you like, and I've always felt that.'[7] The issue of ethnic clannishness
continued to rankle. It was another half century, after a long association
formed through arranging for his East Hills Scouts pipes and drums group to
play at the branch's annual Anzac Sunday march, before he rejoined the
RSL.[8] That first reaction against British clannishness matured for Ron into

resembles the larger animal, and the marsupial mouse. The native birds
are the Kookaburra, whose laugh is internationally known, the Bell Bird,
the Whip Bird, and numerous types of parrots and budgerigars. Of course,
the bush can be dangerous as well as beautiful for many poisonous snakes

*A ' Sydney Morning Herald ' picture of the Finale of the Coronation Pageant
at Sydney Showground. Our contributor is marked by an arrow.*

37 In 1953 Ron Penn headed the Sea Cadet Corps Honour Guard for the Coronation Pageant at
the Sydney Showground, and he proudly sent this photograph to accompany an information piece
about Australia in the magazine of his former English employer. 'Our contributor' is marked by an
arrow amidst formations spelling out 'ER' and depicting the Union Jack

passionate support for migrant assimilation into Australian culture. Describing himself as a 'strong supporter of multiculturalism', he interpreted this as bringing different groups together to share a common Australian identity. As the Assistant Area Commissioner for Ethnic Affairs in scouting, for example, he encouraged different ethnic groups to form mixed ethnic branches rather than branches based on ethnic origin. His discomfort with the complaining passengers on the *Orion* is consistent with this long-standing loyalty to Australia and Australian integration, and he still insists that people who have 'complained their heads off' should go home. 'I feel very strongly about that, sort of people who don't even give the country an opportunity.'

Yet while Ron has no time for overt British clannishness in Australia, he retains a quiet, patriotic pride in his British origins. His earliest memories recall visits with his father, a First World War veteran, to regimental Sunday marches, and he is still stirred emotionally by the marching music from those childhood days. (For so many British migrants music is a potent marker for memory and belonging.) On a visit to Britain in 1988 one of the highlights was his visit to Horse Guards Parade, where he began to relive the old patriotic loyalties: 'everywhere you … could hear bands playing…. I felt I'd never been away and right at that moment that's the only place I wanted to be.' When he and Betty had a rare opportunity to join in a rendition of 'Land of Hope and Glory' at a 'Best of British' concert at the Sydney Opera House, 'the tears rolled down my cheeks (possibly a symptom of older age)'.[9] Those loyalties have been sustained more recently by frequent internet communication with old British friends. Today, Ron proudly combines his British and Australian patriotisms; he supports Australian sporting teams in everything but cricket, and opposes an Australian republic while being resigned to its inevitability. Loath to criticize his adopted country, his only censure dwells on Australians' weak sense of patriotism compared to the British, their reluctance to sing the national anthem, so that nothing 'stirs the feelings in Australia of patriotism'. But while 'Land of Hope and Glory' and 'Jerusalem' stir his emotions, 'another song that moves me considerably is "I still call Australia home". I guess that shows that I am pretty well assimilated.'[10]

The assertion of British identities: 'self-ethnicization'

Ron Penn's expression of his identity as a British Australian bears a uniquely individual stamp; but its subtle combination of British and Australian loyalties and affections echoes our informants' reflections on their identity more generally. The shifting emphasis and slow evolution of Ron's dual loyalties – reinforced by greater travel during retirement – and his suspicion of the ghettoizing tendencies of British loyalty organizations, also form common themes. Curiously, these themes are strikingly absent from recent academic discussion of the place of Britishness, and the British, in Australian life and identity. Since the advent in the 1980s of multiculturalism as a defining feature in Australian national identity, and the strong focus on cultural enrichment from non-English-speaking immigrants, British presence and identity in Australia, academically at least, has come to be defined as a problem.[11]

As cultural studies scholars define it, the 'problem' emerged when the British in Australia lost their centrality as latterday descendants of the 'foundational' core culture in 'Anglo-Celtic' settler Australia. The former privilege of special treatment – the sense, recalled by Ron Penn, that a move to Australia was simply a move to 'another part of Britain' – gave way to a feeling that the British were simply one more minority among many, with no special status and no special claim on the core national identity. 'Taking all together,' Jon Stratton observes, 'all these developments during the 1980s and 1990s produced an increasing sense of self-consciousness among British migrants of themselves as a community.' Increasingly 'denigrated and silenced', and anxious about their marginalization, British migrants asserted themselves as an embattled minority ethnic group deserving of recognition and protection.[12]

One of the prominent lobbyists for specifically English migrants, Geoffrey Partington, illustrated the grievance at the heart of this 'self-consciousness' bluntly: 'There is no desire among Australians born in England or of English descent to form a political party or a faction within the existing parties, but there is a growing resentment that influential parts of the media and many public figures denigrate the British contribution to Australian life.'[13] Partington's blend of references to the English along with the 'British contribution to Australian life' betrays a common confusion about precisely which British groups have begun, belatedly, to 'self-ethnicize' themselves. But scholars like Stratton and Tara Brabazon stress that, while confusion between 'English' and 'British' persists, the reaction is chiefly an English phenomenon. In Britain this relates partly to political developments since the loss of Empire, and partly to more recent moves towards political autonomy evident in developments like the Scottish Parliament and the Welsh Assembly, which have left the English with an uncertain identity of their own. The English uncertainty has been compounded by postwar immigrants from the Caribbean and the Indian sub-continent, and their British-born children, who claim their own British identities. In Commonwealth countries like Australia, moreover, the Scots, Welsh and Irish have remained comparatively secure in an identity clearly distinct from that of the English. Until recently it was easy to confuse 'British' with 'English', and for the English in effect to assume the mantle of Britishness as it suited them. But multiculturalism, according to Stratton and Brabazon, has changed all that. In postmodern language, 'the space between England and Britain is a negotiated territory'; and writers resort to befuddling neologisms like 'Brit/Eng', 'whenever there is a slippery merging of the connotations of British and English'.[14] This confusion is understandable, but it rests on an assumption – usually untested – that the various British migrant identities in Australia are differentiated profoundly by ethnic awareness, with the English, in effect postmodern 'whingers', now seeking special treatment and protection.

The evidence usually cited to support this case derives from a variety of sources, but rarely from personal testimony. Instead, institutions and high-profile public activities emerge as key symptoms of the supposed assertion of a new English 'ethnicization'. Soccer, which, paradoxically, emerged in postwar Australia from non-English-speaking ethnic social clubs, now illustrates the 'imagining' and 'performance' of Englishness, most dramatically in apparent support by the English for the Perth Glory team. Given the well-known high concentration of English migrants in Perth, such English enthusiasms, complete with familiar 'tribal' singing, should not surprise us. But for all the claims that Perth Glory's soccer 'is a marker of English ethnicity as opposed to Australian culture', it remains unclear what role postwar English migrants play in this phenomenon. The emergence of English self-ethnicization during the controversies of Hansonism might suggest a political context and a reaction against the privileges supposedly accorded to other migrant communities. But we need more than a few English songs sung at the game to establish that English migrants are thereby summoning an 'imagined community' of Englishness. No doubt Perth Glory serves various purposes for different supporters, but it is yet to be shown what meaning it has for postwar English migrants.[15]

A more persuasive case might be made for the relevance to migrants of the British loyalty organizations, which have enjoyed something of a revival in Australia in recent years. The United Kingdom Settlers' Association (UKSA), The English in Australia and the Royal Society of St George are a few of the best known. The older ones, like the UKSA, based in Melbourne, have changed their functions substantially over the last few decades. Formed in 1967 to support British migrants, the UKSA gradually evolved into an umbrella for local social clubs, with the accent on dinner dances. The mostly ageing membership still appreciates these activities. A recent edition of the newsletter, *Endeavour*, contained reports of successful dances, one of which, in Springvale, 'had lots of different football clubs represented', complete with team colours, but it also warned of steadily declining patronage. Since the mid-1990s, according to Stratton, the association has taken on a more political focus, in 'an attempt to rebuild the organization on an ethnic basis'. This is evident in *Endeavour*'s close surveillance of media outlets for examples of 'racial vilification directed against the British community'. After a leading feature detailing a Melbourne disk jockey's talkback segment, 'the purpose of which seemed to be to encourage callers to make Anglophobic statements', *Endeavour* launched a sub-committee to investigate such offences, which occur 'almost daily in our media in the form of Anglophobia'. According to the editor, Barrie Hunt, this was 'the single biggest issue on which we get complaints made to the UKSA'.[16]

A more positive and celebratory aspect of the promotion of British ethnicity, according to Stratton, is the 'Britfest', a public display of the ethnic cultures of England, Wales, Scotland and Northern Ireland. These festivals have taken place in Sydney since 1996 and Melbourne since 1998, and the organizers take pride in the varied offerings, from regional cuisine and costume, ethnic dance groups and 'Parramatta Power' soccer demonstrations through to impersonations of Queen Victoria and Beefeaters. Attendance at these festivals testifies to their popularity; their meaning to the crowds attending them is harder to gauge. Stratton argues that various imperial markers, like Queen Victoria, easily 'blur into an Anglo-Saxon nationalism. While not the intention of the organizers of the Britfests, such Brit/Eng ethnic nostalgia can become a glorification of the claimed British heritage of Australia, and of the "Anglo–Celtic" core over the multicultural periphery.' This might well be true. It is also likely that the loyalty associations, virtually by definition, take on a politically conservative outlook and attract conservative support; the former Liberal MP Sir James Killen gave the inaugural UKSA annual dinner address on 'Australian Federation and the British Heritage' and subsequently became the association's patron. But none of this settles the question about the extent of support for such organizations and activities among British migrants, which remains untested by direct testimony. The periodic anxieties of the UKSA about its declining membership suggest that the support might be limited.[17]

'To keep the homesickness at bay': British migrants and loyalty organizations

From their earliest days in Australia the British had a range of loyalty organizations available to them for practical help and socializing with compatriots. Many of these were small, voluntary and short-lived organizations, which thrived briefly among migrants motivated by homesickness and desire for like-minded company. Only a minority of our informants remembers any knowledge of or association with these organizations, and while some received help, most now recall them, with cynicism, as inward-looking havens for the disaffected. Margaret Hill had one brief experience in Adelaide with what she remembered as the 'British Settlers' Association'. After attending one meeting she decided that 'it wasn't my scene'. 'It was Poms sitting round whingeing, and I said "I don't need this", I didn't go again [laughter]. They were just, "Do you remember, do you remember?" And "When are you going home again?".' In Chapter 3 we saw sojourner Joan Pickett's disillusion with Adelaide's Victoria League, which she quickly decided was 'very insular', with people reminiscing about home and discussing the trip back: 'we didn't like the atmosphere at all.' In such cases the uncomfortable 'atmosphere' clashed with the determination of young migrants to meet Australians 'and get accepted'. But the wariness was not confined to young sojourners. In Sydney Albert and Anne Lougher promptly decided to reject an invitation from what they recalled as the 'Settlers' Association'; 'you shouldn't have to have people telling you ... about settlers and meeting each other and whingeing at each other'.[18]

These reactions echo the tensions we saw in hostels between migrants anxious to get established in the community and those they judged to be time-serving 'whingers', simply waiting out their two years before returning. But many of the organizations fulfilled more practical functions, and this is how some migrants remember them. In Launceston Eileen and John Fairbairn established a British migrants' club, meeting weekly for the express purpose of welcoming newcomers. After a year, however, the Launceston Council asked them to disband, worried that other ethnic groups might start similar organizations at odds with assimilationist policies. The club closed without a murmur. John said he felt that it had achieved its supportive aims for new migrants, but he also agreed with the council's priority of cultural assimilation. During the 1950s the Union Jack Club, on Collins Street in Melbourne, was a venue for social events and travel advice for recent migrants. Mildred Hamilton, a young single migrant from Northern Ireland in 1951, promptly discovered the regular dances at the club, where she 'felt quite at home' with young people from all parts of Britain. But once she met her future husband, an Australian, 'that was the finish of the Union Jack Club', as she and Bill enjoyed the larger dances at Box Hill and Hawthorn town halls. The club had served its purpose. In the late 1950s Margaret McClellan knew of the club as a resource for helping recent migrants to make emergency visits back to Britain, but she and her husband never bothered to join. Others visited only 'a few times', had vague memories of its existence, or simply ignored it once they found other outlets. Ivor Miller, a single migrant in the early 1950s, knew that the club offered facilities for billiards, drinks and social nights, but he had already found an active social club and a soccer club through his employer; 'I didn't have to resort to going to the Union Jack.'[19]

These responses speak more to general migrant desires for company and sociability after arrival rather than needs for patriotic expression. Indeed, migrants' relative indifference to such organizations seems to have been a yardstick of their adjustment. So it is not surprising to find that early contacts with clubs and societies were not explicitly oriented around a search for British contacts. In the deeply embedded club culture of New South Wales there were ample opportunities for cheap entertainment and socializing. Yvonne Hoare's parents sought these out in the early 1960s after moving to Sydney from a short residence in Adelaide. Yvonne's father was a Londoner, her mother an Italian, and it is significant that the first club they joined was the Apia Club, an Italian soccer club in Leichardt. But before long they gravitated to RSL clubs, always impressed with the facilities and sociability; 'very much', Yvonne commented, an 'Australian kind of life'. For those who had seen war service it was easy to be drawn to the attractions of RSL clubs, and in the 1950s there were separate branches and services clubs with a British focus. Barbara Doig and her husband, both ex-navy, used the 'Bex Club', or British Ex-Services Club' in Sydney after arrival in 1957, but the association was short-lived.[20] None our informants recalls a significant connection with a British migrant welfare organization. In 1966 researcher James

Jupp argued that British migrant associations were mostly short-lived (except for the British League of Ex-Servicemen, which combined national and service loyalty), and he contrasted the weakness of most British associations with the 'incredible network' of Greek clubs, brotherhoods and newspapers.[21]

For men, of course, Freemasonry could provide a ready social outlet, especially for those who had been members in Britain. While Australian branches were noted for their British loyalties, and some members today make much of their monarchical sympathies, this is not the way our informants remember them.[22] For Grahame Manoy, who was introduced by his Australian father-in-law, membership was a measure of his integration into his new community in Scarborough. George Adam, also in Perth, recalled his five-year membership, partly as Lodge secretary, mainly as a time of unremitting hard voluntary work by his family. He ultimately resigned, regarding it as a 'total waste of time'; 'to my mind it is incredible, primary school kids playing dress-up, you know'. While George expresses strong pride in his Scottish heritage, his experience with Freemasonry did nothing to sustain such pride. On the other hand Freemasonry could prove to be a constructive outlet for what seems to have been a stronger urge of Scottish migrants to express Scottish loyalties. Patricia Wall's father, James Hardie, whose story we told in Chapter 6, promptly used his Masonic attachment in Canberra in the early 1950s to make connections, and set up a new Scottish lodge, the 'Lodge Caledonia'. But even James, intensely attached to his Scottishness, used these outlets to socialize and overcome homesickness, which moderated over time. Patricia recalled her parents' initial membership of the Burns Club: 'They joined the Burns Club more or less to keep, I think, the homesickness at bay. But then they dropped it as they found their niche in society, once they moved over to O'Connor, and they felt that they really were established, they were settled in.' Eddie Carruthers, a Glaswegian, maintained his Masonic membership for only two years, preferring the social activities of the Perth and Perthshire Club with its regular dinner dances.[23]

For British migrants more generally, loyalties were as likely to be local as national, evident in Betty Tilley's short-lived association in the early 1950s with the Leicester Club in Perth; with a membership of about forty at its peak, it, too was a social club. It 'fizzled out' after a few years, but for Betty and her husband it had served its purpose. It is, indeed, difficult to distinguish between the attraction of these organizations for purposes of national loyalty as opposed to their convenience as approachable venues for social events and entertainment. But the general trend for migrants to drop away from them after the initial years suggests their primary function as comfortable agencies of socialization and salves for homesickness. The fact that none of our informants has continued to the present with membership of loyalty organizations suggests that they exerted only a tenuous hold on migrants who were intent on making a new life. Cynical responses to the foundation of The English in Australia (TEA) in the late 1990s underline this reluctance of most migrants of the postwar generation to 'self-ethnicize' in the sense argued by Jon Stratton. Wendy Jay, intensely conscious of her rapid adjustment as a migrant, especially after the early death of her husband, reacted against the apparent promotion of Englishness. After a friend persuaded her to attend the Canberra launch of TEA, she thought, 'Oh God, what do I want to belong to this for? … I thought, God, I've got enough friends of all nationalities of, I really don't think! So I've never, I've never clung to, you know, British ---.' Maggie Campbell, in Sydney, was puzzled by the evident need English people felt to band together in this way, and concluded that her own contentment as a migrant explained her lack of interest. 'I did think, well, maybe it's because, because I've always been so happy and contented here, it hasn't bothered me.' Kate Rowe was similarly perplexed: 'they could talk and whinge among themselves, no, that's not for me'.[24] There is no question that loyalty organizations do appeal to a small section of British Australians, but they provide a misleading guide to the identities postwar migrants have shaped for themselves since the 1940s. The twists and turns of these identities are evident in yet another complicated migrant life history.

Family and national identity: the ambivalent loyalties of Pat Drohan

Like many of the themes we have examined in this book, national identity is frequently bound up with family relationships. For those migrants who have cultivated what is often now referred to as a 'transnational family', their loyalties to both countries evolve with the vagaries of family contacts. Often the family links, along with British attachments, revive in retirement years with more frequent visits to Britain and, as in the case of Ron Penn, email contact. These patterns suggest that understanding of family relationships is an important key to the complicated shaping of British-Australian loyalties. Pat Drohan's story illustrates some of these complex threads over four decades of fluctuating sentiment.

Pat Drohan was single and 24 when she emigrated from Wolverhampton to Australia in 1958, with prearranged secretarial work in the Victorian town of Ballarat.[25] She set out as a classic 'sojourner', intent on an adventurous two-year working holiday, but left behind a large, close-knit and convivial family, none of whom ever emigrated. Her plans shifted dramatically when, before the end of her two years, she met and married an Australian man and settled in Ballarat. At the time it did not matter to Pat that marriage to an Australian set her on a course to permanent residence in Australia. But it marked the beginning of her long struggle to maintain family links, intensified for her by the fact that she left behind a twin sister. The twins had made a pact to be bridesmaids at each other's weddings, but 'I got married, and I had no family, no one at the wedding. And my twin sister and I, we'd always wanted to be bridesmaids.' Pat arranged for the wedding to be taped and sent to her family in England, in an early and innovative use of technology to maintain transnational family communications. But in the initial years much of Pat's life in Australia was defined by separation from her family. Discussing the birth of her two sons, she alluded to her need for her mother: 'the first baby, Michael, was just the – very easy, you know, lovely, but you do miss your Mum. Oh, I'd give anything to have mum. But the second one, Paul, was an absolute nightmare.' Lacking physical closeness, over the years Pat relied on the telephone for the contact which eluded her. Her heartfelt words on the subject betray the emotional depth of a family bond which survived the long years apart.

And over the years the family, with the phone calls and that, they know the time difference and all that, and I've always said to them: 'If anything happens at home, you are, you are to call me, you're to *tell* me; I don't care when. [Include me.]' And they say: 'We *always* include you, Pat, whatever we do, you're always included in what we do, we ring you when...', 'cause I've missed weddings, I've missed births, but I think the worst are the deaths.... But the day I got that phone call ... but I just couldn't describe what it was like, to know Mum had gone, and you, you don't know what to do, there's no one to speak to, just nobody. And then, the calls in the middle of the night, I'll sit up and take the call, I'd, my sons lived at home then and the, my sister died suddenly, with an aneurism ... and what, what do you do? Where do you go? ... And I didn't wake my husband, and it's no good waking my sons, and I sat there crying, and, you can't talk, you can't go round, you can't do anything.

From 1973 Pat was able to begin making return visits, mostly with her husband, to the family in Wolverhampton. Through these return visits Pat came to an awareness of the changes wrought by her emigration. 'When I went back, after fifteen years, the family said: "My word, you've changed!" ... They said I'd become so much more assertive and outspoken ... And I said: "Well you know", I said: "When you go out somewhere that's so far away from home, and you're on your own, you haven't got anybody to stand up and speak for you".'

These trips back to Wolverhampton have also sparked an increasing sense of ambivalence in Pat's attitude to her emigration, encompassing the idea that she has become closer to the family than before leaving. In effect Pat has refashioned her English identity in her later years through telephone contact and return visits. Reflecting about the interview, in which she began to explore some of these feelings in deeper ways than before, she admitted, 'I'm more English now than I was when I left!' As the years have passed and her family have aged, the realization of distance and frequent farewells have brought a new poignancy to her mobility.

My family are now getting old, we are all getting thin in the numbers ... And I ... although it's unspoken, it's there, but, we're, we're all thinking: 'When will the next visit be, will there *be* another one, and who'll be missing...?' And that, that's a fact of life! Somebody *will* be missing – it might even be me. But 'cause you don't know, you meet it, and so you have to make the most of every opportunity.

We can see here in process the gradual weakening of transnational family links over time and through generations, even as the emotional weight these links carry increases. At the same time Pat has been enthusiastically preoccupied with the construction of new Australian family networks. Two married sons and the recent birth of her first grandchild reinforce her awareness of the realities of permanent settlement. Her family and work history are both matters of pride for her, but her identity is inseparable from an acute awareness of her transnational family's dilemma. 'And I certainly couldn't go back there now, because this is, this is my home, I've made it here.... When we come over now, it's not for the big tourist scene.... It's merely to be, make the most of being with the family; it's just the family visit.'

Pat's preoccupation with family attachments in two countries has evolved with her attitude to national identity. She readily admits that at the time of her migration she was not remotely patriotic, her only connection with her homeland being the family attachment. But she also insists that 'I've become more patriotic since I've been away.... I hate anybody saying anything bad about England'; she credits Paul Keating's hostility to Britain with reinforcing her Englishness, but family remains the more tangible motive. Home for Pat remains Wolverhampton, even though she finds it physically unattractive and England today unrecognizable as the country she left. After more than forty years in Australia, 'I think home is always where you've been born'. Yet politically this loyalty has clear limits. When asked about the republican issue, Pat's British loyalty had little relevance.

Well, I think that's fair enough ... you know, British as I am, and the monarchy, I don't think the monarchy has got much relevance now, the way Australia's going, I think it would be good, depending who they had as the head. I, I'd like some connection still to be with England but it, it's no good saying, 'This is another England', because it certainly isn't.

Perhaps a litmus test of Pat's loyalties is her attitude to adopting Australian citizenship. In her reflection that 'I don't think I ever will', she shares her ambivalence with many older migrants, insisting that her loyalty to Australia is best demonstrated by years of being a hard-working citizen.

Well I've been out here forty years, I've worked for most of them, and I, I don't see what a piece of paper saying I've become an Australian is going to change much one way or another. I think I've done my bit for Australia, I think I've *more* than paid them for my passage out. I think they got value for their money, and I don't see any need for it. You know, I'm loyal to Australia, but I, I'm British as well – I keep my British passport. I, I feel Australia and England are just, I've always felt them close.

For Pat the closeness is embodied more in her family ties than in any abstract political ideas. Her family history has been crucial to the moulding of a migrant identity.

Britons and Australians, monarchists and republicans: the complexities of a migrant identity

In recent years debates over an Australian republic have brought new focus to the issue of whether lingering British monarchical loyalties in Australia are a brake on change. During the 1999 republican referendum campaign, media commentary often assumed that British Australians would vote in a solid bloc to defeat the proposal. Britons who had arrived before 1984 retained the vote even if they had not taken Australian citizenship – just one reason why a high proportion (51 per cent in one 1986 survey) are not naturalized – and some republicans even called for the disenfranchisement of non-naturalized Britons.[26] There is no doubt that many British-born voters, and their descendants, like many Australians, were and remain staunch supporters of the monarchy; some of these among our informants expressed their sympathies forcefully. But the equation of British-Australian political identity with monarchism and the anti-republican position is deeply misleading. Even statistical profiles suggest that the trend is much more complicated. Among 138 of our Australian-based interviewees who offered an opinion on republicanism, shortly before or after the referendum, 73 were in favour and 65 opposed. But the raw figures, confined to a simple 'yes' or 'no' response, are themselves misleading, as was evident above with Ron Penn and Pat Drohan. Ron's anti-republican stance was combined with a benign sense of its inevitability, Pat's republicanism with a belated surge of English patriotism. Many interviewees explained similar levels of complex ambivalence. Often this stemmed from the common Australian (and perhaps universal) suspicion of politicians' motives for constitutional change. David Bailey explained his mixed views, encompassing hostility to the monarchy with anti-republicanism, as simply practical self-interest: 'you've got a system and it works, why change it?' Valerie Proverbs qualified her republican support with anxiety about which particular model of choice and presidential powers would prevail; until that was settled 'I've got to reserve my judgement'.[27] But the ambivalence extends well beyond practical questions and encompasses profound emotional loyalties. Such ambivalence, and its mutability, is part of the British–Australian migrant identity; it is a measure of the ways that, years after arrival, the ten pound Poms seek to make meaning of their migrant life histories.

The wide spectrum of British and Australian loyalties among postwar migrants is hardly surprising, from the most intense monarchism to the most robust republicanism. But the process of moulding these sentiments has rarely been straightforward; they might be shaped by complicated dynamics in family networks, as in Pat Drohan's case, or qualified by mixed loyalties developing over time, with retirement years and return visits a crucial phase of reassessment. Variations according to differences of gender and generation underline the importance of the migrant life story to the ongoing process of identity formation. Through all these differences there is an underlying theme in most life stories of a sustained awareness of a migrant identity rather than an exclusively British or Australian one.

Kathleen Barrand, for example, who settled with her parents in Geelong, Victoria, as a 15-year-old in 1949, inherited her mother's overt patriotism and affection for the monarchy (in contrast to her more indifferent father). When the Queen visited Geelong during the 1954 royal tour she attended the procession with her fiancé, her brother and her mother, and recorded the event in detail in her diary. Like so many British and Australian families of her generation, she continues proudly to display her collection of Coronation cups alongside her Royal Albert collection issued during the 1956 Olympics. In these ways Kathleen's sense of her Englishness is tied closely to her domestic and family life. When she organized a family reunion and celebration of the fortieth anniversary of the family's arrival, that too reflected her patriotic sentiments. 'We ... made an exhibition, I got my diaries out and the flag and that, and we sang the royal health, and then we sang "Advance Australia Fair".' Reflecting on her sustained love of England and her monarchist loyalties (in sharp contrast to her republican daughter), she looked back to her fifteen-year upbringing in Essex as 'all my formative years', which left her 'still with a lot of British in me'. Yet even Kathleen views her migration as a privileged experience, which distinguishes her from the British who stayed at home. 'I think it's character building to have come here from another country.... You know, to come over, on a boat ... How many people get the chance, to have those wonderful experiences, and live in another country? But I'm still proud of my heritage.'[28]

Pro-British sentiments vary considerably with age and the time of migration. David Bailey, who came to Sydney with friends in 1968, and in 1998 was again living as a single man, attributes much of his patriotism to sustained anti-English attitudes in Australia. He took to the more relaxed and outdoor Australian life with great enthusiasm, but remains acutely sensitive to persistent 'Pommy bastard' taunts; he reflects that those ingrained prejudices had made him 'more pro-British', and that he 'would have assimilated much better' without them. While he became an Australian citizen purely for the convenience of his frequent travel, he often regrets it: 'sometimes I wish I hadn't done it because I'm not accepted as one, so why should I have one? That's what I feel.' David's views on vilification of the English coincide broadly with those of organizations like the United Kingdom Settlers' Association and The English in Australia, and do much to define his political attitudes. The prejudice, he insists, is directed explicitly at the English rather than the British generally, and leaves the English as the only vilified group in Australia when more recent migrants enjoy legal protection. Like Pat Drohan, David places much of the blame on the multicultural policies of Paul Keating, who, together with Bob Hawke, 'just about ruined this country'. 'It'll never work, this multicultural business, it's like putting a dog and a cat in a kennel.' These views are not uncommon, but usually coexist with comfortable adaptation to life in Australia and a strong aversion against return to Britain. In David's case his more flexible attitude to the future bears all the hallmarks of the younger generation of migrants of the late 1960s, including indifference to the monarchy. While still tied to Sydney by his daughter, he admits that if she married he could quite happily live in England again.

I could quite easily sell this place and, say, move back to England. Or, which would be ideal for me, buy myself a little one-bedroom unit here, let it out and then come back if I want to come back if I could come back. But I could quite easily go and live outside Paris in a little village or something in France.

Here David's voice echoes the sentiments of flexible sojourners rather than staunch British patriots, but it also rests on a strong English identity, a direct outgrowth of his experience as a migrant.[29]

Celtic migrants express their homeland patriotism in both similar and contrasting ways to the English. Alf and Dorothy Floyd, for example, who came to Melbourne from Edinburgh in 1952, echoed the common resentment of the older generation of postwar migrants against pressure to take out Australian citizenship. No passports were required when they came, and, because they regarded themselves as citizens of the British Commonwealth, they insisted that they should automatically be Australian citizens. Alf described the letter he wrote to the Minister for Immigration. 'Having been out here when Ben Chifley was a prime minister, and I've contributed to taxes, and I've defended you against the Japanese, I should be made an honorary; if you don't like it! But there's no way I'm going to front up with some councillor or mayor and pay money.' These views resemble those of many English migrants who claim an old sense of citizenship entitlement from their British status. But in other respects Scots define themselves in Australia as migrants through their difference from the English. Alf and Dorothy, staunch Scottish patriots, albeit both with English fathers, have always bristled against the 'Pom' label, simply 'because we weren't Poms'. For Alf in the workplace this offered the opportunity to define himself as a good adaptable migrant, not simply against whingers 'who missed their pub and missed their football and missed this and missed that', but against the English explicitly; 'and I knew enough about Australians to stick, to be one of them. And I assimilated very quickly.' Over the years Alf and Dorothy continued to celebrate their Scottish loyalty; six years after their arrival they sent their 17-year-old daughter to live with her grandmother for a year to reinforce her Scottishness. But in retirement this now vies with their sense of belonging to Australia. Dorothy recalled that 'when we went back again, you know, we discovered that we'd said: "No, this is home! And this is where our roots are." So we loved always going back again, but — but we were always glad to get back, yes.'[30]

If pro-British patriotism can be complicated by Australian loyalties, robust pro-Australian identities are subject to similar qualifications, often discovered late in life, arising from British sentiments or attachments. We saw in the Introduction how John Cannon's passion for Australia began to be challenged by his rediscovery of a love for the English countryside after return visits later in life. But some of the most deeply felt enthusiasms among our informants emerged in descriptions of their growing love for Australia. The English–Tasmanian author Margaret Scott recounted her own experience of this passion of conversion; after lamenting the 'loss of the known' in her homeland, she recalled:

I was afraid that we would get trapped in Tasmania and never see our native shores again.... Where I went wrong was in imagining that I would remain perpetually miserable, sulky and homesick, persisting in disliking Tasmania as long as I remained upon its soil. Nowadays if anyone offered me a two-year stint in the land of my birth nothing on earth would induce me to live for an extended period in England again or, indeed, anywhere other than Tasmania which I have come to love with the intense – and, for others no doubt wearisome – passion of the convert.[31]

For the generation who emigrated soon after the war a 'conversion' to both love of country and patriotic commitment could be a prompt matter, especially for those, like Maurice Tomlin, who were attracted to Australia by the prospect of greater opportunity for skilled working-class men. The frustrations Maurice experienced in Birmingham at the hands of a still rigid class system were aggravated by a loveless home life and abuse by a stepmother, so it was easier for him to make a complete break with England. Today, while he admits still to being affected by the British national anthem and 'Jerusalem', his patriotism is reserved for Australia, his English origin not mattering 'one iota'. He described his first reaction on a return visit to England as 'Get me on the plane and get me home'. He supports an Australian republic and is proud of the fact that all his family are 'dyed-in-the-wool Australians'. Significantly, too, pride in his complete adoption of an Australian identity coexists with strong views in favour of the need for migrant assimilation generally. 'I don't have much time for the people who want to carry on their Yugoslavian way of life in Australia. If they want to be Australian then come … and be Australian.'[32]

Resentment of old British class distinctions does seem to be one of the most enduring influences among those who have committed themselves to both a whole-hearted Australian identity and relative hostility to Britain. Discussion of the British class system can bring migrants to reflect not simply on waning or waxing patriotisms, but on what it meant for them to become Australian, as much a shedding of Britishness as adoption of Australian characteristics. Shirley Kral, although from a middle-class background, still believed, after a return visit, that 'the class system, is, was still firmly in place', and coupled her conviction with the claim that 'Australia had given me the freedom to grow that I would never have had'. But this insight was slow to come. After her arrival in Sydney with her parents in 1953 at the age of 22, she was hesitant about Australia, especially what seemed to her a creeping Americanization. 'In those first years', she recalled, 'I did sometimes cling to an Englishness.' This was most evident in language, that hazardous terrain for migrants, where their difference from locals is often most exposed. 'I wanted to call things by their English name, like, you know those little grips women used to wear in their hair; it was a "Kirby grip", but here they called it a "bobby pin". And, there was that, within me a little antagonism about having to give up some of my language.' But looking back Shirley now celebrates her gradual adoption of a new identity.

What I think I've always liked from the very beginning, is a kind of relaxed friendliness. A willing to talk to you. And this is apart from gender issues. Australia has helped me to grow, to grow out of being English. And to drop those awful English habits of not speaking first, or wait till you're spoken to, or sitting for hours in a train and not conversing. — I can talk now at the drop of a hat. And I think this is a wonderful thing about Australia, is this easy acceptance of other people, until you're proved wrong.

Shirley's brother, Derek, who had come to Australia by himself in 1947, expressed similar views about social class and growing into an appreciation of

Australia. His early contacts with the hostile parents of a girlfriend, members of the 'squattocracy' (the rural land-owning upper class), shocked him into a fear that the British class system would be replicated in Australia. 'Gradually it dawned on me that, apart from my brush with the aristoc – the *squatt*ocracy – that Australia really was fairly egalitarian. But I wasn't very conscious of it. It gradually dawned on me I think.' It should come as no surprise that both Shirley and Derek are strong republicans, sharply critical – Shirley was 'shattered' – of the forces which combined to defeat the republic referendum.[33]

While these accounts underline the more uncompromising assertions of pro-British and pro-Australian identity and patriotism, few of them are free from qualification. Indeed, the more common stories are those which convey a mixed identity and imply the unfinished process of identity formation. Anne Barkas, who came to Sydney from South Shields in 1960, exemplifies the uncertainty which besets the feelings of numerous migrants when asked to declare their primary national loyalty. This perhaps reflects the continuing regrets of the bulk of migrants who leave family networks and childhood associations behind, while at the same time becoming increasingly committed to new contacts and comforts in Australia. Describing herself as a thorough-going 'Pom', and not remotely Australian, Anne explained this entirely in terms of loss of family and family disruption, for her children as much as herself. 'Parents, generations, yes. And then your, your life that you live, like grandmas, grandads, and that's one thing the kids miss going to when they come here, and they miss their grandmas and grandads.' Yet on reflection that emotional certainty was confounded by divided loyalties, more especially the kind stimulated by patriotic music. 'Well I, I think you're torn between, aren't you? … When I'm in England, I'm all for Australia. And I'm sure if I lived there and I heard "I Still Call Australia Home", it would break me heart! And then you hear, and you hear "Land of Hope and Glory", and then you could break your heart!' Here Anne gives expression to the emotional dilemma of the migrant identity, regretful about her own migration at the later age of 33 ('I think you settle better when you're younger') and thankful that her two sons, thoroughly Australian, won't 'go through that'. Yet in a further contradiction, Anne's loyalty to Britain, evident in her refusal to take out formal Australian citizenship, is confounded by her position on loyalty to the Crown. On the republic issue she declared, 'I think it's got to come. Like Canada and, I, I think it's got to be. We can't evade it, you know.' Anne's ambivalence, her preoccupation with family links over national loyalties, should remind us that the issues of political identity which consume the media are often matters of secondary importance in migrants' lives, and are always subject to modification.[34]

The ethnic mix: multiculturalism in an age of assimilation

The overwhelming bulk of our informants married within their British ethnicity. While we have encountered many in close contact with new non-English-speaking migrants at work and in the community – indeed there is evidence that postwar British migrants were more tolerant towards immigrants of other backgrounds than were native-born Australians[35] – few took these contacts as far as marriage. But some ethnically mixed marriages did occur, even in the relatively intolerant atmosphere of the 1950s and 1960s. A measure of the slight incidence of such marriages is suggested by the fact that out of 140 interviewees who stayed in Australia, only five married non-English-speaking migrants.[36] One of these, Dorothy Roman, married her Polish husband in England before migration. Interestingly, all these marriages involved British women with non-British husbands rather than the reverse; a further story,

38 Rosa Rance on the *Orcades* in April 1951. When she and her brother later went to Bondi Beach wearing similar home-made swimming costumes fashioned from 'leopard skin' material they were sent off the beach: 'our costumes were too brief for Sydney ... bikinis hadn't arrived in Australia'

from Linda Geerling, is of the daughter of a Polish father, whose sensitivity to harsh discrimination against the non-British was particularly acute.[37] All of them allow some insights into the influence of cross-cultural family experience on British migrant identity in Australia.

Rosa Hajinakitas (née Rance) was a 17-year-old Londoner in 1951, 'having too much of a good time in London' to want to emigrate.[38] Like her mother, she was a reluctant migrant, but her father was determined to take his family of four to Sydney, 'and as fathers were head of the house in 1951, we came'. Her father struggled to find suitable employment in their early years, and her mother was conscious of routine 'Pom bashing', but Rosa, employed in office work, thrived in Sydney's outdoor atmosphere and, despite her strict and controlling father, enjoyed the social life. Her youthful exuberance and moderate social defiance against 1950s norms spills out of her written and oral testimony. She went to dances each weekend at the 'Trocadero', which she kept secret from the office because 'a lot of foreigners used to frequent the dance hall and it didn't matter if you had a face like the "back of a bus", you could always get a dance. The men outnumbered the girls.' She also recalls being sent off the beach with her brother, wearing costumes she had made out of 'leopard skin' material; 'our costumes were too brief for Sydney ... bikinis hadn't arrived in Australia' (see Figure 38). Before long, through a Greek acquaintance from the *Orcades* voyage, Rosa befriended a Greek girl, visited her family regularly, and in time began to go out with her friend's older brother, Jim. Her parents made her wait until she was 21 before allowing her to marry Jim, but raised no objections on the ground of ethnic difference. Rosa, too, had experienced a multicultural social life in England, where she mixed with Indian and African students, and was relaxed about interethnic marriage. In a hint of things to come, 110 of the 130 wedding guests were Greek, and the British guests were acutely conscious of cultural difference: 'the majority of the Greek women were dressed in black, (things are different these days), like a row of black crows, someone said'.

Rosa reflects that the culture she married into was more patriarchal than what she had known, most evident in the scrutiny of those Greek women in black. When, after nine years of marriage, she finally gave birth – to a son – the long period of criticism dissolved – 'wasn't I in the good books'. And while she admits that she married a 'dominant man', she notes that this mirrored her mother's experience. The difference between her mother's marriage and her own, she observed, was that 'I always worked, my husband expected me to work.... And my father didn't expect my mother to work.' As we saw in Chapter 5, it was not at all unusual for British migrant wives to take employment, so we should not attach too much significance to the ethnic factors, but wives of non-British husbands themselves tend to see their plight as a product of their 'mixed' marriages.[39] Certainly for Rosa this meant long years of managing the 'dual role' of housework, entirely her responsibility, and employment. After twelve years of employment, Jim began a toolmaking business and Rosa then worked in the family business. Even overseas trips were dedicated to work. 'Whenever I went overseas with my husband I had to work hard all the time, you know trying to get trade and things like that.' At the same time she learnt the language and integrated into Jim's Greek culture. 'I could converse reasonably … was good at Greek dancing and cooking.'

Rosa's multicultural experience was, in some respects, sharply at odds with that of her British peers in Australia. But she fixes her experience in the conditions of the 1950s and 1960s, dominated by assimilationist practices, and a contrast with the multiculturalism of more recent years. She recalls that many of Jim's friends were Australians, and that his marriage 'out of their race', like that of his brothers, distanced them to some degree from ethnic concentration; 'we mixed lightly with the Greeks'. This leads her to reflect on the contrast between the old assimilation, which she approves, and the new multiculturalism.

You'll find that the old new Australians as we know them when we came out in the fifties, forties and the sixties, we'll all still vote for the Queen, to keep the Queen going. Because they came to Australia because they wanted that way of, I mean they are all foreigners you know we mix with, because they came to Australia for that way of life. OK, you will never get assimilation if they keep in their own groups.

As if to fulfil her vision, both her children married non-Greek Australians. And in wistful regret for her entire migrant experience, Rosa now speculates about the middle-class life in the neat houses of north London she might have enjoyed if she had stayed there. She regrets that it was 1982 before she revisited England, and tells her children that if they ever leave the country 'they must revisit Australia every three years or so'. 'I left when I and my cousins were teenagers and returned when we were all middle-aged. I regret those missed years.' Rosa's summary of her relative contentment encapsulates the contingent nature of migrant identity.

I'm happy I came to Australia. I've seen it develop from a 'behind the times' country to a modern, vibrant, easy going place. Our friends are a mixed bunch from different ethnic and social economic backgrounds. When my mother dies, she is now 94 years, I will only have my brother here. I know quite a few migrants who have no relative here. Although I love Australia, I think I could still live happily in England, providing I had central heating.… But I'm sure Jim would never leave Australia and all his family.

Rosa's benign attitude to ethnically mixed marriage is echoed in other cases, and reinforces the impression of migrants' adherence to assimilation practices in the 1950s and 1960s. Margaret Jabour (née Clarke), a 20-year-old Londoner when she came with her parents to Tasmania in 1950, married her Lebanese husband within eighteen months of arrival. For both Margaret and her family neither the migration experience nor her marriage were matters of great disruption or concern. Her father had been in the navy and the family were used to frequent moves, living on numerous naval stations, extending to Canada and New Zealand, during and after the war; in this respect the family had a marked 'modern' approach to their migration. Moreover, even before emigrating Margaret had been dating a Pakistani pilot in London. Her husband, too, who had come to Tasmania as a 9-year-old in 1929, had shed most of his Lebanese identity. He lost his orthodox Christianity largely because there were no suitable places to worship in Tasmania, and converted to Margaret's Catholicism shortly before his death. Margaret considers her marriage to have been affected by a more rigidly gendered division of labour because of his background; her realm, combined with employment, was the domestic, while 'the hard yakka was for the men'. But her experience did not differ radically from the female employment patterns we saw in Chapter 6. Probably the most dramatic impact of their mixed marriage was the discrimination their children experienced at school, where they were routinely subjected to 'wog' taunts. But today, Margaret, a widow, is more conscious of her mixed British and Australian identity. Australia – and more emphatically Tasmania – remains 'home', especially after return visits to England, though she remains uncertain about the republic issue and would prefer to maintain the link with the monarchy. She is now an active member of the British Residents in Tasmania Society, dedicated to maintaining British networks; this is in spite of her children's warning that 'If they're a bunch of whingeing Poms, Mum, I hope you walk out!'[40]

Margaret's experience with the British Residents in Tasmania Society has some parallels with the more politically active loyalty organizations we discussed earlier. She stresses her relatively easy adaptation in the 1950s because of her English background, but notes that for her fellow members today that has changed. In recent contact with the Ethnic Communities Council, she recalled, 'it was made very plain to me that … I was someone whose mother tongue was English and what's more I was Anglo-Saxon. Like it was a dirty word. And that I was accepted because my husband was Lebanese.' But she also underlined the ageing profile of her society's membership, and the way in which heightened awareness of the British connection can be a product of age and retirement, and not far removed from the experience of other migrant groups.

Well, I, I think the older you get the more important it becomes…. Yes, we've discovered that in this society, that you'll have a person who's had no, little or no affiliation with Britain; and, when they get older, or when they become widowed or widowered, they feel they want to be with people that have got some common thread, whether it be the north of England accent.... I mean you get the same in all the other communities, the Polish people, they might have spoken English all the time, but when they get over sixties they want to be with people that speak Polish. And we're finding that with the older British people, or British-*affiliated* people, they want to come back to the situation where they're hearing not, not say their *mother* tongue but the accent they heard when they were young.

None of this, Margaret hastens to add, is inconsistent with the members identifying Tasmania as 'home', most evident during a return visit. An Australian allegiance is deepened for her by the primary Australian commitment of her four children, who retain only casual interest in both their British and Lebanese backgrounds. For Margaret herself, though, an intimate connection with the non-English-speaking migrant world seems to have enhanced her awareness of carrying a migrant identity, a common condition of the British and non-British alike.

Later generations: migrant heritage and the fading attachment

The relative indifference of Margaret Jabour's children to their ethnic background raises the wider issue of the attitude of the second and third generations to their migrant heritage. Assimilationist ideology generally assumes a fading commitment of later generations to the migrant identity, and there are many illustrations of this among our informants. The Butts children, one born in England, one in Australia, both of whom 'don't even think about it', typify this attitude. We have not surveyed or interviewed Australian-born offspring directly, and their attitude to British heritage remains a subject for closer investigation. But Albert Lougher's good-humoured banter with his Australian-born children about being 'an old Pom' hints at the minor curiosity value a British heritage might carry for many descendants. In a similar vein Joyce Dalley laughed off the fact that 'our grandchildren call us aliens'. Sylvia and John Cannon, who prize the intimate relationship they still enjoy with their three Australian-born children, all married, spoke proudly of the children's ongoing interest in their parents' British backgrounds. All of them had hoped to attend the interview. But on reflection Sylvia and John concluded that this interest rarely extended beyond curiosity. John thought it was a 'massive gift' for him to be able to offer them the chance to become British citizens, and to have the convenience of European residence, but 'they're not interested, it's just water off ... they're happy here, they're contented here'. British heritage, Sylvia added, was simply something their children thought was 'cute and quaint and all that'. Indeed, the most routine references to continuing British connections of Australian-born children and grandchildren revolve around the travel convenience of British passports obtained through patriality provisions. This certainly has potential for strengthening connections when it results in the children enjoying working holidays, or something more enduring, in Britain. But the outcome in terms of British loyalties is invariably fragile, as Kathleen Barrand admits ruefully about her republican children, who care nothing for their British heritage.[41]

Many of our informants were young children or adolescents when they moved to Australia with their parents, and their attitudes to national identity today are as varied as their life stories and those of their parents. One of the most common patterns at the moment of migration, of course, is that of the reluctant teenage migrant, sullen and resistant to the parents' determination to emigrate 'for the sake of the children'; while this is more common among girls, it is not exclusive to them. Most commonly it sprang from forcible removal from close friends, family and social life at a crucially formative moment – as we have seen in the story of Janet Francis. But there is no easy equation between initial adolescent hostility to Australia and adult loyalties in later life. Jackie Smith's intense hostility to Australia in 1959 as a 13-year-old, which we saw in Chapter 7, was matched by her passionate attachment to Australia forty-five years later, long after she moved on to Canada. The bitterness provoked by losing her comforting network of extended family and friends in London and the breakdown of her family's intimacy in Adelaide was eventually overcome and transformed, as she now describes it, into a passionate sense of belonging to the land.

You know, there's something about the *land*. The sense … the sense of the land, which, you know, the sense of space…. I did gel there, you know. I became very happy. And … I really loved the land there … and then the sense of being near the ocean, as well, you know, even though Elizabeth was not that close to the ocean, but here in Toronto, when I first came here I was *desperate* to get to the sea.

The strength of these sentiments might well be increased by absence, but after three decades of prosperous life in Canada Jackie continues to identify primarily as Australian. Most significantly, her dilemma of being 'torn' between two loyalties relates only to Australia and Canada. 'I don't identify as English at all, I identify, I actually identify as Australian…. I left there when I was 13, I don't know what it is to be English.' This is, for Jackie, the permanent essence of the dilemma of a migrant identity.[42]

Jackie Smith's robust Australianness is counterbalanced by the ambivalence of those of the younger generation who have long pondered the wisdom of their parents' decision to emigrate. We saw an example of this in Chapter 7 with Ron Benson, whose resentment at being removed from his Durham soccer passions in 1959 never fully faded, despite business success and close community involvement in Perth. His thorough commitment to life in Perth coexists with an avowed mixed identity: a periodic yearning for England, a firm commitment to monarchism and uncertainty about where the best place might be to live. In a jocular reference to the weather, Ron articulated his ambivalence along with the common dream of spending summer in both countries, but with a significant twist, reversing the customary regional loyalty of older migrants. 'June till September, it would just be fantastic, you know. But I couldn't live where I came from; I'd want to be, you know, Surrey or, or Kent, or Hampshire or down on the south, on the south coast … it would be nice to be able to go there and live there for three months of the year.'[43]

Regional British loyalties seem to be less subject to this sort of 'fickleness' among the Scots and Welsh, but here too the sense that national loyalty and belonging is a thing in flux, never final, is as powerful as with the English. Maureen Carter, 19 when she came to Sydney among a Welsh family of ten children in 1964, is still prone to declare her Welsh identity whenever she is taunted as a 'Pom'. 'I get very angry today, even, if somebody calls me a "Pom".… I say, through gritted teeth, "I'm Welsh".… People in Australia don't think of Wales. So my mission is to educate people who call me a Pom, and I'm from that little country on the left.' In other respects her loyalty is proudly Australian, her verdict on migration ultimately that of a 'big success story, because I don't have that "hiraeth", the Welsh for longing, which I had when I left Wales, for so long'. While her parents never took out Australian citizenship, convinced that it would be 'doing the wrong thing by their country of birth', once Maureen visited Wales in 1984 she decided that her 'home' was Australia, and citizenship a natural consequence. 'I saw it in a different light, you know, I saw it as paying my dues, sort of thing, honouring my new country.' Yet now that her children travel and at times reside in Europe and Britain and she visits more frequently, 'it's actually growing, rather than shrinking, because of my children's contacts'.[44]

David Wills, a 12-year-old when he emigrated with his parents from Edinburgh to Hobart in 1950, promptly shifted his loyalty from Scotland to Australia. Unlike his parents, who were resistant to formal citizenship, 'I always denied, through my compliance and change of accent, denied my Scottishness.' But over the years this identity has been subject to uncertainty. 'It is only in recent years', he reflected, 'that I am almost beginning to take some degree of interest in, not quite pride, but bordering on pride, of my Scottish heritage.' This has accompanied his sympathy for Scottish nationalism and independence, just as he supports an Australian republic. He described being 'very choked up, very emotional' on his first visit to Edinburgh: 'I stood in Princes Street and I thought: "I'm home. I'm home." I didn't want to go back to anywhere. Never at all.' Yet, a short time later, 'the next time I went back, no, it was different. I didn't feel that same inflection.'[45]

Margaret Reardon (née Docherty), whose story we have already encountered, brings a fitting conclusion to this scrutiny of British-Australian
migrant identities.[46] Margaret conformed perfectly to the mould of the reluctant teenage migrant in 1951 when she arrived in Sydney from Edinburgh
with her family at the age of 16 (see Figure 39). The family's early difficulties
with employment and housing reinforced the hostility of both Margaret and
her father to the move, and in response each nurtured their pride in their
Scottish heritage. But over the years this moderated for both of them into
recognition of the profound benefits conferred on the family by Mrs Docherty's
courageous move. As Margaret tells it the migrant saga was expressly her
mother's, but Mrs Docherty's emphatic loyalty to Australia gradually infected
the family sceptics. In one of those defining moments of migrant remembering, Margaret recalls the night in 1971 of her family's celebration of the
twentieth anniversary of their arrival, complete with the Australian extended
family of spouses and grandchildren (see Figure 40). Her mother, dressed
impeccably for the occasion, enjoyed the limelight.

She just looked absolutely radiant, and so happy. I thought, how could you, you
couldn't possibly grudge her, or be awful about this happiness that she's got, you
know. And, I mean even Dad looked happy beside her … the happiness was
spilling out over on to him. And she said, 'Well — we had our difficulties.' She
actually made the speech — which I thought was, she was ahead of her time. She
actually, you know, Dad was supposed to say a few words, but she actually said,
'Well, I'd like to say something', you know. And she said — 'We had our difficulties,
but,' she said, 'we would have had them in Edinburgh, and maybe more so, but,'
she said, 'when I look around the table tonight', she said, 'it's all been worthwhile,
really worthwhile'. And she looked across at me, and I was looking at her, and she
gave me this, she just winked at me, across the table [laughs] as much as to say,
'Now come on, you've got to admit it'.[47]

The sight of Edinburgh Castle on Margaret's return visit brought tears
to her eyes; like her father, she retains a deep pride in her Scottish heritage,
although this is little more than a curiosity to her own children.[48] But her
reflections about identity and loyalty now focus more on her attachment to
Australia, and the remembering of her parents' history remains central to this
part of her story. Margaret's mother, while proud of her Scottishness, 'gave
total commitment to her decision', accepting the common view that 'assimilation and integration was the natural follow on from migration'. Her father's
views remained more complex; always a Scot first, he nevertheless accom-
modated to a migrant identity in the context of commitment to his wife and
family. In Margaret's explanation his commitment was symbolic of the
general contribution of the postwar generation of British migrants to Australia.

39 The Docherty family in Aden market place, 1951. Mr Docherty and his teenage daughter Margaret had been reluctant to leave Edinburgh, but Catherine Docherty, matriarch of the family, was determined to get to Australia

40 Catherine Docherty in 1971, dressed specially for the occasion of her family's twentieth anniversary celebration of their arrival in Australia: 'She just looked absolutely radiant, and so happy. I thought, how could you, you couldn't possible grudge her, or be awful about this happiness that she's got'

My father did not take out Australian citizenship – not because he had anything against being known as an Australian citizen – he just had an intense love and loyalty to his Scottish birthplace. The only reason he was in Australia was because he thought it was the place where he should be – with his family – to give us the opportunity to have an even better life than the one we had left behind. Though he was a 'reluctant migrant' he worked hard, obeyed the laws and helped my mother keep a stable home environment for his family. In this way he contributed, as so many other British migrants, like a small cog maintaining and encouraging stability to the betterment of the whole of Australian society.[49]

During this last half century when the British influence in Australia has been notable for its dilution rather than its explicit contribution, Margaret Reardon points to the common migrant commitment of her parents, along with those from other national backgrounds, as the abiding British contribution to their new country. This was symbolized for her by the emotionally affecting ceremony of Australia Day, 1999, when the 'Migrant Wall' – a huge plaque naming several thousand postwar migrants from different national backgrounds – was opened officially by the governor-general in Darling Harbour. The event was a classic multicultural moment, with 'fifty children of the world' in national dress signifying Australia's celebration of national unity in ethnic diversity. 'How proud my parents would have been, as we were,' Margaret wrote, 'to see the clan tartans very prevalent in the parade.' Her own pride was embodied in the Docherty parents' names on the plaque, a testament to their heroic migrant stories, despite the fact that husband and wife carried sharply different migrant identities with them during their long years in Australia.

Peoples from many Lands were gathered as one Nationality – and cheered in unison as one flag, the Australia Flag, was saluted and raised high for everyone to acknowledge. I felt proud that with my sisters' unhesitating encouragement and co-operation when I first broached the idea, I had been able to add my parents' names indelibly to what, I believe, will become an important Australian icon for the future. We had honoured our mother and father in a unique and fitting manner – just as a Lady and Gentleman should be – with class. Ironically their names are on Panel Three, facing directly opposite the dock where the *New Australia* arrived at Piermont, bringing the Dochertys to Australia for the first time, in June 1951.[50]

Margaret's narrative of the diverse ways migration affected her family's fortunes embodies a range of different identities which, at different times, revealed the transformative and fluctuating effects of migration on each family member. Her own teenage resistance evolved into pride in her parents' courage and risk-taking. Her mother, the 'heroine' of her story, stands as a woman 'ahead of her time', explicitly managing and speaking for the family welfare, but also a proud new Australian dedicated to assimilation. Her father's stubborn reluctance and attachment to his birthplace evolved into a recognition shared with his wife of the benefits of her initiative, all the while balancing an abiding Scottish patriotism. Like all migrant identities these were unstable and shifting, never complete, and in Margaret's case the national recognition of the Migrant Wall commemoration has no doubt added a further dimension to her migration story. These rich and complex identities, perhaps, are the point at which British migrants share most, with migrants from other backgrounds, the lifelong effects of migration. The life histories of British Australians, in this respect, are as instructive and powerful as the more visible stories of their ethnically diverse counterparts.

Notes

1 Curthoys, 'Identity Crisis', p. 167. See also Price, *Australian National Identity*.
2 Among an extensive literature, see, for example, Colls, *Identity of England*.
3 Curthoys, 'Expulsion, Exodus and Exile in White Australian Historical Mythology', p. 3.
4 Unless otherwise noted all references derive from the interview with Ron Penn LU.
5 Penn, 'Additional Comments', 24 February 2003, LU.
6 *Forward* (Chiswick Products Ltd), Winter 1953, pp. 84–6, LU.
7 Penn, 'Additional Comments'.
8 *Ibid.*
9 *Ibid.*
10 *Ibid.*
11 The main texts are Stratton, 'Not Just Another Multicultural Story', and Brabazon, *Tracking the Jack*.
12 Stratton, 'Not Just Another Multicultural Story', pp. 38 and 34.
13 Geoffrey Partington, 'The English in Australia', *Adelaide Review*, April 1999, p. 16, quoted in *ibid.*, p. 38.
14 Brabazon, *Tracking the Jack*, p. 13; Stratton, 'Not Just Another Multicultural Story', p. 27.
15 Brabazon, *Tracking the Jack*, pp. 125–37; Stratton, 'Not Just Another Multicultural Story', p. 41.
16 See the UKSA website at www.geocities.com/endeavour_uksa/uksa.html. For discussion see Stratton, 'Not Just Another Multicultural Story', pp. 39–40, and UKSA quarterly newsletter, *Endeavour*: October–November 2001, pp. 12–14; 'Psst! An Anglophobe at Work', August–September 2001, pp. 1–2.
17 Stratton, 'Not Just Another Multicultural Story', pp. 45–7. Despite their undoubted popularity, insurance costs have recently placed their continuance in jeopardy; the 2002 Melbourne Britfest was cancelled for this reason: www.geocities.com/endeavour_uksa/brit2000.html; 'UKSA has a patron!', *Endeavour*, April–May 2002, p. 3.
18 Hill interview LU; Pickett interview US; Lougher interview LU.
19 Fairbairn interview LU; Hamilton interview LU; McClellan interview LU; Mitchell interview LU; Ivor Miller interview LU. See also Margaret Jabour's story of the British Residents in Tasmania Society, discussed below.
20 Hoare interview LU; Doig interview LU.

21 Jupp, *Arrivals and Departures*, p. 40.
22 Letter from Barrie Hunt, president, UKSA, to Hammerton, 31 March 2003.
23 Manoy interview LU; Adam interview LU; Wall interview LU; Carruthers interview LU.
24 Tilley interview LU; Jay interview LU; Campbell interview LU; Rowe interview LU. On Mancunian loyalties see also: Hill interview LU; Pickett interview US.
25 All references in this section derive from the interview with Patricia Drohan LU.
26 James Jupp's pre-1999 research ('Post-War English Settlers in Adelaide and Perth') indicated clear monarchical sympathies among the English-born residents of the South Australian electorates of Canning and Bonython, both with substantial British immigrant populations. Jupp has since noted ('From New Britannia to Foreign Power') the comparatively low republican vote in electorates with a high proportion of British-born constituents.
27 Bailey interview LU; Proverbs interview LU.
28 Barrand interview LU.
29 Bailey interview LU.
30 Floyd interview LU.
31 Scott, *Changing Countries*, p. 12.
32 Tomlin interview LU.
33 Kral and Wrigley interview LU.
34 Barkas interview LU.
35 Jupp, *Australian People*, p. 320.
36 There are two further cases in the written files of English women married to Dutch men.
37 Roman interview LU; Geerling interview LU.
38 The following discussion is based on the interview with Rosa Hajinakitas and her letter to the BBC, 20 December 1996, LU.
39 See Kral and Wrigley interview LU; and, by contrast, Weisinger interview LU.
40 Margaret Jabour interview LU.
41 Butts interview LU; Lougher interview LU; Dalley interview LU; Cannon interview LU; Anderson interview LU; Weisinger interview LU; Barrand interview LU.
42 Jackie Smith interview LU.
43 Benson interview LU.
44 Carter interview LU.
45 Wills interview LU.
46 See chapters 2 and 7. Unless otherwise noted, all references derive from the interview with Reardon, LU.
47 Interview with Margaret Reardon, ABC *Hindsight* programme, 'Ten Pound Poms', Radio National, 19 August 2001.
48 *Ibid.*
49 Written addendum to project interview added by Margaret Reardon.
50 *Ibid.*

Appendix: Statistical summary of project interviews

The following tables provide a statistical summary of the interviews conducted by the teams based at La Trobe University and the University of Sussex. The first two tables refer to total number of interviewees – 181 interviewees, comprising 140 recorded in Australia and 41 recorded in Britain. In Tables A.3–A.7 members of the same family are included within one family unit, with a total of 150 families comprising 119 recorded in Australia and 31 recorded in Britain. All figures are percentages, rounded off to two decimal places where necessary.

Each table also includes a comparison with appropriate and available statistics, including government records and Reg Appleyard's random sample of 20 per cent of assisted British emigrants to Australia in a six-month period in 1959, as detailed in Appleyard's 1964 publication *British Emigration to Australia*.

Table A.1 Gender of interviewees

	La Trobe–Sussex project (%)	Assisted British immigrants 1947–60 (%)	UK home population 30.6.1958 (%)
Male	36.5	53.4	48.2
Female	63.5	46.6	51.8

Note: the higher proportion of females recorded by our project may be due to a combination of female longevity and the propensity for women to come forward more readily for life history projects.
Source: Appleyard, *British Emigration to Australia*, p. 120.

Table A.2 Age on departure

Age	La Trobe-Sussex project (%)	Assisted British immigrants 1947–60 (%)	UK home population 30.6.1958 (%)
0–9	6.08	22.98	15.24
10–14	11.6	9.17	8.07
15–19	9.94	6.45	6.43
20–29	44.2	23.96	12.7
30–39	24.31	21.37	14.07
40–49	3.31	10.63	13.81
50+	0.56	5.25	29.68
Not stated		0.12	

Note: our sample under-represents very young child emigrants (who may be less likely to have clear, detailed memories of their emigration) and emigrants aged over 40 (who are less likely to be alive and available for interview) and over-represents emigrants in their twenties.
Source: Appleyard, *British Emigration to Australia*, p. 120.

Table A.3 Mode of assistance

	La Trobe-Sussex project (%)	Appleyard emigrant sample (1959) (%)
Commonwealth nominee	40	50.11
Personal nominee	42.67	43.62
Employer sponsored	17.33	6.27

Note: in our interviews we sought to ascertain the mode of emigration assistance as accurately as possible, but it may be that some interviewees mistakenly remembered an employer who indicated the availability of work in Australia (but did not provide formal sponsorship) as being as sponsor, and have caused us to over-state that category.
Source: Appleyard, *British Emigration to Australia*, p. 152.

Table A.4 Period of departure

	La Trobe–Sussex project interviews (%)	Sussex project written accounts (%)	UK assisted emigrants to Australia (%)
1945–9	17.33	7.36	7
1950–9	52.67	31.6	24.32
1960–9	26	49.78	48.93
1970+	4	11.26	19.75

Note: our interviews over-represent the earlier decades of British–Australian migration and under-represent the later decades, in part because we were keen to record the stories of the first generation of migrants before it was too late. This imbalance is offset by the written accounts received by the Sussex project from members of 231 migrants families who returned from Australia, for whom statistics for the decade of departure from Britain more closely match the overall picture.
Source: See Table 1, p. 32; Appleyard, *The Ten Pound Immigrants*, p. 160.

Table A.5 Family status at departure

	La Trobe–Sussex project (%)	Total assisted British emigrants to Australia 1955–60 (%)
Families with children	60.67	71.9
Families without children	14.67	11.7
Single adults	24.67	16.4

Source: Appleyard, *British Emigration to Australia*, p. 122.

Table A.6 British region of origin

	La Trobe–Sussex project (%)	Appleyard emigrant sample (1959) (%)	UK home population population 1958 (%)
Scotland	18.67	13.66	10.29
Wales	2.67	2.78	5.2
South Western	4.67	6.89	6.18
Southern	4.67	7.09	5.78
London & South Eastern	36	21.98	21.89
Midlands	10.67	7.71	9.16
North Midlands	5.33	6.43	7.02
Eastern	2.67	7.42	6.99
North Western	12	13.02	12.9
Yorkshire (East & West Ridings)	1.33	7.05	8.22
Northern	1.33	5.97	6.37

Note: to plot the regional origin of our interviewees we used the same categories for Scotland, Wales and the English regions as used by Appleyard and defined in the Registrar General's *Annual Estimates of the Population of England and Wales* (1958). By comparison with Appleyard's snapshot sample of emigrants in 1959 our interviews over-represent London and the south east and, to a lesser extent, Scotland.
Source: Appleyard, *British Emigration to Australia*, p. 115.

Table A.7 Social class at departure

	La Trobe–Sussex project (%)	Appleyard emigrant sample (1959) (%)	UK home population 1951 census (%)
Professional (I)	6.67	2.9	3.2
Semi-professional (II)	23.33	9.1	14.3
Skilled (III)	60	68.2	52.9
Semi-skilled (IV)	6	13.7	16.5
Unskilled (V)	4	6.1	13.1

Note: to define social class at the point of emigration for our interviewees we used the same categories as used by Appleyard and listed in the occupation tables for the 1951 England and Wales census. Note that social class and occupation statistics in the census and Appleyard's sample refer only to males aged 15 years and over. Our own project statistics include single women workers, and the significant number of nurses and teachers amongst single women workers explains the higher proportion of 'semi-professionals' amongst our interviewees.
Source: Appleyard, *British Emigration to Australia*, p. 126.

Bibliography

Archival sources – personal testimony

Battye Library of West Australian History (Perth), Oral History Collection

Bloomfield, Michael and Janet, interview conducted by Bill Bunbury, July 1984, OH 1190ts.
Eadon-Clarke, Charles, 'The World is So Full: A Biography', OH 2675/ttr.
Good, Clifford and Gwendoline, audio tapes and recorded radio talks, OH 1733ts.
Jolley, Elizabeth, interview recorded by Stuart Reid, May–June 1989, OH 2268.
Murphy, Kevin, interview recorded by Theresa Murphy, July 1990, OH 2366/9ts.
Nicholls, Nora Lily, interview and letter, OH 1739.
Thomson, Ian, interview recorded by W. L. Simm for the Harvey Oral History Group, 9.8.1995, OH 2782.

La Trobe University Archive (Melbourne), British Migration Collection

Interviews
(All interviews were conducted by Jim Hammerton unless indicated in brackets.)

Adam, George, Rockingham, WA, 23.3.2000, LU 0003.
Amor, Peggy, Budgewoi, NSW, 19.6.1999, LU 0012.
Anderson, Virgina and George, Scarborough, WA, 12.4.1999, LU 0014.
Armstrong, Daphne, Sandringham, Vic., 29.07.98, LU 0021 (Catherine Coleborne).
Atkinson, Brian, Viewbank, Vic., 17.3.1999, LU 0026 (Helen Gardner).
Bailey, David, Hurstville Grove, NSW, 26.5.1998, LU 0033.
Barkas, Annie, Caringbah, NSW, 8.7.1998, LU 0048.
Barnet, Leslie, Revesby, NSW, 6.6.1998, LU 0050.
Barnett, Joyce, Yokine, WA, 9.3.2000, LU 0051 (Criena Fitzgerald).
Barrand, Kathleen, Hamlyn Heights, Vic., 14.4.2000, LU 0052.
Bate, Gordon, Forest Hill, Vic., 22.3.1999, LU 0053 (Helen Gardner).
Bell, Josephine, Seaford, Vic., 12.4.2000, LU 0060JB (Carole Hamilton-Barwick).
Benson, Ronald, Como, WA, 25.3.2000, LU 0068.
Blackburne, Josephine, Scarborough, WA, 10.4.1999, LU 0076.
Blackmore, Richard and Josephine, Sydney, 17.6.1999, LU 0078.
Bland, Diane, Belmont North, NSW, 21.6.1999, LU 0080.
Bliss, Angela, Sydenham, Vic., 15.9.1998, LU 0081 (Catherine Coleborne).
Boobyer, Maurice, Paddington, NSW, 7.7.1998, LU 0087.
Bradley, Catherine and William, Spearwood, WA, 28.3.2000, LU 0093.
Britton, Joan, Nollamara, WA, 29.3.2000, LU 0103 (Carole Hamilton-Barwick).
Brown, Josephine, Wantirna, Vic., 31.8.1998, LU 0111 (Catherine Coleborne).
Burgess, Robert and Phyllis, Footscray, Vic., 11.11.1999, LU 0122 (Keith Pescod).
Butts, Maureen and John, Waikiki, WA, 27.3.2000, LU 0134.
Calder, Margaret and John, Fremantle, WA, 21.3.2000 and 24.3.2000, LU 0137–8 (Criena Fitzgerald).

Calver, Primrose, Duncraig, WA, 28.3.2000, LU 0140 (Carole Hamilton-Barwick).
Campbell, Joan, North Sydney, NSW, 6.12.1999, LU 0142 (Michelle Arrow).
Campbell, Maggie, Mosman, NSW, 14.7.1998, LU 0143.
Cannon, Sylvia and John, Mount Pleasant, WA, 26.3.2000, LU 0144.
Carr, Maureen, Beacon Hill, NSW, 13.7.1998, LU 0151.
Carruthers, Eddie, Nollamara, WA, 4.8.1999, LU 0154 (Criena Fitzgerald).
Carruthers, Patsy, Nollamara, WA, 25.10.1999, LU 0154a (Criena Fitzgerald).
Carter, Maureen, Picnic Point, NSW, 9.7.1998, LU 0157.
Chatwood, Ruth, Mount Waverley, Vic., 5.11.1998, LU 0169 (Catherine Coleborne).
Clark, John, Croydon Park, SA, 27.9.1998, LU 0175.
Clayton, Mary, Innaloo, WA, 15.9.1999 and 22.9.1999, LU 0180 (Criena Fitzgerald).
Clayton, Terry, Innaloo, WA, 11.11.1999, LU 0180a (Criena Fitzgerald).
Collins, Sylvia, Marburg, Qld, 26.6.1998, LU 0130SC (Carole Hamilton-Barwick).
Cook, Alfred and Winfred, Lindisfarne, Tas., 14.7.2001, LU 0197.
Coventry, Madge, Burleigh, Qld, 23.6.1998, LU 0139MC (Carole Hamilton-Barwick).
Cragg, Emily, Hillarys, WA, 3.10.998, LU 0215 (Carole Hamilton-Barwick).
Crowley, Harold, Mandurah, WA, 24.3.2000, LU 0222.
Curtis, Margaret, Victoria Point, Qld, 9.9.2000, LU 0224 (Carole Hamilton-Barwick).
Dalley, Les and Joyce, Raymond Terrace, NSW, 20.6.1999, LU 0228.
Davies, Mifwany (pseudonym), St Morris, SA, 11.7.2000, LU 1053 (Carole Hamilton-Barwick).
Davies, Rhiannon, Chifley, ACT, 19.5.2000, LU 0233.
Davis, Bunty, Caulfield, Vic., 11.8.1998, LU 0234 (Catherine Coleborne).
Dawkins, Peter, Potts Point, NSW, 27.11.1999, LU 0236 (Michelle Arrow).
Dingle, Margaret, Norwood, SA, 11.7.2000, LU 0253 (Carole Hamilton-Barwick).
Doig, Barbara, Kincumber, NSW, 18.6.1999, LU 0257.
Drohan, Patricia Ballarat, Vic., 13.8.1998, LU 0262 (Catherine Coleborne).
Emery, Joyce, Hamilton Hill, WA, 28.3.2000, LU 0274 (Carole Hamilton-Barwick).
Fairbairn, Eileen and John, Rowville, Vic., 22.2.2000, LU 0284 (Helen Gardner).
Floyd, Alf and Dorothy, Tecoma, Vic., 24.3.1999, LU 0301 (Helen Gardner).
Foster, Marjorie and Dave, Bedfordale, WA, 27.3.2000, LU 0309 (Carole Hamilton-Barwick).
Fowler, Terence, Roseville, NSW, 23.6.1999, LU 0311.
Frost, Jessie, Mornington, Vic., 9.12.1998, LU 0320 (Catherine Coleborne).
Geerling, Linda, Wantirna, Vic., 30.7.1998, LU 0331 (Catherine Coleborne).
Gempton, Elizabeth, Coominya, Qld, 6.9.2000, LU 0332 (Carole Hamilton-Barwick).
Gifford, Margaret, Parkwood, WA, 29.3.2000, LU 0339 (Carole Hamilton-Barwick).
Gittins, Graham, Dickson, ACT, 22.5.2000, LU 0344.
Gray, Gwynneth, Hallett Cove, SA, 28.9.1998, LU 0362.
Grimes, Doreen, Epping, Vic., 14.7.1998 and 17.7.1998, LU 0373 (Catherine Coleborne).
Gursanscky, Pamela, Clifton Springs, Vic., 13.2.2000, LU 0377.
Hajinakitas, Rosa, Dundas, NSW, 16.6.1999, LU 0378.
Hallas, Dot, Mount Waverley, Vic., 27.8.1998, LU 0002 (Catherine Coleborne).
Hamilton, Mildred, Chadstone, Vic., 19.8.1998, LU 0383 (Catherine Coleborne).
Hedges, Leslie, Claremont, Tas., 25.9.1999, LU 0410.
Hewitt, Pat, Traralgon, Vic., 23.11.1998, LU0417 (Catherine Coleborne).
Hill, Margaret Chelsea, Vic., 11.9.1998, LU 0423 (Catherine Coleborne).
Hoare, Yvonne, Coogee, NSW, 24.8.1999, LU 0428 (Michelle Arrow).
Howell, John, Apollo Bay, Vic., 12.2.2000, LU 0444.
Hoyle, Audrey, East Doncaster, Vic., 8.7.1998, LU 0447 (Catherine Coleborne).

Hurst, Rosemary, Sandy Bay, Tas., 2.10.1999, LU 0458.

Jabour, Margaret, Claremont, Tas., 28.9.1999, LU 0466.

Jackson, Patricia, Nambour, Qld, 4.9.2000, LU 0469 (Carole Hamilton-Barwick).

Jaggs, Donnella, Heidelberg, Vic., 30.7.1998, LU 0501DJ (Carole Hamilton-Barwick).

Jay, Wendy, Rivett, ACT, 21.5.2000, LU 0475.

Jennings, Audrey, Flinders Park, SA, 8.7.2000, LU 0477 (Carole Hamilton-Barwick).

Joliffe, Vera, Berwick, Vic., 6.12.2000, LU 0528VJ (Carole Hamilton-Barwick).

Kemp, Frank, Deer Park, Vic., 12.6.1999, LU 0491 (Helen Gardner).

Kendall, Cynthia, Mount Yokine, WA, 28.9.1998, LU 0492 (Carole Hamilton-Barwick).

Kevan, Norah, Aspendale, Vic., 8.9.1998, LU 0496 (Catherine Coleborne).

Knights, Daphne, Purley, Surrey, England, 24.6.2000, LU 0506DK.

Kral, Shirley, and Wrigley, Derek, Pearce, ACT, 20.5.2000, LU 0512.

Ledgett, Ethel, Chatswood, NSW, 8.6.1998, LU 0522.

Logie, William, Narre Warren, Vic., 29.3.1999, LU 0537 (Helen Gardner).

Lougher, Albert and Anne, Balgowlah, NSW, 22.6.1999, LU 0544.

Lowe, Vivienne, Richmond, Vic., 16.6.1998, LU 0546 (Catherine Coleborne).

McCarthy, Noreen, Kooyong, Vic., 16.7.1998, LU 0554 (Catherine Coleborne).

McClellan, Margaret, South Lake, WA, 2.10.1998, LU 0556 (Carole Hamilton-Barwick).

MacDonald, Richard, Rozelle, NSW, 10.7.1998, LU 0585.

McGregor, Mary, Padbury, WA, 1.10.1998, LU 0567 (Carole Hamilton-Barwick).

McGregor, Muriel, Belmont, Vic., 11.2.2000, LU 0568.

McHugh, Margaret, Yass, NSW, 11.7.1998, LU 0570.

Makewell, Vera and Bernard, Newport, NSW, 13.7.1998, LU 0595.

Manoy, Grahame, Scarborough, WA, 8.4.1999, LU 0599.

Martin, Elizabeth, Goorambat, Vic., 8.1.2000, LU 600EM.

Mascall, Peter, Bentley, WA, 27.5.2000, LU 0608 (Criena Fitzgerald).

Middlemiss, Frances and Robert, Ashington, England, 22.1.1999, LU 620FM.

Miller, George and Madge, Northmead, NSW, 28.2.2000, LU 0624 (Michelle Arrow).

Miller, Ivor, Watsonia, Vic., 1.7.1998, LU 0625.

Mitchell, Joan, McKinnon, Vic., 28.7.1998, LU 0629 (Catherine Coleborne).

Monks, Margaret, Chirnside Park, Vic., 22.10.1998, LU 0630 (Catherine Coleborne).

Morphett, Sheila, Elgin, Scotland, 16.1.1999, LU 0637.

Mungeam, Kathleen (pseudonym), Bassendean, WA, 30.3.2000, LU 0214 (Carole Hamilton-Barwick).

Newton-Barnett, Valerie, Scarborough, WA, 11.4.1999, LU 0661.

Noyce, Daphne, Marion, SA, 10.7.2000, LU 0668 (Carole Hamilton-Barwick).

Oakley, Eve, Williamstown, Vic., 3.6.1998, LU 0753EO (Carole Hamilton-Barwick).

Olliff, Roy, Balwyn, Vic., 15.4.2000, LU 0675 (Helen Gardner).

Paul, Jeanne, Prahran, Vic., 22.6.1998, LU 0703 (Catherine Coleborne).

Penn, Ron, Revesby, NSW, 6.6.1998, LU 0713.

Platt, Margaret, Frankston, Vic., 14.12.1998, LU 0726 (Catherine Coleborne).

Pluis, Bridget, Yass, NSW, 12.7.1998, LU 0727.

Pollitt, Jean, Marion, SA, 10.7.2000, LU 0729 (Carole Hamilton-Barwick).

Proverbs, Valerie, Templestowe, Vic., 18.6.1998, LU 0737 (Catherine Coleborne).

Reardon, Margaret, Gundagai, NSW, 12.7.1998, LU 0743.

Richardson, Marjorie, Malvern, Vic., 12.10.2001, LU 0921MR (Carole Hamilton-Barwick).

Roman, Dorothy and Adam, Tullamarine, Vic., 14.8.1998, LU 0767 (Catherine Coleborne).

Rowe, Kate, Petersham, NSW, 12.10.1999, LU 0773 (Michelle Arrow).

Rumsey, David, St Ives, NSW, 18.1.2000, LU 0777.

Sanders, Jim, Wheelers Hill, Vic., 29.2.2000, LU 0786 (Helen Gardner).

Sanders, Kathleen, North Sunshine, Vic., 9.12.1998, LU 0787 (Catherine Coleborne).
Seymour, Vanessa, Mount Stuart, Tas., 27.9.1999, LU 0810.
Simmons, Betty (pseudonym), SA, 29.9.1998, LU.
Simmons, Vida, South Traralgon, Vic., 22.11.1998, LU 0823 (Catherine Coleborne).
Smith, Alan and Joy, Mulgrave, Vic., 21.2.2000, LU 0832 (Helen Gardner).
Smith, Betty, Howrah, Tas., 26.9.1999, LU 0833.
Smith, Jackie, Toronto, Canada, 1.7.2000, LU CS50.
Stringer, Janet, Greenwood, WA, 7.10.1999 and 14.10.1999, LU 0871 (Criena Fitzgerald).
Thomas, Mary, North Hobart, Tas., 13.7.2001, LU 0893.
Tilley, Betty, Ballajura, WA, 9.4.1999, LU 0902.
Tomlin, Maurice, Midland, WA, 9.4.1999, LU 0906.
Turnbull, Grace, East Doncaster, Vic., 3.8.1998, LU 0920 (Catherine Coleborne).
Turnbull, Peter, Mosman, NSW, 19.1.2000, LU 0921.
Wadland, Basil, Mount Waverley, Vic., 28.2.2000, LU 0936 (Helen Gardner).
Walker, Tom and Beryl, Scarborough, WA, 13.4.1999, LU 0940.
Wall, Patricia, Lyons, ACT, 18.5.2000, LU 0944.
Walton, Ruby, Berwick, Vic., 1.5.1999, 1.3.2000 and 1.5.2000, LU 1105RW (Carole Hamilton-Barwick).
Ward, Brian and Connie, Ashburton, Vic., 7.3.2000, LU 0950 (Helen Gardner).
Watton, May, Eumemmerring, Vic., 2.6.1998, LU 1110MW (Carole Hamilton-Barwick).
Watts, Christopher, Chiswick, NSW, 7.61998, LU 0965.
Wayman, Elspeth, Bondi, NSW, 15.9.1999, LU 0968 (Michelle Arrow).
Weisinger, Sheila, Kingsford, NSW, 28.1.2000, LU 0976 (Michelle Arrow).
White, Joanna, South Melbourne, Vic., 24.6.1998, LU 0991 (Catherine Coleborne).
Whitehead, Christine, Mt Gravatt, Qld, 8.9.2000, LU 0992 (Carole Hamilton-Barwick).
Wills, David, Geilston Bay, Tas., 30.9.1999, LU 1009.
Wilson, Carol, Wantirna South, Vic., 4.11.1998, LU 1010 (Catherine Coleborne).
Wilson, Kathleen, Coolbellup, WA, 12.2.2000 and 5.3.2000, LU 1012 (Criena Fitzgerald).
Woolnough, Mary, Como, WA, 21.10.1999, LU 1028 (Criena Fitzgerald).
Wright, Josephine, Shenton Park, WA, 4.10.1998, LU 1030 (Carole Hamilton-Barwick).
Wyse, Hilary (pseudonym), Malvern, Vic., 17.10.2001 and 31.10.2001, LU 1148HW (Carole Hamilton-Barwick).
Young, Joan, Newport, NSW, 14.7.1998, LU 1038.

Unpublished written accounts
Barnet, Leslie, 'The Barnets of Queen Street', Revesby, NSW, LU 0050.
Carruthers, Eddie, 'The Way it Was', Nollamara, WA, LU 0154.
Carter, Maureen, 'Memoir', Picnic Point, NSW, LU 0157.
Cook, Alf, 'The Cook Family Voyage: England to Australia, May–June, 1950', Lindisfarne, Tas., LU 0197.
Dingle, Margaret, 'My Experience as a British Migrant', Norwood, SA, LU 0253.
Duell, Jack, 'Musing', Bongaree, Qld, 1998, LU 0265.
Hajinakitas, Rosa, 'Experiences of a Ten Pound Pom', Dundas, NSW, LU 0378.
Hill, Margaret, Chelsea, Vic., 'Water Under the Bridge', LU 0423.
Kennedy, Valerie R., 'Reflections of a Five Pound Pom', Riverside, Tas., LU 0494.
Kershaw, John, 'Tape – Musical Memoir', Crafers, SA, LU 0495.
Lane, Patricia, 'Life Story', Subiaco, WA, LU 0558PL.
McHugh, Margaret, 'Scenes that are Brightest', Yass, NSW, LU 0570.
Morphett, Sheila, 'Waverley Todd', Elgin, Scotland, LU 0637.
Morphett, Sheila, 'When the Time Comes: An Autobiography, 1961–1985', Elgin, Scotland, LU 0637.

Penn, Ron, 'Additional Comments', 24.2.2003, Revesby, NSW, LU 0713.
Platt, Margaret, 'Our Forty Years in Australia, 1949–1989', Frankston, Vic., LU 0726.
Reardon, Margaret C., 'The Reluctant Migrants', 1998, Gundagai, NSW, LU 0743.
Tomlin, Maurice, 'Memoir', Midland, WA, LU 0906.
Wardle, Hilda, 'Our Memories: Coming to, and Our Life in Australia', Walkerville, SA, LU 0952.

State Library of New South Wales (Sydney), Mitchell Manuscripts Collection

Black, Margery, Diary, 11.1.1949–14.2.1949, MS 4303, 8–435C.
Jolley, Elizabeth, Literary Papers, c 1939, 1950–1987, MS 4880, 9–189C.

State Library of South Australia (Adelaide), J. D. Somerville Oral History Collection

Dean, Jean, interview recorded by Evanka Vodopivec, 31.8.1989, OH 74.
Donn, Les P., interview recorded by Rob Linn, 2.5.1985, Woods and Forestry Dept: An Oral History Project, OH 5/5.
Pirie, Mary, interview recorded by Joan Durdin for the History of Nursing in South Australia Project, 9.8.1987, OH 17/66.
Preston, Betty, interview recorded by June Donovan for the South Australian Women's Suffrage Centenary Project: Oral History of Women's Political Activity Project, 21.1.1994, OH 250/4.
Usher, Ruth Ann, interview recorded by Joan Durdin for the History of Nursing in South Australia Project, 30.8.1988, OH 17/51.
Vaughan, Martha, interview recorded by Joan Durdin for the History of Nursing in South Australia Project, 25.3.1988, OH 17/36.

State Library of Victoria (Melbourne), La Trobe Australian Manuscripts Collection

Anon., Journal, 21.9.1949–14.10.1949, MS 11881, Box 2401/5.
Dickinson, Matt, 'Our Diary of Our Migration from England to Australia, 1955–1956', MS 13116, Box 3805/9.
Marchinton, James Frederick, 'Three Score Years and Ten', MS 11700, Box 1872/7.
Walker, Albert, 'Diaries of Albert Walker, 1946, 1955–56, 1957–58', MS 11509, Box 1776/4–5.

University of Sussex Special Collections (Brighton, England), Mass-Observation Archive, British Australian Migration Collection

The project received written accounts about migration experiences by the following people in the year 2000. The dates for all interviews are noted. All interviews were conducted by Alistair Thomson unless indicated in brackets.

Adams, Marjorie, Bristol, interview, 21.8.2000, US A3.
Adams, Michael, Nottingham, US A4.
Akehurst, Frances, Hove, US A6.
Ashton, John, Blackpool, US A5.
Attwood, Stephan, South Oxfordshire, US A1.
Austin, Anthony, West Sussex, US A2.

Bain, James, Invergordon, Scotland, US B15.

Banks, Georgene, Surrey, US B9.

Banks, John, Lowestoft, US B16.

Barber, Catherine, Longniddry, Scotland, interview 8.9.2000 (Lani Russell), US B12.

Barnes, Patricia, Peterborough, US B13.

Barnes, Peter, Heywood, Lancashire, US B21.

Bates, Alvyn, Wolverhampton, US B7.

Bates, Bruce, Lewes, US B4.

Benson, Douglas, Bath, US B10.

Benson, Ray, Malvern, US B1.

Biggs, Barbara and John, Purley, Surrey, US B17 and B18.

Bird, George and Ray, Hove, interview 20.7.2000, US B6 and B5.

Bishop, Alan, Redditch, Worcestershire, US B11.

Bonnett, Ronald and Jean, Scarborough, US B19.

Borland, Barbara, Stockport, US B14.

Britton, Elizabeth, Stroud, US B20.

Broadbent, E. Robin, Croydon, US B8.

Brooks, Carol, East Sussex, interview 19.7.2000, US B3.

Brown, Pat (pseudonym), Brighton, US B2.

Casson, David, Northampton, US C7.

Caton, George, Blackpool, US C17.

Cave, Phyllis, Isle of Wight, US C3.

Clare, Helen and Maurice, Swadlincote, Derbyshire, US C14 and C15.

Clark, Peter, Worcester, US C16.

Clarke, Robin, Brighton, US C1.

Conley, James, Brighton, US C4.

Coventry, Robert, Bolton, US C13.

Cox, Ann, Shoreham-by-Sea, West Sussex, US C8.

Crooke, Anthony and Seraphine, Penkridge, Stafford, US C11 and C12.

Crooks, Edward, South Croydon, US C9.

Crosby, Wanda, Nottingham, US C10.

Cross, Mike, West Sussex, US C5.

Cudmore, Joyce, Hastings, US C2.

Cullenward, Maureen, Cobar, NSW, Australia, US C6.

Daly, Christina, Burgess Hill, interview 17.7.2000, US D5.

Darroch, George, Greenock, Scotland, US D12.

Davitt, Linda, Northampton, US D10.

Dean, Keith, Woking, US D11.

Devlin, Catherine, Glasgow, Scotland, US D7.

Dickinson, Jennifer, Farnham, Surrey, US D4.

Dickson, Margaret, Matlock, Derbyshire, US D14.

Dixon, Kenneth, Hastings, US D1.

Donaldson, Elizabeth, Orkney Isles, Scotland, US D6.

Dovaston, Jean, Shrewsbury, US D13.

Drake, Geoff and Ruth, Dorset, US D8 and D9.

Duffield, Marjorie, Brighton, US D3.

Dyett, Mike, Farnham, Surrey, US D2.

Easton, Lynford, Stirling, Scotland, US E3.

Egar, Edward and Valerie, Wilmslow, Cheshire, US E4 and E5.

Elleman, Madeline and Thomas, Beckenham, Kent, US E6 and E7.

Ellis, Hazel, Hailsham, East Sussex, US E1.

Enock, Robert, Orpington, Kent, US E2.

Farnfield, Donald and Evelyn (Dorothy), Bexhill, interview 13.7.2000, US F2.

Finch, Ronald, Wolverhampton, US F5.

Finlayson, Elizabeth, Caithness, Scotland, US F9.

Flemington, Annabella, East Kilbride, Scotland, US F8.

Ford, Fred, Manchester, US F11.

Forrest, Margaret, Banffshire, Scotland, US F10.

Forster, James, Wednesfield, West Midlands, US F6.

Francis, Janet, Horsham, interview 8.8.2000, US F4.

Frith, David, Guildford, US F7.

Fuller, Keith, Petersfield, Hampshire, US F1.

Galletly, Alice, Paisley, Scotland, US G5.

Good, Cliff and Gwen, Perth, Australia, interview 30.3.2000, US G2.

Good, Malcolm, Andrew and Robert, Perth, Australia, interview 31.3.2000, US G3.

Gray, Christopher, Manchester, interview 16.12.2000, US G6.

Gray, Christopher (senior), Manchester, US G6.

Gray, Elizabeth, Brighton, interview 5.7.2000, US G1.

Griffiths, Stella, Southampton, US G4.

Hands, Maureen (pseudonym), Stockport, US H15.

Hansford, John, Eastbourne, US H4.

Hardie, John and Margaret, Sauchie, Scotland, interview 9.9.2000 (Lani Russell), US H11.

Hardy, Terry, Brighton, US H3.

Harman, David, Walton-on-Thames, US H7.

Hart, Jennifer, Deal, Kent, US H17.

Hawkins, Ann, Exeter, US H8.

Heath, Nigel, Walton-on-Thames, interview 10.8.2000, US H5.

Higgins, Barbara, Saffron Walden, Essex, US H12.

Higgins, Eric, Hyde, Cheshire, US H4.

Higgins, Lynda (pseudonym), Canterbury, US H2.

Hilliard, Gillian, Brighton, US H1.

Hitchman, Judith, Poole, US H6.

Hogg, Janice and Michael, Kirkcaldy, Scotland, US H9 and H10.

Holborn, Eileen, Scarborough, US H19.

Holborn, George Trevor, Scarborough, US H19.

Holmes, Mary, Monmouthshire, Wales, US H18.

Hood, Sarah, Kilmarnock, Scotland, US H13.

Hutchison, Alfred, Menorca, Spain, US H16.

Irving, John, Blackpool, US I1.

Jack, Susan, Hastings, US J1.

Jackson, Josephine, Gloucestershire, US J5.

Jeffries, Barbara, Brighton, US J4.

Jobling, Dorothy, Bristol, US J3.

Jones, Agnes, Perth, Scotland, US J6.

Jordan, John, Hereford, interview 23.8.2000, US J2.

Kells, Marion, Wolverhampton, interview 20.9.2000, US K5.

Kerr, Irene, Perthshire, Scotland, US K10.

Kimberley, Patricia, Clitheroe, Lancashire, US K9.

King, Arthur, Norfolk, US K1.

Kinross, Carol, Dunning, Scotland, US K8.

Kirby, Audrey, Chertsey, Surrey, US K4.
Kirby, Peggy, Addlestone, Surrey, US K2.
Kitchener, Eric and Florence, Sidmouth, Devon, US K6.
Knights, Daphne, Purley, Surrey, US K3.
Laine, Leslie, Worthing, US L8.
Law, John, Fife, Scotland, US L6.
Lawson, John, Croydon, US L1.
Laycock, Michael, Morayshire, Scotland, US L4.
Leach, Christine, Blackpool, US L5.
Lewis, Elizabeth, London, US L3.
Lucas, Margaret, Sutton Coldfield, US L7.
Luttman, W. G., London, US L2.
M, John (pseudonym), Portsmouth, US M2.
Maile, Phillip, Burgess Hill, US M3.
Maxwell, Gordon, West Sussex, US M5.
McArdle, Maria, Herne Bay, Kent, US M21.
McCherry, Christine, Blackpool, US M17.
McDermott, Avis, Nottingham, interview 20.9.2000, US M10.
McDonald, Brian, Burton-on-Trent, US M22.
McDonald, Maisie, Taunton, US M6.
McGarrity, Eileen, Argyll, Scotland, US M9.
McKechnie, Andrew, West Sussex, US M7.
McKinna, Jessie and Lawrence, Ayrshire, Scotland, US M15 and M16.
McLanaghan, Anne and George, Ayrshire, Scotland, interview 5.9.2000 (Lani Russell),
    US M13.
McNally, Teresa, Alloa, Scotland, US M23.
Miles, Helen, Croydon, US M4.
Miller, Muriel, Hove, US M1.
Miller, Stephanie, Suffolk, US M25.
Morelli, Maureen, Northamptonshire, US M8.
Morrison, Maimie, Argyll, Scotland, US M24.
Morton, Catherine, Lancashire, US M18.
Morton, Iain, Argyll, Scotland, US M12.
Murphy, Anthony, Manchester, US M19.
Musgrve, Beryl, Cheshire, US M20.
Mushet, Katherine, Dumfriesshire, Scotland, US M11.
Myers, Ann, Blackpool, US M14.
Nea, Sheila, Essex, US N4.
Newton, Barbara, Crawley, US N2.
Nicolson, Alice, Isle of Lewis, Scotland, US N3.
Nyman, Hettie, Salisbury, US N1.
Ockenden, Audrey, Hove, US O4.
O'Donovan, Angela, Hove, US O1.
O'Hare, Mary (Kathleen), Manchester, US O3.
O'Neill, Sandra, Sutton Coldfield, interview 21.9.2000, US O2.
Palin, Norma, Lancashire and Queensland, US P17.
Parkinson, Margaret, Seaford, East Sussex, US P5.
Passmore, Edith, Brighton, US P2.
Peirce, Helen, Worthing, US P4.
Penketh, John, Lancashire, US P18.

Perfect, Eileen, Manchester, US P11.
Pester, Cliff, Hampshire, US P16.
Peters, Rose, Worcestershire, US P13.
Phillips, Nellie, Salford, US P15.
Pickett, Joan, Salford, interview 17.12.2000, US P12.
Pike, Wendy, Brighton, US P14.
Pinckney, Gordon and Yvonne, Macclesfield, US P8 and P9.
Pirrie, Ian, Clackmannanshire, Scotland, US P10.
Platt, Mary, Powys, Wales, US P6.
Price, Michael, Hove, US P1.
Price, Ralph, Hove, US P3.
Pritchett, Jean, Bromsgrove, Worcestershire, US P7.
Quillen, Jennifer, Bedford, US Q2.
Qureshi, Judith, Liverpool, US Q1.
Rajan, Marion, Brighton, US R13.
Rayment, Charles, North Cornwall, US R12.
Read, Cynthia, Dorset, US R10.
Rennison, Gloria, Wolverhampton, US R14.
Rigby, Olga, Manchester, US R4.
Rivett, Anne, Ross-on-Wye, US R2.
Roberts, Maureen, Skelmersdale, Lancashire, US R1.
Roberts, Mavis, Gwynedd, Wales, US R11.
Robinson, John, Warlingham, Surrey, US R9.
Robinson, Maggie (pseudonym), Brighton, US R6.
Rooms, Dorothy, Manchester, interview 15.12.2000, US R8.
Roscoe, Jack, Manchester, interview 14.12.2000, US R5.
Ryder, Sylvia and William, Reading, US R3 and R7.
Sandell, Rosemary, Glasgow, US S15.
Schofield, Eric, Lancashire, US S17.
Shaw, Archie, Manchester, interview 18.12.2000, US S18.
Sharples, Olive, Manchester, US S20.
Shearman, Lyndon, Wolverhampton, US S12.
Shirreffs, Wallace, Aberdeen, US S14.
Siberry, Michael, Bexhill, interview 14.8.2000, US S9.
Small, Alexander Verner, Isle of Arran, Scotland, US S21.
Smith, Barry, Hove, US S1.
Smith, Doreen and Len, Rotherham, US S2 and S3.
Smith, Jack, Southport, Merseyside, US S19.
Smith, Margaret and Robert, Edinburgh, interview 7.9.2000 (Lani Russell), US S13.
Smurthwaite, Cornelia, interview 30.8.2000, US S5.
Spencer, Irene and Ray, Bridgend, Wales, interview 22.8.2000, US S7 and S8.
Spencer, Michael, Chichester, US S22.
Spennock, Colin, London, US S10.
Staniforth, Pete, Shoreham-by-Sea, West Sussex, US S11.
Stanyer, Pauline, Cheshire, US S23.
Steel, Barbara, St Leonards-on-Sea, East Sussex, US S4.
Stephens, Ian and Terry, Hove, interview 11.7.2000, US S6.
Stevenson, John, Flintshire, Wales, US S24.
Stirling, Robert, Kilmarnock, Scotland, interview 4.9.2000 (Lani Russell), US S16.
Terras, Edgar, East Kilbride, Scotland, US T4.

Tittle, Sylvia, Leeds, US T5.
Tubb, Derek, Crawley, US T3.
Twiggs, Arthur, Farnham, Surrey, US T1.
Tyas, Irene and Clifford, Eaton, Nottinghamshire, interview 19.9.2000, US T2.
Upton, Kathleen, St Leonards-on-Sea, East Sussex, US U1.
Uttridge, Jim, London, US U2.
Vidler, Sheila, Hastings, interview 1.8.2000, US V1.
Walker, Lamont (William), Edinburgh, US W19.
Warner, Frank, Caterham, Surrey, US W11.
Watkins, Christine, Crawley, US W13.
Webb, Joyce, Hampshire, US W4.
Webb, Alfred, Hampshire, US W5.
Wedge, Christine, Leicestershire, US W20.
Welling, Joyce, Worcestershire, US W14.
Wells, Valerie, Hove, US W17.
Whittle, Gillian and Keith, Brighton, interview 1.8.2000 (Lani Russell), US W6 and W7.
Williams, Barbara, Wallington, Surrey, US W15.
Williams, Cyril, Haywards Heath, US W8.
Williams, Esther, Wales, US W22.
Williams, John, Malvern, US W21.
Williams, Lawrence, Brighton, US W2.
Wilson, John, Devon, US W10.
Wright, Dorothy, Isle of Wight, US W16.
Wood, John, East Sussex, US W9.
Woodhouse, John, Brighton, US W12.
Worsell, Shelagh, Bournemouth, US W1.
Worth, Diana, Hove, US W3.
Wrathall, Anthony, Kendal, Cumbria, US W23.
Wrigley, Janet (pseudonym), London, US W18.
Young, Anne, Wolverhampton, US Y1.
Young, Sue, Henley-on-Thames, US Y2.

Newspapers and periodicals

Adelaide Review
Australian
Australian Women's Weekly
Daily Sketch (London)
Endeavour (Melbourne, Journal of the UK Settlers' Association)
Herald (Melbourne)
Preston Post
Tribune (Melbourne)

Published books and articles

Allery, Linda (ed.), *Elizabeth: From Dusty Plains to Royal Names: Oral Histories from the Elizabeth Community*, Elizabeth, SA, City of Elizabeth, 1996.
Appleyard, Reg, with Ray, Alison and Segal, Allan, *The Ten Pound Immigrants*, London, Boxtree, 1988.

Appleyard, R.T., *British Emigration to Australia*, Canberra, Australian National University, 1964.

Appleyard, R.T., 'Post-war British Immigration', in James Jupp (ed.), *The Australian People: An Encyclopedia of the Nation, Its People and Their Origins*, Cambridge, Cambridge University Press, 2001, pp. 62–5.

Appleyard, R.T., 'Post-war English Immigrants', in James Jupp (ed.), *The Australian People: An Encyclopedia of the Nation, Its People and Their Origins*, Cambridge, Cambridge University Press, 2001, pp. 314–16.

Department of Immigration, Australia, *Australia Ahead*, London, Australian News and Information Bureau, 1950 (1948).

Bain, I., 'Post-war Scottish Immigration', in James Jupp (ed.), *The Australian People: An Encyclopedia of the Nation, Its People and Their Origins*, Cambridge, Cambridge University Press, 2001, pp. 668–74.

Baines, Dudley, *Migration in a Mature Economy*, Cambridge, Cambridge University Press, 1985.

Baines, John E., *Life Wasn't Meant to be Easy*, Geelong, B. Salter & A. McKechnie, [1998].

Baldassar, Loretta, *Visits Home: Migration Experiences Between Italy and Australia*, Melbourne, Melbourne University Press, 2001.

Barker, Dudley, *People for the Commonwealth: The Case for Mass Migration*, London, T. Werner Laurie, 1948.

Barry, Paul, *The Rise and Fall of Alan Bond*, Sydney, Bantam, 1990.

Benmayor, Rina and Skotnes, Andor, 'Some Reflections on Migration and Identity', in Rina Benmayor and Andor Skotnes (eds), *Migration and Identity: International Yearbook of Oral History and Life Stories, Vol. III*, Oxford, Oxford University Press, 1994, pp. 1–18.

Benson, John, *The Rise of Consumer Society in Britain, 1880–1980*, London, Longman, 1994.

Black, Peter, *The Poms in the Sun*, London, Joseph, 1965.

Bodnar, John, *The Transplanted: A History of Immigrants in Urban America*, Bloomington, Indiana University Press, 1985.

Bolton, Geoffrey, *The Oxford History of Australia: 1942–1995, Vol. 5, the Middle Way*, Melbourne, Oxford University Press, 1993.

Bosworth, Richard, 'Australia and Assisted Immigration from Britain, 1945–1954', *Australian Journal of Politics and History*, 34, 2, 1988, pp. 187–200.

Brabazon, Tara, *Tracking the Jack: A Retracing of the Antipodes*, Sydney, University of New South Wales Press, 2000.

Bragg, Melvyn, *The Soldier's Return*, London, Hodder and Stoughton, 1999.

Bragg, Melvyn, *A Son of War*, London, Sceptre, 2001.

Caesar, Andrew, *Life Sentences*, Woden, ACT, Molonglo Press, 1998.

Champion, A. G. and Fielding, A. J., *Migration Processes and Patterns: Vol. 1, Research Progress and Prospects*, London, Belhaven Press, 1993.

Chan, Sucheng, 'European and Asian Immigration into the United States in Comparative Perspective, 1820s to 1920s', in Virginia Yans-McGlaughlin (ed.), *Immigration Reconsidered*, New York, Oxford University Press, 1990, pp. 37–8.

Clapson, Mark, *Invincible Green Suburbs, Brave New Towns: Social Change and Urban Dispersal in Postwar England*, Manchester, Manchester University Press, 1998.

Colls, Robert, *Identity of England*, Oxford, Oxford University Press, 2002.

Committee on Social Patterns, Commonwealth Immigration Advisory Council, *The Departure of Settlers from Australia, Final Report*, Canberra, Department of Immigration, 1967.

Committee on Social Patterns, Commonwealth Immigration Advisory Council, *Inquiry into the Departure of Settlers from Australia, Final Report*, Canberra, Australian Government Publishing Service, 1973.

Curthoys, Anne, 'Expulsion, Exodus and Exile in White Australian Historical Mythology', *Journal of Australian Studies*, June 1999, pp. 1–29.

Curthoys, Anne, 'Identity Crisis: Colonialism, Nation and Gender in Australian History', *Gender and History*, 5, 2, Summer 1993, pp. 165–76.

Davies, Rhiannon, *Wales, The Beloved Country: 'Where There's a Will There's a Way'*, Chifley, ACT, Chifley Publishers, 1999.

Davis, F., *Yearning for Yesteryear: A Sociology of Nostalgia*, London, The Free Press, 1979.

Davison, Barbara and Davison, Graeme, 'Suburban Pioneers', in Graeme Davison, Tony Dingle and Seamus O'Hanlon (eds), *The Cream Brick Frontier: Histories of Australian Suburbia*, Clayton, Vic., Monash Publications in History No. 19, 1995, pp. 41–50.

Department of Immigration, *Consolidated Statistics, Vol. 1*, Canberra, Department of Immigration, 1966.

Erickson, Charlotte, *Invisible Immigrants: The Adaptation of English and Scottish Immigrants in Nineteenth-Century America*, London, Weidenfeld and Nicolson, 1972.

Finnegan, Ruth, *Tales of the City: A Study of Narrative and Urban Life*, Cambridge, Cambridge University Press, 1998.

Frost, Jess, *It Wasn't So Bad After All*, Durham, Pentland Press, 1996.

Gardner, Eunice and Williams, Diana, *The World at Our Feet: The Story of Two Women Who Adventured Halfway Across the Globe*, London, W. H. Allen, 1957.

Gikandi, Simon, *Maps of Englishness: Writing Identity in the Culture of Colonialism*, New York, Columbia University Press, 1996.

Gill, Alan, *Orphans of the Empire: The Shocking Story of Child Migration to Australia*, Alexandria, NSW, Millennium Books, 1997.

Gothard, Jan, *Blue China: Single Female Migration to Colonial Australia*, Melbourne, Melbourne University Press, 2001.

Gray, Bronwyn and Young, Alan, *The Ten Quid Tourists*, Melbourne, New World Arts, 1989.

Haines, Robin F., *Emigration and the Labouring Poor: Australian Recruitment in Britain and Ireland, 1831–1860*, London, Macmillan, 1997.

Hamilton-Barwick, Carole, 'A Ballot Cast for Orestes: Women's Stories of Migration from Postwar Britain', *Journal of the Oral History Association of Australia: Voices of a 20th Century Nation*, 23, 2001, pp. 47–53.

Hammerton, A. James, *Emigrant Gentlewomen: Genteel Poverty and Female Emigration, 1830–1914*, London, Croom Helm, 1979.

Hammerton, A. James, 'Epic Stories and the Mobility of Modernity: Narratives of British Migration to Canada and Australia Since 1945', *Australian-Canadian Studies*, 19, 1, 2001, pp. 47–64.

Hammerton, A. James, '"Family Comes First": Migrant Memory and Masculinity in Narratives of Post-War British Migrants', in A. James Hammerton and Eric Richards (eds), *Speaking to Immigrants: Oral Testimony and the History of Australian Migration*, Canberra, Research School of Social Sciences, ANU, 2002, pp. 21–37.

Hammerton, A. James and Coleborne, Catherine, 'Ten-Pound Poms Revisited: Battlers' Tales and British Migration to Australia, 1947–1971', in Wilfred Prest and Graham Tulloch (eds) *Scatterlings of Empire, Journal of Australian Studies*, 68, 2001, pp. 86–96.

Hart, Sydney, *Pommie Migrant: The Aventures of a British Emigrant 'Down-Under'*, London, Odhams Press, 1957.

Hassam, Andrew, *Sailing to Australia: Shipboard Diaries by Nineteenth Century British Emigrants*, Manchester, Manchester University Press, 1994.

Hassam, Andrew, 'Whingeing Poms and New Australians', paper presented at 'The End of the Affair? Australia and Britain, 1945–1975', Menzies Centre for Australian Studies, London, July 2002.

Hawthorne, Lesleyanne, *Making It in Australia*, Caulfield East, Vic., Edward Arnold Australia, 1988.

Henderson, Anne, *From All Corners: Six Migrant Stories*, St Leonards, NSW, Allen & Unwin, 1993.

Hill, Margaret, *Corrugated Castles*, Manchester, Cromwell Publishers, 1999.

Hugo, Graeme, *The Economic Implications of Emigration from Australia*, Canberra, Australian Government Publishing Service, 1994.

Hugo, Graeme, 'Migration Between Australia and Britain: Past and Present', in David Lowe (ed.), *Immigration and Integration: Australia and Britain*, Bureau of Immigration, Multicultural and Population Research, Carlton, Australia, and Sir Robert Menzies Centre for Australian Studies, London, 1995, pp. 7–96.

Humphreys, Margaret, *Empty Cradles*, London, Doubleday, 1995.

Hussey, Steve, 'Making Television Oral History: An Interview with Paul Neuburg, Producer of *Ten Pound Poms*', *Oral History*, 25, 2, 1997, pp. 90–2.

Hutching, Megan, *Long Journey for Sevenpence: Assisted Immigration to New Zealand from the United Kingdom 1947–1975*, Wellington, Victoria University Press, 1999.

Jenkins, Thomas, *We Came to Australia*, Constable, London, 1969.

Johnson, Les, *The ABC, Albany and Me*, Lower Kalgan, WA, Les Johnson, 1992.

Jolley, Elizabeth, *Central Mischief: Elizabeth Jolley On Writing, Her Past and Herself* (introd. and ed. by Caroline Lurie), Ringwood, Vic.,Viking, 1992.

Jordens, Ann-Mari, *Redefining Australians: Immigration, Citizenship and National Identity*, Sydney, Hale and Iremonger, 1995.

Joutard, Philippe, *Ces voix qui nous viennent du passé*, Paris, Hachette, 1983.

Joynson, Joan, '"Something You Like to Forget, You Know, A Bit like the War": British Assisted Migrants, and Hostels in the 1950s', in Eric Richards and Jacqueline Templeton (eds), *The Australian Immigrant in the Twentieth Century: Searching Neglected Sources*, Canberra, Australian National University, 2002, pp. 106–26.

Jupp, James, *Arrivals and Departures*, Melbourne, Cheshire-Lansdowne, 1966.

Jupp, James (ed.), *The Australian People: An Encyclopedia of the Nation, Its People and Their Origins*, Cambridge, Cambridge University Press, 3rd edn, 2001.

Jupp, James, 'From New Britannia to Foreign Power: The Decline of British Immigration', paper presented at 'The End of the Affair? Australia and Britain, 1945–1975', Menzies Centre for Australian Studies, London, July 2002.

Jupp, James, *Immigration*, Melbourne, Oxford University Press, 2nd edn, 1998.

Jupp, James, 'Post-war English Settlers in Adelaide and Perth', in James Jupp (ed.), *The Australian People: An Encyclopedia of the Nation, Its People and Their Origins*, Cambridge, Cambridge University Press, 2001, pp. 316–21.

Karras, Alan, *Sojourners in the Sun: Scottish Migrants in Jamaica and the Chesapeake, 1740–1800*, Ithaca, NY, Cornell University Press, 1992.

Lack, John and Templeton, Jacqueline, *Bold Experiment: A Documentary History of Australian Immigration since 1945*, Melbourne, Oxford University Press, 1995.

Lewis, Roy, *Shall I Emigrate? A Practical Guide*, London, Phoenix House, 1948.

Little, Graham, *Letter to My Daughter*, Melbourne, Text Publishing, 1995.

Liverani, Mary Rose, *The Winter Sparrows: Growing Up in Scotland and Australia*, Melbourne, Thomas Nelson, 1978.

Lowenstein, Wendy and Loh, Morag, *The Immigrants*, Harmondsworth, Penguin, 1978.

Martin, Harry, *Angels and Arrogant Gods: Migration Officers and Migrants Reminisce, 1945–85*, Canberra, APGS Press, 1989.

Marwick, Arthur, *British Society Since 1945*, London, Penguin, 2nd edn, 1990.

Matless, David, *Landscape and Englishness*, London, Reaktion, 1998.

McLintock, Anne, *Imperial Leather: Race, Gender and Sexuality in the Colonial Context*, New York, Routledge, 1995.

Murphy, John, *Imagining the Fifties: Private Sentiment and Political Culture in Menzies' Australia*, Sydney, University of New South Wales Press, 2000.

Pagram, Edward, *Never Had It So Good*, Melbourne and London, Heinemann, 1968.

Paul, Kathleen, *Whitewashing Britain: Race and Citizenship in the Postwar Era*, Ithaca, NY, Cornell University Press, 1997.

Peel, Mark, 'Dislocated Men: Imagining "Britain" and "Australia"', in A. James Hammerton and Eric Richards (eds), *Speaking to Immigrants: Oral Testimony and the History of Australian Migration*, Canberra, Research School of Social Sciences, Australian National University, 2002, pp. 111–27.

Peel, Mark, *Good Times, Hard Times: The Past and the Future in Elizabeth*, Carlton, Melbourne University Press, 1995.

Perks, Robert and Thomson, Alistair (eds), *The Oral History Reader*, London, Routledge, 1998.

Peters, Michael, *Pommie Bastards*, Crows Nest, NSW, Peter Leydon Publishing and Dingo Books, 1969.

Peters, Nonja, *Milk and Honey – But No Gold: Postwar Migration to Western Australia, 1945–1964*, Crawley, WA, University of Western Australia Press, 2001.

Plowman, Peter, *Passenger Ships to Australia and New Zealand, 1945–1990: Emigrant Ships to Luxury Liners*, Kensington, NSW, NSW University Press, 1992.

Preston, Betty, *Blowing My Own Trumpet*, Christie's Beach, SA, D. Sartain, 1994.

Preston, Betty, *Destination Australia*, Somerton Park, SA, B. Preston, undated.

Price, Charles A. (ed.), *Australian National Identity*, Canberra, Academy of Social Sciences, 1991.

Richards, Eric, 'Annals of the Australian Immigrant', in Eric Richards, Richard Reid and David Fitzpatrick (eds), *Visible Immigrants: Neglected Sources for the History of Australian Immigration*, Canberra, Research School of Social Sciences, Australian National University, 1989, pp. 7–27.

Richards, Lyn, *Nobody's Home: Dreams and Realities in a New Suburb*, Melbourne, Oxford University Press, 1990.

Richardson, Alan, *British Immigrants and Australia: A Psycho-social Inquiry*, Canberra, ANU Press, 1974.

Richmond, Anthony H., *Post-War Immigrants in Canada*, Toronto, University of Toronto Press, 1967.

Robertson, Alex J., *The Bleak Midwinter: 1947*, Manchester, Manchester University Press, 1985.

Roe, Michael, *Australia, Britain and Migration, 1915–1940*, Cambridge, Cambridge University Press, 1995.

Saunders, Gordon and Joan, *Another Fork in the Road*, Launceston, Tas., 1998.

Saxton, James, *Something Will Come to Me*, Ilfracombe, Stockwell, 1981.

Scott, Margaret, 'Changing Countries', *Island*, 52, Spring 1992, pp. 12–14.

Scott, Margaret, *Changing Countries: On Moving from One Island to Another*, Sydney, ABC Books, 2000.

Sharp, Eloise, *The Beginning to the End 1920–1993*, Wickipin, WA, E. M. W. Taylor, 1997.

Sherington, Geoffrey and Jeffery, Chris, *Fairbridge: Empire and Child Migration*, Nedlands, WA, University of Western Australia Press, 1998.

Sherrard, David, *Piddletrenthide to East Intercourse Island*, Northbridge, WA, Access Press, 1991.

Sinfield, Alan, *Literature, Politics and Culture in Postwar Britain*, Oxford, Blackwell, 1989.

Skowronski, Ivy, *I Can't Think of a Title: An Autobiography*, Adelaide, I. Skowronski, 1986.

Sluga, Glenda, *Bonegilla: A Place of No Hope*, Melbourne, History Department, University of Melbourne, 1988.

Snuggs, Olive, *I Came a Migrant*, Norwood, SA, Wednesday Press, 1990.

Stratton, Jon, 'Not Just Another Multicultural Story', *Vision Splendid: Journal of Australian Studies*, 66, 2000, pp. 23–47.

Summerfield, Penny, *Reconstructing Women's Wartime Lives: Discourse and Subjectivity in Oral Histories of the Second World War*, Manchester, Manchester University Press, 1998.

Symes, C., 'The Oz-stracised Pommy', in Millicent E. Poole, Philip R. de Lacey and Bikkar S. Randshaw (eds), *Australia in Transition: Culture and Life Possibilities*, Sydney, Harcourt Brace Jovanovich, 1985, pp. 181–3.

Thomson, Alistair, 'Landscapes of Memory: the Migrations of Elizabeth Jolley', *Meanjin*, 61, 3, 2002, pp. 81–97.

Thomson, Alistair, 'Moving Stories: Oral History and Migration Studies', *Oral History*, 27, 1, Spring 1999, pp. 24–37.

Thomson, Alistair, 'Recording British Migration: Meaning and Identity in the Good Family Audio Letters from Australia, 1963–65', in Wilfred Prest and Graham Tulloch (eds), *Scatterlings of Empire: Journal of Australian Studies*, 68, 2001, pp. 105–16.

Thomson, Alistair, 'Ten Pound Poms and Television Oral History', *Oral History*, 25, 2, 1997, pp. 85–8.

Towler, David J., *Look Mum, I Can Speak Australian!*, Norwood, SA, Wednesday Press, c. 1989.

Tribe, Elizabeth and Derek, *Postmark Australia: The Land and Its People through English Eyes*, Melbourne, Cheshire, 1963.

Turnbull, Paul, '"Jogging Memories": Remembering British Post-War Migration to Australia', *Voices: The Quarterly Journal of the National Library of Australia*, Spring 1996, pp. 9–17.

Upton, Kathleen, *To the Undiscovered Ends: An Accurate and Humorous Account of an Australian Sojourn*, Durham, Pentland Press, 1992.

Walker, David, *We Went to Australia*, London, Chapman and Hall, 1949.

Warden, W. R., *Vale Enchanting*, London, Harrop, 1952.

Whicker, Alan, *Whicker's World Down Under: Australia through the Eyes of Resident Poms*, London, Collins, 1988.

Wiener, Martin J., *English Culture and the Decline of the Industrial Spirit, 1850–1980*, Cambridge, Cambridge University Press, 1982.

White, Richard, *Inventing Australia: Images and Identity, 1888–1980*, Sydney, Allen & Unwin, 1981.

Wilton, Janis and Bosworth, Richard, *Old Worlds and New Australia: The Post-war Migrant Experience*, Ringwood, Penguin, 1984.

Woollacott, Angela, *To Try Her Fortune in London: Australian Women, Colonialism, and Modernity*, New York, Oxford University Press, 2001.

Zamoyska, Betka, *The Ten Pound Fare: Experiences of British People Who Emigrated to Australia in the 1950s*, Harmondsworth, Viking, 1988.

Zion, Lawrence Myer, 'The Pop Music Scene in Australia in the 1960s', Ph.D. thesis, Monash University, 1988.

Zubrzycki, Jerzy, *Settlers of the Latrobe Valley*, Canberra, Australian National University, 1964.

Index

Western Australia House 74
Western Australian 89
Whicker, Alan 24n.7
'whingeing Poms' 6, 10, 12, 14, 144–50,
    165n.43, 167, 171–2, 176, 182–4,
    205, 224, 243, 265, 276, 285, 316–
    17, 334, 349
White, Joanna 80
'White Australia' policy 31, 33, 89–90
Whitlam, Gough 33, 326
Whittle family 71, 109, 121n.44, 131, 206–
    7, 214, 295–6, 304–5
Wilkins, William 101
Williams, Cyril 317
Williams, Diana 257
Williams family 148, 278, 285–6, 289, 301,
    303, 314–15
Williamson, Avis *see* McDermott, Avis 40
Wills, David 352–3
Wollongong 135, 150, 223, 228–9, 292,
    306, 309
Wolverhampton 44, 337–9
women 140–1, 181, 184, 254–6, 260, 285,
    355–6
    childbirth 6–7, 13, 53, 79, 135, 211.
        289, 304, 338
    parenting 8, 54–5, 57–8, 70, 79, 100,
        105–6, 115, 142, 162, 178, 181, 199,

201, 209–14, 223, 226, 230–7, 243–
    5, 271–2, 289, 293–5, 304, 313, 338
work 7, 54, 57, 67, 70, 142, 157–9, 162,
    168, 171, 179, 189, 193, 195–7, 201,
    209–14, 226, 230–2, 236, 249–50,
    257, 260–1, 267, 271, 292–3, 326,
    347–9
    see also femininity; gender and gender
        relationships; gender roles;
        marriage; men; migration, gender
Women's Weekly, Australia 314
Woomera 139, 235
work ethic 67, 199, 206, 208–9, 215, 223–4,
    326

Worsell, Shelagh 314
Worth, Diana 320
Wran, Neville 326
Wright, Dorothy 43–4, 89–90, 100, 101,
    103, 135–7, 278, 281
Wrigley, Derek 344–5
Wrigley, Janet 260–3

Yorke Peninsula 139
youth culture 74–8, 244, 248–63
Yugoslavia 31

Zamoyska, Betka 24n.7